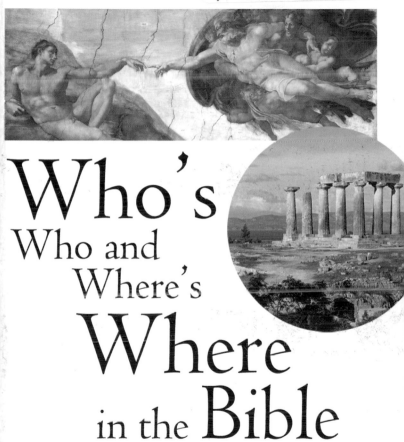

Who's
Who and
Where's
Where
in the Bible

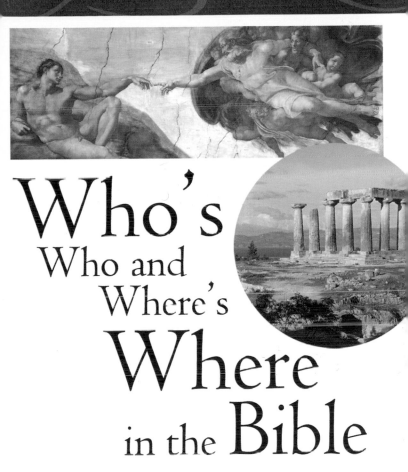

Who's
Who and
Where's
Where
in the Bible

STEPHEN M. MILLER

BARBOUR

ISBN 978-1-59789-687-0

Cover image © Adam/God Painting: Scala/Art Resources, NY
Appolos Temple: Borromeo/Art Resources, NY

Published in association with the literary agency of Alive Communications, Inc., 7680 Goddard Street, Suite 200, Colorado Springs, Colorado 80920.

Published by Barbour Publishing, Inc., P.O. Box 719, Uhrichsville, Ohio 44683
www.barbourbooks.com

Our mission is to publish and distribute inspirational products offering exceptional value and biblical encouragement to the masses.

ecpa Member of the
Evangelical Christian
Publishers Association

Printed in China.

INTRODUCTION

Sorry, folks. It's just not possible for you to enjoy reading this book as much as I enjoyed writing it.

That would be like expecting you to enjoy home videos of our family vacation in Maine as much as we enjoyed being there. But the videos give you only a flickering glimpse of what we enjoyed—and none of the lobster. You had to be there.

To write this book, I rolled out of bed each workday morning for nine months, eager to get to work—and grateful to be eager. I've had the other kind of jobs—eager to clock out. Like that summer job during my college days, running a block of four molds squeezing out rubber car parts. I sweat through my boots in thirty minutes and came home crusted in body salt. I could have been Lot's wife's brother.

Bible folks and scenery—Who's Who and Where's Where—are delightful to study.

There are dramatic stories: Hebrews of the Exodus trembling in terror as they assemble at the base of Mount Sinai to hear the voice of God personally deliver the Ten Commandments—introduced by lightning, a mysterious trumpet, and billows of smoke on the mountain (Exodus 20).

There are funny stories: Jacob working seven years for the privilege of marrying a beautiful woman named Rachel but waking up the morning after with Rachel's older sister, Leah, whose name means "cow" (Genesis 29).

And there are disturbing stories: Joshua and the Israelites wiping out entire Canaanite villages, down to the last breathing child—an Arab holocaust (Joshua 6:21).

Many of the stories are personal for me because I've been to the Bible lands several times. I can't think about the Sea of Galilee without remembering the time I sailed on it with my mom, who for years had been troubled by a problem she couldn't fix but could only worry about. From the boat's railing, she made a slight motion with her hands, as though releasing something invisible into the

ABOUT DATES, MAPS, AND MISTAKES

Dates. You'll come across a lot of dates in this book. Most of them are approximate. Some are hotly debated—especially those related to the Exodus and the Hebrew invasion into what is now Israel. On the other hand, some are precise to the very day because of details in the story that allow scholars to cross-check with other ancient sources inside and outside the Bible.

**MAP 4
B2**
Maps. Most of the towns and cities, rivers and mountains, regions and countries described in this book are represented in a map section on pages 380–385. Place entries in the text are noted with a small logo indicating which map number to consult, and offering a coordinate system to help you find the location. Barbour Publishing appreciates the assistance of the Broadman & Holman company on these maps.

Mistakes. Hopefully, you won't find any. But humans have a way of making them. When we've got more sense than ego, we can learn from our mistakes and fix the future. So if you come across any blunders, please send me a note. I'll let the editor know so we can make the correction before the next printing. You can reach me through the publisher, whose address is in the book, or through my Web site: stephenmiller.info.

water. Only later did I learn what she was doing: "Give all your worries and cares to God, for he cares about what happens to you" (1 Peter 5:7). God lightened her load that day.

And I remember walking in the old part of Jerusalem, following what tradition says was the path Jesus took on his way to execution. Someone spit into our crowd and hit a lady near me. I'll never forget what she said: "They spit on Jesus, too."

There have been lighter moments, as well. Take my advice, if you ever visit the Dead Sea, don't stick your head underwater. I dove in, wanting to see if I could keep from floating in this lake that's four times more buoyant than the ocean. The reason it's four times more buoyant—and why even nonswimmers bob around like a cork—is because it's four times as salty.

Salt burns.

Strangers helped me to the beachfront shower because the salt instantly blinded me with tears that felt squeezed from a jalapeño pepper.

A Word of Thanks

My daughter sings solos once in a while, and she's pretty much on her own when she stands up front and opens her mouth. Producing a book isn't anything like singing a solo. It's more like singing in the choir. That's why the publisher's name is on the cover with mine. So let me thank a few people who sacrificed time, energy, and some stomach lining to help create this book from thin air.

My family: Linda and our two children, Rebecca and Bradley. They sacrificed stomach lining, since writers don't get a steady income. (My last name is Miller, not King.)

Paul Muckley, the editor who stuck his neck out by risking a wad of his boss' money to turn an idea into a book.

Chip MacGregor, the agent who told Paul how far to stick his neck out.

Wilbur Glenn Williams, professor of Old Testament and archaeology, who has made well over one hundred trips to the Bible lands—two of them as my Bible background guide. We got stoned together in Jerusalem: rock in a windshield, not liquid in a bottle. A Palestinian didn't like the car we rented from an Israeli company—the license plates are color-coded to distinguish Israelis from Palestinians. We drove into a Palestinian neighborhood to see Hezekiah's Tunnel. Next time, we'll walk.

The production team from Barbour Publishing—design director Jason Rovenstine, page designer Robyn Martins, editor George Knight, photo editor Lorraine Caulton, typesetter Glady Dunlap, proofreaders Hope Clarke and Aileen Collins, and many others who played smaller but still vital roles in the process.

God bless them, everyone.

And God bless you as you read this book and, more importantly, as you read his Book.

Steve

BIBLE EVENTS	WORLD EVENTS

BC

BC

Before 4000: God creates the world

Before 2500: Flood kills most of humanity

2100: Abraham, father of the Jews, is born

1870: Jacob and family escape drought, moving to Egypt

1440: Moses leads Hebrew exodus out of Egypt. *Many scholars say archaeology supports a date for the Exodus of about 1275 BC, when Rameses II was pharaoh of Egypt.*

1200: Israel led by "judges" instead of kings

4500: Ur, Abraham's hometown, settled in first known empire: Sumer (Iraq)

3400: Massive flood covers Ur

2550: Great Pyramid built at Giza, Egypt

2136: First reported eclipse comes from China

2000: Invaders destroy Abraham's hometown of Ur

2000: First known written story: Babylonian Epic of Gilgamesh tells of tree of life, evil serpent, and great flood

1895: Settlers start moving to Egypt during peaceful reign of King Sesostris II, who starts irrigation project in northern Egypt

1760: Hammurabi's Code with 282 laws, some laws similar to those of Moses

1440: Thutmose III, called the Napoleon of Egypt and who claims he never lost a battle, invades what is now Israel

1450: Hinduism begins

1300: Rameses II of Egypt cultivates apples along the Nile River

1210: In first mention of Israel, Egyptian king Merneptah says, "Israel is laid waste."

1200: Philistines and other "sea people" arrive on coast of Israel and Egypt

1200: Trojan War ends with burning of Troy

BIBLE EVENTS	WORLD EVENTS
BC	**BC**

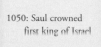

1100: Samson fights the Philistines

1100: Greeks' soaring culture, under Myceneans, plunges into 350-year dark age after Dorian tribes invade from the north

1050: Saul crowned first king of Israel

1000: Chinese cut and store ice for refrigeration

960: Solomon finishes the first Jewish temple

950: Egyptian nobles wear wigs

930: Israel splits in two: Judah in south, Israel in north

776: First Olympics, held in Greece

722: Assyrians exile northern Jewish nation of Israel

701: The Assyrian king Sennacherib says he trapped King Hezekiah "like a caged bird"

586: Babylonians level Jerusalem and temple, exile southern Jewish nation

551: Confucius born

550: Temple of Artemis, one of the Seven Wonders of the World, built in Ephesus, Turkey

539: Cyrus of Persia defeats Babylon and frees the exiles

538: Exiled Jews start returning to Israel

528: Buddha reports attaining enlightenment sitting under a tree

490: Greek runs twenty-five miles to report victory over Persia at battle of Marathon

470: Queen Esther of Persia stops an attempted holocaust

470: Hippocrates, father of medicine, born

110: Romans cultivate oysters as gourmet food

9

BIBLE EVENTS	WORLD EVENTS

BC

63: Roman general Pompey conquers Jerusalem

37: Rome appoints Herod the Great king of the Jews

30: Antony and Cleopatra commit suicide

6: Jesus born in Bethlehem

6: Jupiter and Saturn align to form bright light April 17, 6

5: Exploding star (nova)

4: Herod the Great dies

AD

6: Romans name Caesarea capital of Judea

30: Jesus executed in Jerusalem

26: Pilate begins decade-long rule as Judean governor

35: Paul converts in Damascus, Syria

45: Greek sailors discover monsoon winds and sail from Africa to India in forty days

43: Paul leaves on first missionary trip

47: World's largest library, in Alexandria, Egypt, burns

50: Paul writes first New Testament letter: 1 Thessalonians

50: The French teach Romans to use soap

64: Romans execute Paul and probably Peter

July 18, 64: Rome burns; Nero blames Christians

66: Jews rebel against Rome

June 9, 68: Nero commits suicide

70: Rome destroys Jerusalem and temple

November 1, 79: Mount Vesuvius destroys Pompeii, near Naples

80: Roman Coliseum opens with one hundred days of gladiator fights—thousands of people and animals killed

95: John writes last book of Bible, Revelation

Most dates are approximate.
AD = *Anno Domini*,
Latin for "in the year of the Lord"
BC = Before Christ

105: Chinese make paper from bark, rags

AARON
(AIR un)
Aharon, Hebrew
About 1523–1400 BC
First mention: Exodus 4:14

Aaron was an eighty-three-year-old man when he first appeared in the Bible. Big brother to Moses, he was on a long trek from Egypt to the Sinai desert, looking for his fugitive brother. God sent him: "Go out into the wilderness to meet Moses" (Exodus 4:27). Forty years earlier, Moses had killed an Egyptian foreman for mistreating a Hebrew slave, then ran for his life.

Boldly, the two brothers returned to Egypt and—with Aaron doing most of the talking—demanded that the king free their people, the Hebrews. Ten disastrous plagues later, the king agreed.

Once, on the Exodus out of Egypt, Moses put Aaron in charge—with tragic results. Moses climbed Mount Sinai to receive the Ten Commandments. But he stayed away so long that the people feared he and God had left. They convinced Aaron to build them an idol to lead them—a golden calf like those common in Egypt. When Moses finally returned and saw thousands worshiping the calf, he ordered immediate executions. Three thousand died by the sword. Others died by plague.

Aaron was not only spared; in time God chose him to become Israel's high priest—the first in a tradition that would span some fifteen hundred years. His sons, too, became priests, though his two oldest boys were burned to death after disobeying God by improperly preparing an incense fire.

After lingering forty years in the desert, the Hebrews resumed their march to the Promised Land. Aaron, at age 123, could not join them. At God's

Aaron leads the Israelites in making a golden calf to worship.

As Israel's first high priest, Aaron launched a priestly dynasty that endured more than a millennium—until Romans destroyed the temple in AD 70.

ABEDNEGO

(a BED nee go)
Abed Nego, Hebrew
Arad Nabu, Akkadian
"servant of Nego" (wisdom god)
About 600 BC
First mention: Daniel 1:7

Thrown into a furnace for refusing to worship a gold statue of the Babylonian king, Nebuchadnezzar, Abednego miraculously survived. So did his friends Shadrach and Meshach. His Hebrew name was Azariah. (See *Shadrach.*)

instruction, he climbed Mount Hor, south of Canaan, where he died.

Moses removed the high priestly robes from his brother and put them on Aaron's oldest surviving son, Eleazar—the high priest for a new generation.

AARON'S FAMILY

Father:	Amram
Mother:	Jochebed
Sister:	Miriam
Younger brother:	Moses
Wife:	Elisheba
Four sons:	Nadab,
Abihu, Eleazar, Ithamar	

ABEL

(A bull)
Hebel, Hebrew
"breath"
Before 4000 BC
First mention: Genesis 4:2

The world's first murder victim was Adam and Eve's second son. Abel was a shepherd, while his older brother, Cain, farmed the land. Cain jealously killed Abel. It happened shortly after the two brothers brought gifts to God. "Abel brought several choice lambs" (Genesis 4:4). Cain brought farm produce.

God accepted Abel's offering but not Cain's. Perhaps Cain offered substandard produce or a bad attitude.

Cain's seething jealousy led to a murderous walk in the field with Abel.

ABIGAIL

(AB uh gay il)
Abigayil, Hebrew
"my father rejoices"
About 1000 BC
First mention: 1 Samuel 25:3

Beautiful, sensible, and smart, Abigail was married to a crook. He was Nabal, a rich herder who lived about twenty miles south of David's hometown of Bethlehem. Nabal insulted David by refusing to give his men any food during sheep-shearing season, a time of celebration and prosperity. When David heard this, he led his army to kill Nabal. But Abigail met them on the road and gave them food.

When Nabal discovered how close he had come to dying, he apparently had a heart attack or a stroke and died ten days later. David was so impressed with Abigail that he married her.

ABIMELECH

(uh BIM uh lek)
Abimelek, Hebrew
"my father is king"
About 2100 BC
First mention: Genesis 20:2

The Philistine king Abimelech, of Gerar in southwest Canaan, is best known for trying to add Abraham's wife, Sarah, to his harem.

Abraham moved to the area and told people that the beautiful Sarah was his sister so no one would kill him to marry her. That was half true, since she was his half sister. But in a dream, God warned Abimelech that Sarah was married and her husband was a prophet. Abimelech made a peace treaty with Abraham and showered him with gifts.

ABNER

(AB nur)
Abner, Hebrew
"father is a lamp"
About 1050 BC
First mention: 1 Samuel 14:50

Abner's father and King Saul's father were brothers. In hope of setting up a family dynasty, Abner served Saul as commander and bodyguard. Ironically, Abner's first reported act was presenting to Saul the man who would end that dynasty—David.

After the Philistines killed Saul, Abner backed one of Saul's sons, Ishbosheth, as the new king. Later, in a battle with David's forces, the young brother of David's commander, Joab, chased down Abner. But Abner, a veteran warrior, quickly killed the young man.

Months later, Saul's son accused Abner of sleeping with one of the royal wives. Furious, Abner stormed off to David and vowed to give the nation to him. Joab derailed these negotiations by murdering Abner to avenge his brother's death.

ABRAHAM

(A bruh ham)
Abraham, Hebrew
"father of many"
2100s BC
First mention: Genesis 17:5 (Genesis 11:26
for Abram)

Born and raised in what amounted to the New York City of his day—the world's shoreline hub of culture, power, and wealth—Abraham left his homeland and took everything he owned to a land as rustic and sparsely populated as the Kansas prairies.

Common sense says that a move like that would only doom him to obscurity. Yet, four thousand years later, he is revered as the spiritual father of three major religions: Judaism, Christianity, and Islam.

Before God changed Abraham's name, he was called Abram—meaning "honored father." He grew up in Ur, a city on the west bank of the Euphrates River in southern Iraq. Its ruins today lie just across the river from the modern town of Nasiriya, a hard-fought Iraqi holdout during the 2003 war in which American and British troops ousted dictator Saddam Hussein. In Abram's day, Ur was the control center for the world's first known empire: Sumer.

BOUND FOR CANAAN LAND

Actually, it wasn't Abram who decided to leave home. It was his father, Terah. Why Terah decided to move remains a mystery. The Bible says only that he and his family left "to go to the land of Canaan" (Genesis 11:31). Some scholars guess that Terah, apparently a wealthy man with huge flocks, saw signs of the coming invasion that destroyed Ur in about 2000 BC.

Bound for Canaan, the shortest route was straight west for six hundred miles—almost all of that desert. Not an option for a family with flocks in tow. Terah decided to follow the water supply along one thousand miles of caravan routes. First, he'd walk northwest along the banks of the Euphrates River. Then when he got near the Mediterranean Sea, he would turn south to Canaan.

But he didn't turn south. Instead, he settled in the prosperous town of Haran, about halfway to Canaan. By the time Terah died, Abram was seventy-five years old. God told Abram, "Leave your country, your relatives, and your father's house, and go to the land that I will show you. I will cause you to become the father of a great nation" (Genesis 12:1–2).

Abram did as he was told. He took his wife, Sarai, who was his half sister —Terah's daughter with a second wife. He took his nephew Lot, son of Abram's brother Haran, who had died before the family left Ur. And he took all his livestock and entourage of servants.

PROMISE FOR A CHILDLESS COUPLE

When Abram set up camp at Shechem, in the center of Canaan, God made him a stunning promise: "I am going to give this land to your offspring" (Genesis 12:7).

Abram had no offspring.

And it seemed unlikely he ever would since he was seventy-five and Sarai was sixty-six. Still, Abram built an altar of piled-up stones in honor of God's promise.

Abram's first impression of the land may have left him wondering if God's promise was a blessing or a curse. Famine was squeezing the life out of the land. The drought was so severe that Abram decided to wait it out in Egypt, where the Nile River valley provided water even under the driest conditions.

Abram got in trouble there with the king—serious enough that he was escorted out of the country under armed guard.

His trouble started with a lie that seems strikingly out of character for him. This man who had so much faith in God that he uprooted his family was afraid that some Egyptian would kill him to marry his beautiful senior adult wife. So he and Sarai spread the half-truth that they were brother and sister. True, but the more important half of the truth was that they were husband and wife.

Egypt's king took Sarai into his harem and showered Abram with gifts: livestock and servants, perhaps including Hagar, who is later identified as Egyptian and becomes a surrogate mother for the couple.

A plague struck the king's family. Plagues were often considered punishment from the gods. And the timing apparently led the king to suspect that his marriage provoked the gods.

SURROGATE MOTHER, ANCIENT STYLE

By the time Sarah was seventy-six years old, she felt certain she would never give Abraham a child. "Go and sleep with my servant," she told him. "Perhaps I can have children through her" (Genesis 16:2). Abraham slept with Hagar, and Ishmael was born.

This was a perfectly respectable practice for infertile couples in the ancient Middle East. Similar laws and references show up in many ancient documents from the region where Abraham was born and raised in what is now Iraq: an early Assyrian marriage contract (1800s BC), the Code of Hammurabi, king of Babylon in what is now Iraq (1700s BC), and Nuzi stone tablets from northern Iraq (about 1500 BC).

This is an excerpt of a marriage contract from Nuzi tablets: "If Giliminu [bride's name] will not bear children, Giliminu will take a woman of Lullu-land [apparently famed for excellent slaves] for Shennima [groom's name]."

Law 146 from Hammurabi states: "If a man marries, and his wife gives him her servant to bear children, and then this servant starts acting like she's equal to the wife because of this, the wife isn't allowed to sell her. But she can put a slave mark on her and treat her as a slave."

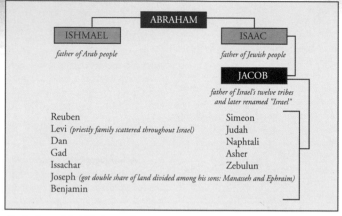

The family tree of the biblical patriarchs.

Abram admitted that Sarai was not only his sister but his wife, as well. That's when the king had Abram and his family escorted to the border, apparently with the king's gifts.

Back in Canaan, years later, the couple used the same ploy with King Abimelech of Gerar, who ruled somewhere along Canaan's southern border. The results were even better this second time around, perhaps because God told the king in a dream that Abram was a prophet. Abram got to keep the bridal gifts from the king, he got extra money as a settlement, he was allowed to stay, and the two men made a peace treaty.

In time, the flocks of Abram and Lot grew so large that it was impossible to graze them in the same fields. So the men separated. Abram gave his nephew first choice of the land, and Lot chose the best pastures in Canaan: the fertile Jordan River valley. Unfortunately for Lot, neighboring kings were eyeing the land, too. An alliance of four powerful kings from the north raided cities of the Jordan valley and plains, carrying off Lot and his family as plunder.

Fortunately for Lot, his uncle was wealthy and well connected. Abram assembled an army of 318 men from his servants alone. Then, with the help of some allies, Abram overtook the raiders, freed the captives, and recovered the plunder. He kept nothing for himself. Instead, he gave a tenth of it to Melchizedek, identified as God's priest living in Salem, an early name for Jerusalem. When Lot's hometown king asked for only the people back, inviting Abram to keep the goods, Abram refused: "I will not take so much as a single thread or sandal thong from you. Otherwise you might say, 'I am the one who made Abram rich!' " (Genesis 14:23). Abram asked only that his allies receive some payment.

ABRAM'S TWO SONS

By the time Sarai reached age seventy-six, she decided that if Abram—then eighty-five—would ever have a son to inherit Canaan, it would be with another woman. So she instructed him to conceive a child with her servant Hagar, an accepted practice for infertile couples in this culture.

Ishmael was born. Though he was not the son destined to inherit Canaan, God made this promise to the boy's father: "I will make a nation of the descendants of Hagar's son because he also is your son" (Genesis 21:13). Many consider Ishmael father of the Arab people.

It was a decade and a half later—when Sarai was ninety and Abram was ninety-nine—that God finally made it clear who would inherit Canaan. It would be the son of Sarai and Abram.

God sealed his promise by changing the couple's names. In ancient times people in authority, such as kings, would often change people's names to mark a turning point in their lives. Abram became Abraham "for you will be the father of many nations. I will give you millions of descendants who will represent many nations" (Genesis 17:5–6). Sarai became Sarah.

This wasn't just a promise. It was an agreement, or covenant, between God and Abraham. For his part, Abraham had to circumcise every male in his family, servants included. And every newborn had to be circumcised on the eighth day after his birth. "Your bodies will thus bear the mark of my everlasting covenant" (Genesis 17:13). Observant Jews today still practice this ritual, called *Berit Mila*, Hebrew for

As God instructed, Abraham's son Isaac is circumcised on the eighth day after his birth—a tradition observant Jews still practice.

"covenant of circumcision."

Not long afterward, the Lord and two others stopped at Abraham's camp on their way to Sodom. Again the Lord promised that Sarah would have a son, but this time he said it would happen within the year. This was apparently the first time Sarah had heard anyone but Abraham say such a thing. Listening from inside the tent, she laughed—as Abraham had done silently when God first made this promise.

So the name God chose for the child was appropriate—Isaac. That's Hebrew for "laughter."

With a son of her own, Sarah no longer had need for the surrogate mother and her son, who was thirteen years old when Isaac was born. In fact, Sarah realized that keeping Ishmael in the family would mean less inheritance for Isaac. (The oldest son generally got a double share of the father's possessions.) So by the time Isaac was weaned, she insisted that Abraham send Hagar and Ishmael away. Abraham certainly loved his oldest son and was heartbroken by the request. But God told him to do as Sarah asked, promising to give Ishmael many descendants, too.

ABRAHAM'S BIGGEST TEST

Isaac was thirty-seven years old when God ordered Abraham to sacrifice him. So says one Jewish legend. It's based in part on the biblical report that Isaac was thirty-seven when Sarah died. The legend says it was the proposed sacrifice that killed her, shocking her to death at age 127.

The Bible never says how old Isaac was. Father and son traveled to a hill of Moriah, three days from their home in Beersheba. That may be the same Mount Moriah where Solomon built the Jewish temple in Jerusalem and where the Islamic Dome of the Rock now dominates the city skyline.

With faithful obedience that seems incomprehensible, Abraham built an altar and raised the knife to kill his son. Suddenly an angel appeared and stopped him, saying, "Now I know that you truly fear God. You have not withheld even your beloved son from me" (Genesis 22:12).

New Testament writers saw in this story the foreshadowing of another Father-Son story. What Abraham was willing to do—sacrifice his son—God did.

Abraham lived almost forty years after Sarah died. Then he was buried with her in the cave of Machpelah near Hebron, which he had bought as a family burial site. Isaac and his wife, Rebekah, were buried there, too. The site today is marked by a huge mosque over what is called the Tomb of the Patriarchs. Built by Herod the Great some two thousand years ago, the building was declared a mosque by Muslims seven hundred years ago. Today, Palestinians control the site, but they permit Jews to worship there under restrictions.

ABSALOM

(AB sah lome)
Absalom, Hebrew
"father is peace"
About 1000 BC
First mention: 2 Samuel 3:3

Though his name bears the Hebrew word for *peace,* Absalom was anything but peaceful. He murdered his half brother and led a coup against his father, King David.

Absalom was David's third son, born to one of his many wives: Maacah, daughter of the king of Geshur, a region along the Sea of Galilee's eastern bank. As David's wives competed for his attention, so did their children. Rivalries churned into hatred, especially among sons who wanted to become the next king.

Absalom, originally third in succession, worked up to first. Kileab, second in succession, apparently died young. Amnon, the oldest, made a fatal decision. He raped Absalom's full sister, Tamar. Amnon lured Tamar into his bedroom by saying he was sick and needed to be fed. By law, Amnon should have married Tamar. Instead, he ordered her out.

REVENGE FOR RAPE

David got angry about the rape but did nothing. Absalom, however, waited for a chance to get revenge. Two years later, during a sheep-shearing celebration, Absalom had his men get Amnon drunk, then kill him. Absalom fled to his grandfather's home in Geshur.

After three years, David missed Absalom. So David's commander, Joab, talked the king into inviting Absalom home. David agreed but refused to see Absalom for another two years. Twice, Absalom asked Joab to intercede. But Joab refused to come. In desperation, Absalom had his servants set fire to one of Joab's barley fields. That brought Joab, who arranged for the son and father to meet.

Reconciliation, however, had no chance against Absalom's bitterness. The crown prince, now first in succession to the throne, decided not to wait for his father to declare him king. Absalom, with his good looks and winning personality, began courting the citizens. Each morning he went to the city gate, where cases were tried, and told the litigants they had a good case and he wished he had the power to give them justice. When people tried to bow before him, he hugged them instead. "In this way, Absalom stole the hearts of all the people of Israel" (2 Samuel 15:6).

COUP AGAINST A FATHER

Absalom crowned himself king in Hebron, his birthplace and David's first capital, about twenty miles south of Jerusalem. This coup was so well planned that David felt compelled to flee Jerusalem. But he left behind a loyal advisor who won the confidence of Absalom and convinced him to mobilize his entire army against David. This bought time for David to muster his own seasoned warriors.

The battle took place in a forest east of the Jordan River. When the battle turned against Absalom, he fled on his mule. But his long, thick hair got caught in an oak tree and left him dangling like an acorn. Despite David's order to spare Absalom, Joab said the order was nonsense, and he plunged three daggers into the rebel's heart.

When David heard his son was dead, he burst into tears: "O my son Absalom! My son, my son Absalom! If only I could have died instead of you! O Absalom, my son, my son" (2 Samuel 18:33).

ACCO

(AK oh)
Akko, Hebrew
First mention: Judges 1:31

MAP 4
B2

Paul, on his third missionary trip, visited this thriving city on the Mediterranean coast. Its ancient ruins lie north of Haifa, Israel, just across the bay. In Paul's day it was called Ptolemais, after the Egyptian king Ptolemy, who rebuilt it. A thousand years later the Crusaders captured it and called it Acre.

ACHAIA

(uh KAY yah)
Achaia, Greek
First mention: Acts 18:12

MAP 5
A2

Paul, during his second missionary trip, became the first Christian on record to introduce Europeans to the Good News about Jesus. He spent a year and a half starting the church in Corinth, bustling capital of the Roman province of Achaia in what is now the southern half of Greece. Two other famous cities in the region were Athens and Sparta.

Upset with Paul's teachings, a group of Jews took him to the new governor, Gallio, and accused him of heresy. Gallio dismissed the case as nothing more than a religious squabble.

ACHAN

(A kin)
Akan, Hebrew
About 1400 BC
First mention: Joshua 7:1

Achan was the first Hebrew in the Promised Land executed for disobeying God. In fact, he got his entire family executed because of his greed.

After the walls of Jericho tumbled down, the Hebrews were supposed to leave without taking anything. The spoils of this battle belonged to God. But Achan stole "a beautiful robe imported from Babylon, two hundred silver coins, and a bar of gold weighing more than a pound" (Joshua 7:21).

Joshua, the leader, didn't suspect a thing until they lost their next battle. Then, using a mysterious system known as lots, perhaps like dice, Joshua narrowed the problem down to the tribe of Judah and eventually to Achan, who admitted his sin.

For disobeying God—an act that cost thirty-six Hebrew warriors their lives—Achan and his family were stoned to death and burned with all his possessions.

ACHOR

(AY core)
Akor, Hebrew
"trouble"
First mention: Joshua 7:24

MAP 1
C5

"Trouble" is Achor's name, with good reason. After the walls of Jericho came tumbling down, one man disobeyed God—Achan. The Hebrews were to take nothing, but Achan couldn't resist a robe imported from Babylon, two hundred silver coins, and a bar of gold. For this, the Hebrews lost their next battle.

When Achan confessed, Joshua replied, "Why have you brought trouble on us? The LORD will now bring trouble on you" (Joshua 7:25). The Hebrews stoned Achan and his family in a valley they named Achor.

Most scholars say Achor is now El Buqeah, "little valley," the only area near Jericho that fits the Bible description of a fertile plain bordered by hills. The plain is about five miles long and two miles wide.

Prophets later used Achor as a symbolic way of promising that God would reverse Israel's hard times. "For my people who have searched for me. . . the valley of Achor will be a place to pasture herds" (Isaiah 65:10).

ADAM

(ADD um)
Adam, Hebrew
"human"
Before 4000 BC
First mention: Genesis 2:19

On the sixth and final workday of Creation, God made Adam and Eve—the world's first human beings. Their assignment: "Be masters over all life—the fish in the sea, the birds in the sky, and all the livestock, wild animals, and small animals" (Genesis 1:26). They were caretakers of the Creation.

In this idyllic world, all seemed perfect. Adam and Eve were like God, "created. . .in his own image; God patterned them after himself" (Genesis 1:27). There was just one rule: "You may freely eat any fruit in the garden except fruit from the tree of the knowledge of good and evil. If you eat of its fruit, you will surely die" (Genesis 2:16–17).

God creates Adam from dust of the earth. Michelangelo painted this masterpiece on the Sistine Chapel's ceiling.

21

A B C D E F G H I J K L M N O P Q R S T U V W X Y Z

They ate the fruit, and in this disobedience they somehow damaged the Creation. The world was no longer perfect, survival became hard work, and death awaited humanity. Expelled from the Garden of Eden, Adam died at age 930.

New Testament writers portrayed Adam as the opposite of Jesus: "Everyone dies because all of us are related to Adam, the first man. But all who are related to Christ, the other man, will be given new life" (1 Corinthians 15:22).

OTHER HUMANS MADE FROM SOIL

God scooped soil from the earth, Genesis 2 says, and created the world's first human. Many other creation stories from the Middle East also tell of humans created from soil.

Some of the oldest come from Sumer, birthplace of the world's first known civilization, in what is now Iraq. One story tells of Enki, Sumerian god of water, ordering the creation of humans: "Mix the heart of the clay that is over the abyss." In another story the goddess Aruru creates the hero Enkidu: She "pinched off a piece of clay, cast it out into the open country. She created a primitive man, Enkidu the warrior."

ADAM

MAP 2
D4

(ADD uhm)
Adam, Hebrew
"human"
First mention: Joshua 3:16

When Joshua led the Hebrews across the Jordan River into the Promised Land, they didn't get wet. In a miracle strikingly similar to the crossing of the Red Sea, God blocked the river. "The water began piling up at a town upstream called Adam" (Joshua 3:16).

Adam was probably an ancient city about eighteen miles north of Jericho, on what is now Jordan's side of the river. The modern city near the ancient ruins is known by its Arabic name, Damiyeh, which sounds similar to the Hebrew word *adamah,* "earth," from which Adam was made.

The Jordan River stopped again in 1927. An earthquake jarred the 150-foot soft soil cliffs near Damiyeh/Adam, producing a landslide that blocked the Jordan River for twenty-one hours.

ADULLAM

MAP 2
C5

(uh DOO luhm)
Adullam, Hebrew
First mention: Genesis 38:1

Insane with jealousy over how the nation loved his son-in-law, David, King Saul sent a detachment of soldiers to assassinate him. But Saul's daughter, David's wife, helped him escape. David fled to one of the many caves near Adullam, a village in the Judean hills about five miles west of his hometown, Bethlehem.

"Soon his brothers and other relatives joined him there. Then others began coming—men who were in trouble or in debt or who were just discontented—until David was the leader of about four hundred men" (1 Samuel 22:1–2),

AHAB

(A hab)
Ahab, Hebrew
Possibly "father's brother"
Reigned about 875–854 BC
First mention: 1 Kings 16:28

Perhaps the most surprising thing about King Ahab—best known for marrying evil and murderous Jezebel—is that he worshiped God. In fact, the names of all his children signified praise of God. But this seventh king of Israel's northern nation also worshiped his wife's god, Baal.

Ahab not only built a temple and shrines for Baal, he stood passively by while Queen Jezebel ordered God's prophets executed. The prophet Elijah stepped in and on Mount Carmel called fire from the sky to prove God's power. In response, the crowd killed Baal's prophets, infuriating Jezebel.

Though Ahab's marriage to Jezebel produced spiritual chaos, it provided at least temporary peace and prosperity. Jezebel was princess of Phoenicia, in what is now Lebanon. This guaranteed peace with seafaring Phoenicia, which included sea trade.

Ahab was a skilled military leader, twice defeating Syrian invaders and once taking part in a coalition that stopped Assyria's push toward Israel. Ahab died in a later battle, however, trying to recapture land east of the Jordan River. A stray Syrian arrow penetrated his armor's seam.

This is his legacy: "Ahab did what was evil in the LORD's sight, even more than any of the kings before him" (1 Kings 16:30).

AHAZ

(A haz)
Ahaz, Hebrew
"God holds"
Reigned about 742–727 BC
First mention: 2 Kings 15:38

Ahaz wasn't just a bad king. He was one of the worst, worshiping idols and "even sacrificing his own son in the fire" (2 Kings 16:3).

The eleventh king of the southern Jewish kingdom of Judah, Ahaz refused to join forces with Israel's northern kingdom and Syria to stop Assyria's advance. When the coalition turned on him, Ahaz asked Assyria for help—not trusting Isaiah's promise that all Judah needed for survival was to worship God.

Assyria defeated the coalition. But they took from Ahaz many temple treasures as payment for protecting Judah. Ahaz ruled for sixteen years, but his nation refused to bury him with other kings. Surprisingly, his son Hezekiah became one of Judah's most godly kings.

Ai

(A eye)
Haay, Hebrew
"ruin"
First mention: Genesis 12:8

MAP 1
C4

It's ironic that Abraham camped in the hills near Ai while scouting the Canaanite land God promised him. Ai is best known for handing Joshua his first defeat.

After Jericho fell, Joshua sent scouts to nearby Ai. The village was small, so Joshua sent only three thousand soldiers to take it. God allowed Ai to chase off the attackers because one Hebrew had disobeyed him: Achan took spoils of war from Jericho. Joshua ordered Achan stoned to death, then he led thirty thousand soldiers against Ai. Most hid in ambush, while Joshua led five thousand in a fake attack followed by retreat. Ai pursued, as before, leaving the village unguarded. The Hebrews in hiding rushed into Ai and set it on fire. Smoke was Joshua's signal to stop running, turn, and fight. The rest of his army joined by attacking Ai's army from the rear, killing them all.

It's unclear where Ai was located. Some scholars in the early 1900s suggested a nearly three-acre mound of dirt covering ruins known by the Arabic name et Tell ("ruin" or "mound"), about ten miles west of Jericho. But excavations show no one lived there at the time.

Aijalon

(AY jah lon)
Ayyalon, Hebrew
"deer field"
First mention: Joshua 10:12

MAP 1
B5

It was in the sprawling valley of Aijalon, about fifteen miles northwest of Jerusalem, that Joshua offered a mysterious battle prayer that still perplexes Bible students: "Let the sun stand still over Gibeon, and the moon over the valley of Aijalon" (Joshua 10:12).

Joshua prepares to execute Canaanite kings after defeating their coalition forces at Aijalon, where "the sun stopped in the middle of the sky."

Joshua's invading army had already taken the cities of Jericho and Ai and was tricked into making a peace treaty with Gibeon. In response, the worried king of Jerusalem assembled a coalition army from several Canaanite cities and led them north to punish their sister city of Gibeon for the betrayal. Gibeonite messengers rushed this news to Joshua, who was camped almost twenty miles east, near the Jordan River.

After an all-night march, Joshua's army took the coalition forces by surprise, routing them, then chasing them west toward the valley of Aijalon. Joshua's prayer may have been a request for God to prolong the day, allowing the Israelites to finish the job of killing their enemies.

"The sun stopped in the middle of the sky. . . . Never before or since has there been a day like that one" (Joshua 10:13–14).

AKKAD

(ACK add)
Akkad, Hebrew
Agade, Akkadian
"fortress"
First mention: Genesis 10:10

Nimrod—one of Noah's descendants —started the first-known Persian Gulf empire by building Akkad, Babel, and other cities. Akkad's location is unknown, though some scholars guess it was near Baghdad.

By 2350 BC—about two centuries before Abraham—Akkad became capital of a powerful dynasty ruled by Sargon I. The region, which took the city's name, covered a hundred-mile stretch of fertile land

along the Tigris and Euphrates rivers. In time, this city and region gave its name to the Akkadian language, used by the Babylonians and Assyrians.

ALEXANDRIA

(al ex AN dree uh)
Alexandreia, Greek
"defender of humanity"
First mention: Acts 6:9

One of the Seven Wonders of the World towered nearly 450 feet above Alexandria, Egypt's shoreline. It was a lighthouse that sailors could see for miles. Paul, on his way to trial in Rome, sailed on a grain ship from this commercial center located where the Nile River drains into the Mediterranean.

Named after Alexander the Great, who conquered Egypt in 323 BC, this city became Egypt's capital during Greek and Roman times. A famed center of learning, Alexandria had the finest library of its time, with more than five hundred thousand volumes. Home to about a million people in New Testament times, these included hundreds of thousands of Jewish immigrants. Here is where Paul's associate Apollos studied and where the first known Bible translation—the Septuagint, a Greek version of Jewish Scriptures—was crafted. Jewish scholars from Alexandria were also among those who debated religion with Stephen, the first Christian martyr.

Alexandria's ancient library was lost in a fire in AD 47, but the city remains a busy port town of more than three million—Egypt's second largest city after the modern capital, Cairo.

AMMON

(uh MAHN)
Ammon, Hebrew
"relatives"
First mention: Deuteronomy 2:19

MAP 1
E4

Today's capital of Jordan—Israel's eastern neighbor—not only preserves the name of an ancient people but is built on the ruins of their capital. Amman was once the capital city of Ammon, homeland of the Ammonites. Jews considered these people their relatives. During the Exodus out of Egypt into the Promised Land, God told the Hebrews, "Do not bother the Ammonites, the descendants of Lot. . . . I will not give you any of their land" (Deuteronomy 2:19).

In the time of the judges, the Ammonites raided Israel for eighteen years. God sent a warrior named Jephthah, who raised an army and stopped the raiders.

AMNON

(AM nahn)
Amnon, Hebrew
"faithful"
About 1000 BC
First mention: 2 Samuel 3:2

David's oldest son, who was first in line to become Israel's next king, didn't live long enough. Amnon cut his life span short by raping his half sister, Tamar. He lured her to his bedroom by pretending he was sick. Disgust

CHOICE WORDS FOR THE RICH

Amos delivered God's stern words to Jewish nobles who oppressed the poor. Here's a sampling:

• "Listen to me, you 'fat cows' of Samaria, you women who oppress the poor and crush the needy. . . . 'The time will come when you will be led away with hooks in your noses'" (Amos 4:1–2).
• "I will destroy the beautiful homes of the wealthy—their winter mansions and their summer houses, too—all their palaces filled with ivory" (Amos 3:15).
• "I hate all your show and pretense—the hypocrisy of your religious festivals. . . . Away with your hymns of praise! They are only noise to my ears. . . . I want to see a mighty flood of justice, a river of righteous living that will never run dry" (Amos 5:21, 23–24).

became his afterglow, and he ran Tamar off instead of agreeing to marry her as Jewish law required (Exodus 22:16).

David became furious but did nothing. So Tamar's full brother, Absalom, patiently plotted revenge. Two years later, when Amnon got drunk at a sheep-shearing festival, Absalom gave his men a signal and they killed the crown prince. Suddenly, Absalom was first in line to become king.

AMOS
(A muhs)
Amos, Hebrew
"cattle's a burden"
About 760 BC
First mention: Amos 1:1

When life was at its best for Jews living in the northern Jewish nation of Israel, a prophet from the southern nation of Judah arrived with unbelievable news from God: "I will bring the dynasty of King Jeroboam to a sudden end" (Amos 7:9).

Jeroboam II was approaching the end of a prosperous forty-year reign (786–746 BC). He had recaptured land once owned by Solomon, in what is now Lebanon, Syria, and Jordan. But rich people oppressed the poor and made a mockery of religion by singing to God as though they were doing nothing wrong.

Amos wasn't a prophet like those of his day who were part of a guild funded by the king. He was a layman who owned herds and an orchard of sycamore figs generally used for cattle feed. Because he cried out for the oppressed poor, some speculate he was poor. But the word used to describe him as a herdsman (*noqed*) is used only one other time in the Bible—referring to a king. In addition, Amos was a masterful writer who apparently read a lot of history. Poor people, however, usually couldn't read. So many today think Amos was rich.

A priest ordered him out of the country, and Amos probably left because he had finished his work there, and his herds needed care. But he may have lived long enough to see his prophecy come true. In 722 BC, Assyria crushed Israel, exiling the survivors and repopulating the region with Assyrian settlers.

An outspoken critic of the rich, Amos called pampered wives of wealthy landowners fat cows who crush the poor and then ask their husbands for another drink.

ANAB

MAP 1 C6

(A nab)
Anab, Hebrew
First mention:
Joshua 11:21

A fierce race of giants lived in several cities throughout Canaan, including Anab on Canaan's southern border. Those giants spooked the Hebrews, who decided to stop the

Exodus. God punished their lack of faith by sentencing them to forty years in the southern badlands. When the next generation of Hebrews finally invaded the Promised Land, led by Joshua, they wiped out the giants and destroyed their towns.

ANANIAS

(an uh NI us)
Hananias, Greek
Perhaps from *Hananeyah,* Hebrew
"God is merciful"
1. About 30 AD
2. About 35 AD
First mention:1. Acts 5:1
2. Acts 9:10

1. **Dropped dead.** The first reported Christian convert to die did so immediately after giving a donation to the church. Ananias died where he stood, condemned by the apostle Peter. His death terrorized believers because they thought God had killed him.

Apparently, it all began when Ananias and his wife, Sapphira, saw the accolades showered on Barnabas for selling some property and donating the money for believers in need. So Ananias and his wife decided to do the same. They, however, kept some money for themselves but told the apostles they were donating all the proceeds.

"Ananias, why has Satan filled your heart?" Peter asked. "You lied to the Holy Spirit, and you kept some of the money for yourself" (Acts 5:3). In what may have been a massive heart attack, Ananias instantly dropped dead. Three hours later, the same thing happened to his wife after she arrived and repeated the exaggerated claim of generosity.

2. **Healed Paul.** For three days, the man who would later become known as the apostle Paul lay blind in Damascus —the result of seeing Jesus in a vision. God instructed a believer, Ananias, to go to Paul and lay prayerful hands on him to heal him.

"But Lord," Ananias replied, "I've heard about the terrible things this man has done to the believers in Jerusalem!" (Acts 9:13). In fact, Paul had come to Damascus to arrest believers. But God explained that Paul would take the message of salvation to Jews, non-Jews, and even royalty.

Ananias obeyed, and when he touched Paul, something like scales fell from Paul's eyes so he could see again.

ANDREW

(AN droo)
Andreas, Greek
"manly"
First century AD
First mention: Matthew 4:18

Peter's brother, Andrew, followed John the Baptist before leaving to become one of the first of Jesus' twelve disciples. The switch took place when John pointed him out as "the Lamb of God" (John 1:36). Andrew spent the rest of the day with Jesus, then went to Peter and declared that he had found the Messiah. Apparently later, Jesus saw the brothers fishing and called out: "Come, be my disciples, and I will show you how to fish for people!" (Matthew 4:19).

Andrew is the disciple who brought to Jesus a boy with some bread and fish that Jesus used to feed thousands. In the late 200s, a story called the Acts of Andrew reported that a Roman official ordered him crucified on an X-shaped cross in southern Greece.

ANTIOCH

(AN tee ahk)
Antiocheia, Greek
First mention:1. Acts 6:5
2. Acts 13:14

MAP 5
F3, D2

A general and successor of Alexander the Great—Seleucus—apparently admired his father, Antiochus, because he named many cities Antioch. There were sixteen. Two show up in the Bible.

1. Antioch, Syria. It's called Hatay, Turkey, now. In Bible times, Antioch was the third largest city in the Roman Empire (population about five hundred thousand), following Rome and Alexandria, Egypt. After Jews in Jerusalem killed Stephen and began persecuting other Jewish Christians, many believers fled some three hundred miles north to the more tolerant Jewish communities in Antioch, Syria.

An amazing thing happened there. Jewish Christians accepted non-Jews into their movement without requiring them to observe circumcision or other Jewish traditions. In time, the apostles sent one of their ministers, Barnabas, to investigate. He became the pastor and soon recruited Paul to help him.

Here is where believers were first called "Christians," perhaps a belittling term like "Moonies" for followers of Sun Myung Moon. Here, too, is where missions began. The church, guided by the Holy Spirit, commissioned Barnabas and Paul to travel abroad, spreading the news about Jesus.

2. Antioch, Pisidia. During Paul's first missionary trip, he and Barnabas sailed to the southwestern coast of what is now Turkey, apparently wasting no time getting out of the swampy area famous for its mosquito-bred malaria. They moved north into the highland city of Antioch (now ruins near Yalvac), in a small region called Pisidia in Rome's province of Galatia.

Synagogue leaders invited the travelers to address Sabbath worshipers, as was the custom. Initially, the people liked what they heard and invited them back for the next Sabbath. Most of the town showed up. Suddenly jealous, the Jewish leaders "slandered Paul and argued against whatever he said" (Acts 13:45).

Welcome mat withdrawn, the two moved on, vowing to take their message to non-Jews. Still, Paul returned during his second and third missionary trips to visit those who believed his teachings.

APHEK

(AY fek)
Apeq, Hebrew
"fortress"
First mention: Joshua 12:18

Israel lost its holiest object—the gold-plated ark containing the Ten Commandments—in a battle with the Philistines at Aphek, a village whose ruins (Ras el Ain) rest along the Yarkon River in what is now the eastern outskirts of Tel Aviv. It was after losing the first battle that soldiers decided to use the ark as a charm to help win the next offensive. Two sons of the ninety-eight-year-old high priest, Eli, who was Samuel's mentor, took the ark into battle. But the Philistines won, stole the ark, and killed Eli's sons. When Eli heard the news, he fell off his chair, breaking his neck and dying. The Philistines returned the ark after an outbreak of tumors.

Years later, the Philistines assembled another army at Aphek—the one that killed Saul, opening the door for David's dynasty.

APOLLOS

(uh PAH luhs)
Apollos, Greek
First century AD
First mention: Acts 18:24

When the troubled church of Corinth split into factions, some supported their founding pastor, Paul, and others supported a newcomer named Apollos. He was an eloquent speaker from the Oxford of the ancient world—Alexandria, Egypt—an educator's paradise, with the world's biggest library.

As a polished speaker, Apollos may have left Paul sounding dirt dry in comparison. Paul did put at least one person to sleep with a long-winded sermon (Acts 20:9). And he said he knew what his critics were saying about his sermons: "I am bold in my letters but timid in person" (2 Corinthians 10:1).

There's no hint in the Bible that Apollos encouraged this rift. On the contrary, Paul's later supportive words about Apollos suggest he didn't.

The Bible says Apollos spent time in Ephesus, Turkey, before moving on to Corinth, Greece. Why he strayed so far from his Egyptian home is uncertain. Perhaps his top-notch education combined with his public speaking skills assured him an eager audience as a traveling teacher.

APPIAN WAY

(APE ee un)
Via Appia, Latin
"Appius Road"
First mention: Acts 28:15

When Paul, under arrest and headed for trial, reached port in Italy's Bay of Naples, he walked north to Rome on one of the world's oldest known roads: the Appian Way. Named after the official in charge of the project, Appius Claudius, it was built in 312 BC. In Paul's day, the stone-paved road spanned some 130 miles to Capua, just north of Naples. It later extended about 350 miles to Italy's boot heel city called

Brindisi, on the Adriatic Sea. This was the main trade route to Greece and the eastern part of the empire.

One of the world's oldest roads, this stone-paved Appian Way led Paul on the final leg of his trip to Rome for trial.

crucified some twenty years earlier—was the Messiah.

The couple moved to neighboring Greece and set up their tent-making business in Corinth. There they met the apostle Paul, a fellow tent maker who worked with them to support himself while he started the Corinthian church. The couple later went with Paul to Ephesus in Turkey and taught the traveling minister Apollos about the Christian faith. They eventually returned to Rome about a year after Claudius died in AD 54. They were the first people Paul greeted in his New Testament letter to believers in Rome.

AR

(ARE)

Ar, Hebrew

"city"

First mention: Numbers 21:15

MAP 1
D6

AQUILA

(uh QUILL uh)

Akylas, Greek

"eagle"

First century AD

First mention: Acts 18:2

Aquila and his wife, Priscilla, may have been church leaders in Rome before Claudius Caesar ordered them out of town. In AD 49, Caesar ordered all Jews to leave, perhaps because of violent clashes between tradition-minded Jews and those who believed that Jesus—

On their march to the Promised Land, Moses and the Hebrews passed through the Moabite town or perhaps region called Ar, along the northern border with Ammon. Moab and Ammon, in what is now Jordan, were nations descended from Lot's sons. God told the Hebrews to pass through these lands peacefully because they belonged to Lot's descendants. Exactly where Ar was remains a mystery.

ARABIA

(uh RAY bee uh)
Arab, Hebrew
"ambush"
First mention: 1 Kings 10:15

In Bible times, Arabia wasn't the Saudi Arabian desert nation we know today that's more than four times the size of Texas. It was bigger. "Arabia" meant nearly all the desert east of Israel as well as the Sinai Peninsula in the south. The queen of Sheba came from Arabia, bringing "a great caravan of camels loaded with spices, huge quantities of gold, and precious jewels" (1 Kings 10:2). A spider web of caravan routes covered Arabia, connecting Mediterranean people with Persian Gulf cultures. Paul, after his conversion in Damascus, retreated to Arabia—perhaps an oasis town to the east or south.

ARAD

(AY rad)
Arad, Hebrew
First mention: Numbers 21:1

After the Hebrews had lived forty years in the desert south of Canaan, God gave them approval to resume their trip toward the Promised Land. The king of Arad, a fortified city about thirty-five miles south of Jerusalem and just inside Canaan's border, decided to launch a preemptive strike. His army succeeded in taking prisoners, but his entire city was wiped out in a Hebrew counterattack. Ruins of the ancient city lie near the modern town of Arad.

Snow-capped Mount Ararat, photographed from a space shuttle, is the highest mountain in the Ararat range.

ARARAT

(AIR ah rat)
Ararat, Hebrew
Urartu, Assyrian
First mention: Genesis 8:4

It surprises many people, but the Bible doesn't say that Noah's ark came to rest on Mount Ararat. "The boat came to rest on the mountains of Ararat" (Genesis 8:4). Like the Rockies, Ararat is a mountain range. It runs along the border of Turkey, Iran, and Armenia —just south of the Black Sea and the Caspian Sea.

In a conservative estimate, the Ararat mountains cover territory about the size of Kansas. But not everyone agrees on where one range ends and another begins, so some estimates more than double that territory.

Noah's ark before the flood, as envisioned by an artist, based on the Bible's description. The Bible says this covered barge ran aground somewhere in the Ararat mountains—many speculate at Mount Ararat.

There is, however, one standout mountain with twin peaks. For at least the last thousand years, this extinct volcano in eastern Turkey has been known as Mount Ararat (Agri Dag by Turks). Its tallest peak, Great Ararat, towers nearly seventeen thousand feet and is always covered in snow. The second peak, Little Ararat, rises almost thirteen thousand feet. A harsh mountain known for its earthquakes, avalanches, and shifting glaciers, Ararat has earned a nickname by locals: Painful Mountain. These grueling conditions, however, haven't stopped explorers from trying to find Noah's ark somewhere on the slopes.

In the third century BC, a Babylonian priest named Berossos reported that mountain people of the region said they knew where to find the ship described in the Babylonian flood story. He said they even wore charms made from the ship's waterproofing material, bitumen, which is naturally occurring tar or asphalt.

In the last two hundred years, many explorers have chased clues like these up one side of the mountain and down the other. Some have claimed astonishing discoveries, such as pieces of wood from Noah's ark or photographs of the hull. But so far, no discovery has produced convincing evidence that Noah's ark ever came anywhere near this mountain. Still, people continue their search—nowadays using high-tech methods such as ice-penetrating radar and satellites that map suspicious bulges beneath the snow.

HAND-CUT TIMBER AT 13,000 FEET

In 1955, a French explorer, Fernand Navarra, pulled pieces of wood from a glacier thirteen thousand feet up Mount Ararat. One piece was a hand-cut board five feet long. Carbon 14 tests, however, showed the wood was no more than twelve hundred years old. But a question remains: What was cut timber doing that high up on an inhospitable mountain? Some speculate it may have been part of an ark-like monument that Crusader-era monks built for visiting pilgrims.

AREOPAGUS

(AIR ee OP uh gus)
Areios pagos, Greek
"Ares Hill," after the Greek god of war, or
"Mars' Hill," after Roman god of war, or
"Hill of Curses [Arai]"
First mention: Acts 17:19

See Athens

MAP 5
B2

While visiting Athens during his second missionary trip, Paul piqued the curiosity of philosophers by telling them about Jesus' resurrection. Most educated Greeks didn't believe in the resurrection of the body. So they brought him to a meeting place for philosophers: a flattop, limestone hill called the Areopagus. After climbing steps chiseled into the side of this lone outcropping that rose some 370 feet high, Paul told these elite thinkers about the one they had already honored with an altar inscribed "To an Unknown God" (Acts 17:23). Some laughed. Others believed.

ARIMATHEA

(air uh mah THEE uh)
Arimathaia, Greek
First mention: Matthew 27:57

MAP 4
B4

Mentioned only once in each Gospel, Arimathea was the hometown of Joseph, the rich man who donated his tomb for the burial of Jesus. Joseph of Arimathea was a member of the Sanhedrin, the Jewish high council that pressured Pilate into crucifying Jesus. It's uncertain where Arimathea was, but the name was apparently a Greek adaptation of a somewhat similar-sounding Hebrew name, much like Munich is the English version of Munchen. Among many possibilities are Ramallah, eight miles north of Jerusalem; er-Ram, five miles north of Jerusalem; and Rentis, fifteen miles east of Tel Aviv.

ARMAGEDDON

(are muh GED un)
Armagedon, Greek
Har Megiddo, Hebrew
"mountain of Megiddo"
First mention: Revelation 16:16

See Jezreel Valley

MAP 4
B3

In a vision about how the world as we know it will end, John of Revelation sees a global gathering of "all the rulers and their armies to a place called Armageddon in Hebrew" (Revelation 16:16). What follows is a massive battle in which heaven's armies wipe out the armies of earth.

Actually, there's no such place on the map.

Armageddon—a word used only once in the Bible—is supposed to be a Greek spelling that mimics the sound of a particular Hebrew phrase. Which phrase is uncertain. The most popular guess is that the Greek word is a mispronunciation of two Hebrew words: "har Megiddo" (mountain of Megiddo). Another possibility is "ir Megiddo" (city of Megiddo).

Megiddo was an ancient fortress built on a hundred-foot-high hill in the line of rolling hills called the Mount Carmel range. Megiddo controlled a major route through these hills. Romans called this route the "Way of the Sea" because it paralleled

"The perfect battlefield" is what Napoleon called this sprawling Jezreel valley, which some Bible experts say is the Bible's Valley of Armageddon.

the coastline. Beneath the fortress sat a sprawling, triangle-shaped valley called by various names: Jezreel valley, Esdraelon, and Valley of Armageddon. The valley has three legs: (1) twenty miles, running southwest along the foot of the Carmel range, (2) twenty miles, extending north to Mount Tabor, (3) twelve miles, stretching west toward the coast along the Nazareth ridge.

When Napoleon saw this valley, he declared it the world's most perfect battlefield. In fact, more than thirty major battles have been fought there. Joshua captured Megiddo. Deborah's Hebrew militia charged down Mount Tabor and routed a chariot corps bogged down at the Kishon River. Gideon overpowered the Midian raiders. And Jewish king Josiah died in a battle with Neco of Egypt. In 1918, British general Edmund Allenby

charged into this valley from the east, with the rising sun to his back, and liberated the region from the Turks of the Ottoman Empire.

Some scholars say John of Revelation was describing yet another battle to come. Others say John used this valley as an excellent symbol of the final battle between good and evil. In either case, John made this much clear. God wins. Good prevails. (See also *Megiddo*.)

ARNON RIVER

MAP 1
D6

(R nahn)
Arnon, Hebrew
First mention: Numbers 21:13

One spectacular site in the Middle East is a massive gorge, three miles wide in some places and up to half a mile deep. It was formed by the Arnon River, which flows west across Jordan and empties into the Dead Sea. Today called Wadi

Mojib, this stream provided a natural boundary between the Ammonite kingdom in the north and the Moabites in the south. Arnon's gorge made it nearly impossible to travel north and south along the east bank of the Dead Sea. The main route—the King's Highway—lay about fifteen miles farther east.

ASA

(A sah)
Asa, Hebrew
"healer"
Reigned 913–873 BC
First mention: 1 Kings 15:8

King Asa of Judah deposed his grandmother, Maacah. She served as queen mother but made the mistake of erecting an obscene pole used in fertility rituals. And she did it when Asa was leading a reform to draw people back to God.

Asa also had troubles with King Baasha of Israel—the Jewish nation in the north—especially boundary squabbles. Once, Baasha captured Ramah. That was a village just seven miles north of Asa's Jerusalem capital. Asa emptied the temple treasury to pay Syria's king to attack Baasha. The Syrian agreed, and Baasha retreated.

ASAPH

(A saf)
Asap, Hebrew
"collector"
About 1000 BC
First mention: 1 Chronicles 6:39

Of the four Bible men named Asaph, the best known is a musician David appointed music minister in Jerusalem.

It was Asaph who led the Jews in praise when Israel's most sacred object—the ark containing the Ten Commandments—arrived in Jerusalem. A dozen psalms bear his name, perhaps written by him or in his style (Psalms 50, 73–83). His family became one of three Levite clans in charge of music after Solomon built the temple.

ASHDOD

(ASH dod)
Asdod, Hebrew
First mention: Joshua 11:22

MAP 1
B5

One of five key Philistine cities along the Mediterranean coast, Ashdod is most famous for what happened after Philistine soldiers captured the Jewish ark containing the Ten Commandments. They set the ark in Ashdod's temple, beside an idol of their god Dagon. By morning, the idol had fallen on its face. Then came an epidemic of tumors throughout the town. The Philistines returned the ark.

Amos and other prophets predicted Ashdod's fall. It came within a generation, in 712 BC, when the Assyrian king Sargon II captured the city. In 1956, the modern port city of Ashdod was founded near the ruins of the old city. The current population of Ashdod is about 190,000.

ASHER

(ASH ur)
Aser, Hebrew
"happy one"
First mention: Joshua 17:7

After capturing the Promised Land, Joshua divided the region among Israel's twelve tribes, or extended families, descended from Jacob's twelve sons. The tribe of Asher got a small but fertile strip of land along what is now Israel's northern coast—from Haifa and the Mount Carmel range to the tip of Canaan, into what is now Lebanon. This strip of land, about fifteen miles wide and fifty miles long, is excellent for growing olives and grapes.

ASHKELON

(ASH kuh lon)
Asqelon, Hebrew
First mention: Joshua 13:4

When Joshua and the Israelites were settling in Canaan's central highlands, a seafaring people called the Philistines were settling in five cities along the coast. At 150 acres, Ashkelon was the largest of the five and the only one on the beach. Throughout most of ancient Israel's history, Ashkelon stayed independent. But from time to time, strong Jewish kings such as David controlled it. Crusader battles destroyed the city in 1191; the Muslim warrior Saladin leveled it as Richard the Lionheart approached.

Famous for its onions, the city gave us the word *scallion* from a version of its name: Ascalon. Today, a new Ashkelon—a busy resort town about thirty miles south of Tel Aviv—has grown up around the ancient ruins.

ASHURBANIPAL

(ASH ur BAN uh pul)
Assur-bani-apli, Assyrian
"Ashur [a god] created an heir"
Reigned 668–626 BC
Only mention: Ezra 4:10

Last of Assyria's powerful kings, Ashurbanipal left documents claiming he was the king who captured Judah's most notorious king, Manasseh. The Bible confirms that "the Lord sent the Assyrian armies, and they took Manasseh prisoner. They put a ring through his nose, bound him in bronze chains, and led him away" (2 Chronicles 33:11).

An educated man, Ashurbanipal created a massive library of clay tablets, part of which survives and provides incredible insight into Assyrian life. The empire survived only fourteen years after him, with the capital falling to Babylon in 612 BC.

ASIA

(AY shuh)
Asia, Greek
First mention: Acts 2:9

When John wrote the last book in the Bible, he addressed it to "the seven churches in the province of Asia" (Revelation 1:4). In New Testament times, Asia was a Roman province in what is now western Turkey. Before, it was the kingdom of Pergamos, ruled by a dynasty known as "the kings of Asia." But

37

A B C D E F G H I J K L M N O P Q R S T U V W X Y Z

when King Attalus III died in 133 BC, he willed his kingdom to the Romans. They named it after his dynasty and adopted the kingdom's capital of Pergamum. Later they moved the capital to the coastal city of Ephesus, where Paul spent more than two years in ministry —longer than at any other church he helped start.

ASIA MINOR
(AY shuh)
Asia, Greek

MAP 5
D2

Though the phrase "Asia Minor" doesn't show up in the Bible and probably wasn't even invented until the AD 400s, the territory that it points to plays an important role in Bible stories. The Roman province of Asia covered just the western tip of what is now Turkey, but Asia Minor was more than twice Asia's size. It swallowed all of Asia and stretched farther east to encompass the entire Turkish peninsula—the huge footprint that separates the Black Sea in the north from the Mediterranean Sea in the south. The apostle Paul grew up there, in the southeast city of Tarsus, and later traveled throughout the region during his three missionary expeditions.

ASSYRIA
(uh SEER ee uh)
Assur, Hebrew
First mention: Genesis 10:11

MAP 3
D2

Israel's ten lost tribes are lost because of Assyria, the world's first megaempire, which brutalized the Middle East for about three hundred years.

In its heyday (934–612 BC), beginning a few decades after David and Solomon, the Assyrian Empire cut a huge swath through the population centers of the Middle East—from what is now Iran in the east to Israel in the west, and from Turkey in the north to Egypt in the south.

Genesis 10 says that Nimrod, a descendant of Noah, planted the seed for this empire by building what would become its capital, Nineveh, on the Tigris River near what is now the city of Mosul in northern Iraq. The oldest references to Assyrian kingdoms go back to the 1700s BC, several hundred years before Moses. But it took Assyria almost a millennium to emerge into a world power.

Even then, with an expansive territory to police, it was hard for Assyria to keep its servant nations in line. Whenever a weak Assyrian king came to the throne or a major power challenged Assyria, some of the servant kingdoms rebelled and refused to pay taxes in an attempt to regain independence. That's what killed Israel, the northern Jewish kingdom that had split from Judah in the south. Judah refused to join the rebel coalition. But Israel did. And in 722 BC, Assyria overran Israel. Most survivors were exiled, and the land was repopulated with Assyrian pioneers. Israel was wiped off the world map, and the ten tribes living there were scattered and assimilated into other cultures.

About a century later, Assyria slipped off the map, too. Warriors from Babylon united with Medes from what is now Iran and overran the Assyrian capital, Nineveh, in 612 BC. Out of the Assyrian ashes grew the Babylonian Empire.

THE EVIL EMPIRE

How to treat a prisoner of war—Assyrian style: Stake them to the ground. Sew wild, live cats inside their abdomen. Watch the cats claw their way back out. Assyrians did this at least once to survivors of a city that resisted their invasion. The intent was to terrify future enemies.

Battlefield terrorism like this also earned Assyria its reputation as the most evil and brutal empire in the ancient world. It's a reputation they acclaimed. Artwork on Nineveh's palace walls showcased graphic scenes. One famous scene chiseled into stone is of dead Jews from Lachish, a city about thirty miles from Jerusalem, pierced through their chest with stakes as thick as a fencepost. Crucified with this single pierce, they hang in rows outside the city walls. (See photo page 238.)

ATHALIAH
(ath uh LIE yuh)
Atalyah, Hebrew
Possibly "God is strong"
Reigned 842–837 BC
First mention: 2 Kings 8:26

There was a time when the southern Jewish nation of Judah had a queen instead of a king. Not just any queen. She was the daughter of King Ahab and possibly Jezebel, the notorious couple who ruled the northern Jewish nation of Israel.

Athaliah didn't come by her throne honestly. She had to murder her family.

Her story began when Ahab and King Jehoshaphat of Judah made a peace treaty. They sealed their treaty with the marriage of their children: Baal-worshiping princess Athaliah to the God-worshiping prince Jehoram. Nearly twenty years later, Jehoram became king. After he died, his son took over but was assassinated. When the queen mother learned her son was dead, she rounded up all possible heirs she could find and killed them. Then she ruled.

One infant grandson, Joash, escaped. A priest raised him secretly for six years before declaring him king with cooperation from the military. The grandmother queen was executed.

Dedicated to goddess Athena more than four hundred years before Paul arrived in Athens, the Parthenon rests like a crown on the Acropolis hilltop.

ATHENS

(ATH ins)
Athenai, Greek
Probably named for Athena,
goddess of wisdom
First mention: Acts 17:15

MAP 5
B2

About the time Joshua and the Hebrews began settling in the Promised Land (1400s BC), another group of people nearly a thousand miles to the west were settling in what would become the seaside capital of modern Greece—Athens. And about the time the Jews were picking up the pieces of their nation that for a generation had been wiped off the map by Babylonian invaders (500s BC), Athenians were inventing democracy.

The apostle Paul was not impressed.

When he arrived there in about AD 50, on a mission to spread Christianity, "he was deeply troubled by all the idols he saw everywhere in the city" (Acts 17:16). One shrine, however, provided a perfect springboard for Paul's message—so he dove in: "Men of Athens, I notice that you are very religious, for as I was walking along I saw your many altars. And one of them had this inscription on it—'To an Unknown God.' You have been worshiping him without knowing who he is, and now I wish to tell you about him" (Acts 17:22–23).

Many in his audience of Greek philosophers, in this emerging college town, laughed when Paul said Jesus had risen from the dead. Others believed him, but apparently just a few. Paul moved on to Corinth about fifty miles west, where he found a receptive audience and stayed for a year and a half.

ATTALIA
(AT uh LIE uh)
Attaleia, Greek
First mention: Acts 14:25

MAP 5
D3

At the end of his first missionary trip, to Cyprus and then on to southern Turkey, Paul sailed back to his home church. He set sail from Attalia, chief port of the small Roman district of Pamphylia—notorious for its swampland humidity and malaria.

AUGUSTUS
(uh GUS tus)
Augustus, Latin
"sacred" or "revered"
September 19, 63 BC–August 19, AD 14
Only mention: Luke 2:1

As emperor of Rome when Jesus was born, it was Caesar Augustus who issued the decree that fulfilled a prophecy about Christ's birth. "You, O Bethlehem Ephrathah, are only a small village in Judah. Yet a ruler of Israel will come from you, one whose origins are from the distant past" (Micah 5:2).

Augustus ordered a census to register people for taxes. A census, by Jewish custom, took place in the ancestral home of the family head. For Joseph, that meant Bethlehem, birthplace of his most famous ancestor, King David.

Augustus, the great-nephew and adopted son of Julius Caesar, was born Gaius Octavius. Senators gave him the deity-like title "Augustus" in 27 BC, after he beat back rebellions and consolidated his near-dictatorial power.

He was only nineteen when Julius Caesar was assassinated. But Augustus quickly crushed the rebellion led by assassins Cassius and Brutus. Later, he defeated the combined forces of his former brother-in-law, Mark Antony, and Antony's new wife, Cleopatra, queen of Egypt.

Caesar Augustus, ruler of Rome when Jesus was born

B

BAAL
(BAY ul)
Baal, Hebrew
"lord," "master," "husband"
First mention: Numbers 25:3

Canaanite god of fertility in family, field, and flock, Baal was often worshiped with sex rituals. Baal followers might have sex with male or female priests or with one another—as

happened during the Exodus into the Promised Land: "Some of the men defiled themselves by sleeping with the local Moabite women. . . . Before long Israel was joining in the worship of Baal" (Numbers 25:1, 3).

Perhaps because rain was so crucial to crops and livestock, Baal was also considered the god of weather. Statues and pictures of Baal often show him holding lightning bolts.

Some Israelites worshiped God and Baal, perhaps figuring that Canaanite success in farming was due to Baal rather than to generations of practice. For these Israelites with a limited understanding of theology, God seemed mainly a go-to god in times of war.

BAAL-HAZOR
(BAY ul HAY zor)
Baal hasor, Hebrew
"Lord of Hazor"
First mention: 2 Samuel 13:23

MAP 1 C4

On rugged slopes about fifteen miles north of Jerusalem, one son of King David murdered the other. Revenge was the motive. Two years earlier, Amnon—first in line to become king—raped his half sister, Tamar. Her full brother, Absalom, invited Amnon to a sheep-shearing party near the limestone mountain now called Jebel el-Asur, the highest point in Palestine's West Bank: elevation 3,333 feet. Once Amnon got drunk, Absalom ordered his men to kill the rapist.

Storm god Baal waves a club and holds a spear that resembles a bolt of lightning.

BAAL-PEOR

MAP 1
D5

(BAY ul PEE or)
Baal peor, Hebrew
"Lord of Peor"
First mention: Deuteronomy 4:3

At a mountain known as Baal-peor, somewhere east of the Jordan River in what is now Jordan, the Hebrews following Moses on their final leg to the Promised Land experienced a miracle one day and a plague another.

The miracle: Moab's king hired a seer named Balaam to stand on the mountain and pronounce a curse on the approaching Hebrews. At God's order, Balaam blessed them instead.

The plague: Afterward, crowds of Moabite women seduced Hebrew men into what was probably ritual sex, to worship the fertility god Baal of Peor. God sent a plague on the Hebrews, killing twenty-four thousand. This plague ended after Aaron's grandson, Phinehas, charged into the tent of a Hebrew man who blatantly escorted a Moabite woman right past Moses. Phinehas thrust a spear "all the way through the man's body and into the woman's stomach" (Numbers 25:8).

BAASHA

(BAY uh shuh)
Basa, Hebrew
"Baal hears"
Reigned about 900–877 BC
First mention: 1 Kings 15:16

Baasha started a violent tradition for selecting Israel's kings.

The successor was the person who assassinated the king.

Baasha lived in the northern Jewish nation of Israel, which had split from the southern nation of Judah ruled by David's descendants. Baasha became Israel's third king after murdering the son of the nation's founding king, Jeroboam. Baasha's dynasty ended when his son Elah was assassinated.

BABEL

See Babylon

MAP 3
D3

(BAY bull)
Babel, Hebrew
"confused"
Bab-ilu, Akkadian (Babylonian language)
"gate of god"
First mention: Genesis 10:10

When Jews in Bible times spoke of Babylon, the ancient empire's capital that now lies in ruins near Baghdad, they used the word *babel*, as in "babble on." That's because this word sounds so much like the Hebrew word *balal*, which means "confused." And confusion is a good way to describe what happened there. The citizens decided

The Tower of Babel—a project God stopped by confusing the languages of the workers.

to "build a great city with a tower that reaches to the skies—a monument to our greatness!" (Genesis 11:4). God stopped them by changing their single language into many, and they scattered abroad by language groups.

Babylonians had another name for their capital. That name referred to a gateway leading to their chief god, Marduk. In fact, among Babylon's ruins stands an impressive stair-step tower called a ziggurat devoted to Marduk. It was only one of fifty in the city, according to Babylonian texts. Some temples in the region were built as early as 2300 BC—a couple of centuries before Abraham and nearly two thousand years before Babylon's famous king, Nebuchadnezzar.

the land of Babylonia, with the cities of Babel [Hebrew for "Babylon"], Erech, Akkad, and Calneh" (Genesis 10:10). When the city was built is anyone's guess. Archaeologists say people were living in the region as early as 5000 BC and that Babylon is mentioned by name as early as about 2200 BC.

King Hammurabi united the region four centuries later and governed it with a set of laws known as Hammurabi's Code, which shares a few notable similarities to the law of Moses that came later. Both, for example, call for fair punishment: "an eye for an eye."

Yet this wanna-be empire faded in and out of history—depending on the ruler. It took a thousand years for

BABYLON

MAP 3
D3

(BABB uh lawn)
Babel, Hebrew
"confused"
Bab-ilu, Akkadian (Babylonian language)
"gate of god"
First mention: Joshua 7:21

A warrior hero built this city. How fitting since Babylon— one of the oldest cities on the planet—eventually flexed its muscles and conquered most of the Middle East to become the sprawling Babylonian Empire, stretching from Iran to Egypt.

Nimrod was that warrior. A descendant of Noah's second son, Ham, Nimrod "built the foundation for his empire in

The Euphrates River runs through the heart of ancient Babylon, alongside a temple complex devoted to the god Marduk.

The Hanging Gardens

You wouldn't expect to find a forest-covered mountain in the Baghdad suburbs. But twenty-five hundred years ago, it was there. Considered one of the Seven Wonders of the World, it was actually a garden that King Nebuchadnezzar reportedly built for his homesick queen. She was a mountain woman from what is now Iran. Babylon's flat desert and flat-topped buildings depressed her. Like a Colorado lady transplanted in Kansas, she missed her mountains.

Nebuchadnezzar brought the mountain to his queen by building a terraced tower some four hundred feet square and seventy-five feet high, covered in dirt deep enough to support massive trees. Buckets on pulleys hidden behind foliage lifted water from the Euphrates River nearby and carried it up to irrigation pools on the artificial mountain.

Greek historian Diodorus Siculus, from the first century BC, described the Wonder this way: "The approach to the Garden sloped like a hillside and the several parts of the structure rose from one another tier on tier. . . . On all this, the earth had been piled. . .and was thickly planted with trees of every kind that, by their great size and other charm, gave pleasure to the beholder."

Babylon to emerge as a stable, world-class power. In 612 BC, Babylon conquered the Assyrian Empire.

Babylon's greatest king

Nebuchadnezzar ruled during the new empire's glory days (605–562 BC). Under his rule, the six-square-mile city of Babylon never looked richer. Double walls surrounded the entire city. And the Euphrates River flowed right through the heart of town, nourishing the Hanging Gardens, splashing on the brick pillars supporting the bridge between Old and New Babylon, and shimmering beneath the thirty-story ziggurat topped with a temple for the national god, Marduk.

This is the empire that wiped the Jewish nation off the map in 586 BC and enslaved many of the survivors. Fifty years later, however, Babylon fell to the Persians, who would later lose to Alexander the Great. Alexander died young, in Babylon, before he could follow through with his plans to make the city his new capital. Babylon slowly faded away after one of Alexander's succeeding generals built another capital nearby. The city that endured at least two thousand years was deserted by AD 200, and its ruins now lie on the outskirts of Baghdad.

BALAAM

(BAY lum)
Bilam, Hebrew
About 1400 BC
First mention: Numbers 22:5

As Moses and the Hebrews advanced toward the Promised Land, the king of Moab in what is now Jordan decided to stop them. He sent for Balaam, a seer who lived hundreds of miles north, near the Euphrates River along the Turkey-Syria border. The king wanted Balaam to put a curse on the Hebrews, which he thought would ensure victory for his army.

God sent an angel to Balaam, but at first only his donkey could see it. The irony was that a dumb animal could see what a seer couldn't. Miraculously, the donkey spoke and suddenly Balaam saw the angel, too. The angel ordered Balaam to deliver only the message God gave. So Balaam ended up blessing the Hebrews —four times—predicting their victory.

Hebrew soldiers later killed Balaam during a battle with Midian, Moab's neighbor to the south. Midian's people had lured many Hebrews into idol worship.

BALAK

(BAY luck)
Balaq, Hebrew
1400s BC
First mention: Numbers 22:2

King Balak was terrified when he saw the swarm of Hebrew refugees camped on his doorstep in what is now Jordan. Moses was leading them to the Promised Land by way of Balak's kingdom, Moab.

Conventional warfare alone would not stop them, Balak must have concluded. He knew how they overran his northern neighbor, the Ammonites. So he sent for a seer named Balaam to put a curse on them. But an angel told Balaam to bless the Hebrews instead. King Balak tried four times to convince Balaam to curse the invaders, offering to pay a huge fee and taking him to different locations to perform the ritual. But each time, Balaam blessed the Hebrews.

BALAAM OUTSIDE THE BIBLE

Balaam's name and part of the Bible story about him has shown up on a plaster wall from about the 700s BC. Archaeologists found it in 1967 in what is now Jordan, the region Balaam visited on his mission to stop the Hebrew march to the Promised Land. Written in red and black ink on white plaster walls, the story identifies Balaam just as the Bible does—as a "seer of the gods" and the "son of Beor" who had a vision in the night.

BARABBAS

(bah RABB us)
Barabbas, Greek
"son of father"
First century AD
First mention: Matthew 27:16

Four words in the Gospel stories about Jesus describe Barabbas: criminal, robber, insurrectionist, murderer. Some of the words in Greek resemble those used to describe gangs of rural bandits who operated much like Robin Hood—stealing from the rich and making life miserable for political leaders.

Once caught, people like that were usually crucified. And it often happened at the crime scene or at a busy crossroads —to warn other would-be criminals.

On the religious holiday of Passover, however, it was Roman custom to release one Jewish prisoner. So Pilate, the Roman governor, gave the crowd a choice: Jesus or Barabbas. Fresh from the trial of Jesus, Jewish leaders convinced the crowd to choose the killer over the healer.

Given the choice of saving Jesus or Barabbas from crucifixion, the crowd chooses the murderer Barabbas.

BARAK

(BEAR ak)
Baraq, Hebrew
"lightning"
1100s BC
First mention: Judges 4:6

A chickenhearted general who wouldn't go to war unless a woman went with him—that's how Jewish history remembers Barak.

About a century before Israel had a king, a Canaanite king was terrorizing Jewish settlers in the north. He fielded a corps of nine hundred iron chariots— eliciting a battlefield fear factor comparable to foot soldiers facing tanks today. Deborah, a leader among the Jews, ordered Barak to mass an army on the steep slopes of Mount Tabor. He agreed, on the condition that she join him.

"Since you have made this choice," she replied, "you will receive no honor" (Judges 4:9).

When the enemy heard of this gathering force, they rushed their chariots into battle positions near Mount Tabor, in the Kishon River valley. A rainstorm trapped the chariots in mud about the time ten thousand Israelites charged down the hill and routed the panicked Canaanites.

BARNABAS

(BARN uh bus)
Barnabas, Greek
Bar nebua, Aramaic
"son of encouragement"
First century AD
First mention: Acts 4:36

Paul is famous for taking the story of Jesus to non-Jews, but Barnabas did it first. A compassionate man, Barnabas first shows up in the Bible as the Jerusalem convert who "sold a field he owned and brought the money to the apostles for those in need" (Acts 4:37). Barnabas also had compassion for outsiders. An outsider is exactly what the apostles thought of the Christian persecutor, Paul—even after he converted. They thought he might be a spy. But Barnabas convinced the suspicious apostles to meet him.

Later, the apostles showed their confidence in Barnabas again when they sent him on a fifteen-day trip north (three hundred miles) to Antioch, Syria.

His controversial mission was to investigate rumors that non-Jews were converting. Christianity began as a Jewish movement, and many tradition-minded Jews thought all converts needed to obey Jewish laws, including those about circumcision and kosher food. Barnabas reported that Gentiles were indeed among the believers, and they were enjoying God's favor without obeying Jewish rules.

Barnabas stayed in Antioch as a minister. When the congregation swelled, Barnabas recruited Paul as an associate. Antioch became the sending church for Paul's three famous missionary trips. Barnabas and Paul went on the first one together, sailing to Barnabas' home island of Cyprus and then on to Turkey.

But on the second trip, the two couldn't agree about taking Barnabas' cousin John Mark, who had gone on the first trip but abandoned them partway through. Paul didn't want a repeat, so he chose Silas as a partner and went to Turkey, while Barnabas and John returned to Cyprus.

BARTHOLOMEW

(bar THAH low mew)
Bartholomaios, Greek
Bar-Talmai, Aramaic
First century AD
First mention:
Matthew 10:3

The first missionary stop of Barnabas and Paul was the scenic Mediterranean island of Cyprus, Barnabas' homeland.

Bartholomew was one of Jesus' twelve disciples. That's all the Bible says. He appears only in lists of the apostles' names. Eusebius, a church historian and scholar in the AD 300s, said Bartholomew became a missionary to India. From at least the 800s, scholars have speculated that Bartholomew and Nathanael were the same person. (See *Nathanael*.)

BARUCH
(bah RUKE)
Baruk, Hebrew
"blessed"
600s–500s BC
First mention: Jeremiah 32:12

A secretarial writer by trade, Baruch is one of the few Bible people whose existence is confirmed outside the Bible.

Archaeologists found a clay impression from one of his personalized tools: the seal he used to press his mark onto plugs of soft clay that sealed the scrolls he wrote. The impression reads: "Belonging to Baruch, son of Neriah, the scribe." There are also whorls of a fingerprint on the clay—perhaps Baruch's.

Seal impression of Baruch, a writer who assisted the prophet Jeremiah

The seal impression tracks with the Bible's description of him: "Baruch son of Neriah" (Jeremiah 32:12). Dating of the impression also matches Baruch's time. Jeremiah dictated to Baruch a first draft of the book of Jeremiah in about 605 BC.

Officials read the scroll to King Jehoiakim, who didn't appreciate the prophecies about his kingdom's destruction. After each section, the king cut off a piece of the scroll and tossed it in a fire he was using to keep warm. Jeremiah dictated a new version with more prophecies. Many scholars say Baruch probably wrote the history sections between the prophecies.

After Jerusalem fell in 586 BC, a group of Jewish survivors forced Jeremiah and Baruch to flee with them to Egypt, where prophet and scribe were never heard from again.

BASHAN
(BAY shun)
Basan, Hebrew
"smooth plain"
First mention: Numbers 21:33

MAP 1
D2

East of the Sea of Galilee, in southern Syria, lies a sprawling plateau so fertile that it became the prize in wars between Israel and Syria. Bashan's elevation of roughly two thousand feet, along with its frequent rain and its rich, volcanic soil, made it ideal for crops and livestock. It was famous for cattle. The prophet Amos once called the rich and pampered women of Israel "cows of Bashan" (Amos 4:1 NRSV). King Og, a giant with a bed more than thirteen feet long and six feet wide, ruled sixty cities in this region before the Israelites captured it on their way to the Promised Land.

BATHSHEBA
(bath SHE buh)
Bat-seba, Hebrew
Perhaps "daughter of abundance"
About 1000 BC
First mention: 2 Samuel 11:3

When Bathsheba makes her first appearance in the Bible, she's not wearing any clothes. She's taking a bath. Outside. Within eyeshot of the very married King David—seven wives at least—who is strolling around on what was probably the flat roof of his home. Roofs were used much like we use porches and decks.

Bathsheba takes a bath outside, perhaps in her courtyard. King David, looking down from his palace, likes what he sees—with tragic results.

Bathsheba was married to Uriah the Hittite, a soldier in David's elite corps known as the Thirty. A three-day march away, Uriah was with the Israelite army, laying siege to the city of Rabbah (near modern Amman, Jordan).

"David sent for her; and when she came to the palace, he slept with her" (2 Samuel 11:4). That bath she took was after her menstruation—probably about a week later, since that's how long a woman had to wait before performing her purification rituals. That put Bathsheba in her fertile period. She got pregnant.

When David got the bad news, he called Uriah home, saying he wanted a war report. Actually, he wanted Uriah to sleep with Bathsheba. No chance. Even drunk, Uriah honored the Jewish

tradition of sexual abstinence during war (1 Samuel 21:5). This prods some Bible students to draw the conclusion that Uriah drunk was more righteous than David sober.

David resorted to murder. Uriah carried the secret order himself. He would take a frontline position in an assault on the city, then commander Joab would pull back the support troops. Uriah and several others died.

Bathsheba observed the mourning rituals, which generally lasted a week, then joined David's harem.

The prophet Nathan confronted David, vowing that God would not allow this child to live. David admitted his sin, sought God's forgiveness, and pled for the child's life. But Bathsheba's son lived only seven days. Bathsheba, however, gave David four more sons: Shimea, Shobab, Nathan, and Solomon—whom David promised would become the next king.

When the elderly David lay dying, his oldest son—Adonijah—threw himself a coronation party. Bathsheba rushed to David's bedside and urged him to honor his promise, which he did.

Later, Adonijah asked Bathsheba to intercede for him with Solomon. Since Solomon took what Adonijah thought was his throne, Adonijah asked for at least the right to marry one of David's secondary wives, a concubine. Bathsheba agreed, perhaps out of ignorance or out of a desire for revenge. Solomon reacted with rage. When a conqueror took a kingdom, he often married the former king's wives—to prove his authority. Solomon apparently thought his older brother was trying to assert his right to rule. Solomon killed him, and we can only guess if Bathsheba saw it coming.

BEER

MAP 2
D5

(BEE ear)
Beer, Hebrew
"well"
First mention: Numbers 21:16

It's stretching it to say that the Bible has a beer song. But when thirsty Israelites on their way to the Promised Land dug for water somewhere in Jordan's desert—and quickly found it—they burst into song: "Spring up, O well!" (Numbers 21:17). The exact location of this place they named Beer

is uncertain. They arrived there after passing the Arnon River but before reaching Mattanah. Scholars say it might have been any number of dry riverbeds, called wadis, where water often lies near the surface. One possibility is Wadi eth Themed, about twenty miles south of Jordan's capital, Amman.

BEER-LAHAIROI

MAP 1
A7

(BEE ear la HI roy)
Beer lahay roi, Hebrew
"well of the Living One who sees me"
First mention: Genesis 16:14

Pregnant Hagar, a surrogate mother carrying a child for Abraham and Sarah, ran away after Sarah started mistreating her. Hagar stopped beside a desert well in what is now the Negev, in southern Israel. There, an angel appeared and told her to go back to camp. He promised that her son, Ishmael, would give her many descendants. Hagar named the well Beer-lahairoi in honor of this holy encounter. But it was Sarah's son, Isaac, who later lived near the well.

BEERSHEBA

MAP 1
B6

(BEE ear SHE buh)
Beer seba, Hebrew
"well of the seven" or "well of the oath"
First mention: Genesis 21:14

Three miles outside Beersheba, Israel's capital of the Negev desert region in the south, there are ruins of an ancient Beersheba with a tamarisk tree planted beside a well. This isn't the tree the Bible says Abraham planted about four thousand years ago, but it could be the well he dug. And it might be the spot where he and King Abimelech pledged loyalty, and where Abraham gave him seven lambs. That's how the city got its name. Beer is Hebrew for "well." Seba can mean "seven" or "oath."

Here is where Abraham camped when he ordered Hagar to take her son and leave. And on the outskirts is where God showed Hagar a well when she and her son were dying of thirst. Later, God appeared to Isaac there and promised him many descendants. God also appeared there to the elderly Jacob, assuring him that he could move his family to Egypt during a drought.

Modern Beersheba—home to some two hundred thousand Israelis—is a transportation and industrial center, with railroads, oil pipelines, and chemical companies that draw from the rich minerals in this area near the Dead Sea. But there's still the flavor of Bible times, with a camel market every Thursday morning.

BELSHAZZAR

(bell SHAZ ur)
Belsasar, Aramaic
"Bel [a god] protect the king"
Coruler from about 545–539 BC
First mention: Daniel 5:1

On the night the Babylonian Empire died, King Nabonidus' son, who was also the coruler, hosted a party for a thousand nobles. Belshazzar and his guests drank from gold and silver cups that Babylonian soldiers looted from the Jewish temple some fifty years earlier. Suddenly, a disembodied hand wrote mysterious words on the wall. Daniel was called in to interpret. He

Horrified, Babylonian king Belshazzar watches a disembodied hand scrawl a message on the palace wall.

said the words meant the Persians and Medes would divide the empire. Belshazzar died that night as invaders stormed the capital.

BEN-HADAD

(ben HAY dad)
Ben-hadad, Hebrew
"son of Hadad," a god
Ruled about 860–843 BC
First mention: 1 Kings 15:18

Two or three kings named Ben-hadad ruled Syria from Damascus. Best known is the second one. He repeatedly raided the northern Jewish nation of Israel, until King Ahab defeated his army and captured him. The two kings made peace, with Ben-hadad agreeing to trade relations and to return Jewish cities he had taken. He may also have been the king who got sick and sent an official—Hazael—to ask Elisha if the king would recover. Elisha said Hazael would soon rule. Hazael returned and suffocated the king with a wet blanket, then became king himself.

BENJAMIN

(BEN juh muhn)
Binyamin, Hebrew
"my right-hand son"
About 1800s BC
First mention: Genesis 35:18

Benjamin was the last of Jacob's twelve sons who became founding fathers of Israel's twelve tribes. He never knew his mother, Rachel, Jacob's favorite wife. She died giving birth to him somewhere on the twenty-mile journey between Bethel and Bethlehem.

Jacob favored Benjamin and Joseph, the two sons of Rachel. When jealousy drove his ten other brothers to sell Joseph to slave traders and report that animals killed him, Jacob was devastated. Joseph became an Egyptian leader. Without revealing his identity, he ordered his ten brothers who had come for grain to go home and get their youngest brother. Jacob initially refused but finally agreed—leading to a happy reunion.

BENJAMIN

MAP 1
C5

(BEN juh muhn)
Binyamin, Hebrew
"my right-hand son"
First mention: Joshua 18:11

When it came time to divide Canaan among the twelve tribes of Israel, one of the tiniest strips went to descendants of Jacob's youngest son, Benjamin. Plotted on a map, it looks like a tongue flailing west out of the Jordan River. It extended about twenty miles long halfway to the Mediterranean Sea—and about ten miles at its widest. Yet within those boundaries lay several key cities, including Jerusalem, Jericho, and Gibeon.

BETHANY

MAP 4
C5, B5

(BETH uh nee)
Bethania, Greek
First mention: 1. John 1:28
2. Matthew 21:17

Two towns called Bethany were important to Jesus' ministry. One witnessed the beginning of his mission. The other saw the end.

1. **Bethany east of the Jordan River.** John the Baptist baptized people near a village called Bethany on the east side of the Jordan River, in what is now Jordan. God sent John to prepare people for the coming of Jesus. And it was in Bethany that John said, "I baptize with water, but right here in the crowd is someone you do not know, who will soon begin his ministry. I am not even worthy to be his slave" (John 1:26–27). Bethany's exact location is uncertain, but a Christian tradition

dating to at least the AD 200s says John baptized Jesus near a monastery about five miles north of where the Jordan River empties into the Dead Sea.

2. **Bethany near Jerusalem.** Whether today or in Bible times, people standing on the Temple Mount in Jerusalem and looking east toward the rising sun would see about a mile away a ridge of hills called the Mount of Olives. On the opposite slopes, hidden from view, is Bethany:

- Hometown of Mary, Martha, and Lazarus
- Where Jesus raised Lazarus from the dead
- Headquarters of Jesus the week of his crucifixion
- Where a woman anointed Jesus with ointment
- Where Jesus ascended to heaven

The village isn't called Bethany today. Located in the Palestinian West Bank, this Arab village of about two thousand people is Al-Azariyeh—Arabic for "the place of Lazarus." His tomb attracts tourists. Actually, scholars aren't certain this was *the* tomb, but Christians did build a church near it in the AD 300s, soon after Rome legalized Christianity. Today, there are churches and a mosque nearby. Visitors walk down twenty-two winding steps into an underground vestibule. From there, they can stoop and duck-walk into what may have been the tiny crypt that once reverberated with three remarkable words: "Lazarus, come out!" (John 11:43). (See photo page 239.)

BETHEL
(BETH uhl)
Bet el, Hebrew
"house of God"
First mention: Genesis 12:8

MAP 1
C4

After sleeping here with a rock for a pillow, Jacob renamed the village—from Luz ("almond tree") to Bethel. This was to commemorate his famous dream of God standing at the top of a stairway to heaven. Jacob's grandfather, Abraham, had camped near this village years before while scouting the land God promised to give his descendants.

In Bible times, Bethel was perched

On a rock pillow, Jacob dreams of a stairway to heaven.

on a high ridge of rolling hills, honey-combed with plenty of springs. Settlers planted themselves there a thousand years before Abraham arrived—as early as 3200 BC. A crossroads town twelve miles north of Jerusalem, Bethel lay on the north-south road to the Samaritan hills and on the east-west road connecting Jericho with the sea. Today Bethel is an Arab village called Beitin, with a Jewish settlement about a mile away called Beir El—both preserving the meaning of the ancient name.

BETHLEHEM
(BETH le hem)

MAP 4
B5

Beit Lahm, "house of meat," Arabic
Beth Lehem, "house of bread," Hebrew
First mention: Genesis 35:16

In a cave beneath the oldest church in the world, priests sometimes get into a fistfight while worshiping at the birthplace of the Prince of Peace.

There, where an ancient tradition says shepherds stood together and admired the Christ child in a manger, priests over the centuries have occasionally argued about who has the right to stand where and when. Three denominations are responsible for taking care of the church: Greek Orthodox, Armenian Orthodox, and Roman Catholic. One fracas at Christmastime, reported in the *Jerusalem Post* newspaper, started after some visiting monks conducting prayers moved a chair reserved for the Greek patriarch.

Over the centuries, armies have seized and besieged this church. In 2002, Israeli soldiers surrounded it

BIBLE EVENTS:

- Ruth and Boaz become great-grandparents of David, ancestors of Jesus
- David born, raised, and anointed king
- Jesus born

HOLY SITES:

- Church of the Nativity, over birthplace of Jesus
- Shepherds' Field, where angels announced Jesus' birth

STATISTICS:

- Population—27,000
- Elevation—nearly half a mile above sea level, about twenty six hundred feet, on a ridge in the Judean hills
- Location—six miles south of Jerusalem

during a campaign to round up terrorists. Two hundred and forty gunmen and bystanders ran into the church and holed up for five weeks, until thirteen leaders agreed to deportation.

IN BIBLE TIMES

Ruth. Here is where widow Ruth sneaked under the covers at the feet of a sleeping Boaz, calling on him to fulfill his obligation as her next of kin and marry her. Her bold action, which seems out of character, was apparently the custom. It's similar to a Middle

Greek Orthodox priests in Bethlehem's most popular tourist attraction, the Church of the Nativity.

Eastern marriage custom today in which the groom extends his arm and uses the cloak he is wearing to cover his bride. When Ruth proposed, it was with a phrase that used a play on words: "Spread the corner of your covering over me" (Ruth 3:9). In Hebrew, the word for "corner" can also mean "wings." She was calling on Boaz to become God's wing of protection for her.

The interracial marriage of this woman from what is now Jordan with a Hebrew man from Bethlehem produced Obed, grandfather of Israel's most respected king: David.

David. Ruth's great-grandson was born in this obscure little village of not more than a few hundred people. There, in the fields surrounded by terraced hillsides of olive trees and vineyards, David kept watch over his father's sheep. And it was there that the prophet Samuel anointed this boy as God's chosen, future leader of Israel.

Jesus. Bethlehem became the birthplace of Jesus because of a pagan ruler so superstitious he carried a sealskin to ward off lightning strikes. Caesar Augustus, the former general who defeated Antony and Cleopatra, ordered a census. This required Joseph and Mary to leave their Nazareth home and register at the hometown of Joseph's ancestor David, a three-day trip to the south.

Descendants of David were apparently numerous enough to fill the lodging facilities in this hilltop village that had become a last-chance supply station for caravans traveling south to Egypt or Arabia.

AFTER BIBLE TIMES

The cave stable. Christian writers reported the birth took place in a cave used as a stable. The hillsides around Bethlehem are honeycombed with caves. The earliest known reference to a nativity cave comes from Justin Martyr, a Samaritan-turned-Christian. He was born about the time the apostle John died, around AD 100. John had been a close friend of Jesus and was probably the disciple who took care of Mary after the Crucifixion (John 19:27). So it seems reasonable that Mary told John where Jesus was born and that Christians living in the Jerusalem-Bethlehem area knew the site.

After crushing a Jewish revolt in AD 135, the Roman emperor Hadrian began destroying all sacred sites, Jewish and Christian. He replaced them with Roman shrines. Over a cave stable in Bethlehem, he built a temple to Adonis—ironically, a god known for his death each winter and his resurrection each spring.

Two centuries later, the Roman emperor Constantine replaced the shrines with churches. The Church of the Nativity was built in about AD 325. Persian invaders in the 600s left it untouched when they saw in it a mosaic of the three wise men wearing Persian clothes.

Today

Nearly all Bethlehem residents are Palestinian Arabs. Israel captured the city from Jordan in the Six-Day War in 1967, and Bethlehem now makes up part of the Occupied West Bank. Until 1995, the Israeli government administered Bethlehem. But in 1995, as part of a peace plan negotiated with Palestinians, Israel turned control of the city over to the Palestinian Authority.

Most residents are Muslim, though some are Christian. When Palestinian-Israeli clashes don't dominate headlines, Bethlehem hosts two million visitors each year. Tourism is a major source of income. Citizens, often working out of their homes, make religious souvenirs sold in local shops. Nativity scenes carved from the hard and fine-grained wood of the olive tree are especially popular.

Church of the Nativity. This is the busiest place in this town. Stairs under the front altar lead to candlelit caverns below. The first room is the Grotto of the Nativity, a cavern about forty feet long by ten feet wide. Embedded on the floor is a silver star, reminiscent of the Star of Bethlehem. Many believe this is the very spot where Jesus was born. (See photo page 164.)

In a nearby chamber, Jerome translated the Bible into Latin in the AD 300s. He chose to work there because he said it was "the earth's most sacred spot."

Shepherds' Field. It's at the eastern edge of town, on the only level field in the area, where tradition says Ruth met Boaz and that on the night of Jesus' birth "some shepherds were in the fields outside the village, guarding their flocks of sheep" (Luke 2:8).

Christians visiting Bethlehem cannot be certain they are standing exactly where the shepherds stood or where Mary delivered her Child. But somewhere in this hilltop village, the Prince of Peace was born. And those who have heard the Good News have been coming ever since.

BETH-PEOR

See Baal-Peor

(BETH pee or)
bet paor, Hebrew
"temple of Peor," a god
First mention: Deuteronomy 3:29

MAP 1
D5

Ten miles from the Promised Land, near the village of Beth-peor in what is now Jordan, Moses gave his farewell speech. This settlement, captured by the Hebrews, sat on the western edge of a large plateau that sloped down into the Jordan River valley. On a clear day, the Hebrews could have seen their future homeland. Moses got an even better look from Pisgah Peak on nearby Mount Nebo but then died and was buried in a valley near Beth-peor.

BETHPHAGE

(BETH fah gee)
Bethphage, Greek
"house of the early figs"
First mention: Matthew 21:1

Long since erased from Israel's map, the village of Bethphage has just one claim to fame: a donkey. When Jesus rode into Jerusalem before his crucifixion, he rode on a donkey's colt that his disciples got from Bethphage.

Like Bethany—home of Mary, Martha, and Lazarus—Bethphage was on the Mount of Olives near Jerusalem. Perhaps it was on the main road into the city, between Bethany and Jerusalem. That's where the Crusaders said it was, about half a mile down the eastern slopes of the ridge. A Franciscan chapel marks the area that archaeologists say was occupied in Jesus' time and where a chapel stood in the AD 300s when Rome first legalized Christianity.

BETHSAIDA

(beth SAY uh duh)
Bethsaida, Greek
"house of the fisherman"
First mention: Matthew 11:21

It's not surprising that three of Jesus' disciples—fishermen Philip, Andrew, and Peter—all came from Bethsaida. It was a fishing village somewhere along the northeast shore of the Sea of Galilee. Perhaps the grassy, rolling hills and the lakefront view are why Herod Philip, Roman governor and son of Herod the Great, built it into a city and chose to be buried there.

On the slopes near Bethsaida is where Jesus fed more than five thousand people with "five loaves of bread and two fish" (Luke 9:13). Later, he healed a blind man there and walked on the water nearby.

The people were apparently unimpressed, because Jesus warned that Sodom-like horror was headed their way. "If the miracles I did in you had been done in wicked Tyre and Sidon," Jesus complained, "their people would have sat in deep repentance long ago" (Matthew 11:21).

Three ruins are suggested for Bethsaida. Two are neighbors on the shoreline and may have been one large city: el-Araj and el-Misadiyye. The other is a mile and a half inland: twenty-acre et Tell (the Mound), favored by the Israel Antiquities Authority. Some archaeologists argue that this site was on the lakefront until an earthquake and landslide pushed the shoreline away—perhaps the horror Jesus predicted. People deserted the city in the AD 200s.

BETH-SHAN

(beth SHAWN)
Bet san, Hebrew
"house of quiet"
First mention: Joshua 17:11

The corpses of King Saul and his son Jonathan were hung as trophies on

Beth-shan's city walls. The Philistines had killed them in a nearby battle. But Saul's loyalists stole the bodies and buried them.

Beth-shan was a garden paradise and busy crossroads town at the intersection of Israel's two main valleys: the north-south Jordan River valley and the east-west Jezreel valley, sometimes called the Valley of Armageddon. Joshua's invaders never captured this city that, archaeologists confirm, was controlled by Philistines in Saul's day. By New Testament times, the population moved down from the mound that had gradually developed from more than a dozen settlements building on top of each other's ruins. In the plain below, the city expanded to more than three hundred acres, becoming the chief city of ten known as the Decapolis. Romans renamed it Scythopolis.

BILDAD
(BILL dad)
Bildad, Hebrew
Perhaps about 2000 BC
First mention: Job 2:11

When Job suddenly lost his family, flocks, and health, three friends came to comfort him: Eliphaz, Bildad, and Zophar. Better accusers than comforters, all three insisted that Job must have brought this tragedy on himself by some terrible sin.

"Your children obviously sinned against him, so their punishment was well deserved," Bildad callously concluded. "But if you pray to God and seek the favor of the Almighty. . .he will

rise up and restore your happy home" (Job 8:4–6). God eventually put Job's friends in their place by ordering them to ask Job to pray for them.

BOAZ
(BO as)
Boaz, Hebrew
Possibly "in him is strength"
1100s BC
First mention: Ruth 2:1

It was about midnight in Bethlehem, and wealthy Boaz—who would become King David's great-grandfather—was sleeping near his barley fields during harvest. To his shock, he woke to find a widow under the covers with him. Lying at his feet was Ruth, freshly bathed, perfumed, and dressed in her best.

Ruth's mother-in-law, Naomi, told her to do this. It was apparently an acceptable way for a widow to propose to her dead husband's relative. Under Jewish custom, a close relative was obligated to marry the widow. Naomi wisely realized that Boaz would gladly accept his duty, for he had already shown kindness to Ruth. Farmers were supposed to let the poor glean harvest leftovers, but Boaz told his workers to leave extra for Ruth.

Boaz married Ruth and had a son, Obed, the father of Jesse and grandfather of David.

CAESAREA
(cess uh REE uh)
Kaisareia, Greek
First mention: Acts 8:40

MAP 4
B3

For a thousand years Israel had no harbor. If sailors wanted to stop and buy or sell something, they had to drop anchor and wade to shore or take a small boat. Generally, they kept sailing.

Herod the Great changed that when he built a harbor worthy of his name—three walled acres accommodating three hundred ships. Caesarea by the Sea, as the city was sometimes called, was built around a former trading post midway between what is now Tel Aviv and Haifa. Caesar Augustus gave the coastland to Herod, and the king chose this run-down anchorage to become a port town so grandly Roman —with a theater, palaces, and temples—that it served as Rome's capital of Palestine for more than six hundred years. Herod named the city after his benefactor, and he even named the harbor Sabastos, Caesar's Greek name.

Caesarea was Paul's port of arrival after two of his missionary trips, and it's where he spent two years in jail before sailing to the appeals court in Rome. This was also where Peter baptized the first non-Jewish Christian on record: a Roman commander. That opened the church door to Gentiles.

CAESAREA PHILIPPI
(cess uh REE uh FILL uh pie)
Kaisareia he Philippou, Greek
First mention: Matthew 16:13

MAP 4
C2

One day's walk north of the Sea of Galilee, Jesus stood at the foot of Mount Hermon, near Caesarea Philippi, and asked his disciples who they believed he was. "You are the Messiah, the Son of the living God," Peter answered. "You are Peter," Jesus replied, "and upon this rock I will build my church" (Matthew 16:16, 18).

One of the largest springs feeding into the Jordan River is here, in this fertile region. Greeks worshiped the pagan god Pan at the spring and named the city Panias.

To supply his new oceanfront city of Caesarea with water, Herod the Great built an aqueduct that carried water from springs six miles to the north.

Herod Philip, son of Herod the Great, renamed it Caesarea after Caesar. Philippi was added later, to distinguish it from Caesarea by the Sea. Today it's called by an Arab variation of the Greek name: Banias.

CAIAPHAS

(KYE uh fuss)
Kaiaphas, Greek
High priest about AD 18–37
First mention: Matthew 26:3

Caiaphas' stone coffin, containing the bones of a man about sixty years old.

Oddly enough, it was after Jesus raised Lazarus from the dead that the Jewish high priest—Caiaphas—decided Jesus had to die.

Perhaps Caiaphas feared the people would rally around Jesus and start a disastrous war of independence. The Jewish Revolt forty years later ended with Rome destroying the last Jewish temple. Caiaphas' position depended on Rome; a Roman official appointed him, and the successor of Pilate, who governed the region, later deposed him.

It was in Caiaphas' home that Jewish leaders tried Jesus and found him guilty of a capital offense: claiming to be God's Son, which Caiaphas considered blasphemy.

The first-century Jewish historian Josephus implied that Caiaphas was a family name. Josephus referred to the high priest as "Joseph, who was called Caiaphas." In 1990, an ornate, first-century family burial box was found beneath Jerusalem. Inscribed on it were the words "Joseph son of Caiaphas."

Inside were the bones of six people, including a man of about sixty, who scholars say was likely the high priest himself.

CAIN

(KANE)
qayin, Hebrew
Possibly "metalworker," and the original smith, short for blacksmith
Before 4000 BC
First mention: Genesis 4:1

Cain, humanity's first child, grew up to become the first murderer. In a quick read, the story sounds a bit like a Western: Rancher versus farmer, and the farmer wins. That's what the first son of Adam and Eve was—a farmer. Their second boy, Abel, herded flocks. When it came time to thank God, Abel sacrificed "choice lambs from the best of his flock" (Genesis 4:4). Cain brought "farm produce" (Genesis 4:3). God accepted Abel's offering but

THE MARK OF CAIN

The mark of Cain wasn't a curse; it was a blessing. God used it to protect Cain: "The LORD put a mark on Cain to warn anyone who might try to kill him" (Genesis 4:15).

In years past, some Christians argued that this mark was black skin and that enslaved people of African heritage were simply living out their destiny as Cain's descendants. In fact, God put a curse on one man in Cain's family tree—Ham—whose descendants included people of Africa. The curse reads, "May they be the lowest of servants" (Genesis 9:25). But the curse was directed at Ham's son, Canaan, and it was fulfilled when the Israelites took over their land of Canaan.

The Bible doesn't say what the mark of Cain was, other than it was a mark of mercy.

rejected Cain's.

Since there's no explanation of why God rejected Cain's offering, some have speculated it was because Abel offered blood and Cain didn't. Not likely. For one thing, God accepted crop offerings in later times, as well as animal sacrifices. And for another, God had shown throughout Bible times that he cared more about motives than rituals. As an ancient songwriter put it: "If I brought you a burnt offering, you would not accept it. The sacrifice you want is a broken spirit. A broken and repentant heart, O God" (Psalm 51:16–17).

Many Bible clues suggest Cain's motive was distorted. When God saw Cain's anger, he said he would accept Cain—if Cain did what was right. Cain's crime is another clue about the kind of person he was. New Testament writers added their judgment, saying Abel was good, while Cain was evil.

God's punishment for Cain was not a life for a life. Instead, because Cain polluted the ground with his brother's blood, the ground would not produce adequate crops. Cain could farm no longer. He became a homeless fugitive. Cain is considered the ancestor of all smiths because his name

Cain, in a jealous rage, murders his brother.

62

comes from a root word meaning "metalworker," and his descendant Tubal-cain was "the first to work with metal, forging instruments of bronze and iron" (Genesis 4:22).

CALEB
(KAY luhb)
Kaleb, Hebrew
"faithful dog"
1400s BC
First mention: Numbers 13:6

Vineyard workers prepare their grapes for shipping to a winery. In Cana, Jesus skipped a lengthy process and turned water into wine.

From an oasis near Canaan's southern border, Moses sent twelve scouts on a mission into what is now Israel—the land God promised to give the Hebrews. But the majority report from ten of the scouts spooked the people: walled cities, powerful armies, and giants. Only Caleb and Joshua had encouraging words. "Let's go at once to take the land," Caleb said. "We can certainly conquer it!" (Numbers 13:30).

The people refused. So God sentenced the entire generation to live their lives in the desert—forty years, one year for each day the scouts were gone. Of all the adults who left Egypt in the Exodus, only Caleb and Joshua would set foot in the Promised Land.

CANA
(KAY nuh)
Kana, Greek
"reed"
First mention: John 2:1

MAP 4
B3

After his baptism, Jesus returned home to Galilee, where he joined his mother at a wedding in Cana, somewhere near their hometown of Nazareth. There, Jesus performed his first reported miracle: turning water into wine. This was also where a Roman official asked Jesus to heal his son, who was about a day's walk away in Capernaum.

Two sites are contenders for Cana: Kafr Kanna, an Arab village five miles from Nazareth that sells "wine from Cana," and Khirbet Qana, an uninhabited mound eight miles away. Many scholars favor Khirbet Qana partly because Cana means "reed," and this mound is in a valley where reeds grow.

CANAAN
(KAY none)
Kenaan, Hebrew
Perhaps "bend"
Before 2500 BC
First mention: Genesis 9:22

Noah's grandson Canaan was the father of the Canaanite people. But he's better known for getting cursed by his grandfather for something he didn't do. Canaan's father, Ham, was the culprit. Ham—Noah's youngest son—treated his father disrespectfully when he found him drunk and naked. He gawked and called his brothers to have a look. Noah put a curse on Ham's youngest son: "A curse on the Canaanites! May they be the lowest of servants to the descendants of Shem and Japheth [Noah's other sons]" (Genesis 9:25). For failing his father, Ham's own family would fail.

CANAAN
(KAY none)
Kenaan, Hebrew
Perhaps "bend"
First mention: Genesis 10:19

"Leave your country," God told Abraham, "go to the land that I will show you" (Genesis 12:1). That land was Canaan, roughly the same territory as modern Israel—with parts of Syria and Lebanon added in the north.

From north to south, Canaan stretched about 250 miles. But east to west, it narrowed to as little as forty miles on the strip between the Jordan River in the east and the Mediterranean Sea in the west.

It wasn't much bigger than New Jersey, and most of the land wasn't much to brag about: rocky hills, parched fields with no major rivers except the Jordan on the border, and very little rainfall—especially in the deep south,

with one to four inches a year.

Yet Canaan was a prize. Not only did it enjoy fertile land in the river valleys and along the coast; it had location. It was the only hospitable land bridge connecting Egypt and Arabian countries in the south to empires such as Assyria and Babylon in the north. Travelers wanting to avoid Canaan had two choices: the sea or the desert.

In fact, trade propelled Israel into a golden age. Solomon received vast amounts of income "from merchants and traders, all the kings of Arabia, and the governors of the land" (1 Kings 10:15). (See *Israel*.)

CAPERNAUM
(kuh PURR nay um)
Kapharnaoum, Greek
Kepar Nahum, Hebrew
"village of Nahum"
First mention: Matthew 4:13

Capernaum saw the best Jesus had to offer: profound teachings, countless healings, and astonishing exorcisms. Yet Capernaum also drew his worst

The fishing village of Capernaum, once the headquarters of Jesus' ministry. The octagonal building marks the site of Peter's house. In the foreground stands all that's left of the synagogue.

rebuke: "You people of Capernaum, will you be exalted to heaven? No, you will be brought down to the place of the dead. For if the miracles I did for you had been done in Sodom, it would still be here today. I assure you, Sodom will be better off on the judgment day than you" (Matthew 11:23–24).

Of all the cities Jesus could have picked as his ministry headquarters, why move to this boondocks community of the stonehearted? At least two reasons:

First, nearly half of his disciples lived there: fishermen brothers Peter and Andrew, fishermen brothers James and John, and tax man Matthew.

Second, Capernaum probably wasn't a backwoods fishing village, but a busy border town with a customs station for merchants traveling to and from Syria. The village lay on Galilee's eastern border, on a branch of the main trade route called the Way of the Sea, linking Egypt and Arabia in the south with all the nations north of Israel. So Jesus had plenty of people coming and going whom he could teach—and he could do it without the political scrutiny he would face at Galilee's capital in neighboring Tiberias, along the shoreline ten miles south.

IN BIBLE TIMES

Jesus' new home. After Jesus was baptized, then tempted in the desert—both of which probably took place in southern Israel—he returned to his home region of Galilee in northern Israel. But he didn't go back home to

BIBLE EVENTS:

- Jesus heals man lowered through roof
- Jesus heals Peter's mother-in-law
- Jesus heals servant of Roman commander
- Peter catches fish and finds money inside to pay tax
- Jesus teaches in the synagogue

HOLY SITES:

- Peter's home, where Jesus stayed
- Synagogue where Jesus taught

STATISTICS:

- Excavation of village ruins begins 1905
- Size of ancient village—300 yards by 200 yards (about 15 acres)
- Population—perhaps 1,500 (in late Roman times)
- Abandoned—AD 600s, during Arab invasion
- Elevation—686 feet below sea level
- Location—one day's walk (20 miles) northeast of Nazareth, along the Sea of Galilee's north shore

Nazareth, a hilltop village off the main roads. He moved a day's walk away to Capernaum, known as a trading hub

PETER'S HOUSE

About thirty yards from the city synagogue are ruins of what many believe was Peter's house. Several clues point to this:

• The first-century house was large enough for Jesus and his disciples to stay with Peter, as the Bible says they did. There were several roofed buildings arranged around three courtyards. Total area: about eighty-four square yards.

• After Christianity became legal in the AD 300s, the house was expanded into a church.

• Graffiti etched into the plastered walls read: Jesus, Lord, Christ, and Peter. Also, a Spanish pilgrim named Lady Egeria visited Capernaum in the AD 380s and described the "House of Simon, called Peter." She said it had been turned into a church, with the original walls still standing.

In the 500s, church leaders leveled Peter's original house and the church, filled in the ruins with dirt (which preserved the building's outline), and constructed an octagon-shaped church on top.

Today, that octagon building is also a ruin. Sitting above it, on pillars, is an octagon-shaped memorial center with a see-through floor in the middle, allowing visitors to see the ruins below.

and a fishing village but also known for farming and light industry, such as processing olive oil. Capernaum became "his own town" (Matthew 9:1).

Jesus and the apostles apparently lived at Peter's house: "After they arrived at Capernaum, Jesus and his disciples settled in the house where they would be staying" (Mark 9:33). Archaeologists claim to have found the ruins of this house. If they're right, Peter had room for all of the disciples and more.

Roman officer. After Jesus' most famous message—the Sermon on the Mount, which tradition says took place on a shoreline slope just a couple of miles from Capernaum—a Roman military officer sent some Jewish leaders to ask Jesus to heal his servant. The Jews said this officer deserved help because he built the village synagogue. As Jesus approached the house, the officer sent others to tell Jesus he didn't need to come in to perform the healing—perhaps not wanting Jesus to become ritually unclean by entering the house of a non-Jew. The Roman said Jesus could simply speak the healing into reality. Amazed, Jesus replied, "I haven't seen faith like this in all the land of Israel!" (Luke 7:9).

Peter's mother-in-law. Afterward, when Jesus arrived at Peter's house, he found Peter's mother-in-law in bed with a fever. "When Jesus touched her hand, the fever left her. Then she got up and prepared a meal for him" (Matthew 8:15). That same day, people began bringing the sick and demon-possessed to him. The Bible says he healed them all.

Paralyzed man lowered from rooftop. As word spread of Jesus' power, people swarmed the house where he was staying—presumably Peter's house. Four men carrying a paralyzed man on a mat couldn't get through the crowd. So they carried their friend up the staircase to the flat-top roof, dug through it, and gently lowered him. Amazed at this expression of faith, Jesus caused a stir by telling the man his sins were forgiven. When Jewish leaders objected, saying only God could forgive sins, Jesus asked which was easier, to forgive sins or to heal the man. And at his order, the man promptly jumped up and carried away his mat.

AFTER BIBLE TIMES

Death of Capernaum. The village remained exclusively Jewish, according to Epiphanius, a church leader born in the country in the AD 300s. In time, many Capernaum Jews converted to Christianity and are referred to in Jewish writings as *minim,* or heretics. By the AD 400s, Gentiles were living there. That's when a church was built around Peter's house—and archaeologists say Gentiles did the building.

Jesus predicted death for Capernaum. That came in the AD 600s, with Arab invaders. Residents abandoned their homes. In time, wind and earth consumed the village. It lay dead and buried for more than a thousand years.

Synagogue discovered. A British mapmaker discovered Capernaum's synagogue in 1866. Initially, archaeologists couldn't agree on when this synagogue was built. But the general consensus today is that the synagogue, which has been partly restored, was built in the AD 300s to 400s.

Though it wasn't the synagogue in which Jesus taught Capernaum citizens about the "bread of life," there was another synagogue underneath. Visitors who look closely at the west foundation wall can see blocks of black stone about four feet long and a foot high. Those are most likely foundation stones from the synagogue in Jesus' day.

TODAY

Franciscan monks in Capernaum. The city's resurrection as a venerated ruin began in 1894 when Franciscans hoping to preserve sacred sites in the Holy Land bought the property from Arabs. Exploratory excavations began eleven years later and continued until World War I. But it wasn't until the eighteen years of excavations beginning in 1968 that archaeologists discovered ruins of Peter's house as well as the first-century synagogue.

Franciscan monks still own and manage the property. They built a small monastery next to the site and oversee tourists, requiring them to follow a strict dress code. No shorts. No sleeveless shirts or blouses. For the Franciscan fathers, it's a matter of showing respect for a gentle slope of land that was once the home of Jesus.

CAPPADOCIA

(cap uh DOE she uh)
Kappadokia, Greek
First mention: Acts 2:9

Jews from Cappadocia, a mountainous area in central Turkey, were among the pilgrims who came to Jerusalem for the Pentecost festival and heard Peter's sermon that launched the Christian church. They must have taken the news of Jesus home because the letter of 1 Peter is addressed to them and other Jews abroad. Islamic faith was imposed on the people after nomadic Turks crushed Rome's Byzantine Empire in 1071. Today, 99 percent of the population is Muslim.

CARCHEMISH

(CAR kuh mish)
Karkemis, Hebrew
"city of Chemosh," a god
First mention: 2 Chronicles 35:20

In a battle here—one of history's most important—three world powers fought for control of the Middle East. In 605 BC, Nebuchadnezzar of Babylon marched toward busy Carchemish along the Euphrates River in Turkey. He intended to destroy the last of Assyria's army. Pharaoh Neco of Egypt rushed north, hoping to save Assyria as a weak buffer country—which would insure Egypt's independence. He didn't get there in time, perhaps slowed by King Josiah's unsuccessful attempt to stop him as he marched through Israel. Neco lost at Carchemish. The winner, Babylon, dominated civilization's Fertile Crescent, from Iran to Egypt.

CARMEL

(CAR mull)
Karmel, Hebrew
"garden"
First mention: Joshua 12:22

Besides the wooded Carmel Mountains in northern Israel, there was also a Carmel village twenty miles south of Jerusalem. Though the name means "garden," this Carmel—now known by its Arabic name el-Kirmil—sits in a dry wasteland. Once, however, it was a fertile pasture for livestock. Here Nabal, a sheepherder, refused to give supplies to David's men. When Nabal died, David married his wife, Abigail. Earlier, Saul built a monument there to commemorate victory over the Amalekites.

CENCHREA

(sin CREE uh)
Kenchreais, Greek
First mention: Acts 18:18

Corinth, a port city located on a four-mile-wide finger of land separating two seas, enjoyed access to harbors in both seas. Cenchrea served as the eastern port, into the Aegean Sea. Paul shaved his head there one day, before sailing to Ephesus. Earlier, he apparently took a vow that was somewhat like a haircut fast. He refused to trim his hair, perhaps to express his desire that God bless his mission. Paul shaved his head to mark the end of the vow and of a successful mission.

Invaders during the AD 580s chased Cenchrea's residents into the countryside. Its harbor ruins are now under water. Kechriais, Greece, is the modern city near the ancient site.

CHALDEA

MAP 3
E4

(cal DEE uh)
Kasdim, Hebrew
First mention: Isaiah 23:13
("Babylonia" in some translations)

Chaldea's fertile river valley was home to the world's first known civilization, as well as to Abraham—who hailed from "Ur of the Chaldeans" (Genesis 11:31). This kingdom emerged in southern Iraq, where the lower Tigris and Euphrates rivers empty into the Persian Gulf. In time, the Chaldeans took control of Babylonia in the north and expanded it into the vast Babylonian Empire. By then, "Chaldean" meant the same thing as "Babylonian."

CILICIA

MAP 5
E2

(suh LEE she uh)
Kilikia, Greek
First mention: 1 Kings 10:28

Paul grew up in the river-rich territory of Cilicia, a two-hundred-mile-long strip of land on the Mediterranean Sea in what is now Turkey. Paul's hometown, Tarsus, was capital of this Roman province famed for its crops—especially grapes, grain, and flax. A narrow mountain pass called the Cilician Gates leads through the

Shaped a bit like Florida, David's Jerusalem made up just the bottom half of this ridge (below the white dots). His son Solomon later added the temple on the squared section above, where the gold Dome of the Rock now sits.

Taurus Mountains. Paul traveled through this pass on his missionary journeys, as did Alexander the Great on his conquests.

CITY OF DAVID

See Jerusalem

MAP 2
C5

Ir Dawid, Hebrew
First mention: 2 Samuel 5:7

It was a small village David captured: Jebus, which soon became the City of David and later Jerusalem. No more

BIBLE EVENTS:

- Paul starts the Corinthian church
- Paul writes two letters about troubles in the church

STATISTICS:

- Excavation of ruins begins—1886
- Size of city—2.5 square miles, surrounded by 6-mile wall
- Population—100,000 or more (estimates vary widely)
- Abandoned—1858, destroyed by earthquake
- Elevation—about 400 feet above sea level
- Location—45 miles south west of Athens, 4 miles from modern Corinth

good choice. It was well protected, nestled on the crest of a ridge that rose steeply above the Kidron valley. Though its water supply—the Gihon Spring—lay in a hidden cave just outside the city walls, the people had access to it through an underground shaft inside the city. This shaft was their downfall. David found out about it. His men scaled it and took the city by surprise. (See *Jerusalem*.)

COLOSSE

MAP 5
C2

(coh LAH see)
Kolossai, Greek
First mention: Colossians 1:2

Within perhaps a few months after Paul wrote the church at Colosse, praying they would have all the patience and endurance they needed, an earthquake demolished their city—in about AD 60.

There's no indication Paul ever visited the small town of Colosse, in what is now western Turkey. But he spent two years in the region's chief city, Ephesus. And his influence reached out the 120 miles to Colosse and its neighbor cities in the Lycus River valley. In fact, the Colossian pastor Epaphras was a student of Paul's.

Sometime after the earthquake—perhaps because of it—the citizens abandoned Colosse and moved three miles south to a city now called Honaz. All that remains of Colosse is a mound waiting for archaeologists to begin excavating it, to discover what lies beneath.

than twenty-five hundred people lived on this eleven-acre piece of ground roughly two hundred yards wide and six hundred yards long.

Though it was small, David wanted it for his capital. Jebus was an excellent choice for uniting the nation. First, it rested near the center of the country. And second, there would be no hint of tribal favoritism since it lay on the border of two tribes that hadn't been able to capture it from the Canaanites.

There's another reason it was a

Pillars that supported the Temple of Apollos tower over the fractured ruins of Corinth—once a busy seaport town where Paul ministered to the most troublesome church in the Bible.

CORINTH
(COOR enth)
Korinthos, Greek
First mention: Acts 18.1

MAP 5
A2

Why would Paul, on his first preaching mission into Europe, treat Athens like a rest stop on the way to Corinth?

Athens was an Oxford of its day—a thinking man's town. Some of the world's brightest educators lived there, in the Roman province of Achaia in what is now southern Greece. Yet Paul spent perhaps just a few days there before pressing on to neighboring Corinth, where he spent a year and a half starting what would become the most famous church in history.

What did Corinth have that Athens didn't?

While Athens had the brains, Corinth had the muscle. A working-man's town, Corinth was the region's capital, and one of the top-ten busiest cities in the Roman Empire. And though Athens had a fine location on the sea, Corinth had a better location on two seas—with a harbor in each one. That guaranteed Corinth throngs of people. And it guaranteed Paul an ample audience.

IN BIBLE TIMES
Caesar's resurrected city. People have lived in and around Corinth for six thousand years or more. Its rich soil attracted farmers and herders. And its location on a four-mile-wide strip of land separating the Aegean Sea in the east from the Adriatic Sea attracted sailors and merchants. It was a perfect crossroads town—a bridge linking not only southern Greece to northern Greece, but the western world to the eastern world.

Eight hundred years before Christ, the Greek poet Homer was already calling the busy two-harbor town "wealthy Corinth." Shipbuilding was a specialty. So were pottery and bronze work. But when Corinth took a stand against the emerging Roman Empire, Rome all but wiped Corinth off the map. That was in 146 BC, when most of the men were killed and the women and children were sold as slaves.

A century later, in 44 BC, Julius Caesar ordered the city rebuilt. Colonists included a diverse mix of freed slaves from many nations, along with retired

71

SHIPS ON WHEELS

Many ships didn't bother sailing two hundred miles around the southern cape of Greece. They took a shortcut only four miles long—across land.

Corinth had two harbors—one in the Aegean Sea in the east (toward Turkey) and another in the Adriatic Sea in the west (toward Italy). Smaller ships loaded with cargo were hauled up out of the ocean, tugged onto rollers, and pulled along a rock-paved trail into the opposite sea. Ships too large for this often unloaded their cargo and had it carried to the opposite port for other ships waiting to continue the transport.

This shortcut wasn't just a matter of cutting several days off the trip; it was a strategy for reducing risk. Pirates and sudden storms plagued the area. One ancient saying among Greek sailors confirms it: "Let anyone who sails around [Cape] Malea first make a will."

Paul, in fact, was one of the entrepreneurs. To finance his preaching ministry, he teamed up with a couple who had recently arrived from Rome—Aquila and Priscilla—and made tents.

Athens propaganda? Corinth has gotten bad press throughout the ages. It's hard to know how much of it is true because most of it comes from writers in the rival town of Athens. Here's a sampling of how Athenian writers contributed to Corinth's twisted-sister image:

- Aristophanes coined a Greek verb built on Corinth's name, translated "corinthianize." Its modern equivalent has various "wild party" meanings, including a crass word for "fornicate."
- A writing team wrote a play with a title based on Corinth's name. The title's translation: "Whore Lover."
- Even Plato got in the act. The way Valley Girl used to mean bubbles for brains, Plato used Corinthian Girl (*korinthia kore*) to mean prostitute.

Many scholars insist that Corinth was no better or worse than any other busy commercial city and that reports from Paul's day of one thousand sacred prostitutes in Aphrodite's temple is make believe—perhaps leftover rumors from Greek times centuries earlier. On the other hand, there were enough problems there—including a church member who was sleeping with

soldiers. Next came immigrants from the east—including Jews—along with entrepreneurs and trading companies. By the time Paul arrived in the early AD 50s, business was again booming with taverns, temples, theaters, markets, and bathhouses.

his stepmother—that Paul wrote the church two letters of advice, with some stern rebuke.

Olympic-like games. Athletes met every two years in Poseidon's sanctuary at Isthmia—one of Corinth's neighbor cities—to begin the Isthmian Games. Paul may have attended some competitions, because after visiting Corinth, he started using athletic images in his writing. One, for example, may have been a reference to the crown of withered celery that winners at Isthmia received: "All athletes practice strict self-control. They do it to win a prize that will fade away, but we do it for an eternal prize" (1 Corinthians 9:25).

Erastus was here. Paul wrote that a man named "Erastus stayed at Corinth" (2 Timothy 4:20) and that he was "the city treasurer" (Romans 16:23). Erastus was a rare name, but it has shown up as a pavement inscription in Corinth—dating to the AD mid-50s, the very time of Paul's ministry. The inscription also confirms that he was a city official.

AFTER BIBLE TIMES

An earthquake ending. Corinth survived many waves of destructive invaders: Goths, who were north Europeans such as Germans and Swedes, in the AD 200s and 300s; Crusaders in the 1100s; Turks in 1458; Venetians in 1687; and Turks again in 1715, who were finally ousted by the Greeks in 1822.

What Corinth didn't survive was an 1858 earthquake that decimated the city. The entire region, stretching into Turkey, sits on active and violent rifts in the earth's crust.

TODAY

Tourist stop. About a one-hour bus trip from Athens will bring tourists to the ruins of ancient Corinth. Only about 1 percent of the large city has been excavated—the city center—but visitors can see the remains of several temples, shops, paved streets, and fountains. They can even see the meat market Paul spoke about, along with the platform where he likely stood trial before "Gallio. . .governor of Achaia" (Acts 18:12).

In the background stands the Acrocorinth, a hill towering some fifteen hundred feet above the city. Set like a jewel on the highest of the two peaks was a temple to Aphrodite,

A WARNING ABOUT CORINTH

"Not for everyone is the voyage to Corinth." That was a common saying, a word to the wise. Horace, a Roman writer who died about the time Paul was born, explained: Competition was cutthroat, and you could lose your shirt. Geographer Strabo, living at the same time, applied the saying another way: Sex was everywhere, and you could lose your virginity.

goddess of love and Corinth's patron deity.

Some four miles from the ruins is where residents chose to rebuild after the 1858 earthquake. Today, the city that Roman writer Cicero once called "light of all Greece" is the tiny town of Korinthos. It has a population of about thirty-two thousand—far from the number-one city of Athens, with a population of about three-quarters of a million.

Canal shortcut. Ships can skip the voyage around Greece's southern tip by crossing the four-mile isthmus at Corinth. They can sail through a seventy-five-foot-wide canal that Nero started in AD 66, using Jews captured in the Jewish War. He abandoned the job when scientists warned the Adriatic Sea would rush in from the west and flood the nearby island of Aegina in the east. The project was renewed in 1882 and finished eleven years later. Aegina survived.

CORNELIUS
(cor NEE lee us)
Kornelios, Greek
First century AD
First mention: Acts 10:1

Christianity was a Jews-only movement until God kicked open the door for a Roman commander and his family.

Cornelius lived in Caesarea, a thoroughly Roman city that served as Rome's seaside capital of what is now Israel. He worshiped God, praying regularly and giving to charity. But he wasn't a full convert who had been circumcised and ate only kosher food.

Yet, in a vision, God told him to send for Peter, a day's walk south in Joppa. God also told Peter, in a vision, to go with the messengers. Peter obeyed, taking some fellow believers with him. Jews were supposed to avoid non-Jews, who were considered spiritually impure and unfit for worshiping God until they converted to Judaism. Peter's vision indicated otherwise. Peter said, "God has shown me that I should never think of anyone as impure" (Acts 10:28).

When Peter told Cornelius about Jesus, the Holy Spirit filled the soldier and his family. Suddenly, all who heard the message began speaking in a heavenly language. Peter and his colleagues recognized this as God's doing and baptized them all.

CRETE
(CREET)
Krete, Greek
First mention: Deuteronomy 2:23

MAP 5
B3

"Liars, cruel animals, and lazy gluttons." That's what a hometown boy—Cretan poet Epimenides—had to say about his fellow islanders in 800 BC. Paul not only quoted him when writing a letter of advice to Titus, a pastor on this Mediterranean island south of Greece. Paul added, "This is true" (Titus 1:13).

In the Bible, Crete is most famous for the autumn gale that snatched Paul's ship from the shoreline and drove it five hundred miles in two weeks, before running it aground off the island of Malta, south of Italy.

CUSH
(COOSH)
Kus, Hebrew
First mention: Genesis 2:13

When the Bible speaks of a land called Cush, it's hard to know whether to look north to the Persian Gulf area or south to Egypt and Ethiopia.

The confusion may stem from the fact that the land gets its name from Cush, one of Noah's descendants. Those descendants may have dispersed to both regions. The warrior hero Nimrod was a northland descendant of Cush who "built the foundation for his empire in the land of Babylonia" in what is now Iraq (Genesis 10:10). Also, one river in the Garden of Eden flowed around "the entire land of Cush" (Genesis 2:13). The Garden of Eden, many believe, was in Persian Gulf territory.

Yet when the prophet Ezekiel warned of Egypt's destruction, he said God would destroy it as far south as the border of Cush—translated "Ethiopia" in many Bible versions (Ezekiel 29:10).

CYPRUS
(SI prus)
Kypros, Greek
Kittim, Hebrew
First mention: Numbers 24:24

Paul's first missionary stop was this Mediterranean island sixty miles off Syria's west coast. Paul and his partner

Barnabas likely chose this hilly island because it was Barnabas' home. The two landed at the eastern port of Salamis and preached their way west across the 138 mile-long island, converting the Roman governor at the capital city of Paphos, on the island's western tip.

Mountains dominate the land, providing a wealth of cypress, cedar, and other valuable timber. In ancient times, minerals were a major export, and Cyprus was the world's main source for copper. In fact, "copper" evolved from Rome's Latin word *Cyprium*, which means "Cyprus metal."

Jerusalem-area Christians fled to this island when Jews began persecuting them after Jesus' crucifixion. Today, the two main religions of the 723,000 Cypriot people are Greek Orthodox (78 percent) and Muslim (18 percent).

CYRENE
(si REE ne)
Kyrene, Greek
First mention: Matthew 27:32

A Libyan carried the cross for Jesus. At least on today's map, that's where the mysterious man called Simon from Cyrene lived. Cyrene was a seaside city and educational center for medicine and philosophy, located on a lush tableland about ten miles inland and nearly half a mile above North Africa's beachfront. Simon may have been one of many Jews who lived there and who made a nearly thousand-mile pilgrimage to Jerusalem for the Passover festival. Jews in Cyrene revolted against Rome in AD 115 and were brutally suppressed—two hundred thousand died. The city began declining, and Arab invaders finished it off in 642. Today, nomads graze their flocks there.

CYRUS

(CY russ)
Kores, Hebrew
Reigned from 559–530 BC
First mention: 2 Chronicles 36:22

It was Cyrus, a Persian king in what is now Iran, who put Israel back on the map.

Babylon had wiped out the last remnants of the Jewish nation, beginning with deportations in 605 BC and ending with the decimation of Jerusalem and the exile of most survivors about twenty years later. The prophet Jeremiah, who witnessed the destruction, promised that after seventy years God would bring the people home.

Seventy years after the first deportations, Cyrus defeated the Babylonians and gave their captives permission to go home. His emancipation order appears in 2 Chronicles 36:22–23 and Ezra 1:2–3. And a clay cylinder from his reign confirms that he freed the people captured from west of the Tigris River "and returned them to their homes."

This nine-inch-long Cylinder of Cyrus, dating from 536 BC, confirms the Bible's report that the Persian king Cyrus freed political captives such as the Jews.

DAGON
(DAY gahn)
Dagon, Hebrew
First mention: Judges 16:23

Idols of Dagon, the chief Philistine god, towered above several Israelite symbols of strength at one time or another. Samson, captured and blinded, was paraded as a trophy in Dagon's temple. King Saul's severed head was fastened to a temple wall. And the sacred ark containing the Ten Commandments was stored at the idol's foot. But Samson demolished the temple by pushing on two support pillars. And the ark mysteriously seemed to topple the idol—two nights in a row.

It's unclear what kind of god Dagon was. There are three theories based on possible meanings of Dagon's name: fish, grain, or rain.

DAMASCUS
(duh MAS cuss)
Dammeseq, Hebrew
First mention: Genesis 14:15

MAP 1
E1

An oasis on the edge of a vast desert, Syria's capital of Damascus is one of the oldest continually occupied cities in the world—with good reason. Built on the banks of the only year-round river in the region, the city's soil is among the richest in the Middle East—making it prime agricultural and grazing land. Damascus was also a caravan crossroads for people traveling north and south along the King's Highway in what is now Jordan, and to and from the Mediterranean Sea about sixty miles west.

In Bible stories, Damascus is best known as Saul's destination on a mission to arrest Christians. Jesus appeared to him and asked, "Why are you persecuting me?" (Acts 9:4). This was an experience that transformed Saul into Paul, the emerging church's most dynamic minister.

The city, occupied at least a

Samson pushes down the support pillars in Dagon's temple.

thousand years before Abraham showed up in 2100 BC, was also home to Abraham's trusted servant, Eliezer. Throughout Israel's history Damascus was often either an ally of Israel, fighting a common foe, or an enemy competing for control of the region.

DAN
(DAN)
Dan, Hebrew
"judge"
1800s BC
First mention: Genesis 30:6

Dan was a child born of desperation. Jacob had two wives: sisters Leah and Rachel. After Leah delivered four sons, Rachel wanted a child of her own so badly that she told Jacob to use her servant Bilhah as a surrogate mother. Bilhah delivered a son. Rachel named him Dan, meaning "judge," because God judged her worthy of a son. Dan became the ancestor of one of Israel's twelve tribes.

DAN
(DAN)
Dan, Hebrew
"judge"
First mention: Genesis 14:14

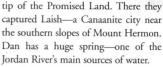

MAP 1
B5, D1

Even with help from their hero Samson, the Israelite tribe of Dan never captured their assigned territory on the coast of what is now central Israel, around Tel Aviv. Philistines lived there, forcing the Danites to stay in the hilly part of their territory. Many Danites migrated more than one hundred miles north, to the

tip of the Promised Land. There they captured Laish—a Canaanite city near the southern slopes of Mount Hermon. Dan has a huge spring—one of the Jordan River's main sources of water.

A fifty-acre mound is all that's left of the ancient city. Archaeologists have been excavating it since 1966 and have found a platform that many say was the shrine where Israel's King Jeroboam erected a golden calf (1 Kings 12:29).

DANIEL
(DAN yull)
Daniel, Hebrew
"God is my judge"
600s–500s BC
First mention: Daniel 1:6

On the most famous night of his life, Daniel found himself sealed inside the rock den of lions. An old man, perhaps eighty, Daniel must have wondered if he would get any older. His friend, the king, surely wondered the same. Manipulated into imposing this punishment on Daniel, the king spent the tense night fasting—hoping the lions would do the same. No doubt, however, he expected the lions would do what they do best—kill.

Daniel's journey to this pivotal night began more than sixty years earlier, probably as a teenager living a thousand miles away.

NOBLE CAPTIVE
Prince Daniel. That's probably who he was in his Jewish homeland—a nobleman who may have been part of

the king's extended family. That wasn't a safe connection in 597 BC, when the Babylonian king Nebuchadnezzar arrived at Jerusalem determined to punish the king for refusing to pay Babylon's imposed taxes. Actually, the rebellious king, Jehoiakim, had recently died. His eighteen-year-old son, Jehoichin, was the new ruler. Until he wisely surrendered.

Nebuchadnezzar looted the palace and temple. He also took "ten thousand captives from Jerusalem, including all the princes and the best of the soldiers, craftsmen, and smiths. So only the poorest people were left in the land" (2 Kings 24:14).

Daniel's long night in the lions' den.

Daniel, probably no older than his teenage king, was among them. Both were treated royally. That's because Babylon had a practice of taking home with them the best people in a conquered land, with the intent of using them to improve Babylonian society.

ELITE PALACE TRAINING

Once in Babylon, near what is now Baghdad, the king ordered his officer in charge of palace officials to select the best from Judah's nobility to serve his own palace. These nobles would enter a three-year training program.

"Select only strong, healthy, and good-looking young men," the king said. "Make sure they are well versed in every branch of learning, are gifted with knowledge and good sense, and have the poise needed to serve in the royal palace. Teach these young men the language and literature of the Babylonians" (Daniel 1:4).

Among these elite were four familiar names—Daniel and three who would later survive a walk in a furnace: Shadrach, Meshach, and Abednego.

The king ordered the best food for his future advisors. But Daniel refused to eat meat, apparently so he could observe a kosher diet. Jews weren't supposed to eat certain common meats, such as pork and rabbit. And other meats had to be drained of blood.

RESURRECTION TO COME

You won't find much in the Old Testament about the afterlife. Those Scriptures usually talk about the godly dead as resting or going to be with their fathers.

But by Daniel's time, Jews began hearing about a new teaching: resurrection.

A heavenly messenger brought Daniel this prophecy, recorded in visions that conclude the book: "Many of those whose bodies lie dead and buried will rise up, some to everlasting life and some to shame and everlasting contempt" (Daniel 12:2).

As for Daniel, the messenger said, "You will rest, and then at the end of the days, you will rise again to receive the inheritance set aside for you" (Daniel 12:13).

Daniel and his four friends ate only vegetables and looked healthier than those who ate the rich food at the king's table.

After the three-year program, all four men so impressed the king that he appointed them to his regular staff.

DREAM INTERPRETER

During his more than sixty years as a royal advisor, Daniel earned fame not only for his sage advice but for his ability to interpret the supernatural— notably two dreams in which God communicated to Nebuchadnezzar and one paranormal event in which God wrote four mysterious words on King Belshazzar's palace wall.

Daniel correctly described Nebuchadnezzar's dream about a gigantic statue made of various materials. The king had refused to describe his dream, perhaps to test the skill of the dream interpreters. Daniel then explained that the different materials represented the inferior kingdoms that would follow him. Though Daniel didn't name the kingdoms, history does. Silver and bronze represented the next two kingdoms: the Medes and the Persians. Daniel said they would be crushed by an iron kingdom: Greeks led by Alexander the Great. The statue's clay feet and toes represented the kingdom divided: Alexander's generals divided his empire among themselves.

Nebuchadnezzar's second dream revealed that insanity would drive him to live like an animal for seven years. Though history says nothing of this, Daniel reported it happened and that afterward the king returned to the throne and praised God.

For a later king, Belshazzar, Daniel interpreted four words that a disembodied hand wrote on the palace wall: Mene, Mene, Tekel, Parsin. Daniel said the words meant "numbered, numbered, weighed, divided" (Daniel 5:26–28). The explanation was that Belshazzar's days were numbered. He had been spiritually weighed and found lacking. So God would divide his kingdom among the Medes and Persians.

The capital fell that night, and Belshazzar died.

FASTING LIONS

The new king of what became the Persian Empire recognized the elderly Daniel's wisdom and planned to put him in charge of all other officials. Jealous, the officials hatched a plot that depended on Daniel's faith and the king's ego. They convinced the king to declare an irrevocable law: People could pray to no one but him for thirty days. Lions got the violators.

Daniel prayed to God, and the king had no choice but to impose the teeth of his law. But the lions didn't eat. Not until the next morning, after the king retrieved Daniel and had the conniving officials take his place.

DANIEL THE DRAGON SLAYER

Daniel's life inspired more stories than those in the book named after him. One such story, preserved in Catholic and Eastern Orthodox Bibles, is about Daniel killing a "dragon" that the Babylonians worshiped. The dragon was probably a huge snake.

Daniel killed it with a hairball—a lethal concoction of tar, fat, and hair. The dragon exploded, proving it was no god.

DARIUS
(duh RYE us)
Dareyawes, Hebrew
Reigned 521–486 BC
First mention: Ezra 4:5

This Persian king's name is usually followed by two words: the Great. The Bible says he authorized Jews to rebuild the Jerusalem temple. Cyrus, an earlier king, had done this, too. But opponents of the Jews convinced a later king to stop the work. Darius found the original order and reissued it.

A shrewd administrator, Darius divided his empire into twenty provinces for easier taxing and governing—a system that lasted two hundred years. He also set up a broad legal code based on Babylonian laws and standardized a system of weights and measures throughout the empire.

DARIUS THE MEDE
(duh RYE us the MEED)
Dareyawes madaja, Hebrew
Possibly reigned from 559–530 BC
First mention: Daniel 5:31

History and the Bible clash over Persian king Darius the Mede. The Bible says he was sixty-two when he ousted the last Babylonian king, Belshazzar, and that he appointed Daniel as an advisor and was manipulated into putting Daniel in the lions' den. Ancient historians never seemed to mention him and reported that Cyrus conquered Babylon. Some scholars suggest Darius was another name for Cyrus and that Daniel 6:28 should read much like this footnote from the New Living Translation: "So

Daniel prospered during the reign of Darius, that is, the reign of Cyrus the Persian."

DAVID
(DAY vid)
Dawid, Hebrew
"beloved one"
Reigned 1010–970 BC
First mention: Ruth 4:17

David was a shepherd boy in Bethlehem who traded his pasture for a palace and became Israel's second king—the most honored in all the nation's history. With good reason.

During his forty-year reign, David managed to unify a loose-knit coalition of family tribes into an empire, the likes of which Israel has never seen since. A warrior king, David tamed the regional powers such as the Philistines, who had plagued Israel for centuries. Then he pushed out the boundaries of Israel's domination north beyond Lebanon to the upper tip of Syria, south to Egypt, east into Jordan, and west to the Mediterranean Sea.

His astonishing success is one important reason why centuries later, when Israel was occupied and oppressed by invaders, the people prayed for God to send a "son of David" to free them.

SHEPHERD BOY
Raised in the rolling hills of Bethlehem, David was the youngest son of a herder named Jesse. David had at least seven brothers and two sisters. Surprising to many, David was not entirely Jewish. His great-grandmother, Ruth, came from what is now the Arab country of Jordan.

THE MUSICIAN

Before David became a giant killer, he was a music therapist. Palace officials periodically called in the shepherd boy to treat King Saul with soothing harp music when Saul got depressed.

David not only played music; he wrote it. When Saul and Jonathan died in battle, David composed a funeral song with memorable lyrics: "How the mighty heroes have fallen!" (2 Samuel 1:27). Before David died, he wrote a song expressing his wish to be remembered as "the sweet psalmist of Israel" (2 Samuel 23:1).

This wish seems to have come true. Seventy-three of the 150 songs in the Psalms, Israel's hymnal, are titled "a psalm of David." The word "of" doesn't necessarily mean "by." It could mean "about," "for," or "to" David. But at the very least, David's life inspired some of Israel's most cherished music.

David loved music so much that he set up a music ministry at the worship center, appointing the musicians and their assistants.

The shepherd boy David, with the trophy that launched his fame: the head of Goliath, a Philistine champion that even King Saul was afraid to fight.

In ancient Middle Eastern families, the youngest child was usually considered the least important—so Jesse reported that his youngest son, David, was watching the sheep. That freed the more important family members to meet with Samuel. But as another citizen of Bethlehem and a descendant of David would say a thousand years later, in God's eyes the last are sometimes first (Matthew 20:16). That was the case with David, a young boy "ruddy and handsome, with pleasant eyes" (1 Samuel 16:12). Samuel immediately recognized that David was God's choice. So Samuel poured olive oil over David. "And the Spirit of the LORD came mightily upon him from that day on" (1 Samuel 16:13).

Israel's first king, Saul, persistently disobeyed God. So God set in motion a plan to replace him. God sent the prophet Samuel to Bethlehem on a secret mission to anoint one of Jesse's sons as the future king. God warned Samuel not to judge the sons by their looks or height—a temptation because Saul was tall and handsome. Instead, God told Samuel, "the LORD looks at a person's thoughts and intentions" (1 Samuel 16:7).

Jesse paraded his sons before the prophet. Though Samuel saw great potential when judging by the looks of the boys, he didn't sense God selecting any of them. "Are these all the sons you have?" he asked Jesse (1 Samuel 16:11).

GIANT KILLER

It must have given David incredible confidence to know that God had chosen him and would bless his life. Perhaps he felt nearly invincible—more so than a typical young boy. When lions and bears charged into his herd and latched onto lambs, David snatched back his lambs. And when a predator turned on him, he grabbed it by the jaw and clubbed it to death.

David offered to do the same thing to a towering Philistine champion warrior named Goliath, who stood nearly seven feet tall—or nearly ten feet

DAVID WAS HERE

King David's exploits were no more real than King Arthur's legends. That's what many scholars once concluded, since there was no solid proof David existed.

Now there's rock-solid proof—three discoveries in the 1990s of David's name engraved in rock.

• In 1993, archaeologists found a foot-high section of a victory monument in the ruins of Dan, a city in northern Israel. The engraving dates to about a century after David and refers to the "House [meaning Dynasty] of David" and the "King of Israel." The words were written only in consonants, as was the custom then. So "House of David" appears as bytdwd. Byt stands for beit (a form of bayit), or "house of." Dwd stand for Dawid, or "David." Some scholars argue that the letters could mean something else, but others insist that in the context of the other words, "House of David" is the more likely translation.

• The identical phrase has been discovered on a second stone from a century after David—this one from Moab, now Jordan. The Moabite Stone was found in 1868, but the reference to David was discovered only recently, after studying a paper impression made of the stone before it was smashed.

• Egyptologist Kenneth A. Kitchen of the University of Liverpool reported that a stone hieroglyphic telling about the victories of Pharaoh Sheshonk—who lived a few decades after David—includes a reference to "the heights of David," perhaps talking about the hilltop city of Jerusalem.

tall (the oldest Bible manuscripts report the shorter number).

Jesse had sent David to deliver some roasted grain and bread to David's brothers, camped with Saul's militia a little more than half a day's walk west of Bethlehem, in the valley of Elah. The Israelite and Philistine armies were staged on opposite sides of the valley, preparing for battle. David arrived in time to see what had become a daily ritual: Goliath came out to challenge an Israelite to mortal combat—winner take all. No one dared accept, even though Saul offered a royal reward—one of his daughters in marriage and a tax-free life for the warrior's entire family.

David accepted, though he wasn't strong enough to wear body armor and he seemed no match for a giant whose coat of mail alone probably weighed as much as the shepherd boy—125 pounds. Perhaps even more intimidating was Goliath's towering spear. Its shaft looked like a weaver's beam, which at roughly six inches thick is about half the thickness of a telephone pole. Mounted on the tip was a fifteen-pound iron spearhead. Philistines guarded the secret of iron making because iron could cut through the bronze weapons that Israel had.

David dropped Goliath with a stone. He flung it from a slingshot, then cut Goliath's head off, using the giant's own sword. Panicked, the Philistines turned and ran. The Israelites ran after them, killing them all along the retreat to their stronghold cities of Gath and Ekron, several miles away.

That day, David moved into the palace with Saul and became best friends with Saul's son, Jonathan. Whatever Saul asked David to do, David did it well. So Saul made David a military commander, which soldiers and citizens applauded.

FUGITIVE

A song pushed Saul over the edge: "Saul has killed his thousands, and David his ten thousands!" (1 Samuel 18:7).

That's what people sang. Saul, livid with jealousy, began looking for ways to kill David. He tried pinning him to the palace wall with a spear while David played the harp. He missed. Then he sent David on dangerous missions, hoping David would die. He didn't, and his popularity soared. One mission was to kill one hundred Philistines for the privilege of marrying Saul's daughter, Michal.

David killed two hundred and married the princess.

In time, Saul resorted to a bold misuse of his power. He ordered some of his troops to go to David's home and assassinate him. Michal bought David time to escape by putting a decoy statue in their bed and convincing the troops he was too sick to move.

David remained a hunted fugitive for the rest of Saul's life.

But David wasn't alone for long. His brothers joined him in hiding. "Then others began coming—men who were in trouble or in debt or who were just discontented—until David was the leader of about four hundred men" (1 Samuel 22:2).

Saul doggedly pursued them and once had them trapped in the caves of En-gedi, about a day's walk—twenty miles—southwest of Bethlehem near the shores of the Dead Sea. But Saul didn't realize it. He relieved himself in the very cave where David and his men were hiding. When David's men urged him to kill the king, David refused to harm the "LORD's anointed one" (1 Samuel 24:6). Instead, he cut off part of Saul's robe. When the king left, David called him from a distance and held up the robe piece. Saul replied with tears, "You are a better man than I am, for you have repaid me good for evil" (1 Samuel 24:17). And he went home.

Saul soon resumed the hunt, forcing David and his men into Philistine territory. Ironically, the king of Goliath's hometown—Gath—let them stay because he believed they were raiding Israelite settlements. Actually, they were clearing Israel of non-Jewish communities such as Amalekites.

When it came time for a showdown between the combined Philistine armies and the Israelite army led by Saul, David was still in Philistine territory. So he marched with them, at the rear. Some Philistine commanders objected, perhaps rightfully fearing that David would attack them from behind while Saul's men attacked from the front. They sent David home and defeated Saul, leaving the king and three of his sons dead—Jonathan among them.

David mourned the death of Saul and his sons, even executing the messenger who brought the news and claimed to have killed "the LORD's anointed one" (2 Samuel 1:14–15). David may have felt especially sensitive about leaders anointed by God since he was one of them, and he knew how that anointing changed his life.

KING

In the power gap that followed, the people of Judah, an Israelite tribe in southern Israel, crowned David as their king. But in the north, Saul's military commander proclaimed one of Saul's sons, Ishbosheth, the new king. Civil war broke out, but it ended when two of Ishbosheth's commanders assassinated him, cut off his head, and took it with them to show David. Never fond of people who killed his in-laws,

David ordered them executed.

With Saul's dynasty gone, Jewish elders from all twelve tribes assembled in Hebron, David's capital in southern Israel. There, they installed him as king of a united Israel.

To lead a united nation, David wanted a neutral capital—one that wouldn't suggest he was favoring one tribe over another. He chose Jerusalem because it was a Canaanite holdout that hadn't been captured by any tribe. Also, it sat near the center of Israel, on the border between the tribes of Judah and Benjamin.

Jerusalem captured, David brought in the most sacred Jewish relic, the ark containing the Ten Commandments—considered the earthly throne of God. So Jerusalem became the political and religious center of Israel.

For the first time in Israel's history, the twelve tribes were united. And David the giant killer turned them into a powerful war machine. With Egyptian and Assyrian empires in temporary decline, David's armies stormed out to control all the land God promised to Abraham's descendants—and then some, capturing parts of what are now Lebanon, Syria, and Jordan.

FLAWED FAMILY MAN

By the time David saw Bathsheba taking a bath, he already had at least seven wives. It was late in the afternoon, when David rose from a nap and took a walk on the flattop roof of his palace. From there, he saw Bathsheba, perhaps in her walled courtyard. He sent for her, they had sex, and she became pregnant.

David called her husband, Uriah, home from the battlefront, hoping he would sleep with her and think the child was his. But Uriah insisted on honoring the Jewish tradition of abstaining from sex during a battle. David sent Uriah back to the battlefield with sealed orders for the commander to put him at the front of the attack, then retreat, leaving him stranded. He died in battle, and David married his widow, Bathsheba.

Many people wonder how David could get away with such blatant sin. He didn't. There were immediate and long-term consequences. Though David repented, the child died. Also, this sin marks a turning point in David's story: A lifetime of blessing unravels. Instead of reading more success stories, we start to read about David's debilitating family troubles. His oldest son raped a half sister. David did nothing. So the sister's full brother, Absalom, murdered her rapist and fled the country. Three years later, David called Absalom home but refused to see him for another two years. By then, the rift was so wide that Absalom launched a near-successful coup, forcing David to flee Jerusalem. The coup stopped only after Absalom was killed, against David's order.

Years later, as the elderly David lay dying, his oldest surviving son—Adonijah—threw a party to declare himself king. Bathsheba pleaded with David to remember an earlier promise he had made to transfer the reign to her son, Solomon. David honored that promise,

and in time Solomon felt compelled to execute his half brother to keep the brother from launching a coup.

DYING WORDS

"I am going where everyone on earth must someday go," David on his deathbed told Solomon. "Take courage and be a man. Observe the requirements of the LORD your God and follow all his ways" (1 Kings 2:2–3).

"David died and was buried in the City of David" (1 Kings 2:10).

The epitome of saintly perfection, he was not. David was a flawed human —but a human who trusted God, did his best to serve him, and asked for forgiveness when he failed. A great man, David knew the Source of his greatness.

DEAD SEA

Yam Hammelah, Hebrew
Salt Sea
First mention: Genesis 14:3

MAP 1
C5

When David fled to escape assassination from the jealous king Saul and hid in the caves of En-gedi, along the Dead Sea shoreline, he certainly felt low. If he were hiding there today, he could slip over to one of the beachfront stores and pick up a tee shirt that reads, "Lowest spot on earth." That would describe his feelings and the geography. At about thirteen hundred feet below sea level, the beach along the Dead Sea is the lowest stretch of dry land on the planet.

In Bible times, the Dead Sea was known by many names, especially the

Salt Sea as well as the Sea of Arabah and the Eastern Sea. But today it's called the Dead Sea. That's because nothing lives there. If a fish is unlucky enough to follow the Jordan River's current into the Dead Sea, which is at least 25 percent salt (four times higher than the ocean), it dies almost instantly.

Dead Sea floaters can't possibly sink because the water—25 percent salt—is incredibly buoyant.

This saltwater lake, about fifty miles long and ten miles wide, separates Israel from Jordan. Because it's the lowest spot on earth, it's the drainage tank for all rivers and streams in the region. Water pours in then has nowhere to go but up—in evaporation. That keeps the mineral concentration high.

In the shallows along the southwestern shore, the Dead Sea Works company extracts some of these minerals, especially potassium compounds used in making fertilizer and other products. Mining isn't new to the Dead Sea. In ancient times, people camped along the shore and waited for boat-size globs of bitumen, a tarry asphalt substance, to pop up and float. Miners would hack these tarbergs into hunks, load them on their boats, and sell them as waterproofing and mortar.

A DEAD SEA FLOAT

Doctors in Israel sometimes tell patients to soak their head in a large body of water that instantly kills marine life. In fact, minerals in the Dead Sea do seem to have therapeutic value for treating certain ailments, especially some skin disorders.

This has spawned a health resort boom along the shores. Guests from around the world coat themselves with lake mud or float on their backs in the lake. The water is so salty that people bob around like corks and can't sink. But if they get any of the concentrated saltwater in their eyes, they're headed to the beachfront showers to put out the fire.

DEBORAH

(DEB uh rah)
Debora, Hebrew
"bee"
1100s BC
First mention: Judges 4:4

In a day when men ruled families and nations and women were typically considered minors in court, Deborah became one of Israel's most charismatic judges. A prophet as well as a judge, she held court under a palm tree in the hills of central Israel. How she rose to power in a male-dominated society is anyone's guess, but it may have to do with the kind of God-connection and determination she showed in calling her people to battle.

Deborah sent for a general named Barak and told him that God wanted Barak to lead an army of ten thousand against the Canaanite king Jabin, who had been oppressing the Israelites with his army of nine hundred chariots.

Barak agreed, but only if Deborah joined him.

"I will go with you," she replied. "But since you have made this choice, you will receive no honor" (Judges 4:9). A sudden storm drenched the battle-field, flooding the nearby river and sucking Jabin's chariots deep into the mud. Deborah's army won, and her victory song is preserved in the Bible as one of the oldest surviving Hebrew poems.

DECAPOLIS
(duh CAP oh liss)
Decapolis, Greek
"ten towns"
First mention: Matthew 4:25

MAP 4
D4

When Jesus started his ministry, one of the places he visited was a predominately non-Jewish area known as the Decapolis. It was located east and south of the Sea of Galilee—partly in what is now Israel, but mostly east of the Jordan River in what is now northern Jordan. This territory was home to ten towns that preserved the Greek way of life. Alexander the Great introduced

Greek culture when he conquered much of the Middle East. The list and number of towns in the Decapolis region changed over time, and it's difficult to know which ones were there in Jesus' time. The Roman scholar Pliny, writing about fifty years after Jesus' time, listed these ten: Canatha, Damascus, Dion, Gardara, Gerasa, Hippos, Pella, Philadelphia (modern Amman, Jordan), Raphana, and Scythopolis (Beth-shan, Israel).

DELILAH
(dee LIE lah)
Delila, Hebrew
Perhaps "loose hair" or "small"
About 1075 BC
First mention: Judges 16:4

The strong man Samson had one weakness—unsavory women. The Bible tells of three, all of whom got him into violent trouble. But the Bible names only one—skipping even his wife, but naming Delilah. Perhaps her name served as a foreshadowing in this dramatic story—a hint that Samson's lights were about to go out. His name is connected with "sun." Her name sounds like the Hebrew word for night: *layla*.

Some time after visiting a prostitute in Gaza, about thirty miles south of his hometown, Samson fell in love with Delilah. The Bible doesn't say Delilah was a Philistine, but it's likely because she lived in Philistine territory in the Sorek valley, west of Jerusalem. That placed her just a few miles from Samson's hometown, along the Philistine border.

By this time, Samson was a living legend because of his extraordinary strength. But money has power, too. So a group of Philistine leaders offered Delilah a reward if she could find out what made Samson so strong and deliver him tied securely. The price of this betrayal was that each leader would give her 1,110 silver coins (weighing a total of 28 pounds). That's about $1,500 today, when silver is selling at $4.50 a troy ounce. Deal.

"So day after day she nagged him until he couldn't stand it any longer. Finally, Samson told her his secret" (Judges 16:16–17). She alerted the Philistines to wait nearby, and while Samson slept on her lap, she had a servant shave his hair. Samson was captured, blinded, and put to work grinding grain at a prison in Gaza. He died a prisoner. But he took thousands of Philistines with him—perhaps Delilah, too—when he used a surge of strength to topple support pillars in a temple during a festival.

DEMETRIUS

(duh ME tree us)
Demetrios, Greek
"belongs to Demeter," a goddess
First century AD
First mention: Acts 19:24

Paul did such a good job converting citizens in Ephesus, a leading city in Rome's empire, that a man who owned an idol-making business started a riot to protect his revenue. Demetrius hired artisans to make silver idols of the city's patron goddess, Artemis, also called Diana. He gathered his craftsmen, along with everyone connected to the industry. When he warned that business was crumbling and Artemis' prestige was fading, the growing crowd

Artemis, the many-breasted fertility goddess worshiped in Ephesus. Demetrius earned a living by making and selling figurines of her.

began chanting, "Great is Artemis of the Ephesians!" (Acts 19:28). This went on for two hours. An official eventually dispersed the crowd. Paul left town, as he had been planning to do before the riot.

DERBE
(DUR bee)
Derbe, Greek
First mention: Acts 14:6

MAP 5
E3

Only one of the four cities Paul and Barnabas visited in what is now Turkey didn't run them out of town when they arrived on the first missionary trip. Derbe, the last stop on the circuit, was that one. Paul's later associate, Gaius, came from there. And Paul returned to Derbe on his second trip.

Two inscriptions naming Derbe and found in a mound near Kerti Huyuk—about fifteen miles from the larger city of Karaman—suggest this mound was ancient Derbe.

DINAH
(DIE nah)
Dina, Hebrew
"judge"
1800s BC
First mention: Genesis 30:21

For the love of Dinah—daughter of Jacob and Leah—a village was wiped out. The village was Shechem, in what is now central Israel. Jacob had camped nearby. When Dinah went to visit some women there, the prince raped her. But he fell in love with her. So he asked to marry her, and he invited Jacob's family to settle in the area. Dinah's brothers, however, wanted only revenge. They convinced the prince to have all the village men circumcised. While the men were still hurting from the procedure, Dinah's brothers Simeon and Levi killed them all. The other brothers joined in, plundering the village and taking the women and children as slaves.

DOTHAN
(DOE than)
Dotan, Hebrew
First mention: Genesis 37:17

MAP 1
C3

Sent to check on his sheepherding brothers, the teenager Joseph walked some seventy miles—probably for about four days—only to end up getting sold to slave traders. His father, Jacob, sent him from their home in Hebron in southern Israel to Shechem in central Israel. But Joseph's brothers had moved the flocks farther north to Dothan. That's where his brothers, jealous of the way their father treated him, sold him to slave traders who took him to Egypt.

Dothan was also where Syrian soldiers tried to capture Elisha. Instead, he captured them. Elisha blinded the army and led them as prisoners some eleven miles to Samaria. A twenty-five-acre mound marks the site of ancient Dothan.

EBENEZER

MAP 2
C4

(eb uh NEE zur)
Eben haezer, Hebrew
"the stone of help"
First mention: 1 Samuel 4:1

Of all the names the prophet Samuel could have given a stone monument he erected after Israel beat the Philistines in battle, "Ebenezer" has to be among the most ironic. It means "the stone of help." Samuel gave it this name because "the LORD has helped us!" (1 Samuel 7:12).

But twenty years earlier, Israel's most sacred stones—the Ten Commandments carried in a chest called the Ark of the Covenant—were no help at all. Israel had lost a battle with the Philistines at what is now the outskirts of Tel Aviv. So they decided to bring the ark with them in a second attack. They lost the battle and the ark. The Philistines took it but gave the ark back after an outbreak of disease. Perhaps Samuel's subtle message was that Israel's source of help was God, not sacred objects.

EDEN

See Tigris River
MAP 3
D3

(EE den)
Eden, Hebrew
Possibly "flatland"
First mention: Genesis 2:8

This homeland of the first humans—Adam and Eve—may have been paradise for them, but it's torment for Bible experts. Scholars can't figure out where it was or even what it was. At times, the Creation story in Genesis says Eden was a garden. Other times, Eden was a region that had a garden: "God planted a garden in Eden" (Genesis 2:8). Perhaps it was both—the name of the garden and the territory, the way "Babylon" once described an empire and its capital city.

Eden's garden was a lush and fertile land fed by an unnamed river that nourished fruit trees, animals, and the first couple—until the couple ate forbidden fruit. Then God banished them to east of Eden.

LOOKING FOR EDEN

Eden hunters have two main clues.

1. God planted the garden "in Eden, in the east" (Genesis 2:8). But east of what? East of Israel? The east side of Eden?
2. The garden's unnamed river branched into four more: Tigris, Euphrates, Pishon, and Gihon. Only the first two are known today. They course through Iraq and drain into the Persian Gulf.

Eden hunters can choose from many theories about where to find humanity's first home. Here are two.

Eden underwater. One theory says Eden lies flooded beneath the Persian Gulf, which was once the garden river. That was before floods filled the river valley and linked with the Arabian Sea. Ancient Persian Gulf lore tells of a lost island where people never died.

The lost river of Gihon that ran through "Cush" is the Karun River of Iran. Nimrod, a descendant of Noah's son Cush, settled in western Iran. The lost river of Pishon is the dry riverbed called the Kuwait River. Both rivers join the other two and empty into the gulf. That's the trouble. The Bible has the current running the other way—the garden river that is now the Persian Gulf flowed into the other rivers. Some wonder if the writer reversed the current in the story as a symbolic way of saying Eden is gone forever and impossible to find.

Eden in the hills. Another theory starts at the source of the Tigris and Euphrates, in the mountains of Ararat where Noah's ark ran aground. Here, seven hundred miles north of the Persian Gulf in northern Iran, is a highland plain described in a five-thousand-year-old Sumerian story as "eden," the Sumerian word for flatland.

The lost Gihon is the similar-sounding Giahum. That's what Arab geographers called it in the AD 600s. Today it's Aras. A Cush connection? Rising high above the river is Kusheh

Degh—the "Mountain of Kush." The lost Pishon is a river formerly called Uizhun, before the "P" was switched to "U" to accommodate the Iranian alphabet. It's now called Kezel Uzun. Eden's main river was a mountain stream.

On the east side of this Iranian plain was a village settled by a tribe of fierce warriors, the Kheru. Some scholars say this may be a version of *keruvim,* the Hebrew word for cherubim. The Bible says that after God banished Adam and Eve, he stationed a sword-carrying cherubim east of the garden.

The Garden of Eden, says this theory, was probably on the site of what is now an industrial city on the plain's east side: Tabriz. If so, paradise is lost—buried beneath urban sprawl.

Edom

(EE dum)
Edom, Hebrew
"red"
First mention: Genesis 25:30

MAP 1
D7

For a bowl of red stew, Esau traded his privileged rights as the family's first son. That earned him a nickname, Edom, meaning "red." The name stuck, and the land where Esau's descendants settled, south of the Dead Sea, became known as Edom. The sandstone hills there and much of the soil bear a reddish hue. The one-time capital of Edom was Petra, today a tourist attraction with massive rock carvings in the cliffs.

Edom refused to let the Hebrews pass through their land on the way to Canaan. But God told the Hebrews not to bother them since they were relatives.

EGLON

(EGG lon)
Eglon, Hebrew
Perhaps "calf" or "rounded"
First mention: Joshua 10:3

Eglon was a Canaanite settlement that Joshua's forces completely wiped out—to the last person. After citizens of Gibeon tricked Joshua into making a treaty with them, Jerusalem's king decided to punish Gibeon. He gathered a coalition army from five villages—including Eglon—and marched to Gibeon. Joshua came to the rescue of his allies, defeating the coalition forces. Then he wiped out each of the coalition cities except heavily fortified Jerusalem.

delta in the north, where the river splits into streams that empty into the Mediterranean Sea. Egypt's livable land was only about the size of Maryland. The rest was desert.

That worked to Egypt's advantage. They built their cities along the river and used the river as their superhighway. Almost every year, the Nile flooded just enough to water the plain and lay down a fresh blanket of rich soil. Egyptians called their seven-hundred-mile-long valley *kemet,* "the black land." Protecting this valley were sprawling deserts that warded off all but the most persistent invaders. That helps explain why Egyptian civilization has survived for about fifty-one hundred years.

EGYPT

(EE jippt)
Misrayim, Hebrew
Aigyptos, Greek
First mention:
Genesis 12:10

Egypt looks large as it sits on the northern tip of Africa. Egypt's chunk of ground is nearly the size of Texas, Oklahoma, and Kansas combined. But that's an optical illusion. The only land people could live on in Bible times was about a ten-mile-wide strip along the Nile River and the fan-shaped

Egyptians in Bible times lived on the ten-mile-wide strip of fertile land along the Nile River. Beyond that lay desert—a natural boundary discouraging invaders.

SAFE HAVEN FOR JEWS

Throughout Israel's ancient history, spanning the two thousand years from Abraham to Jesus, Egypt often hosted Jewish refugees during droughts or oppression. Abraham traveled there to wait out a drought. Jesus' family fled there to wait out King Herod's life. Between those years, many other Jews took refuge in Egypt. Jacob brought his extended family there during a seven-year famine, grazing their flocks in the delta territory called Goshen. Jeremiah and other survivors of the Babylonian invasion also escaped there.

Egypt and Israel weren't always gracious to each other. Jacob's family wore out their welcome as guests and became city-building slaves who languished in Egypt some 430 years. Later, the two nations sometimes fought each other, often with Egypt marching up the coastline road into Israel. Shortly after the Israelites settled in Canaan, Pharoah Merneptah inscribed this exaggerated claim in stone: "Israel is laid waste, his seed [people] no longer exists."

EHUD

(EE hud)
Ehud, Hebrew
"where is the glory?"
About 1300 BC
First mention: Judges 3:15

Second of Israel's twelve champion leaders, called judges, Ehud freed his people from eighteen years of foreign rule by assassinating King Eglon of Moab, now in Jordan. Ehud took Israel's taxes to the king—along with an eighteen-inch dagger strapped to his leg. After delivering the money, Ehud told the king he had a message from God. King Eglon cleared the room, and Ehud thrust the dagger into the obese king's abdomen. Ehud locked the door and escaped through the indoor toilet. Back in Israel, he rallied the men and defeated the Moabites, ushering in eighty years of peace.

EKRON

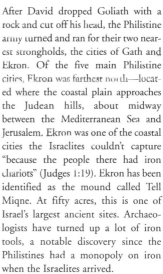

(ECK ron)
Eqron, Hebrew
Akkaron, Greek
First mention: Joshua 13:3

MAP 1
B5

After David dropped Goliath with a rock and cut off his head, the Philistine army turned and ran for their two nearest strongholds, the cities of Gath and Ekron. Of the five main Philistine cities, Ekron was farthest north—located where the coastal plain approaches the Judean hills, about midway between the Mediterranean Sea and Jerusalem. Ekron was one of the coastal cities the Israelites couldn't capture "because the people there had iron chariots" (Judges 1:19). Ekron has been identified as the mound called Tell Miqne. At fifty acres, this is one of Israel's largest ancient sites. Archaeologists have turned up a lot of iron tools, a notable discovery since the Philistines had a monopoly on iron when the Israelites arrived.

A B C D E F G H I J K L M N O P Q R S T U V W X Y Z

ELAH VALLEY

MAP 2
B5

(EE lah)
Ela, Hebrew
"oak"
First mention: 1 Samuel 17:2

Young David, perhaps still a teenager, picked up five stones from a stream now called Brook Elah. Then he used his slingshot to drive one of those stones into the forehead of Goliath. This mortal combat that David won over the Philistine champion took place about fifteen miles west of David's Bethlehem home, in the Elah valley. Philistine soldiers camped on the gently rolling hills overlooking the wide valley from the south. Saul staged his Israelite troops on the north hills. Both had a great view of the short battle. Tourists today visit the valley and pluck pebbles from the brook as souvenirs.

ELAM

MAP 3
E3

(EE lam)
Elam, Hebrew
"highland"
First mention: Genesis 14:1

In the Bible's first mention of war, a Persian Gulf coalition raided what is now Israel, looting Sodom along with other cities and kidnapping citizens including Lot. Among the invaders were soldiers from Elam, a kingdom in what is now southwest Iran. Abraham and his allies chased down the raiders, rescuing the captives and stolen goods. Elam's recorded history started about 3200 BC—more than a thousand years before Abraham—and ended with the arrival of Alexander the Great in 331 BC.

ELEAZAR

(el ee A zur)
Elazar, Hebrew
"God has helped"
1400s BC
First mention: Exodus 6:23

When Aaron died, Israel needed a new high priest to take responsibility for the tent worship center known as the tabernacle. The job fell to Eleazar, the number-three son of Aaron's four. All of Aaron's sons helped him as priests, but the two oldest—Nadab and Abihu—died when they built a ritual fire different from the kind God commanded. So Eleazar became the oldest surviving son. As high priest, he led the tribe of Levi, which became a group of families that helped take care of the worship center and perform the worship rituals.

ELI

(EE lie)
Eli, Hebrew
"Exalted"
1100s BC
First mention: 1 Samuel 1:3

Eli was an Israelite high priest whose sons turned out so badly that God killed them both in a single day. Yet Eli also raised Samuel from a toddler to become one of Israel's most respected prophets.

Eli's story begins with him scolding

Samuel's mother, Hannah. She was childless at the time and tearfully praying about it at Israel's worship center in Shiloh, near the center of Israel. Her family came there once a year to offer sacrifices. Eli saw her mumbling and thought she was drunk. But when she assured him she was only praying in anguish, he responded with encouragement: "Cheer up! May the God of Israel grant the request you have asked of him" (1 Samuel 1:17).

Samuel was born within the year. In gratitude, Hannah took him to the worship center after he was off breast milk. She gave him to Eli to raise him in God's service.

SEX-HUNGRY PRIESTS

Eli's sons were a shameful embarrassment. They seduced young women who helped at the worship center and took prime-cut sacrificial meat intended only for God. Yet Eli did nothing but ask them to stop. They didn't. In time, a prophet arrived with horrifying news: Eli's sons would die on the same day, and no one else in Eli's family would live a long life.

War broke out with the Philistines. After losing the first battle, Israel's soldiers called up their most sacred object to lead them: a chest containing the Ten Commandments.

Eli's sons helped carry it and were lost in the battle along with the chest and thousands of Israel's soldiers.

Eli—ninety-eight years old, blind, and fat—sat on a chair by the road, waiting for news of the battle. When it came, he fell backward off his chair, breaking his neck.

On a mission to find a wife for forty-year-old Isaac, Eliezer meets Rebekah. She not only gives him a drink but waters his camels—a clue that she'll make a hard-working wife.

ELIEZER

(el uh EE zur)
Eli ezer, Hebrew
"my God helps"
About 2100 BC
First mention: Genesis 15:2

Several Bible men were named Eliezer, including a son of Moses. But the best known is an old slave from Damascus, the faithful servant of Abraham. He was the one Abraham thought would inherit his land and wealth—until the unexpected birth of Isaac when

Abraham was one hundred years old. Childless couples often willed their property to a servant.

It was probably Eliezer, identified as Abraham's "oldest servant" and "in charge of his household" (Genesis 24:2), who went on a mission some five hundred miles north to Abraham's relatives in Haran, in what is now southern Turkey. He returned with a wife for Isaac.

ELIHU

(ee LIE hew)
Eliu, Hebrew
"it was God indeed"
Perhaps about 2000 BC
First mention: Job 32:2

After Job's three friends tried unsuccessfully to convince him that he lost his health, children, and flocks because he had sinned, young Elihu got mad at all of them. He was mad at Job for not admitting his sin and mad at the three friends for not being smart enough to out-argue a sick man. "Job," Elihu said, "you deserve the maximum penalty for the wicked way you have talked" (Job 34:36). God, however, rewarded Job with restored health, more children, and larger herds.

ELIJAH

(ee LIE jah)
Eliyah, Hebrew
"my God is the Lord"
Ministered from about 865–850 BC
First mention:
1 Kings 17:1

Elijah is perhaps the only wonder worker in Old Testament times who could give Moses a run for his

ELIJAH'S RETURN

"Look, I am sending you the prophet Elijah before the great and dreadful day of the LORD arrives" (Malachi 4:5).

Because of that prophecy, some four hundred years after Elijah, Jews began looking for him as one who would pave the way for the Messiah. Jews set a place for him at the annual Passover meal. And they kept a chair for him at each circumcision ceremony.

Elijah did return. Literally and figuratively.

Literally. He and Moses appeared with Jesus. In that meeting, Jesus' clothes became "dazzling white, far whiter than any earthly process could ever make it" (Mark 9:3).

Figuratively. The angel Gabriel announced the birth of John the Baptist by saying, "He will be a man with the spirit and power of Elijah, the prophet of old. He will precede the coming of the Lord, preparing the people for his arrival" (Luke 1:17). Jesus confirmed that John fulfilled Malachi's prophecy (Matthew 17:11–13).

money—both in astounding miracles and legacy. Elijah is the prophet who called down fire from heaven after 850 Canaanite prophets couldn't. He raised a widow's son from the dead and rode to heaven on a whirlwind that churned in the wake of a fiery chariot.

He was the first—and possibly the most spectacular—in a long line of prophets God sent to win back the hearts of the Jewish nation. The people had forgotten their history and were worshiping other gods. Elijah's job was to remind the people of God's power and to convince them that there were no other gods.

This was an impossible mission. Politicians of the day didn't care about respecting God's power. They cared about preserving their own.

RAIN GOD IN A DROUGHT

Ahab and Jezebel—king and queen notorious—were ruling the northern Jewish nation of Israel. Jezebel wasn't Jewish. She came from what is now Lebanon and brought her Canaanite gods with her: Baal and the mother of gods, Asherah. King Ahab—not famed for his theological acumen—saw no problem worshiping Israel's God alongside other gods. So he allowed his wife to finance 450 Baal prophets and 400 Asherah prophets. He also let her nearly wipe out the competition: God's prophets.

One who escaped was Elijah from Tishbe, an otherwise unknown village on what is now Jordan's side of the Jordan River.

After running for his life from Queen Jezebel, Elijah stops one hundred miles later, exhausted and hungry. An angel arrives to feed him.

In a bold appearance before the king, Elijah announced that the God of Israel would shut off the dew and rain. The theological challenge would have been obvious, even to Ahab. Baal was the rain god. Fertility in flock, field, and family was his specialty.

It didn't rain for nearly three years.

Ahab, however, didn't seem to blame it on Israel's sin and Baal's impotency. He blamed it on Elijah's sin of blaspheming Baal and Baal's anger. So Ahab launched a manhunt, and Elijah went into hiding.

The drought was a killer. Even in Jezebel's homeland, in the village of Zarephath about twenty miles south of Beirut, Elijah came upon a widow scrounging for sticks to build a fire. She wanted to make one last meal before she and her son starved. But she fed the meal to Elijah. He showed his appreciation and God's power by miraculously filling her flour and olive oil containers—and keeping them full for the duration of the drought. Later, when her son became sick and stopped breathing, Elijah stretched himself out on the boy and prayed for his life to return. It did.

Life was soon to return to Israel's parched fields, as well.

BATTLE OF THE GODS

At God's instruction, Elijah went to see Ahab. " 'So it's you, is it—Israel's troublemaker?' Ahab asked when he saw him. 'I have made no trouble for Israel,' Elijah replied. 'You and your family are the troublemakers, for you have refused to obey the commands of the LORD and have worshiped the images of Baal instead' " (1 Kings 18:17–18).

Elijah then leveled a challenge to settle the matter of who deserved worship—God or the Canaanite gods. Elijah and God would take on all 850 of Jezebel's Canaanite prophets and their gods in a contest on Mount Carmel. The object was right up Baal's alley: Send fire from the sky to light a sacrificial altar. No big deal for a rain god often depicted slinging lightning bolts.

The prophets pled with their god to send fire. They prayed, danced, and cut themselves, all morning, afternoon, and into the evening. Finally, Elijah built a simple altar of twelve stones, one for each tribe of Israel. He stacked wood and bull pieces on top, then drenched it with water three times. He prayed a short prayer, asking God to "prove today that you are God in Israel" (1 Kings 18:36).

Fire flashed from the sky, incinerating even the stones. Jews watching fell on their faces, and Elijah ordered the false prophets rounded up and executed in compliance with God's law: "Anyone who sacrifices to any god other than the LORD must be destroyed" (Exodus 22:20).

Elijah then prayed for rain, and the drought ended.

PROPHET ON THE RUN

Awestruck at God's power doesn't describe Jezebel. She was livid about Elijah's attack on her power. He had slaughtered her herd of sacred cows, so she vowed to slaughter him—before sundown.

Shocked that Jezebel couldn't see God's power in the Mount Carmel miracle, Elijah must have felt his mission was hopeless. He ran for his life.

He didn't stop until he got to the desert of Beersheba one hundred miles away. Sleep and food became his spiritual first aid. Then God directed him to Mount Sinai, where he would encounter the Lord in the same place Moses did. A windstorm hit the mountain, followed by an earthquake and a fire. God was not in any of them. He came in a gentle whisper. This was perhaps a hint that God works not only in the occasional high drama, but in the quiet of the everyday.

God gave Elijah a new assignment—one that promised hope even in the face of unyielding rulers. He would anoint the next king of Israel and of neighboring Syria, as well.

In time, Elijah returned to Ahab's palace with a warning: God would destroy the king's family. Elijah lived to see it.

CHARIOTS OF FIRE

Elijah knew the very day God would take him. So did other prophets in the region, including Elijah's new disciple, Elisha.

God directed Elijah back to his homeland east of the Jordan River. As the two prophets reached the Jordan River, Elijah rolled up his cloak and touched the water with it. The water stopped flowing, and a path opened before them, as it had done for Joshua and the Israelites when they first entered the Promised Land. Here, though, Elijah was leaving—but for what people of faith believe is a better Promised Land.

Young Elisha asked if he could become Elijah's successor. Elijah put the matter in God's hands, saying Elisha would get his request only if God allowed him to see what was about to happen. "Suddenly a chariot of fire appeared, drawn by horses of fire. It drove between them, separating them, and Elijah was carried by a whirlwind into heaven. Elisha saw it and cried out, 'My father! My father! The chariots and charioteers of Israel!' " (2 Kings 2:11–12).

Elisha picked up Elijah's cloak and headed home. When he came to the river, it parted again when touched by the rolled-up cloak. Elisha knew then that God had granted his request. So did a group of prophets who had been waiting by the river to see what happened. They arranged for fifty men to search the area for Elijah.

They found nothing.

ELIPHAZ

(EL i faz)
Elipaz, Hebrew
Possibly "God is fine gold"
Perhaps about 2000 BC
First mention: Job 2:11

Job's main comforter—first of three to advise him—Eliphaz came from a region famed for wisdom, Teman—probably in what is now Jordan. Instead of comforting Job, however, Eliphaz paved the way for accusations: "My experience shows that those who plant trouble and cultivate evil will harvest the same" (Job 4:8). Bildad and Zophar also insisted that Job had lost his family, flocks, and health because he sinned. God later revealed otherwise, ordering the three to ask Job to pray for them.

ELISHA

(ee LIE sha)
Elisa, Hebrew
"my God is salvation"
Ministered from about 850–800 BC
First mention: 1 Kings 19:16

Elisha gets lost in the shadow of his mentor, Elijah, and by comparison almost seems like a second-rate prophet. For example:

- Elisha parted the Jordan River.
- Elijah did it first.
- Elisha purified some bad spring water. Elijah stopped a three-year drought.
- Elisha defied gravity by making an ax head float. Elijah flew to heaven with an escort of fiery chariots.

Even so, Elisha would have won the popularity showdown. He was the people's prophet during a fifty-year ministry, while Elijah spent much of his fifteen-year ministry in seclusion.

Elisha was no second-rate prophet among his people—or in Jesus' eyes. Jesus used Elisha's healing of a Syrian soldier with leprosy to justify healing non-Jews. And though Jesus fed a crowd with one boy's bread and fish, Elisha did it first, feeding a crowd with a few loaves and a sack of grain.

FROM PLOWBOY TO PROPHET

Elisha was part of God's remedy for Elijah's depression. The older prophet, Elijah, had run to the desert after Jezebel, queen of the northern Jewish nation of Israel, vowed to kill him for executing her 850 Canaanite prophets. God assured Elijah that Jezebel would die and have no lasting successor, but Elijah's successor would be Elisha.

At the first reported meeting of these two men, on the farm of Elisha's father, the young Elisha marched last in a line of twelve farmers plowing with oxen. Elijah threw his cloak on the young man's shoulders, a symbol of anointing or calling that Elisha understood. When Elijah started walking away, Elisha was to follow. Instead, he asked if he could kiss his parents good-bye. Elijah sensed indecision or perhaps a tactic for getting the parents to help work up a good excuse. Elijah replied that young Elisha could walk one way or the other, following his

MIRACLES OF ELISHA

Elisha led a group of prophets—and many scholars say these prophets likely preserved Elisha's story. These are the miracles of Elisha, recorded in 1 Kings 19 and 2 Kings 2–13:

- Parted the Jordan River
- Purified bad water in a spring, using salt
- Punished a gang of boys with a curse that brought a bear attack
- Provided pools of water for a coalition army
- Filled jars with olive oil so a prophet's widow could sell it to pay her debts without selling her sons into slavery
- Made an infertile couple able to have a son
- Brought the son back to life after he died of what may have been heatstroke
- Neutralized poison gourds put in a stew, using flour
- Fed one hundred prophets with twenty loaves of bread and a sack of grain
- Healed a Syrian commander of leprosy
- Punished his servant with leprosy for charging the Syrian
- Made a lost ax head float
- Blinded an attacking army
- Predicted the end of a siege
- Dead and buried, he revived a dead man whose body touched his bones after being buried in the same tomb

parents or following God. Jesus later drew from this very scene when a disciple wannabe asked to say good-bye to his family: "Anyone who puts a hand to the plow and then looks back is not fit for the Kingdom of God" (Luke 9:62).

Elisha killed his oxen, burned his plowing equipment, and used the fire to roast the meat as a farewell meal. With no looking back, he followed Elijah as an apprentice.

HEALING AN ENEMY SOLDIER

Though there are many stories about Elisha, none is better known than his healing of a Syrian commander, Naaman, who had what the Bible calls leprosy. Actually, Naaman may not have had what we now call Hansen's disease. He may have had nothing more than dry skin that afflicts some people living in a dry climate. But that doesn't minimize what happened.

Naaman's slave girl, captured in a raid of Israel, said Elisha could heal him. Naaman set out for Israel, with his king's blessing along with incredible gifts: ten sets of clothing, 750 pounds of silver ($40,500 today when silver sells for $4.50 a troy ounce), and 150 pounds of gold ($630,000 today with gold at $350 a troy ounce).

Elisha told Naaman to wash seven times in the Jordan River. The commander stormed off, apparently expecting a more regal therapy. His officers convinced him to give it a try, and he was healed. Naaman returned to Elisha to give him the gifts, but the prophet refused, and Naaman headed home vowing to worship only God. Elisha's servant, Gehazi, chased down Naaman and said Elisha changed his mind and wanted just a token gift. He got two sets of clothes and 150 pounds of silver. Elisha found out about this and gave Gehazi another gift: Naaman's skin disease. Gehazi passed the disease on to his kids and grandkids.

ELIZABETH

(ee LIZ uh beth)
Elisabet, Greek
"my God is my oath"
First century AD
First mention: Luke 1:5

The angel Gabriel made two unusual birth announcements in a year. One was about the birth of Jesus to a virgin named Mary. And the other was about the birth of John the Baptist to an old and childless woman named Elizabeth, a relative of Mary.

Elizabeth was in the sixth month of her pregnancy when Mary came to visit. At the sound of Mary's greeting, Elizabeth's baby moved. And Elizabeth, suddenly filled by God's Spirit, became the first person on earth to publicly declare Jesus as the Messiah: "What an honor this is, that the mother of my Lord should visit me!" (Luke 1:43).

About thirty years later, Elizabeth's son baptized Mary's son, launching the ministry of Jesus.

EMMAUS

(em MAY us)
Emmaous, Greek
First mention: Luke 24:13

On the first Easter Sunday, after Jesus appeared to several woman at the garden tomb, he met two of his followers walking on the road to Emmaus, a village about seven miles from Jerusalem. They didn't recognize him until they reached Emmaus and sat down to eat. That's when Jesus disappeared.

Emmaus hasn't been identified yet. Crusaders, favoring the Arab village of El-Qubeibeh seven miles northwest of Jerusalem, built a fort there and named it Castle Emmaus. But the first-century historian Josephus said a village called Ammaous was three and a half miles from Jerusalem—making the round-trip seven miles.

ENDOR

(en DOOR)

En dor, Hebrew

Perhaps "spring of the settlement"

First mention: Joshua 17:11

MAP 1
C3

It was the end of time for Saul, in a place some call the Valley of Armageddon. Saul brought his army to Mount Gilboa in northern Israel to counter a Philistine offensive. When he looked down into the expansive Jezreel valley, as it's often called, he was terrified by the number of Philistines camped on the slopes of the neighboring Mount Moreh. When night fell, he snuck behind enemy lines to the village of Endor on the opposite side of Mount Moreh. Saul asked a village medium to conjure up Samuel's spirit for advice. Samuel arrived, to the medium's shock, and announced that on the next day Saul would be joining him in the place of the dead.

EN-GEDI

(en GED ee)

En gedi, Hebrew

"spring of the young goat"

First mention: Joshua 15:62

MAP 1
C6

Some folks who have climbed up the steep, winding trail around massive boulders to reach the spring-fed pools at the En-gedi oasis understand why it's named after a goat. The lush oasis thirty-five miles southeast of Jerusalem lies hidden beneath towering cliffs about a mile from the Dead Sea

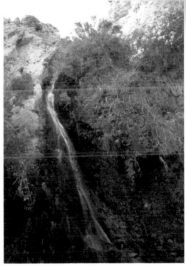

En-gedi's waterfall nourishes a hidden oasis nestled in a craggy canyon of the Judean badlands, alongside the Dead Sea.

shoreline and some 650 feet above it. Rainwater runoff filters through the rocks and collects in the underground springs that nourish date trees and vineyards, along with a wide array of tropical and desert plants and animals.

David hid from King Saul among the cliff caves at "the wilderness of En-gedi" (1 Samuel 24:1). Saul stepped into the very cave where David hid, and relieved himself. David quietly clipped off part of Saul's robe as evidence that he could have killed the king. Then, from a distance, David called out and raised the robe clipping. Humiliated, Saul went home.

ENOCH
(EE nuck)
Hanok, Hebrew
Perhaps "founder"
Before 4000 BC
First mention: Genesis 4:17

Born seven generations after Adam, Enoch was not only part of the first group of humans who lived incredibly long lives—he was one of the elite who never died.

Ruins are all that's left of Ephesus, one of the Roman Empire's greatest cities. This remnant of a library is one of the best preserved buildings.

At age 365, "he disappeared because God took him" (Genesis 5:24). One New Testament writer explained how most Jews understood the disappearance. God didn't use conventional means—death—to take him. "It was by faith that Enoch was taken up to heaven without dying" (Hebrews 11:5).

Among the children Enoch left behind was his son Methuselah, who lived longer than any other human— 969 years.

EPHESUS
(EFF uh suhs)
Ephesos, Greek
First mention: Acts 18:19

MAP 5
C2

There were Seven Wonders of the World, but the most beautiful was a temple in the city of Ephesus. At least that's how some writers of the day described the Temple of Artemis, called Diana by Romans.

Here's what Greek scientist and mathematician Philon of Byzantium, writing in the 200s BC, said about the temple: "I have seen the walls and hanging gardens of ancient Babylon, the statue of Olympian Zeus, the Colossus of Rhodes, the mighty work of the high pyramids, and the tomb of Mausolus. But when I saw the temple at Ephesus rising to the clouds, all these other wonders were put in the shade."

It was for love of this temple that Ephesus rioted, driving Paul out of town. He was converting Artemis worshipers.

With Paul gone, the citizens probably thought they had beaten back the competition and their temple was safe. Today, however, all that remains of this ancient wonder are the foundation blocks—uncovered beneath twenty feet of topsoil—and a single, white pillar. This pillar was pieced back together and erected as a glimpse of past glory. But it juts up from the ground like a broken, lone tooth. The elegance of Paul's teaching in Ephesus, however, is gloriously preserved in the New Testament book of Ephesians.

In Bible times

The golden years. Not even Rome likely saw as much wealth per year as the port city of Ephesus. Third largest city in the vast empire—after Rome and Alexandria, Egypt—the Ephesus of Paul's day was a funnel. People and merchandise passed through its port on their way to and from Europe in the west or Turkey and beyond in the Middle East. Ephesus owed its traffic to its harbor, built in the bend of the Cayster River. Workers straightened the bend and dredged the river to widen and deepen the river's mouth into a bay that opened to the Mediterranean Sea.

A melting pot of cultures and religions, Ephesus was already at least a thousand years old by the time Paul arrived during his third missionary journey in the AD 50s. What he saw was Ephesus at its best, during its more than fifteen-hundred-year history. The sights included many temples, a theater seating 25,000, gymnasiums, public baths, fountains, aqueducts, a library large enough to hold 15,000 scrolls, a 360-foot-square market center surrounded by shops, and elegant homes with beautiful wall paintings and mosaics. The Temple of Artemis—four times larger than the Parthenon—stood 130 yards long, 70 yards wide, 6 stories high, and was majestically

Signs in the Sky

Ephesians would have read their daily horoscope if they could have. Like other people in the region, many Ephesians—including Jews—lived in fear of heavenly powers they thought controlled their fate. They even kept in the first Temple of Artemis a sacred stone—probably a meteorite—they said fell from Zeus in the heavens.

A statue of Artemis recovered at Ephesus shows her wearing signs of the zodiac, perhaps a symbol of the belief that as Zeus' daughter, she had the power to change fate.

Alexander the Great was born the very day an early version of the temple burned. Perhaps seeing himself tied by fate to this great building, he offered to pay for the reconstruction if he got credit. The Ephesians tactfully replied, "It's not fitting that one god should build a temple for another." Then they spent the next twenty years restoring it to the peak of its grandeur—the temple Paul would have seen.

framed with rows of 127 pillars 6 feet thick and 60 feet high.

Riot over Paul. The apostle stayed about three years. He converted so many people that he got the attention of Demetrius, a businessman whose company made silver shrines of Artemis. Sales plummeted. Demetrius called a meeting of everyone connected in any way with the business and warned that their jobs were on the line—and that "the great goddess Artemis" would lose influence and "be robbed of her prestige" (Acts 19:27). A crowd grew, chanting, "Great is Artemis of the Ephesians!" (Acts 19:28). They managed to find a couple of Paul's associates and drag them to the amphitheater, but an official calmed the riot. Paul left town to finish his final missionary trip.

Paul's last known words to the Ephesian Christians, written from prison in Rome, is the New Testament letter of Ephesians, urging them to devote themselves to God.

AFTER BIBLE TIMES

Hometown of church leaders. Church tradition says Mary the mother of Jesus moved to Ephesus and lived in the home of John, the apostle who is likely the one Jesus, while on the cross, asked to care for his mother. This may be the same John who wrote Revelation while exiled on a small island off the coast of Ephesus.

Perhaps the Mary connection is why the church maintained a strong presence in Ephesus even during intense persecution. A long line of bishops lived there. And it was there, in AD 431, that the Council of Ephesus condemned a heresy that taught Jesus was two people in one—

human and divine—and that Mary was not the mother of God.

Surviving the plague, but not bad politics. Ephesus survived a plague that Roman soldiers brought back in the late AD 100s, after defeating Parthians in what is now Iran and Afghanistan. But it started crumbling after continual assassination of the city's best leaders along with aggressive attacks on Christians.

Raiders started coming. In one sea attack in 262, Goths from what is now Russia destroyed much of the town and the Temple of Artemis. Ephesus was rebuilt, but it never fully recovered.

The river silted up, filling the bay and choking the trade. By the 500s, the people moved to a new location in the nearby hills, but Turks overran it in 1090. When the Crusaders arrived a short time later, they couldn't believe Ephesus was gone. And the locals had no memory of their once glorious Temple of Artemis.

TODAY

Stone piles in swampland. Tourists visit the ruins of Ephesus. They walk along ancient stone-paved roads and visit the amphitheater where the people rioted against Paul. But the sea is gone. Silt has pushed the coastline back several miles.

The once bustling Ephesus, home to perhaps the most amazing of all the Seven Wonders of the World, is little more than a tumble of rocks sitting motionless in a poorly drained marsh.

Visitors today might ask the same bewildered question a Crusader commander did of a local more than a thousand years ago: "Sir, is this the city of Ephesus?"

EPHRAIM
(EE fray im)
Eprayim, Hebrew
Perhaps "fertile place"
First mention: Genesis 48:6

MAP 1
B4

Descendants of Joseph's son Ephraim got Israel's heartland. The tribe of Ephraim lived on a swath of rugged highland country a little north of Jerusalem. Ephraim's land stretched some twenty miles north and thirty miles west into part of the coastland.

It was an important, central location. There, in the city of Shiloh, Israelites pitched the tent worship center they used during the Exodus. Joshua and Samuel both belonged to this tribe. So did Jeroboam, who led a rebellion against Solomon's son that split Israel into two kingdoms. Jeroboam became the first king of the northern kingdom of Israel.

EPHRATH
(EE frath)
Eprata, Hebrew
First mention: Genesis 35:16

See Bethlehem

MAP 1
C5

In early Bible times, Ephrath was another name for Bethlehem. It's unclear why the tiny village had two names. Scholars guess that Ephrath was the name of an extended family, or clan, that once lived there. That would help explain why King David's father, Jesse, was described as an "Ephrathite from Bethlehem" (1 Samuel 17:12). Jesse was probably part of the Ephrath family still living there. (See *Bethlehem.*)

ESAU
(EE saw)
Esaw, Hebrew
Perhaps "hairy"
1900s BC
First mention: Genesis 25:25

First of twin boys born to Isaac and Rebekah, Esau was in line to become a patriarch—one of the Jewish founding fathers: Abraham, Isaac, and Esau. But it didn't work out that way.

Even in the uterus, Esau and his brother, Jacob, jockeyed for position—to the discomfort of their mother. When Rebekah asked God what was going on, he said her sons would become rival nations, and the older son would serve the younger.

At the delivery, Esau arrived first, but Jacob latched his tiny fingers onto Esau's heel and arrived a close second. This arrival order was important. It meant that Esau, as the firstborn, owned the family birthright. When his father died, he would get twice as much inheritance as Jacob.

As a newborn, Esau "was covered with so much hair that one would think he was wearing a piece of clothing" (Genesis 25:25). His parents gave him a name that sounded like the Hebrew word for hair.

DADDY'S BOY

Esau grew into a hairy outdoorsman who loved hunting. Isaac favored him because of the savory meat he brought home. Jacob grew into a smooth-skinned homebody. Rebekah favored him perhaps because they spent so much time together and because she remembered what God had said about him.

One day while Jacob was cooking some red stew, Esau returned from a hunt, famished. Jacob wouldn't share unless Esau traded his birthright. Esau made the trade and earned a nickname, Edom, meaning "red"—after the stew.

Esau still owned the right of the firstborn's blessing—a prayer from his father that gave Esau authority to lead the family. People believed this prayer of blessing had power to make things happen. Jacob stole it with his mother's help. Old Isaac, blind and thinking he was near death, asked Esau for some wild meat before giving the blessing. While Esau hunted, Rebekah cooked two goats. Then, with hairy animal skins on his arms, Jacob served the meat, pretending he was Esau. Isaac blessed him with prosperity and authority over his brother.

When Esau found out, he vowed to kill Jacob as soon as Isaac died. Jacob ran away. By the time he returned twenty years later, with a big family and massive herds, Esau had forgiven him. The two embraced, then settled in separate regions. Esau became the father of the Edomites, who lived south of the Dead Sea. Jacob became one of Israel's three founding fathers: Abraham, Isaac, and Jacob.

ESTHER
(ES tur)
Ester, Hebrew
Perhaps "star"
Her husband ruled 485–465 BC
First mention: Esther 2:7

It was a Jewish orphan in what is now Iran who risked her life to save the Jews

A girl dresses up as Esther during the Jewish festival of Purim, which marks the holocaust that Queen Esther prevented.

from an ancient holocaust. Persian officials had plotted to wipe out all Jews in the empire, from India in the east to Egypt in the west. But Esther, who grew up beautiful and became queen, took a risky stand and declared herself a Jew.

Whether Esther's elevation to queen was a result of God's doing or the king's drunkenness is a matter of debate. After all, God's name never appears in this story preserved in the book of Esther. Many, however, see God at work behind the scenes.

FROM ORPHAN TO QUEEN

Esther's family came from Israel, exiled a century earlier when Babylon wiped the Jewish nation off the map. Her parents died when she was young, so her cousin Mordecai adopted her. They lived in Susa—Persia's capital. Though Esther went by her Persian name to hide her Jewish identity, she also had a Jewish name, Hadassah.

It was King Xerxes' drunken request at the end of a six-month celebration that landed her in his harem. Partying with a group of men, Xerxes ordered his favorite wife, the beautiful Queen Vashti, to make an appearance. He wanted to show her off. She refused. So he banished her forever from his presence and launched an empirewide queen hunt.

Many lovelies joined his harem as secondary wives, but only Esther became queen.

CELEBRATING A HOLOCAUST MISSED

The most jubilant holiday on the Jewish calendar is a springtime Mardi Gras–style festival that Jews have been celebrating since Esther's day. It marks a Persian holocaust avoided. Kids wear costumes and friends exchange gifts.

It's called Purim (PEW rim), the Hebrew word for "lots." Haman used dicelike lots to decide what day to kill the Jews. "Haman," by the way, is a name not heard at the festival. Esther's story is read out loud, but when the reader comes to Haman's name, noisemakers and screaming voices drown it out.

HOLOCAUST PLANNED

Persia's top official under the king was Haman, an Amalakite—bitter enemies of the Jews. When Haman walked by, most people bowed. Not Mordecai, probably because of bitterness between their races. Mutual hatred would help explain Haman's final solution to the problem—wipe out all Jews.

Haman got the king's approval to rid the empire of a "certain race of people" who "refuse to obey even the laws of the king" (Esther 3:8). Neither of them knew the queen belonged to this race. Extermination was set for March 7.

Mordecai convinced Esther to appeal to the king, even though Xerxes killed people who showed up uninvited. Fortunately, Xerxes asked Esther what he could do for her. Esther invited him and Haman to a pair of banquets—sudden queenly attention that delighted Haman. Esther dropped the bomb at the second banquet by asking the king if he would kindly spare her and her people from Haman's exterminators.

Xerxes hung Haman right away. But his order to annihilate the Jews was irrevocable. So he issued a new order allowing the Jews to defend themselves with the help of Persian forces. Jews throughout the empire killed some seventy-five thousand enemies.

ETAM
(EE tum)
Etam, Hebrew
First mention: Judges 15:8

Samson set fire to Philistine fields. Then the Philistines set fire to Samson's family—his ex-wife and father-in-law. Samson retaliated in a one-man assault on the Philistine nation, killing many before retreating to a cave at Etam, somewhere in the Judean hills.

Etam was probably east of Jerusalem, in the hill country where Samson grew up. Philistines followed him into Israel and raided a village. To stop the violence, some of Samson's countrymen went to Etam and convinced him to give himself up. Once

in Philistine custody, however, Samson broke free and killed a thousand Philistine soldiers with a donkey's jawbone.

ETHIOPIA
(eeth ee O pee uh)
Aithiopia, Greek
Possibly "land of people with burnt faces"
First mention: 2 Kings 19:9

When Philip baptized an Ethiopian palace treasurer who was headed home after worshiping in Jerusalem (Acts 8:27), the official didn't have to travel half as far as he would today. Ethiopia in Bible times was in what is now southern Egypt and Sudan to the south. Ethiopia's northern border began at the Nile's first waterfall (cataract) in Aswan, Egypt. Modern Ethiopia is farther into the Nile, southeast of Sudan. Old Testament and Egyptian writings often referred to Ethiopia as Cush, which was the homeland of Moses' wife—perhaps a second wife.

EUPHRATES RIVER
(you FRAY tees)
Euphrates, Greek
Perat, Hebrew
First mention: Genesis 2:14

Human civilization, as far as historians can tell, got its start in Mesopotamia—a word that means "between the rivers." Those rivers are the Tigris and Euphrates. Iraq is the main country between these rivers, and it was the birthplace of such early empires as Sumer, Babylon, and Assyria.

The Euphrates River, which flows about seventeen hundred miles, is longer and wider than the Tigris. Plotted on a map, it looks like an archer's bow. It begins as snowmelt in the Turkish mountains and flows southwest into Syria before curving back to the southeast through Iraq. It eventually joins the Tigris and empties into the Persian Gulf. Ancient cities built along the Euphrates included Babylon and Abraham's hometown of Ur. God promised the Hebrews land from the Red Sea to the Euphrates (Exodus 23:31).

EUTYCHUS

(U tuh cuss)
Eutuchos, Greek
"fortunate"
First century AD
First mention: Acts 20:9

Eutychus was a young man who fell asleep during a sermon. He was sitting on a windowsill at the time. He fell three stories to his death. So reports Luke, a physician.

Paul was the speaker of the hour. Hours, actually. It was the last day of his weeklong visit to Troas, a city on Turkey's coast. So he talked until about midnight. When Eutychus fell, Paul ran and hugged him. Eutychus revived, as happened centuries earlier when the prophets Elijah and Elisha hugged young ones who had died.

Paul and the group ate. Then Paul talked until dawn.

EVE

Hawwa, Hebrew
"life-giving"
Before 4000 BC
First mention: Genesis 3:22

In the beginning, Eve was not her name.

Eve wasn't even second choice for the name of humanity's mother. It was third. Adam came up with it only as they were leaving the Garden of Eden, forced out by God.

After creating Eve from Adam's rib, God called them both by the same name: Adam, meaning "human." Eve's mate, however, fresh off the chore of naming all creation's animals, gave her a name, too: "She will be called 'woman' [*issa* in Hebrew], because she was taken out of a man [*is*]" (Genesis 2:23).

Eve plucks forbidden fruit at the urging of a snake. The Bible doesn't say what kind of fruit it was.

A FULL PARTNER

Eve was human number two, created from Adam as a "companion." Throughout the ages, many have argued this means women should defer to men. Even Paul used that argument: "God made Adam first" (1 Timothy 2:13).

"Companion," however, is from the Hebrew word *ezer*. There's no subordination in the word. In fact, it's the same word often describing God as Israel's "helper."

A BITE OUT OF SIN

Eve took the first bite of the forbidden fruit. God said it would kill her. But the snake said it would make her like God, opening her eyes to good and evil.

She bit and gave her husband a bite, too.

The snake was partly right. Innocence gone, they could see they had done wrong, they realized they were naked, and they were afraid of God—but not his equal.

God ordered them out of Eden's garden. In time, they would die. But Eve would be able to continue the race by bearing children. Perhaps that's why Adam renamed her Eve, because it sounds like the Hebrew word for "the living."

EZEKIEL

(ee ZEEK ee ul)
Yehezqel, Hebrew
"God strengthens"
Ministered from 593–571 BC
First mention: Ezekiel 1:3

Ezekiel, a young priest, lived through the worst catastrophe in ancient Israel's history—an event throbbing with holocaust horror.

Babylon wiped the Jewish nation off the map and leveled Solomon's majestic Jerusalem temple, which many Jews considered God's earthly home—the only place they were allowed to worship him.

Ezekiel warned it was coming—God's punishment for the nation's legacy of sin.

GOOD-BYE, JERUSALEM

Ezekiel was twenty-five years old and serving in Jerusalem's temple when King Nebuchadnezzar's army arrived.

The Babylonians had come from what is now Iraq to enforce their right to collect taxes from Judah and to crush any hope of Jewish independence. It was 597 BC, and Babylon's strategy for derailing the drive to independence included taking hostages—ten thousand of the Jewish elite: royalty, soldiers, artisans, and priests, Ezekiel among them.

Five years later and a thousand miles from home, Ezekiel saw a vision of God telling him to prophesy to the Jews in Babylon. In this vision, God fed Ezekiel a honey-sweet scroll—a

EZEKIEL'S STRANGE BEHAVIOR

Sunday school psychologists reading Ezekiel's story have words to describe him: paranoid, psychotic, schizophrenic.

Actually, his bizarre behavior was God's doing. It was street theater, in which Ezekiel acted out prophecies so people would never forget them. It worked, since we're reading about them some twenty-five hundred years later.

Among his many bizarre behaviors, Ezekiel:

- Slept on his left side for 390 days and his right side for 40 days. Each day represented a year of sin—the left side for the northern Jewish nation of Israel, and the right side for the southern Jewish nation of Judah.

- Shaved his head and divided the hair into three piles. He burned one pile, symbolizing Jews who would die inside Jerusalem when Babylon attacked. He cut a second pile with a sword, representing Jews who would die outside the city walls. He scattered the last pile to the wind, illustrating those who would be exiled.

- Didn't mourn his wife. The Jews wouldn't be able to perform customary mourning rituals for their dead thousands, perhaps because of the shock or because Babylonian soldiers wouldn't give them the time.

symbol that Ezekiel's words would come from God.

Doom describes the prophecies. In perhaps Ezekiel's most troubling vision, he witnessed the glowing cloud of God's glory leaving the Jerusalem temple. God was gone, and worse: "I am your enemy, O Israel, and I am about to unsheath my sword to destroy your people" (Ezekiel 21:3).

It happened in 586 BC, when Babylonian soldiers crushed a revolt by leveling Judah's cities and burning Jerusalem to the ground—just as Ezekiel had started predicting about seven years earlier. Suddenly, this prophet, ridiculed for his bizarre visions and acted-out prophecies, gained an eager and respectful audience.

HELLO, JERUSALEM

Doomsday over, it was time for Ezekiel to deliver a new and startling message.

In a vision, God transported him to a valley littered with human skeletons. It must have looked like a massacre from many years earlier.

"Son of man," God asked the

A B C D E F G H I J K L M N O P Q R S T U V W X Y Z

prophet, "can these bones become living people again?" (Ezekiel 37:3).

Within moments, bone-clack rattling echoed through the valley as skeleton pieces snapped together. Soft tissue latched the bones in place and organs filled the skeletal cavities. Then flesh erupted and spread over each lifeless corpse. Decay reversed.

Wind rushed into the valley of the shadow of death, restoring breath and life. This was supernatural CPR. The massive crowd stirred and stood.

"Son of man, these bones represent the people of Israel," God explained. "They are saying, 'We have become old, dry bones—all hope is gone' " (Ezekiel 37:11). But God told Ezekiel to deliver this message: "I will put my Spirit in you, and you will live and return home to your own land" (Ezekiel 37:14).

Ezekiel probably didn't live to see it. His ministry seemed to end about thirty years before Babylon fell and the new world dominator—Persia—released the Jews to go home and rebuild their country. But the people remembered Ezekiel's words, which had poured like honey from the scroll of God.

EZRA

(EZ ruh)
Ezra, Hebrew
"help"
Arrived in Jerusalem 458 BC
First mention: Ezra 7:1

Judging from the standout scene in his life, Ezra makes a horrible first impression.

The books of Ezra and Nehemiah —originally one book—describe him kindly. He was a priest and scholar "well versed in the law of Moses" (Ezra 7:6). He lived in what is now Iraq, among Jews banished more than a century earlier.

But his standout scene—ordering Jewish men to run off their non-Jewish wives and children—makes him seem intolerant at best. Even racist.

SCHOLAR IN CHARGE

In fairness, Ezra's plan was to help the Jewish nation get back on its feet. About one hundred years after the first wave of exiles returned home and started rebuilding their nation, Ezra led a new group. With nearly four tons of gold and twenty-four tons of silver supplied by the Persian king Artaxerxes, Ezra planned to restore the temple's wealth and refurnish it with elegant utensils.

In addition, Ezra had the king's authority to govern everyone west of the Euphrates River (flowing through Syria and Iraq) and to teach them the Jewish law.

When Ezra arrived in Jerusalem, some officials reported what they considered terrifying news: Many Jewish men had married non-Jewish locals. "The holy race has become polluted by these mixed marriages," they complained (Ezra 9:2).

It was a worry because that's how pagan religions had first crept into Israel. God had already destroyed the nation for idolatry once, and the Jews didn't want a repeat.

Ezra fell on the ground in front of the temple, crying and praying as a crowd gathered. One man, Shecaniah, urged Ezra to order all Jewish men to divorce their non-Jewish wives, sending them and their children away. "It is your duty," Shecaniah insisted (Ezra 10:4). Ezra complied.

Oddly, included on the list of 113 Jewish offenders was Shecaniah's father, Jehiel of Elam's family. Perhaps Jehiel had more than one wife and Shecaniah was his son by a Jewish woman. If so, Shecaniah may have been less concerned about Jewish law than about family tension or his share of an inheritance.

Later, Ezra read to the people the entire Law of Moses, and they vowed to obey it all—including what was by then an outdated ban from Moses' day on Jews marrying the non-Jews they were supposed to wipe out (Deuteronomy 7:1–4). King David's great-grandmother, after all, was a non-Jew from what is now Jordan. Her name was Ruth. And she loved God.

FAIR HAVENS
Kaloi Limenes, Greek
"fair harbor"
First mention: Acts 27:8

MAP 5 B3

Sailing to Rome for trial, Paul probably didn't expect to arrive before the winter storms. His ship left Caesarea too late in the season. By October—well into the risky season for sailing—his ship approached the island of Crete, south of Greece. Paul, a seasoned traveler, advised the captain to winter in Fair Havens, a Crete harbor. The captain said it was too exposed and sailed toward Crete's harbor at Phoenix. A gale, however, snatched the ship and battered it for two weeks before running it aground near an island south of Italy.

FELIX
(FEE licks)
Phelix, Greek
Ruled AD 52–60
First mention: Acts 23:24

Paul spent two years in a Judean prison while the governor, a former slave named Felix, "hoped that Paul would bribe him" (Acts 24:26).

It started when Paul returned to Jerusalem after his last missionary trip, and Jews mobbed him for teaching heresy. Roman soldiers intervened and took him to Caesarea, Rome's Judean capital. Festus inherited the case after Rome recalled Felix and charged him with abusing authority. Among his crimes was arranging the murder of a high priest who criticized him. Felix escaped execution only after his brother appealed to Emperor Nero.

FESTUS
(FESS tuhs)
Phestos, Greek
Ruled AD 60–62
First mention: Acts 24:27

Festus succeeded Felix as governor of Judea and inherited the two-year-old case against Paul. Though Paul was never charged, Jewish leaders said he taught heresy and was a troublemaker. The Jews asked Festus to move the trial from Rome's Judean capital of Caesarea to Jerusalem—secretly intending to ambush and kill Paul. Festus asked Paul if he would agree. Paul apparently sensed the danger and invoked his right as a Roman citizen to appeal his case to Caesar. Festus approved and sent Paul to Rome.

GABRIEL
(GAY bree uhl)
Gabriel, Hebrew
"God is my warrior"
First mention: Daniel 8:16

"I am Gabriel! I stand in the very presence of God" (Luke 1:19).

That's the only description the Bible gives of the angelic messenger God sent to earth on at least four occasions, spanning almost six hundred years. The Bible names only one other angel, Michael, but early Jewish and Christian writings say four archangels stood in God's presence: Gabriel, Michael, Raphael, and Uriel.

Gabriel's most notable message was his last one found in the Bible: "Greetings, favored woman!" he said to Mary. "God has decided to bless you! You will become pregnant and have a son, and you are to name him Jesus" (Luke 1:28, 30–31).

Six months earlier, Gabriel announced another birth and again named the child. The mother would be Elizabeth, an elderly and childless relative of Mary. Gabriel appeared to Elizabeth's husband, a priest named Zechariah. "Your wife, Elizabeth, will bear you a son! And you are to name him John," Gabriel said. "He will

Daniel's vision was about a two-horned ram so powerful that it butted everything out of the way. Then a goat, looking something like a unicorn, came and defeated the ram. Gabriel said the two-horned ram was the empire created by the Persians and Medes. The goat that defeated it was the Greek Empire, probably referring to Alexander the Great's conquests.

Later, Gabriel explained some cryptic numbers Daniel read from Jeremiah about when to expect the rebuilding of Jerusalem and the arrival and execution of "the Anointed One" (Daniel 9:25).

Scholars today would appreciate an explanation of Gabriel's explanation. Though the numbers can be finessed to point to Jesus' time, most scholars say it probably points to the Jewish war of independence more than a century earlier and that the Anointed One refers to a high priest who was killed.

Early Christian writings outside the Bible say that the last musical note the world hears will be played by Gabriel, blowing a trumpet to announce Judgment Day.

The angel Gabriel—on his most famous mission—tells young Mary that she will give birth to the world's Savior.

precede the coming of the Lord, preparing the people for his arrival" (Luke 1:13, 17).

AN ANGELIC TUTOR

Gabriel may have appeared many times in the Bible. He may have been the "angel of the Lord" who announced the births of Samson and Ishmael and who stopped Abraham from sacrificing Isaac. But Gabriel is identified by name in only two other passages—both of them helping the prophet Daniel understand messages about the future, first a vision, then a prophecy Daniel read from Jeremiah.

GAD

Gad, Hebrew
"fortunate"
1800s BC
First mention: Genesis 30:11

Gad was seventh of the twelve sons Jacob had with four women. Jacob's two wives, sisters Leah and Rachel, tried to outdo each other producing children.

Each one even used her personal maid as surrogate mother. Gad was born to Leah's servant, Zilpah. When Leah saw the child was another boy she exclaimed, "How fortunate I am!" (Genesis 30:11), then named him accordingly.

GAD

Gad, Hebrew "fortunate"
First mention: Numbers 1:14

When the Israelites came to the doorstep of the Promised Land, on what is now Jordan's side of the Jordan River, the tribes of Gad and Reuben were ready to stop. They had vast herds, and the land was ideal for grazing. Men of the two tribes, however, helped the remaining tribes capture cities throughout Canaan. Gad took much of the Jordan River valley's fertile east bank, along with forests and fields of the plateau farther east.

GALATIA

(guh LAY shuh)
Galatia, Greek
First mention: Acts 16:6

On their first missionary trip, Paul and Barnabas visited cities in Galatia, a Roman province in what is now central Turkey. The original Galatians were fierce Celtic raiders from central Europe, but they didn't have the discipline to stop the Roman legions. Caesar Augustus annexed their kingdom in 25 BC and established it as a province. Of the four Galatian cities Paul and Barnabas visited—Antioch, Iconium, Lystra, and Derbe—all but the last one ran them off. Undeterred, the team backtracked through each city on their way home.

Sloping gently toward the Sea of Galilee, a hillside called the Mount of Beatitudes is where an old tradition says Jesus preached the Sermon on the Mount.

GALILEE

(GAL uh lee)
Galila, Hebrew "circle"
First mention: Joshua 11:2

Jesus grew up and ministered mainly in Galilee, a beautiful region of green rolling hills in northern Israel.

Ruled in Jesus' day by Herod the Great's son, Herod Antipas, this swath of fertile farmland started along the western banks of the Jordan River and the Sea of Galilee, stretching some thirty miles farther west toward the Mediterranean coast and extending some fifty miles north and south. A Jewish historian of the day, Josephus, said there were 240 villages in the area. But most were small, giving the region a rural character. Most people made their living growing crops such as grapes, olives, and barley. Many fished in the Sea of Galilee—as did most of Jesus' disciples.

After Rome destroyed Jerusalem and its temple in AD 70, Jewish scholars moved north to Galilee. It became the new center of Jewish religion and the place where the Mishnah and Talmud—revered Jewish commentaries and other sacred writings—were compiled.

GAMALIEL
(guh MAY lee uhl)
Gamaliel, Hebrew
"reward of God"
First century AD
First mention: Acts 5:34

Unlike most Pharisees in the New Testament, Gamaliel—the top Jewish scholar of his day—had a reputation for tolerance and compassion.

Gamaliel, a mentor of Paul, showed his tolerance when he defended Jesus' disciples, who disobeyed orders to stop preaching about the Resurrection. Gamaliel urged his fellow members of the Jewish governing council to let them go, arguing that if their teaching was man-made, the movement would die, and if it was of God, no one could stop it. The council accepted his advice.

Jewish writings report that Gamaliel

also advocated helping non-Jews in need and improving women's rights.

GATH

MAP 2
B5

Gat, Hebrew
"winepress"
First mention: Joshua 11:22

The hometown of Goliath, Gath was one of five major Philistine cities somewhere along Israel's Mediterranean coast. Exactly where is uncertain. The top contender at the moment is a mound ruin called Tel es-Safi. Rich in Philistine pottery and art, it lies about twenty miles southwest of Jerusalem. That would place it near the border with Israel. Surprisingly, David fled to Gath when he was on the run from King Saul. For a time, David and his band of six hundred men served as mercenaries for Gath's king.

GAZA

MAP 2
B6

(GAH zah)
Azza, Hebrew
Gaza, Greek
First mention: Genesis 10:19

Often in the news in recent years, the city of Gaza in 1994 became headquarters of the Palestinian Authority that rules the Gaza Strip and other Palestinian regions throughout Israel. In Bible times, it was one of five main Philistine cities. This is where the Philistines took Samson after they blinded him, forcing him to grind grain in the prison.

Gaza is about forty miles south of Tel Aviv and three miles from the

Mediterranean Sea, on the main coastal road to Egypt. This proved a dangerous location, since armies coming or going to Egypt often overran Gaza.

GEDALIAH
(ged uh LIE ah)
Gedalyah, Hebrew
Appointed 586 BC
First mention: 2 Kings 25:22

After Babylon wiped the Jewish nation off the map in 586 BC, burning the cities and exiling most survivors, only the poorest people remained. Babylon's king appointed a Jew named Gedaliah to govern them. Like the prophet Jeremiah, Gedaliah had advised the Jews not to resist the Babylonians. Within a few months, Judean guerrillas assassinated him.

GEHAZI
(guh HAZE eye)
Gehazi, Hebrew
"valley of vision"
First mention: 2 Kings 4:12

Elisha's servant, Gehazi, seemed like a fine assistant—right up until Elisha felt like he had to curse him with a skin disease.

Earlier, Gehazi showed incredible compassion for an elderly couple in the north Israel village of Shunem. They had prepared a guest room for Elisha to use whenever he passed by. So Elisha wanted to show his gratitude. Gehazi reminded him that they had no son. So Elisha told the woman she would have a son the next year. And she did.

Gehazi got himself in trouble after Elisha refused payment for healing a Syrian commander of a skin disease. Gehazi chased down the departing soldier and said Elisha changed his mind. Gehazi ended up with two sets of clothes and 150 pounds of silver. When Elisha found out, Gehazi also got the soldier's skin disease, then passed it on to his family.

GEHENNA
(guh HEN nuh)
Ge hinnom, Hebrew
Gehenna, Latin
"valley of Hinnom"
First mention: Joshua 15:8

See Jerusalem
MAP 4
B5

Hell can't be plotted on a map, but the symbol for it is in Jerusalem.

That symbol—which Jesus frequently used—was the Valley of Hinnom. It's south of the hilltop temple where Jews once worshiped and where Muslims and tourists today visit the thirteen-hundred-year-old Dome of the Rock shrine.

Gehenna, as the valley is called by its Latin name, was the place where some Jews once burned their children to death as sacrifices to the Canaanite god Molech. The ritual apparently conveyed the idea of passing the child through the fire and into the hands of the god. At least two Jewish kings—Ahaz and his grandson Manasseh—sacrificed their own children this way.

Exactly how the valley developed into a symbol for hell is unclear. It may have grown out of the child sacrifices. There's also speculation that the valley served as an ever smoldering garbage dump. Whatever the reason, as the Jews grew in their understanding of an afterlife, Gehenna became one of the words they used to describe the punishment that evil people can expect.

"How terrible it will be for you teachers of religious law and you Pharisees. Hypocrites!" Jesus said. "How will you escape the judgment of hell [*Gehenna*]? (Matthew 23:29, 33). (See *Hades; Hell; Hinnom.*)

GERAR

(GEE rarr)
Gerar, Hebrew
First mention: Genesis 10:19

MAP 1
A6

Abraham and Isaac both lied about their wives in Gerar, a city about forty-five miles southwest of Jerusalem, near the coastal city of Gaza. Abraham first and Isaac decades later both claimed that their wives were their sisters. They did this to protect themselves from being killed by men who might want to marry the beautiful women. Each time the king discovered the truth.

Gerar is thought to be the forty-acre mound of ruins known as Tel Haror. Pottery fragments there date back to about the time of Abraham.

GERSHOM

(GUR shom)
Gersom, Hebrew
"a stranger there"
1400s BC
First mention: Exodus 2:22

When Moses fled from Egypt after killing a foreman who mistreated the Hebrew slaves, he settled along what is now the western border of Saudi Arabia (Midian). There, he married a shepherd's daughter, Zipporah, and had a son. "Moses named him Gershom, for he said, 'I have been a stranger [*ger* in Hebrew] in a foreign land [*som* literally means "there"]' " (Exodus 2:22).

GETHSEMANE

(geth SEM uh nee)
Gethsemani, Greek
"olive press"
First mention: Matthew 26:36

See *Jerusalem*
MAP 4
B5

On the night Jesus was arrested, he led the disciples on a short walk out of Jerusalem, down into the Kidron valley, and just a little way up the slopes of the Mount of Olives. There—if Christian tradition is right—they came to a familiar, peaceful olive grove where they had rested and prayed before. This is where Jesus chose to spend his last minutes, in prayer, before his all-night trial and

Gnarled old olive trees frame the path through a garden on the Mount of Olives, the hillside where Jesus prayed the night of his arrest.

morning crucifixion.

When Rome legalized Christianity in the AD 300s, Emperor Constantine's mother visited the Holy Land and designated many locations as sacred. One such site was the place tourists today visit as the Garden of Gethsemane—a tiny grove of olive trees in the courtyard of the Church of All Nations. Trees there could be hundreds of years old and perhaps a thousand or more. But it seems unlikely they are living witnesses of Jesus, since the Roman general Titus reportedly cut down all the nearby trees as he laid siege to Jerusalem in AD 70.

Several other sites are suggested as the authentic Gethsemane, but none of the others has a tradition dating all the way back to the beginning of Roman Christianity.

GEZER

(GEEZ ur)
Gezer, Hebrew
First mention: Joshua 10:33

After destroying Jericho, the Israelites swept through southern Canaan, wiping out cities and clearing the land for settlement. During one battle, the king of Gezer arrived with his army to reinforce his Canaanite allies. He and his men died in the lost cause, but it seems the Israelites didn't conquer Gezer. An Egyptian pharaoh did that several hundred years later and gave the city to his daughter. That daughter married Solomon, who rebuilt Gezer.

Located about midway between Jerusalem and the modern coastal city of Tel Aviv, Gezer guarded one of the main roads branching off the coastline road and leading inland. What remains of the city is a thirty-three-acre mound called Tell Jezer.

GIBEAH

(GIB ee uh)
Gibah, Hebrew
"hill"
First mention: Joshua 15:57

It's not surprising that the Bible talks about four places named Gibeah, since the name means "hill" and Israel is full of hills. The most famous Gibeah was King Saul's birthplace and capital, a few miles north of Jerusalem, in the tribal territory of Benjamin. This was also the infamous Jewish town where some men raped to death the secondary wife, called a concubine, of a Jewish traveler. The widower cut his wife's corpse into twelve pieces and sent them to tribal leaders as a call for justice. Tribal leaders refused to turn over the guilty men of Gibeah, so the other tribes nearly annihilated Benjamin's descendants.

Some scholars say Gibeah's ruins lie in a mound called Tell el-Ful, three miles north of Jerusalem. Others point to a mound called Tell el-Jib, three miles farther north.

GIBEON

MAP 1
C5

(GIB ee uhn)
Gibon, Hebrew
"hill place"
First mention: Joshua 9:3

Cunning and decep-
tive, people of the hill-
top village of Gibeon
quickly hatched a plot
to stay alive after they
saw what Joshua and
the Israelites did to
their neighbors in
Jericho. The Gibeon-
ites heard that Israel
planned to wipe out all
Canaanites, making no peace treaties.
So Gibeon's peace delegation said they
came from far away. They wore ragged
clothes and carried moldy bread. Only
after the deal was done did Joshua discover the deception.

Gibeon's neighbor cities felt betrayed. Five attacked, and Gibeon sent
for their new allies. Joshua took the
attackers by surprise, overwhelming
them. In the heat of battle, he asked
God to stop the sun, apparently to give
the Israelites time to finish the battle.
"So the sun and moon stood still until
the Israelites had defeated their enemies" (Joshua 10:13).

The ancient ruin identified as
Gibeon is Tell el-Jib, about six miles
north of Jerusalem. The prophet Jeremiah spoke of a huge pool there
(Jeremiah 41:12). Archaeologists found
a large pool cut thirty-five feet deep
and thirty-seven feet in diameter—
through solid rock. It's actually a

*Gibeon's city water was stored in this huge cistern, cut thirty-five feet
into solid rock.*

cistern connected by tunnel to an
underground water chamber.

GIDEON

(GID ee uhn)
Gidon, Hebrew
"hacker"
1100s BC
First mention: Judges 6:11

Gideon's story begins with what sounds
like an angel making a wisecrack.

For seven years, raiders on camel-
back had swarmed into Israel like
locusts. They came at harvest time
from Midian, which is now western
Saudi Arabia, and they snatched all the
livestock and crops they could get their
hands on.

The Israelites hid. When an angel
arrived at the farm of Gideon's father,
Gideon was hiding, threshing grain in
the bowels of a winepress so raiders
wouldn't spot him. The farmer must
have looked cowardly, which makes the

CAMELS TAMED TO RAID

When camel-riding raiders stormed in from the Arabian Desert to plunder crops from Gideon and his Israelite neighbors, it marked a turning point in history. It became the first time, as far as historians can tell, that camels were used in warfare. That was in the mid-1100s BC.

Camels gave the raiders an incredible edge over Israelite farmers and militia on foot. Some seven feet tall at the shoulders, camels can sprint up to forty miles per hour, maintain twenty-five miles per hour for an hour, and cover one hundred miles in a day.

Gideon's savvy tactic was to take the raiders by surprise while they were camped and bedded down for the night.

angel's greeting sound more sarcastic than prophetic: "Mighty hero, the LORD is with you!" (Judges 6:12).

The angel then announced that God had chosen Gideon to defeat the raiders. Gideon wanted proof since he was low man on the family totem pole, in the weakest clan among his tribe of Manasseh. Gideon prepared an offering of meat and bread, and the angel touched it with a staff, setting it aflame, then disappearing. Later, at Gideon's

insistence, God made overnight dew fall on nothing but fleece left on a patch of ground. And the following night, God did the opposite—dew on the ground, not the fleece.

WAR CRY

Gideon sent word to neighboring tribes in northern Israel that he was amassing an army to fight back. Tens of thousands came, but God said with this many, the Israelites would credit the victory to their military power instead of God's power. God told Gideon to send home anyone who was afraid. Twenty-two thousand left, leaving only ten thousand. At God's instruction, Gideon reduced the group to three hundred by releasing those who drank spring water by lapping it up like a dog instead of using cupped hands. This probably wasn't a test to find only the most alert fighters, since that could have been seen to reduce God's role in the battle. It was probably just a quick way of drastically cutting the size of the army.

Gideon found the raider camp in a valley and surrounded it. Equipping his men with torches, empty jars, and rams' horns, he waited for darkness to fall. About midnight, Gideon's army held lit torches under the jars. At his signal, they broke the jars, blew the horns, and screamed: "For the LORD and for Gideon!" (Judges 7:18).

This sound-and-light show was terrifying to the raiders. And in the pitch black of the valley, they started killing each other. Those who survived ran for home, as Gideon's army ran them down.

THE UNHAPPY ENDING

Back home, Gideon used forty-three pounds of gold from enemy earrings to make a sacred ephod, a lavish vest worn by royalty or priests. It's unclear if this means he accepted the grateful nation's offer to become king—replacing God—or if he wore it himself or put it on an idol. "But soon all the Israelites prostituted themselves by worshiping it, and it became a trap for Gideon and his family" (Judges 8:27). And it was a large family since Gideon had many wives, seventy sons, and perhaps as many daughters.

GIHON

(GUY huhn)
Gihon, Hebrew
"gusher"
First mention: 1. Genesis 2:13
2. 1 Kings 1:33

See Jerusalem

MAP 2
C5

The Bible mentions two Gihons, both of which were sources of water.

1. **Gihon River.** One clue to locating Eden is the Gihon River. Four rivers branched off the unnamed river flowing out of Eden: Tigris, Euphrates, Pishon, and Gihon (Genesis 2:13). The first two rivers run mainly through Iraq, but Pishon and Gihon remain a mystery. (For speculation on Gihon's location, see *Eden*.)

2. **Gihon Spring.** A second Gihon is a spring just outside the walls of ancient Jerusalem. As King David lay dying, he ordered his officials to take Solomon out to this popular gathering spot and, in front of all the people, anoint Solomon the next king. Years later, King Hezekiah had miners chisel nearly six hundred yards through solid rock to make a tunnel from Gihon Spring into the city, to provide water during a siege. The spring doesn't produce a steady flow. It gushes from a sixteen-foot crack in a rock about twice a day during the dry season and four or five times a day in the rainy season.

GILEAD

(GILL ee add)
Gilad, Hebrew
"stone pile as a reminder" or "rough terrain"
First mention: Genesis 31:21

MAP 1
D3

East of the Jordan River, in what is now Jordan, lies about a twenty-mile-wide strip of land known in Bible times as Gilead. Rich in grazing land and heavily forested, it was a place where many people fled for safety: Jacob from his father-in-law, Israelites from Philistine soldiers, and King David during a revolt by his son, Absalom. In the forest there is where Absalom's long hair got stuck in a branch, yanking him off his mule during a battle and leaving him dangling, where David's soldiers found him and killed him. Gilead was also where the medicinal tree sap called the balm of Gilead was produced.

GILGAL

(GILL gal)

Gilgal, Hebrew

"circle"

First mention: Deuteronomy 11:30

MAP 1
C5

When the Israelites crossed the Jordan River into the Promised Land, they made camp at a place they called Gilgal. The name probably refers to a circle of stones they piled up. A representative from each of the twelve tribes picked up a stone from the riverbed. Joshua, their leader, piled up the stones and said, "In the future, your children will ask, 'What do these stones mean?' Then you can tell them, 'This is where the Israelites crossed the Jordan on dry ground.' For the LORD your God dried up the river right before your eyes, and he kept it dry until you were all across, just as he did at the Red Sea" (Joshua 4:21–23).

GOD

Yahweh (YAH-way), Hebrew

"the Lord"

First mention: Genesis 1:1

In the beginning, God turned on the lights of the universe. In the end, he'll turn them out.

That's the short version of Genesis and Revelation—the first and last books of the Bible. Between lies the story of God at work on his creation.

It's a story that doesn't reveal nearly enough about God to satisfy our curiosity. There's no description of what he looks like, where exactly he lives, or what he does to pass eternity.

But the story makes this much clear: "God is love" (1 John 4:8).

And that love is directed at humanity: "God so loved the world that he gave his only Son, so that everyone who believes in him will not perish but have eternal life" (John 3:16).

A GOOD CREATION GOES BAD

"Let there be light" (Genesis 1:3). With that single sentence, God began his masterful creation: the sky draped in stars, oceans teaming with life, land blanketed in plants and animals—and humans to take care of it all.

The big question is why. Why did God create all of this? We can only guess. But if God is love, perhaps he wanted someone he could love and someone to love him in return.

For whatever reason God created us, we are one of the best clues about what he's like. For when God made us, he said, "Let us make people in our image, to be like ourselves" (Genesis 1:26). Scholars debate what God meant by that. It might mean we look like him. But since God is a spirit being—not limited to the physical—it might mean we share some of his spiritual characteristics: an eternal soul and the ability to reason, love, and forgive.

There's another human trait that God and humans share. And the fact that God built that trait into us reveals something about him. God gave us the freedom to choose—between good and bad, up and down, left and right, yes and no. Though he wanted a

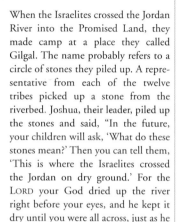

GOD'S MANY NAMES

When Moses and God had their first talk—at a burning bush—Moses asked God his name.

God was sending Moses back to Egypt to free the enslaved Hebrews. So Moses wanted to tell the people who sent him. "I AM THE ONE WHO ALWAYS IS," God replied. "Just tell them, 'I AM has sent me to you'" (Exodus 3:14).

God immediately added another name—one more personal: "Tell them, 'The LORD, the God of your ancestors—the God of Abraham, the God of Isaac, and the God of Jacob—has sent me to you.' This will be my name forever; it has always been my name, and it will be used throughout all generations" (Exodus 3:15).

In ancient Hebrew, written only in consonants and no vowels, that name is "YHWH." Scholars are left to guess which vowels to insert but have come up with the word "Yahweh," translated into English as "the Lord" or "Jehovah." Used nearly seven thousand times in the Old Testament, it's the Bible's most common name for God. But in time, out of reverence, many Jews stopped speaking this name. Instead, they used other names or titles, such as:

Abba: Father (used by Jesus)
Adonai: my Lord (very common)
El: God
El elyon: God Most High
El shaddai: God Almighty
Elohim: God (perhaps emphasizing His supremacy)
Theos: God (in Greek)
Yahweh jireh: the Lord will provide
Yahweh shalom: the Lord is peace

relationship with humans, he wanted it to be our choice.

If God made a mistake in creation, that was it.

Yet if God is all-knowing, as the Bible portrays him, he would have known where this would lead—to a rocky and sometimes broken relationship. But he would have known, too, that his persistent love would eventually draw us back to him.

For humanity, choice dangled from a fruit tree.

"You may freely eat any fruit in the garden except fruit from the tree of the knowledge of good and evil," God said. "If you eat of its fruit, you will surely die" (Genesis 2:16–17).

Humanity might never have bothered with this poisonous fruit, given all the savory food in the Garden of Eden. But they had help from a snake,

God at work creating the universe, as imagined by artist Michelangelo.

identified by a New Testament writer as "the ancient serpent called the Devil" (Revelation 12:9), whom Jesus said fell from heaven "as a flash of lightning" (Luke 10:18).

" 'You won't die!' the serpent hissed. 'God knows that your eyes will be opened when you eat it. You will become just like God, knowing everything, both good and evil' " (Genesis 3:4–5).

When Adam and Eve bit into the fruit—humanity's original sin—it didn't just poison them. Somehow, it poisoned the Creation. The couple died, in time. Trust between God and humanity evaporated. Trust among humans got swallowed up in jealousy, as Cain murdered his brother. And life on the planet became harsh, with women suffering in childbirth and men struggling against the earth to survive.

God's good creation was poisoned.

RECLAIMING THE CREATION

If you had only one sentence to sum up the Bible's plot and God's goal from this point on, it might be this: God gets rid of sin and restores his good creation—people and all. That's a tall order, but God has a plan. And the Bible is the story of God working his plan—past, present, and future.

God begins small, with one man—Abraham. The idea seems ludicrous, that God could restore all of creation through one man. What God saw in Abraham, we can't be certain. Perhaps God saw a bit of himself. This seems likely, given Abraham's near sacrifice of his son, Isaac. This dramatic story reads like a lived-out prophecy about God and his Son, Jesus. What Abraham was willing to do—sacrifice his son—God did.

On Abraham's remarkable faith—a faith that may have expected God to raise Isaac from the dead just as God later did for his own Son—God would build a nation.

Abraham's descendants are the Jews.

God had one essential rule for all of them to follow: "You must be holy because I am holy" (Leviticus 11:44).

Unfortunately, scholars don't agree on what it means to be holy. "Perfect" doesn't seem adequate because we know all too well that humans can't be perfectly behaved unless they're heavily sedated. Some say that God's holiness means he's one of a kind—transcendent and above anything else in creation. We, then, become holy when we worship him as such. This worship makes us a one-of-a-kind people—different from others because we're devoted to the one-of-a-kind God.

Rules to live by

Within about seven hundred years, Abraham's family had grown into a nation known as Hebrews. God chose Moses to lead them to the Promised Land, now called Israel. And God gave them a set of rules to live by and to make it clear to other nations that these people were unlike any other on the planet.

There were over six hundred rules to follow, with the Ten Commandments as the bedrock foundation. Because of these rules, people knew if their neighbors were Hebrews. The Hebrews worshiped only one God. They circumcised their baby boys. And they didn't work from sundown Friday until sundown Saturday.

MYSTERY OF THE TRINITY

Even Jesus didn't try to explain how there could be one God in three persons: Father, Son, and Holy Spirit.

Knowing full well that the most important Jewish teaching was that there is only one God, Jesus offered only a single, cryptic statement: "The Father and I are one" (John 10:30).

Perhaps he didn't explain it because physics-bound humans have no frame of reference for understanding it.

Though the word Trinity doesn't appear in the Bible, there is clearly a divine trio at work: "Go and make disciples of all the nations," Jesus told the apostles, "baptizing them in the name of the Father and the Son and the Holy Spirit" (Matthew 28:19).

For centuries, Christian scholars debated the idea of a Trinity and came up with lots of theories. Some said Jesus was simply God on earth and that the Holy Spirit was another name for God. Yet at the baptism of Jesus, God spoke and the Spirit descended.

In time, scholars gave up trying to explain it. They just believed it because it was taught in the Bible.

Summing up the consensus in the AD 400s was a theologian named Augustine: "The Father is God, the Son is God, the Holy Spirit is God. . .yet we do not say that there are three gods, but one God, the most exalted Trinity."

Heaven mourns the death of Jesus, crucified as part of God's plan to save humanity from its sin.

The Hebrews became God's dramatic example to the world of how good it was to be God's people. With God on their side, there was no stopping them. The Red Sea opened a corridor. Jericho's walls collapsed. And Joshua stopped the sun with a prayer so he could finish a battle.

God's plan for this emerging nation that became Israel was a lofty one: "You will be a light to guide all nations to me" (Isaiah 42:6).

Israel failed. They failed as miserably as Adam and Eve.

Just as the first couple was banished from the Garden of Eden, the Jewish people were banished from the Promised Land. But not before God sent generations of prophets pointing out the nation's sins—the biggest of which was turning their backs on God and walking away to worship make-believe gods.

In time, many Jews repented, and God allowed them to come home and rebuild their nation. The image of them returning home from exile in Babylon is reminiscent of Jesus' story about a prodigal son, welcomed home by his forgiving father.

SENDING THE LIGHT

Though Israel failed to become a light to all nations, God's Light did come from that nation. The Light was born to a Jewish woman.

"I am the light of the world," Jesus said. "If you follow me, you won't be stumbling through the darkness, because you will have the light that leads to life" (John 8:12).

The best way to find out what God is really like is to look at his Son. Jesus healed the sick, fed the poor, taught the uneducated, and ate with prostitutes. Criticized by religious leaders for not realizing that people judged him by the company he kept, Jesus replied, "Healthy people don't need a doctor—sick people do" (Matthew 9:12).

From one man, to one nation, God's plan was about to embrace the whole world. Crucified and resurrected, Jesus ascended into the clouds leaving this commission to his stunned disciples: "Go into all the world and preach the Good News to everyone, everywhere" (Mark 16:15).

WHAT GOD SAID
ABOUT HIMSELF

- "Is anything too hard for the LORD?" (to Abraham; Genesis 18:14)

- "I am the LORD, the merciful and gracious God. I am slow to anger and rich in unfailing love and faithfulness. I show this unfailing love to many thousands by forgiving every kind of sin and rebellion. Even so I do not leave sin unpunished" (to Moses; Exodus 34:6–7).

- "You must worship no other gods, but only the LORD, for he is a God who is passionate about his relationship with you" (to Moses; Exodus 34:14).

- "Do not treat my holy name as common and ordinary. I must be treated as holy" (to the Israelites; Leviticus 22:32).

- "It is I, the LORD, who makes you holy" (to the Israelites; Leviticus 22:32).

- "Who is this that questions my wisdom with such ignorant words? ...Where were you when I laid the foundations of the earth? Tell me, if you know so much" (to Job, who questioned God's fairness; Job 38:2, 4).

- "Am I a God who is only in one place? ...Am I not everywhere in all the heavens and earth?" (to a prophet; Jeremiah 23:23–24).

- "How can you say the LORD does not see your troubles? ...Don't you know that the LORD is the everlasting God, the Creator of all the earth? He never grows faint or weary. No one can measure the depths of his understanding. He gives power to those who are tired and worn out; he offers strength to the weak. Even youths will become exhausted, and young men will give up. But those who wait on the LORD will find new strength. They will fly high on wings like eagles. They will run and not grow weary. They will walk and not faint" (to discouraged Israelites exiled in a foreign land; Isaiah 40:27–31).

It took some prodding. Peter needed a vision to convince him that it was okay to baptize non-Jews. And Paul needed an appearance by the ascended Jesus himself before launching a ministry that would eventually convert the Roman Empire to Christianity.

A NEW CREATION

From one man to one nation to the entire world, God's plan continues to unfold. The final moment—yet to come: God's new creation.

We catch a glimpse of what it will be like through the end-time visions of a Christian prophet named John: "I saw a new heaven and a new earth, for the old heaven and the old earth had disappeared. . . . I heard a loud shout from the throne, saying, 'Look, the home of God is now among his people! He will live with them, and they will be his people. God himself will be with them. He will remove all of their sorrows, and there will be no more death or sorrow or crying or pain. For the old world and its evils are gone forever' " (Revelation 21:1, 3–4).

In this future scene, God has turned out the lights of the universe. But they're not needed in his new creation: "There will be no night there— no need for lamps or sun—for the Lord God will shine on them [people devoted to God]. And they will reign forever and ever" (Revelation 22:5).

GOG
Gog, Hebrew
First mention: Ezekiel 38:2

Gog may never have been a person, but only a symbol of evil pitted against God and his people.

God told the prophet Ezekiel, "Prophesy against Gog of the land of Magog, the prince who rules over the nations of Meshech and Tubal" (Ezekiel 38:2). Scholars have theories about who Gog was—including a king from Turkey in Ezekiel's time. But the prince's name and the locations mentioned remain puzzling. The writer of Revelation—a book about end times—says Gog and Magog represent nations all over the world that are convinced by Satan to attack God's people. God destroys them with fire.

GOLAN
(GO lawn)
Golan, Hebrew
First mention: Deuteronomy 4:43

MAP 1
D3

If Jews accidentally killed someone, they could escape vengeance-seeking relatives by fleeing to a city of refuge, where they could get a trial. People found innocent of murder were protected as long as they stayed inside the city. Golan was one of six such cities scattered throughout Israel, three of which—like Golan—were east of the Jordan River. Many scholars place the city east of the Golan Heights, at the modern Syrian city of Sahem el-Joulan—near where the borders of Israel, Syria, and Jordan meet.

GOLIATH
(go LIE uhth)
Golyat, Hebrew
1000s BC
First mention: 1 Samuel 17:4

A giant of a man, Goliath was a Philistine champion warrior bristling with the best weaponry of his day—including the new secret metal, iron. But he lost in mortal combat to a boy brandishing a slingshot.

It's unclear exactly how tall Goliath was. The Hebrew manuscript used to translate the King James Version of the Bible says he stood about nine feet, nine inches. But several older manuscripts—including a Dead Sea Scroll copy of the Bible story that's about thirteen hundred years older—put him at about six feet, nine inches. At either height, he was an intimidating enemy.

Goliath's hometown was Gath, one of five major Philistine cities on what is now Israel's coastal plain. The boy he fought, David, came from Bethlehem. They met in a valley about midway between the two cities, with the Philistine and Israelite armies staged on opposing hillsides.

Each day for forty days Goliath challenged the Israelites to send a champion who would fight him to the death. The loser's nation would serve the winner's nation. No Israelite volunteered, even though the king offered a reward: one of his daughters in marriage and no taxes for the warrior's

David finishes off Goliath, a giant of a Philistine champion who stood nearly seven feet tall—nearly ten feet by some accounts.

family—rewards of no use with Goliath's fifteen-pound iron spearhead in your chest and your head on a pole.

David, probably still a teenager, dropped Goliath with a single stone to the forehead. Then, using the Philistine's own sword, David cut off Goliath's head. The sword became a trophy stored at the Jewish worship center. Years later, David took it back and may have used it in battle, since it was made of iron and the Israelites were still using bronze.

GOMER
(GO mur)
Gomer, Hebrew
700s BC
First mention: Hosea 1:3

"Go and marry a prostitute, so some of her children will be born to you from other men" (Hosea 1:2).

That's the word of the Lord.

He gave this order to the prophet Hosea—who dutifully married Gomer.

God explained his extraordinary request: "This will illustrate the way my people have been untrue to me, openly committing adultery against the LORD by worshiping other gods" (Hosea 1:2). And so, Hosea's family life became a parable written in flesh—a dramatic and continuing message for Israel.

Gomer delivered three children. Hosea gave them symbolic names:

- Jezreel, after the valley where Israel's army would die
- Lo-ruhamah, meaning "not loved," because God rejected Israel
- Lo-ammi, meaning "not my people," God's description of Israel.

Hosea possibly kicked Gomer out for adultery, and she sold herself into slavery to one of her lovers. At God's order, Hosea bought her back—just as God would one day take Israel back. "I will show love to those I called 'Not loved.' And to those I called 'Not my people,' I will say, 'Now you are my people.' Then they will reply, 'You are our God!' " (Hosea 2:23).

GOMORRAH

(guh MORE uh)
Amora, Hebrew
"flooded place"
First mention: Genesis 10:19

Sodom and Gomorrah were twin cities of sin that God burned off the planet in the days of Abraham and Lot. At sunrise, "the LORD rained down fire and burning sulfur from the heavens on Sodom and Gomorrah. He utterly destroyed them. . .eliminating all life—people, plants, and animals alike" (Genesis 19:24–25). Both cities live on only as a symbol of sin and where it leads. (For more, including theories about the location of these cities and the natural resources God could have used in their destruction, see *Sodom*.)

GOSHEN

(GO shun)
Gosen, Hebrew
First mention: Genesis 45:10

It seemed like a great place to wait out a drought, but the Jews really didn't intend to stay 430 years. Joseph was Pharaoh's top official, and he invited his father, Jacob, to bring the entire family down until the dry spell was over.

"You will live in the land of Goshen," Joseph said, "so you can be near me with all your children and grandchildren, your flocks and herds, and all that you have. I will take care of you there, for there are still five years of famine ahead of us" (Genesis 45:10–11).

Goshen was drought-proof, with lush pastures on the east side of Egypt's sprawling delta—where the Nile River fans out into gentle streams that empty into the Mediterranean Sea. It was prime land for shepherds, but not of much use to most Egyptians, who preferred cities along the Nile. Egyptian records confirm that foreign shepherds

The Greek warrior Alexander the Great spreads his native language throughout the Middle East—which is why Jewish writers penned the New Testament in Greek instead of Hebrew.

came there in times of drought.

Scholars debate the time line, but Jacob's family may have arrived in about 1750 BC or earlier. Eventually the Egyptians enslaved them and didn't let them go until Moses pried them loose in the 1400s or the 1200s.

GREECE

Hellas, Greek
First mention: Isaiah 66:19

By the time Greece started to emerge as a nation, Israel was nearly dead. That was in about the 800s BC. Greece had just started building city-states, and Homer was writing his famous epic, the *Iliad.* But nearly one thousand miles to the southeast, in the two Jewish kingdoms of Israel and Judah, prophets warned the end was coming. Israel fell in 722 BC, and Judah followed in 586 BC.

Alexander the Great carried the Greek language and culture throughout the Middle East in the 300s BC, which is why the New Testament was originally written in Greek instead of Hebrew. The apostle Paul, in return, carried the Christian faith back to Greece—distinguishing Philippi as the hometown of the first church in Europe. Paul's work in Greece spawned several New Testament letters: Philippians, 1 and 2 Thessalonians, along with 1 and 2 Corinthians.

Today, the mountainous peninsula, a little smaller than Florida, is home to more than ten million people—98 percent of whom claim to be Christians who follow the teachings of the Greek Orthodox Church.

HABAKKUK
(huh BACK uck)
Habakkuk, Hebrew
"embrace"
Probably 600s BC
First mention: Habakkuk 1:1

"How long, O LORD, must I call for help? But you do not listen! 'Violence!' I cry, but you do not come to save" (Habakkuk 1:2).

That's one of the hard questions this prophet asks God in the years shortly before Babylon invaded the Jewish nation of Judah in 586 BC and erased it from the map. We know almost nothing about this prophet, other than what he reveals in his short book of fifty-six verses.

What he reveals is sharp thinking, poetry, and faith. He asks why God would send an evil nation like Babylon to punish a Jewish nation not nearly as evil. God replies that the Babylonians will be punished eventually, but in the meantime, "the righteous will live by their faith" (Habakkuk 2:4).

The prophet responded with an eloquent poem of faith that describes what the landscape will look like after the Babylonians invade: "Even though the fig trees have no blossoms, and there are no grapes on the vine; even though the olive crop fails, and the fields lie empty and barren; even though the flocks die in the fields, and the cattle barns are empty, yet I will rejoice in the LORD! I will be joyful in the God of my salvation. The Sovereign LORD is my strength! He will make me as surefooted as a deer and bring me safely over the mountains" (Habakkuk 3:17–19).

HADAD
(HAY dad)
Hadad, Hebrew
"the one who smashes"
900s BC
First mention: 1 Kings 11:14

Hadad, the prince of Edom, was only a child when King David and his army crossed the border into

Invaders level the Jewish nation and take survivors captive. The prophet Habakkuk couldn't understand why God would allow this.

what is now Jordan and spent six months killing nearly all the men of Edom. Hadad and a few of his father's officials fled to Egypt. Pharaoh grew fond of Hadad and gave him a home, food, and land. When Hadad grew up, he married the queen's sister.

After David died, Hadad moved back to Edom and "made trouble" for Israel's new king, Solomon.

HADES
(HAY dees)
Hades, Greek
First mention: Matthew 11:23

Location Unknown

Hades is not another word for hell.

It's a word describing the place where all dead people go—not just the bad ones. Hades is the Greek word for a Hebrew term, *Sheol.* Jesus illustrated the Jewish understanding of *Sheol* in a parable about two men who died—a rich man and a beggar named Lazarus. Flames tormented the rich man, but he could see Lazarus in a comfortable place with Abraham. The rich man asked for a taste of water, but Abraham explained it was impossible: "There is a great chasm separating us" (Luke 16:26).

Jewish writers often portrayed Hades as a kind of waiting room, where the dead awaited God's coming judgment, with rewards for good people and punishment for bad ones.

Hades was a fitting Greek word to translate *Sheol.* In Greek mythology, Hades was the god of the dead. When he and his brothers divided the universe, Hades got the underworld, Poseidon got the sea, and Zeus got the heavens.

The underworld itself was often called Hades, and it had various regions where the good lived in comfort and the evil lived in torment. (See *Hell.*)

HAGAR
(HAY gar)
Hagar, Hebrew
Perhaps "splendid"
2100s BC
First mention: Genesis 16:1

When Abraham's wife, Sarah, reached her midseventies, she resigned herself to the fact that if Abraham was ever going to have a child, it would be with another woman. As was common among wealthy, infertile wives, Sarah chose her servant as a surrogate mother. That servant was Hagar, from Egypt.

Hagar gave birth to Ishmael. Amazingly, however, Sarah gave birth fourteen years later—at age ninety-one. Her son was Isaac.

Sarah didn't want Isaac to share the family inheritance with his older half brother, who by custom would have gotten twice as much as the younger son. She insisted that Abraham order Hagar and Ishmael to leave. Abraham resisted because he loved Ishmael.

"Do just as Sarah says," God instructed Abraham, "for Isaac is the son through whom your descendants will be counted. But I will make a nation of the descendants of Hagar's son because he also is your son" (Genesis 21:12–13).

Many consider Isaac father of the Jews and Ishmael father of the Arabs.

HAGGAI

(HAG eye)
Haggay, Hebrew
"festive"
Prophesied August 29–December 18, 520 BC
First mention: Ezra 5:1

Haggai's ministry as a prophet spanned less than four months—with dates uncommonly precise because of several historical landmarks in the story that match Persian records. His ministry may have been this short because he was an old man. Haggai apparently remembered seeing Solomon's temple nearly seventy years earlier, before Babylonian invaders leveled it.

Despite his apparent age and his short ministry, his words—preserved in the book of Haggai—prodded the Jews to rebuild their temple.

Persia had defeated Babylon and freed the exiled Jews to go home. That was twenty years earlier. Now, at the end of another bad harvest scorched in the fields, Haggai said God would end the drought as soon as the Jews rebuilt the temple. That was August 29, 520 BC. They started construction on September 21 and laid the foundation on December 18, with Haggai promising God's blessing "from this day onward" (Haggai 2:19).

HAM

Ham, Hebrew
"hot"
Before 2500 BC
First mention: Genesis 5:32

One of Noah's three sons, Ham is the one who saw his father drunk and naked, then apparently called his brothers to come and look. But his brothers Shem and Japheth, showing respect for their father, walked backward into Noah's tent and covered him with a robe.

When Noah found out what had happened, he put a curse on Canaan, one of Ham's sons: "A curse on the Canaanites! May they be the lowest of servants to the descendants of Shem and Japheth" (Genesis 9:25). Ham's other descendants included the Egyptians and Ethiopians.

HAMAN

(HAY mon)
Haman, Hebrew
Perhaps "illustrious"
400s BC
First mention: Esther 3:1

Nearly twenty-five hundred years before Hitler's Holocaust, a Persian prime minister tried to rid the empire of all Jews. Haman was the top official under King Xerxes, and he planned the holocaust after a Jew refused to bow before him. Haman's ancestors, the Agagites, had been enemies of the Jews since King Saul fought King Agag of the Amalekites.

Without knowing that Queen Esther was a Jew, Haman set the extermination date for March 7. All Jews, young and old, were targeted. Their property would go to the people who killed them.

When Esther told the king that she was a Jew and that Haman had plotted to annihilate her people, the king jumped to his feet in rage. Haman was hanged that day on gallows he built for the Jew who refused to bow to him—Mordecai, Esther's cousin. The Jewish festival of Purim celebrates this holocaust missed.

HANNAH
(HAN nah)
Hanna, Hebrew
"grace"
1100s BC
First mention: 1 Samuel 1:2

For years before Hannah gave birth to Samuel, she pled with God to let her have a child. She was one of Elkanah's two wives. The other wife, who could have children, made fun of her, reducing her to tears.

In desperation, Hannah went to the worship center in Shiloh. In prayer, she promised if God let her have a son, she would give him back for a lifetime of service to God. As she mumbled her tearful request, the priest Eli accused her of being drunk.

"I'm not drunk!" she said, "I was pouring my heart out to the LORD" (1 Samuel 1:15).

"Cheer up!" Eli responded. "May the God of Israel grant the request you have asked of him" (1 Samuel 1:17).

Samuel was born within a year. After he was able to eat solid food, Hannah took him to Eli, who raised him to serve God. Hannah brought Samuel a new robe each year and had three more sons and two daughters.

HARAN
(HAIR uhn)
Harranu, Akkadian
"road"
First mention: Genesis 11:31

For some mysterious reason, Abraham's father, Terah, decided to move his entire extended family from the hub of civilization to the boondocks about a one-thousand-mile walk away. By today's map, what he planned was a move from Iraq to Israel. But he ended up in Haran, a village in south Turkey, near the Syrian border.

It could be that Terah saw signs of the invasion that destroyed his riverside hometown, Ur, in about 2000 BC. For whatever reason, he decided to follow the caravan routes up the Euphrates River valley, then down the Mediterranean coastline to Canaan. But he apparently liked the wonderful pastures and plentiful water he saw in Haran some six hundred miles upriver. So he stayed. After he died, Abraham finished the journey, at God's instruction. Canaan became the land God promised to Abraham's descendants, the Jews.

HAROD SPRING
(HAIR uhd)
Harod, Hebrew
"trembling"
First mention: Judges 7:1

Harod Spring, in northern Israel, is where Gideon cut the size of his army to three hundred by watching the men drink water. He kept only those who drank from their hands, sending home those who drank with their faces in the water.

An old tradition puts the spring at Ain Jalud, in what is now an Israeli park at the north end of a chain of Samaritan hills. That's just a few miles from the hill of Moreh, where Gideon's enemy was camped. Here, rainwater filters through the hills, and one of the places where it comes out is this spring, which tourists visit.

HAZAEL
(HAY zay el)
Hazael, Hebrew
"God has seen"
Reigned about 842–800 BC
First mention: 1 Kings 19:15

Hazael stole Syria's throne by suffocating the ill King Ben-hadad with a wet blanket. Assyrian records confirm Hazael didn't inherit the throne, calling him "the son of a nobody."

The prophet Elisha likely gave Hazael the motivation. Elisha predicted Hazael would become Syria's next king. Then Elisha wept. He knew God would use Hazael to punish Israel: "You will burn their fortified cities, kill their young men, dash their children to the ground, and rip open their pregnant women!" (2 Kings 8:12). And Hazael did.

HAZOR
(HAY zor)
Hasor, Hebrew
First mention: Joshua 11:1

It wasn't enough for Joshua's Israelites to kill everyone in Hazor and burn the city. Hazor bounced back.

Located about ten miles north of the Sea of Galilee, Hazor was a leading city in the northland and well fortified. Hazor's king assembled a coalition army from more than a dozen kingdoms to run off the Israelites—but they lost. Perhaps a couple of centuries later—during the time of Israel's heroic leaders called judges—the Canaanites resettled Hazor, oppressing the Israelites. But Deborah's forces crushed them at Mount Tabor, and King Solomon later rebuilt the city into a military outpost. What's left today is a twenty-five-acre mound of ruins called Tell el-Qedah.

HEAVEN
Samayim, Hebrew
Ouranos, Greek
First mention: Genesis 14:19

Abraham didn't go to heaven when he died. Not according to the oldest books in the Bible.

Neither did Moses, David, or other ancient heroes. The only contenders were Enoch, who didn't die, and Elijah, taken to heaven by a whirlwind and flaming chariots. But even in Elijah's story, *heaven* could have meant the sky, with the writer trying to say that God transported Elijah to another place on earth.

Throughout most of the Old Testament, heaven wasn't seen as the eternal home for good souls. *Heaven* referred to the sky, or to God's home. When Abraham died—as far as devout

Jews were concerned in Old Testament times—he went to the mysterious place of the dead, wherever and whatever that was.

A psalmist summed up the ancient understanding this way: "The heavens belong to the LORD, but he has given the earth to all humanity. The dead cannot sing praises to the LORD, for they have gone into the silence of the grave. But we [the living] can praise the LORD both now and forever!" (Psalm 115:16–18).

HUMANS IN HEAVEN

This perception of heaven started changing near the end of the Old Testament, thanks to an angel's end-time message: "Many of those whose bodies lie dead and buried will rise up, some to everlasting life and some to shame and everlasting contempt. Those who are wise will shine as bright as the sky, and those who turn many to righteousness will shine like stars forever" (Daniel 12:2–3).

Jesus confirmed that heaven isn't just a place for God: "There are many rooms in my Father's home, and I am going to prepare a place for you. If this were not so, I would tell you plainly. When everything is ready, I will come and get you, so that you will always be with me where I am" (John 14:2–3).

Jesus backed up those words with convincing proof: He rose from the dead, then ascended into the sky. This convinced the disciples that they would one day join him.

Angels carry souls of the dead to heaven, in a painting by Dutch artist Hieronymus Bosch (1450–1516).

WHAT HEAVEN IS LIKE

If the scholars are right, don't expect pearly gates, golden streets, and jasper walls—even though that's what John, writer of the book of Revelation, said he saw in his vision of heaven.

Some Bible experts say John was trying to describe the indescribable. But there's nothing on earth to compare it to. So the best John could do was draw from images of earth's most precious objects.

John also said heaven was a cube, fourteen hundred miles in every direction. Don't take that literally, either, many scholars advise. A cube symbolized the perfect sacred space. The holiest room in the Jewish temple was a cube that contained the chest with the Ten Commandments. That room measured only thirty feet in every direction. Heaven is unimaginably more than the holiest spot on earth.

Even though John didn't say much about what heaven looks like, he said plenty about what it's like to live there:

"The home of God is now among his people! He will live with them, and they will be his people. God himself will be with them. He will remove all of their sorrows, and there will be no more death or sorrow or crying or pain. For the old world and its evils are gone forever" (Revelation 21:3–4).

HEBRON
(HE bron)
Hebron, Hebrew
First mention: Genesis 13:18

MAP 2
C5

After Abraham and his nephew Lot separated so their flocks wouldn't have to compete for grass and water, Abraham set up camp in an oak grove on the crest of a ridge about twenty miles south of Jerusalem. That spot near the crossroads of two caravan routes became known as Hebron. Abraham was buried there with several

of his family. Hebron was also David's first capital, before Jerusalem. Herod the Great built a massive building around Abraham's burial cave, and it's still standing. Tourists often bypass it, though, because of clashes between Jews and Palestinians. Hebron, controlled by the Palestinian Authority, is home to about seventy thousand Palestinians—and to a settlement of about one thousand Jews.

Souls tormented in a fiery hell.

HELL
Hel, Old English
"the hidden place"
First mention: Matthew 5:22

Location
Unknown

Hell isn't in the Bible. At least not in the original languages.

Hell is an English word that Bible experts today use to translate a couple of Bible terms about the afterlife: Gehenna and Tartaros.

Gehenna refers to a valley outside of Jerusalem where Jews once burned humans as sacrifices to a Canaanite god. By Jesus' time, the name of this valley had become a symbol. Just as

Sodom symbolized evil, Gehenna symbolized the terrible punishment that evil people could expect after God's judgment. Jesus used this symbolism many times, for example: "If your hand causes you to sin, cut it off. It is better to enter heaven with only one hand than to go into the unquenchable fires of hell [*Gehenna*] with two hands" (Mark 9:43).

Tartaros appears only once in the Bible and refers to the place God will send rebel angels: "God did not spare even the angels when they sinned; he threw them into hell, in gloomy caves and darkness until the judgment day" (2 Peter 2:4).

Oddly, the original English word —*hel*—didn't mean what it does today. It meant to cover or hide, and it generated related words like *helmet* and *hole*. But given how little we know about hell, the root word seems fitting.

HELL: FIGURATIVE OR REAL?

Conventional wisdom says hell is a place where sinners suffer forever in flames. Many scholars aren't so sure.

Certainly Jesus spoke of hell as though it was real. And he described it as a place of fire. John, who saw the end-time visions recorded in the last book of the Bible, also spoke of fire. He said the Devil will be thrown into "the lake of fire that burns with sulfur, joining the beast and the false prophet. There they will be tormented day and night forever and ever" (Revelation 20:10).

But some scholars wonder if this is figurative language that tries to

WHERE DID PURGATORY COME FROM?

Many believe that purgatory—a word that can mean "purge" or "cleanse"—is a place where Christians go after they die to purify themselves for heaven. From there, believers who committed only minor sins that were not forgiven on earth are quickly ushered into heaven. But Christians who committed serious sins have to linger and undergo punishment as penance.

The Roman Catholic Church and Eastern Orthodox churches teach that purgatory exists. They base the teaching partly on the fact that the book of 2 Maccabees which is part of their Old Testament though missing from most Protestant Bibles—tells of a Jewish commander offering sacrifices for the sins of the dead. Also, some early Christian leaders urged their people to pray for the souls of dead loved ones.

In the Middle Ages, many Catholic leaders used this belief for fund-raising. They sold indulgences—fast-pass tickets out of purgatory which the living could buy for the dead. Reformers—such as Martin Luther—said this was exploitive nonsense. And the Protestant churches were born.

describe a spiritual reality that earthbound humans can't really understand. After all, the Bible sometimes describes hell as a dark place—though fire dispels darkness. You can't have both.

Bible experts offer lots of theories about what hell is really like:

- It's a real place. And people who end up there suffer forever in flames.
- There's no physical fire, just the torment of being forever separated from God.
- Fire symbolizes annihilation. Sinners won't suffer endlessly. They'll be destroyed. And it's the destruction—not the suffering—that will last forever.
- God will keep even the sinners alive forever—not to punish them, but to allow reconciliation. (See *Gehenna; Hades*.)

HEROD AGRIPPA I
(HAIR uhd uh GRIP uh)
Herodes Agrippas, Greek
Reigned AD 37–44
First mention: Acts 12:1

The grandson of Herod the Great, Herod Agrippa is best known for being the first to execute one of Jesus' disciples. "He had the apostle James (John's brother) killed

Coins struck during the reign of Herod Agrippa I, the first ruler to execute a disciple of Jesus.

with a sword. When Herod saw how much this pleased the Jewish leaders, he arrested Peter" (Acts 12:2–3). An angel freed Peter.

Herod rose to power the same way his grandfather did—through Roman connections. Educated in Rome, he grew up with Caligula and Claudius, who became emperors. Caligula named Herod king over some of the Jewish territories, and Claudius later added the rest, uniting the Jews under one king for the first time since Herod the Great died nearly a half century earlier.

In AD 44, at age fifty-four, he got deathly sick after a crowd in Caesarea cheered him as a god. "An angel of the Lord struck Herod with a sickness, because he accepted the people's worship instead of giving the glory to God. So he was consumed with worms and died" (Acts 12:23). His grandfather died in a similar way, with maggot-infested gangrene.

HEROD AGRIPPA II
AD 28–93
First mention: Acts 25:13

Herod Agrippa II was only seventeen when his father, King Herod Agrippa I, died. Emperor Claudius, a close friend of Herod's father, wanted this young man educated in Rome to assume his father's throne. But advisers convinced Claudius that the boy was too young. Six years later, in AD 50, Claudius gave Herod some territory to rule in what is now Lebanon. Herod later traded that for regions in northern Israel and Syria.

Herod happened to visit Caesarea while Paul was in prison there, just before the apostle sailed to Rome and a trial in Caesar's court. Herod was intrigued by Paul's case and asked to hear what the apostle had to say for himself. Paul told his story about seeing Jesus while traveling to Damascus and about prophecies fulfilled by Jesus. When Paul asked if Herod believed the prophets, Herod replied, "Do you think you can make me a Christian so quickly?" (Acts 26:28).

John the Baptist criticizes Herod Antipas for breaking Jewish law by marrying his own brother's ex-wife.

Herod remained loyal to Rome—even when the Jews rebelled in AD 66 and temporarily overpowered Rome's occupying forces. For his loyalty, Herod received more territory and was allowed to rule until he died in AD 93.

HEROD ANTIPAS

(HAIR uhd AN tuh puhs)
Herodes Antipas, Greek
Reigned 4 BC–AD 39
First mention: Matthew 14:1

There are two reasons to remember Herod Antipas, son of Herod the Great.

• He ordered John the Baptist beheaded.

• He made fun of Jesus by dressing him in a royal robe on the morning of the Crucifixion.

Though Jesus once called him "the fox," it probably wasn't to compliment his cunning as much as to tag him a chicken thief. "Cunning" doesn't fit this ruler who got booted off his throne and exiled to France.

When Herod the Great died in 4 BC, he split his kingdom among his three sons. Antipas got a northern region, including Galilee, where Jesus lived. Although he called himself a Jew, Antipas built his capital in Tiberias, over a burial ground. Just walking there made a Jew unclean and unfit to worship God until cleaning rituals were completed. Antipas also divorced his wife and married his sister-in-law, Herodias.

This marriage upset many people, including Herod Agrippa I—the new

CAESAR'S OPINION OF HEROD

"I would rather be Herod's pig than his son!"

That's what Caesar Augustus said, according to Roman writer Macrobius, living in the AD 400s and apparently drawing on historical records.

What made the line funny was that it was true. As at least a marginally practicing Jew, Herod would never have ordered a pig butchered—pork wasn't kosher. But he ordered three of his sons executed.

bride's brother, who was also Antipas' nephew. He showed his disgust by later accusing Antipas of treason, eventually prompting Rome to exile Antipas.

John the Baptist was upset, too, insisting that it was against Jewish law for a man to marry his brother's wife. Herodias got John's head on a platter for that remark. Her daughter, Salome, danced so well at Antipas' birthday party that he offered her anything. She consulted her mother and requested John's head.

Later, Herod Antipas was in Jerusalem for the Passover celebration when Jewish leaders arrested Jesus and asked Pilate to crucify him. Since Jesus was from Galilee, Pilate sent him to Herod, who was delighted and hoped "to see him perform a miracle" (Luke 23:8).

Jesus just stood there. Herod dressed him in a king's robe and sent him back to Pilate—a joke that turned the two rulers into friends. Herod was deposed several years later, in AD 39, after Agrippa I convinced his childhood buddy, the new emperor Caligula, that Antipas was stockpiling weapons and making alliances to fight Rome. Agrippa got Antipas' territory.

HEROD THE GREAT
(HAIR uhd)
Herodes, Greek
Reigned 37–4 BC
First mention: Matthew 2:1

By the time King Herod tried to kill the baby Jesus in Bethlehem, Herod had already executed two of his own sons, one wife, and a mother-in-law for the same reason he tried to kill Jesus —to protect his hold on power as king of the Jews.

Wise men had arrived in Herod's Jerusalem capital from an eastern country—probably what is now Iran or Iraq. They said they had followed a new star and believed it marked the arrival of a future king, so they brought gifts and asked where the child was. Herod consulted with his scholars, who told him what ancient prophets had predicted: Israel's long-awaited Messiah king would be born in nearby Bethlehem.

Shrewdly, Herod told the visitors to go there and report back so he could honor the king, too. But God warned them in a dream not to return. So Herod ordered the slaughter of all Bethlehem boys ages two and under, since it was apparently two years earlier that the star first appeared. Joseph and his family escaped, however, fleeing to Egypt after God warned Joseph in a dream of Herod's plot.

Herod wasn't always as paranoid as he became during these, his senior years. But he was controlling and vicious from the earliest days of his political career. He probably felt he had to be. This king of the Jews, after all, was an Arab.

ROMAN CONNECTIONS

Jews never did warm up to Herod, an outsider from the neighboring nation of Edom, called in the New Testament by its Greek name, Idumea. Edomites once lived in what is now Jordan, but by New Testament times had migrated into southern Israel. How Herod got himself named king of the Jews is a tribute to his cunning, connections, and brutality.

About a century before Herod's birth in the late 70s BC, the Jews won a war of independence from Greek rulers who were trying to impose their religion on Israel. The Jews quickly imposed their religion on others, forcing the Edomites to convert—Herod's aristocratic forefathers among them. Herod's

grandfather and father both served as military commanders under the liberated Jews. But in a cunning move, Herod's father—Antipater—switched loyalties after Roman legions invaded Judea, their name for what is now the general region of Israel. He started fighting alongside the Romans because he considered them unstoppable.

As a reward, Rome appointed him military governor of Judea. Antipater named his oldest son—twenty-five-year-old Herod—governor of Galilee, a region in northern Israel. Herod soon made a name for himself by crushing a revolt and hunting down criminals.

A palace fortress called the Herodium once topped this artificial hill near Bethlehem. Herod the Great built it and used it as a quiet getaway.

When Antipater died of poisoning in 43 BC, descendants of the former Jewish rulers and freedom fighters allied themselves with Parthians—a kingdom in what is now Iran and Afghanistan—and staged a comeback. The Roman Senate retaliated by naming Herod king of the Jews and sending an army to wipe out the rebels.

HEROD'S MISERABLE DEATH

At about seventy years of age, King Herod died from what some physicians say could have been chronic kidney disease made worse by maggot-infested gangrene of the genitals.

Josephus, a Jewish historian writing a few decades after Herod, described the symptoms: "intense itching, painful intestinal problems, breathlessness, convulsions in every limb, and gangrene of the genitals."

Herod's gangrene, some doctors say, could have been caused by gonorrhea, persistent scratching, or an abdominal infection that spread to his groin.

It's hard to know how long Herod suffered. But Dr. Philip Mackowiak told ABC News at an annual conference to diagnose historical figures that it was "probably months, possibly a couple of years."

If the disease lasted two years, Herod's problems may have started at the birth of Jesus—when the wise men first saw the Star of Bethlehem.

SWAGGERING DICTATOR

Once in control of Jerusalem, in 37 BC, Herod moved quickly to silence dissension. Leaders he couldn't bribe into supporting him, he killed. He executed forty-five nobles who had backed the rebellion, then confiscated their wealth. He appointed an old friend as the Jewish high priest—though Jewish law called for this to be a lifetime office passed down from family to family.

Herod then married Mariamne, of the former Jewish ruling family, and a granddaughter of the former high priest. He thought this would help bridge the rift between him and the Jews. But Mariamne, whom Herod deeply loved, began lobbying for the rights of her Jewish family. She even went over Herod's head to the Roman commander Mark Antony, who controlled the Middle East, and succeeded in getting her teenaged brother named high priest. Mariamne's victory was short-lived—and so was her brother. Herod considered the seventeen-year-old boy a threat to his power and arranged to have servants drown him during a rough game in the Jericho palace pool.

Though Herod denied any connection to the "accident," Mariamne believed otherwise. In 29 BC, Herod accused his wife of adultery and of plotting to kill him. He had her executed but mourned her the rest of his life—even naming his next wife after her.

Grief didn't dull Herod's political senses. He proved this after finding himself on the losing side of a Roman civil war. His patron Mark Antony, along with Cleopatra, lost to Octavius—who became Emperor Augustus. Herod dressed himself in a slave's collar and pleaded his case to Octavius. The king of the Jews argued that he had been loyal to Antony when Antony was Rome's legally appointed leader of the region and that he would be loyal to any future leader Rome would appoint. Herod also reminded Octavius that Jewish forces hadn't actually fought in the battle between the two Roman generals.

Octavius allowed Herod to remain king of the Jews.

BUILDER KING

It took Herod about ten years—from 37 to 27 BC—to firm up his grip on the nation. That done, what followed were about fourteen years of prosperity along with furious and lavish building that would have shamed Solomon: temples, theaters, hippodromes for gladiator contests, miles of aqueducts to carry water, palaces, fortresses, even entire cities, and one artificial, flattop mountain he built as a combination palace and fortress: the Herodium, near Bethlehem.

In a nation without a harbor and a port city, Herod built both. And he named the city after Caesar: Caesarea—a Mediterranean jewel so beautiful and thoroughly Roman that Rome adopted it as capital of Judea.

Yet Herod's most famous project was thoroughly Jewish: the Jerusalem temple. He wanted to expand and re-model the existing temple. Babylonian invaders had destroyed Solomon's temple, and the Jews had rebuilt a modest one that needed repairs after nearly five hundred years.

Jerusalem's main hilltop wasn't big enough to accommodate Herod's vision. So he widened the hill by creating an earth platform shored up by retaining walls of massive stone blocks. One of these walls still exists as Judaism's most sacred site: the Western Wall (or Wailing Wall). This is all that remains of the Jewish temple. Romans destroyed the temple in AD 70 during a Jewish rebellion, and it has never been rebuilt. A thirteen-hundred-year-old Muslim shrine—the famous Dome of the Rock—now sits on the hilltop.

Many scholars say Herod's ambitious building program was all about himself—about wanting to rule a glorious kingdom. Even the temple, they suggest, was more practical than religious—a way to seduce the Jews. For compelling evidence that Herod's world revolved around himself, there's probably no better place to look than his family tree.

A KILLER FAMILY MAN

Whenever Herod thought people posed a risk to his dictatorial power, he killed them—family or not.

Here's a sampling of executed family members, most of whom had ties to his favorite wife who was the second of ten wives:

• Mariamne, his favorite wife

- Mariamne's grandfather, John Hyrcanus II, who had been high priest and a member of the ruling Jewish family before Rome took over
- Mariamne's mother, Alexandra
- Mariamne's brother, Aristobulus
- His two sons by Mariamne: Alexander and Aristobulus
- A third son, Antipater, by his first wife, Doris

When Herod died, he divided his kingdom among three of his four surviving sons. Herod II was disinherited. Herod Archelaus became king of Judea in southern Israel. Herod Antipas became ruler of Galilee in northern Israel and Perea, in what is now Jordan—but with the title of tetrarch, which carried less prestige than "king." Herod Philip ruled as tetrarch over several regions in what is now Syria.

Herod wanted people to grieve when he died—even if they weren't really grieving for him. So as death approached, he ordered Jewish nobles locked in a Jericho hippodrome. They were to be executed the moment he died. It was a godlike command reminiscent of Egypt's ego-driven pharaoh builders who took their servants to the grave with them.

The nobles, however, were freed. And Jews throughout the country celebrated the end of Herod's violent rule.

HERODIAS
(huh ROW dee us)
Herodias, Greek
Born about 8 BC
First mention: Matthew 14:3

A scheming woman, notorious for stopping at nothing to get her way, this granddaughter of Herod the Great managed to get the head of prophet John the Baptist on a platter.

In an arranged marriage, Herodias wed her half uncle who was Herod the Great's disinherited son: Herod II, also known as Philip. Herod II had a daughter by him—Salome. But when Herodias was approaching forty, she divorced Herod and married his more prosperous brother, Herod Antipas, ruler of Galilee.

Jewish law considered it incest for a man to marry his living brother's wife. John the Baptist condemned the marriage. For that, Herodias wanted him dead. But Antipas refused to kill the popular prophet. Herodias found a way. Salome danced so well at Antipas' birthday party that he offered her anything. Her mother told her to request John's head.

Herodias later talked Antipas into going to Rome to seek the title of king. She was jealous that her brother, Herod Agrippa I, was named king of a neighboring region. The strategy backfired. Agrippa accused Antipas of plotting to fight Rome. So Emperor Caligula—Agrippa's childhood friend—exiled Antipas to France in AD 39. Herodias joined him.

HERODIUM
(hair ROW dee um)

MAP 4
B5

When King Herod the Great wanted to get away from noisy Jerusalem, he sometimes traveled eight miles south to a hilltop palace he built beyond Bethlehem. This palace is not mentioned in the Bible. Called the Herodium, this monument to him looks like a hill with the peak sheared off. Tourists who climb the hill can walk down inside the hollowed-out top and explore the ruins, including a pool, a Roman bathhouse, mosaic pavement, and a synagogue. The palace was round, circled by double walls sixty yards in diameter, and guarded by four towers equally spaced around the walls.

Herod built the fortress on the site of a military victory that helped bring him to power. He enjoyed the palace so much that he chose it as his burial place. His tomb hasn't been found yet. Jews who rebelled against Rome took control of the fortress in AD 66 and held it until AD 72—two years longer than Jerusalem survived. (See photo phage 149.)

HEZEKIAH
(hez uh KIH uh)
Hizqiyahu, Hebrew
"strong"
Reigned 715–687 BC
First mention: 2 Kings 16:20

Survival of the Jews—threatened with extinction by the Assyrian Empire—depended on a twenty-five-year-old king. That was Hezekiah's age when he inherited Judah's throne from his father, King Ahaz.

The odds seemed stacked against young Hezekiah, in heaven and on earth.

God was upset because Hezekiah's father worshiped Canaanite gods, even sacrificing one of his own sons. And Judah followed the king's lead, abandoning God.

The threat on earth came from Assyrians who dominated the Middle East, forcing weaker nations like

Wading through knee high water, a visitor explores the spring-fed tunnel that King Hezekiah built to make sure Jerusalem had water during a siege.

153

HEZEKIAH'S TUNNEL

King Hezekiah didn't want his people inside Jerusalem to die of thirst, once Assyrian soldiers surrounded the city. It was a good guess the Assyrians would come since he intended to stop paying taxes to the empire. Unfortunately, there was no water source inside Jerusalem.

There was, however, a hidden spring just outside. So he put miners to work—one team chiseling through solid rock from the Siloam Pool inside the city and another team swinging picks from Gihon Spring. In a surprising feat of ancient engineering, they met in the middle of a 582-yard-long tunnel.

The tunnel was rediscovered in 1880, with a stone plaque briefly describing "the story of its cutting." Tourists have been wading through the tunnel ever since.

Judah to give up their independence and pay annual taxes to the empire. Rebellion was met with annihilation—as the northern Jewish nation of Israel discovered in 722 BC. Assyrian soldiers overran the Jewish cities, deported the captured people into what are now Syria, Iraq, and Iran, then repopulated the Jewish nation with Assyrian settlers.

Israel was off the map, and the southern Jewish nation of Judah seemed doomed to follow.

REDISCOVERING GOD

As the Bible tells it, Hezekiah's devotion to God produced miracles that allowed the young king to overcome the stacked odds.

Hezekiah didn't approve of his father's pagan religious practices, which included sex rituals. The first thing the Bible says Hezekiah did as king was to destroy pagan shrines throughout the country. He even crushed the more than seven-hundred-year-old bronze serpent that Moses had made because Jews were worshiping what they nicknamed "the Brass Thing."

"Hezekiah trusted in the LORD, the God of Israel. . . . He remained faithful to the LORD in everything, and he carefully obeyed all the commands the LORD had given Moses. So the LORD was with him, and Hezekiah was successful in everything he did" (2 Kings 18:5–7).

In a move that was politically risky, Hezekiah invited Jewish survivors in the northland—which Assyria had resettled—to worship in Jerusalem as their ancestors had done before the Jewish nation split in two. Assyria could have interpreted this as a first step toward resurrecting the united nation of Israel.

SAYING NO TO ASSYRIA

Like most rulers bullied by a foreign

nation, Hezekiah wanted to free his country. Though tiny Judah seemed no match for an empire stretching from Egypt in the west to Iran in the east, Hezekiah made plans to break free.

He reinforced Jerusalem's walls and added a second wall inside the first. He stockpiled weapons and food. He also built a tunnel to a hidden spring so the people inside Jerusalem would have water. In addition, he plugged and hid other springs surrounding the city so the invaders couldn't use them.

It's unclear exactly when Hezekiah started withholding Judah's imposed taxes to Assyria. But it was likely some time after the Assyrian emperor Sargon II died in a battle in 705 BC. Neighboring kingdoms joined the rebel movement, including Philistine cities and Tyre, in what is now Lebanon.

Sargon's son, Sennacherib, took on his father's dual role of emperor and tax collector. In 701 BC, he mobilized his fierce army and invaded what was left of the Jewish world after quickly crushing Tyre and Philistine rebels.

Sennacherib's own records tell the story in words and pictures: "I approached Ekron [a Philistine city] and killed the governors and nobles who had rebelled," reads a clay prism reporting the campaign, "and hung their bodies on stakes around the city." Horrifying images carved into stone and displayed as a trophy in the king's palace show similar scenes from the battle of Lachish, a Judean city about

thirty miles southwest of Jerusalem.

Forty-six walled cities of Judah fell, one by one, until only Jerusalem was left.

SAYING "I'M SORRY"

While Sennacherib was finishing off Lachish, Hezekiah sent him a message: "I have done wrong. I will pay whatever tribute money you demand if you will only go away" (2 Kings 18:14).

The angry Assyrian demanded a ton of gold and more than eleven tons of silver, forcing Hezekiah to empty both the palace and temple treasuries and to peel gold overlay off the temple doors.

Sennacherib accepted the wealth but came anyway—apparently to root out the source of the rebellion. His armies surrounded Jerusalem and began building dirt ramps that would allow attackers to charge up and over the city walls.

Representatives from both sides met outside the city to negotiate an end to hostilities. The Assyrian envoy spoke loudly and in Hebrew for the benefit of Jews listening on the walls. He told them to give up and accept deportation rather than death.

"Have the gods of any other nations ever saved their people from the king of Assyria?" barked the representative. "Name just one! So what makes you think that the LORD can rescue Jerusalem?" (2 Kings 18:33, 35).

The prophet Isaiah comforted

King Hezekiah: "This is what the LORD says: Do not be disturbed by this blasphemous speech against me from the Assyrian king's messengers. Listen! I myself will move against him, and the king will receive a report from Assyria telling him that he is needed at home. Then I will make him want to return to his land, where I will have him killed with a sword" (2 Kings 19:6–7).

That night, "the angel of the LORD" moved through the Assyrian camp (2 Kings 19:35). By daybreak, 185,000 soldiers were dead. Sennacherib hastily broke camp and scurried home, where he was murdered by two of his sons.

DEATHLY ILL

About this time Hezekiah became ill. Isaiah arrived with terrible news: "Set your affairs in order, for you are going to die. You will not recover from this illness" (2 Kings 20:1).

As Isaiah walked sadly away, Hezekiah began a prayer that changed his destiny. He asked God to remember his devotion and obedience. Isaiah didn't even get out of the palace before God gave him a new message.

KING IN A CAGE

"As for Hezekiah," the Assyrian king Sennacherib bragged, "I made [him] a prisoner in Jerusalem, his royal residence, like a bird in a cage. I surrounded him."

Sennacherib's bragging is preserved on a six-sided clay prism, commemorating his Judean invasion of 701 BC. (See photo page 342.) His words add credence to a remarkable Bible story about God miraculously scaring away the Assyrians, for although Sennacherib said he conquered forty-six cities, he stopped short of saying he conquered Jerusalem.

With good reason, according to the Bible: "The angel of the LORD went out to the Assyrian camp and killed 185,000 Assyrian troops. When the surviving Assyrians woke up the next morning, they found corpses everywhere. Then King Sennacherib of Assyria broke camp and returned to his own land" (2 Kings 19:35–36).

The Greek historian Herodotus, who wrote about 250 years later, added more support to the story. He said Sennacherib's army, headed for Egypt, was stopped one night by an invasion of mice. The mice ate bowstrings, leather shields, and other equipment and killed many soldiers. Some scholars suggest it's likely that the mice brought disease, such as the bubonic plague.

Hezekiah would live another fifteen years. To prove it, God made the shadow on some kind of a sundial—perhaps a staircase—move backward ten steps.

Later, representatives arrived from the emerging empire of Babylon. Hezekiah welcomed them and led them on a tour of his treasures. When Isaiah heard this, he predicted that one day Babylon would take all the Jewish treasures and lead Hezekiah's descendants into captivity. Though troubled by this news, which was fulfilled a century later, Hezekiah took comfort in the peace his people would enjoy during his lifetime.

After ruling Judah for twenty-nine years, Hezekiah died—revered as one of the godliest kings in Jewish history. His son, however, became one of the worst. Manasseh reverted to his grandfather's pagan religion, to the point of burning one of his sons as a sacrifice.

HIERAPOLIS
(HI ur OP o lis)
Hierapolis, Greek
"sacred city"
First mention: Colossians 4:13

MAP 5
C2

While sitting in prison awaiting trial, Paul wrote what became the New Testament letter to Christians in Colosse, in what is now Turkey. Paul expressed concern about heretical teachings worming their way into the church and neighboring churches, such as in Hierapolis, about twelve miles north. Ancient Hierapolis lies in ruins, probably

destroyed in an earthquake that devastated the region about the same time Paul wrote his letter, in AD 60.

HINNOM
(HEN nom)
Hinnom, Hebrew
First mention: Joshua 15:8

See Jerusalem

MAP 1
G5

In the Valley of Hinnom, in Jerusalem, at least two Jewish kings each burned one of his sons in sacrifice to Canaanite gods. The valley is better known by its Roman name, Gehenna, which is translated into English as *hell*.

By the time of Jesus, the valley had become a symbol of punishment that evil people can expect from God.

The infamous kings who led their people into human sacrifice were Ahaz and his grandson Manasseh. Surprisingly, Ahaz's son and Manasseh's father, Hezekiah—sandwiched between the two—was one of Israel's most revered kings.

The Hinnom valley, shaped like an L, ran for about half a mile alongside two of Jerusalem's ancient walls—west and south—before connecting with the larger Kidron valley that meanders at the foot of the Mount of Olives. The valley begins as a shallow trough outside what is now Jaffa Gate and gradually deepens into a gorge. (See *Gehenna; Hell.*)

HIRAM

(HI rum)
Hiram, Hebrew
"my brother is exalted"
Reigned about 969–936 BC
First mention: 2 Samuel 5:11

Arabs helped build Israel's first temple and palace. Hiram, king of the seaside city of Tyre in southern Lebanon, was a good friend of Israel's two most famous kings—David and Solomon. When David wanted a palace, Hiram sent him cedars of Lebanon, with carpenters and stonemasons.

Years later, Hiram did the same when Solomon wanted to build the temple. In return, Solomon sent Hiram food and ceded him twenty cities in northern Israel. In a profitable joint venture, Hiram provided sailors for Solomon's fleet of ships that brought back gold and other riches from the nation of Ophir, location unknown.

HOLY SPIRIT

Ruah, Hebrew
Pneuma, Greek
"wind" or "breath"
First mention: Genesis 1:2

Classic paintings don't do justice to family portraits of God the Father, Son, and Holy Spirit. They're usually painted as two men and a bird.

There's a reason for that.

The Bible says the Father and Son each took human form at one time or another. But the closest the Bible comes to describing the Spirit as a physical being is when the Spirit showed up at the baptism of Jesus: "The Holy Spirit descended on him in the form of a dove" (Luke 3:22). Many scholars argue that the translators got this scene wrong and that the Spirit descended as gracefully as a dove—not in the feathered form of a dove.

The image of a dove isn't normally how the Bible describes the Spirit. Unfortunately, the more common description isn't suitable for framing. He's invisible—often described as wind or breath, which is the literal meaning of "spirit."

As hard as it is to describe the Spirit, it's perhaps just as hard to explain what he does. That's because it seems as though his work has changed over the ages.

SPIRIT OF CREATION

In the beginning, it's sometimes tricky to tell the difference between God and the Holy Spirit.

For one thing, their names—"Spirit of God" and "Spirit of the Lord"—often seem woven together. "Holy Spirit" appears only three times in the Old Testament (Psalm 51:11; Isaiah 63:10, 11).

For another thing, their names sometimes seem interchangeable. One example: When "God created the heavens and the earth. . .the Spirit of God was hovering over its [earth's] surface" (Genesis 1:1–2).

It would be easy to read those two references to God as though the writer were talking about one entity, since

SEEING GOD FACE-TO-FACE

"You may not look directly at my face," God told Moses, "for no one may see me and live" (Exodus 33:20).

That seems a strange thing to say since the Bible reports elsewhere that Moses and others did talk with God "face to face."

- "I have seen God face to face," Jacob said after wrestling a mysterious man, "yet my life has been spared" (Genesis 32:30).
- "Inside the Tent of Meeting, the LORD would speak to Moses face to face, as a man speaks to his friend" (Exodus 33:11).

God can certainly present himself in ways that humans can handle: visions, voices, even in physical form as a traveler eating with Abraham (Genesis 18). But His celestial appearance—perhaps similar to the glowing form of Jesus during the Transfiguration—is something humans apparently can't handle.

God is a spirit being. But the general agreement among scholars is that this Spirit is the one later identified as the third person in the Godhead. If so, this verse places the Holy Spirit at the Creation, just as John's Gospel does for Jesus. "He created everything there is" (John 1:3).

Three divine persons at Creation spawned a theory that God was referring to all three when he said, "Let us make people in our image, to be like ourselves" (Genesis 1:26). Other theories, however, suggest that the three-in-one God may have been addressing the heavenly court, or perhaps using the plural to identify himself as royalty—just as rulers sometimes did.

SPIRIT FOR EXTRAORDINARY PEOPLE

The Spirit wasn't available to just anyone in Old Testament times. Kings, prophets, champion warriors, and people in extraordinary circumstances were the only ones receiving the Spirit, as far as the Bible reports.

The Spirit could:

- Remain with a person for life, as with Israel's most celebrated king, David: "And the Spirit of the LORD came mightily upon him from that day on" (1 Samuel 16:13).
- Leave when a person disobeyed God: "Now the Spirit of the LORD had left Saul" (1 Samuel 16:14).

- Prepare a warrior for battle: "Then the Spirit of the LORD took possession of Gideon. He blew a ram's horn as a call to arms" (Judges 6:34).
- Inspire ordinary people to deliver messages from God: "The Spirit of God came upon Saul's men, and they also began to prophesy" (1 Samuel 19:20).

SPIRIT FOR EVERYONE

In time, one prophet said, this would all change. God's Spirit would be available to everyone: "I will pour out my Spirit upon all people. Your sons and daughters will prophesy. Your old men will dream dreams. Your young men will see visions. In those days, I will pour out my Spirit even on servants, men and women alike" (Joel 2:28–29).

Disciples of Jesus marked this event fifty days after the Crucifixion and ten days after Jesus ascended into heaven. Jesus had told his followers to go to Jerusalem during the springtime festival of Pentecost. There they would receive a "Counselor, who will never leave you. He is the Holy Spirit, who leads into all truth" (John 14:16–17).

The Spirit caught their attention when he arrived. "Suddenly, there was a sound from heaven like the roaring of a mighty windstorm in the skies above them, and it filled the house where they were meeting. Then, what looked like flames or tongues of fire appeared and settled on each of them. And everyone present was filled with the Holy Spirit and began speaking in other languages, as the Holy Spirit gave them this ability" (Acts 2:2–4).

With what appears to have been a temporary gift of language skills, the disciples began telling the festival pilgrims about Jesus—speaking in the pilgrims' own languages.

From that day on, the Bible says the Spirit has been available to everyone—with one condition, identified by Peter in an astonishing sermon he preached that day. "Each of you must turn from your sins and turn to God, and be baptized in the name of Jesus

In the form of a dove, the Holy Spirit descends at the baptism of Jesus.

Christ for the forgiveness of your sins. Then you will receive the gift of the Holy Spirit. This promise is to you and to your children, and even to the Gentiles—all who have been called by the Lord our God" (Acts 2:38–39).

Three thousand people that day followed Peter's advice, and the Christian church was born.

Several years later, Paul taught what it meant to be filled with the Holy Spirit. "When the Holy Spirit controls our lives, he will produce this kind of fruit in us: love, joy, peace, patience, kindness, goodness, faithfulness, gentleness, and self-control" (Galatians 5:22–23).

HOPHNI

(HOFF nee)
Hopni, Hebrew
"tadpole"
1100s BC
First mention: 1 Samuel 1:3

Though there were good priests in ancient Israel, Hophni wasn't one of them. Neither was his brother Phinehas.

These sons of the devout priest Eli "were scoundrels who had no respect for the LORD" (1 Samuel 2:12). They exploited their office, seducing women who worked at the worship center and helping themselves to the most savory sacrificial meat, intended for God. Both died in a battle with the Philistines while carrying the chest that held the Ten Commandments. When ninety-eight-year-old Eli got the news, he fell backward off his seat and died of a broken neck.

HOSEA

(ho ZAY uh)
Hosea, Hebrew
"the Lord has saved us"
700s BC
First mention: Hosea 1:1

So deplorable was God's request to the prophet Hosea that many Bible scholars don't believe it. It's a parable, they say. It never really happened.

The request? "Marry a prostitute, so some of her children will be born to you from other men. This will illustrate the way my people have been untrue to me, openly committing adultery against the LORD by worshiping other gods" (Hosea 1:2).

HUSBAND AND FATHER

The Bible says almost nothing about Hosea's background. But it does place him in the final decades of the northern Jewish nation of Israel. God brought this shocking request to Hosea sometime during the reign of King Jeroboam II (786–746 BC). Clues in the story—scenes of prosperity and complacency—suggest it was near the end of this king's golden reign. The nation disappeared in 722 BC, after Assyria invaded.

"Hosea married Gomer, the daughter of Diblaim, and she became pregnant and gave Hosea a son" (Hosea 1:3). That's the first of three children—and the only one identified as Hosea's. Yet the grammar doesn't guarantee that even this child was legitimate. In some ancient manuscripts, Hosea isn't mentioned in any of the pregnancies.

God gave each child a symbolic name to convey a message about Israel's doom.

- *Jezreel* means "God sows," as in scattering seeds. The name certainly describes what happened to the Jews: Abraham's seed was deported and scattered abroad. But Jezreel valley was also where Assyria robbed Israel of independence by crushing their armies in 733 BC.
- *Lo-ruhamah* means "not loved," showing that God rejected Israel.
- *Lo-ammi* means "not my people," which is God's description of Israel.

RUNAWAY BRIDE

Gomer disappears in chapter 1. Hosea may have run her off because of her habitual adultery, as chapter 2 implies: "Call Israel to account, for she is no longer my wife, and I am no longer her husband" (Hosea 2:2).

Whatever happened, God told Hosea to buy Gomer back. Apparently, she sold herself into slavery. Hosea bought her for a few ounces of silver, five bushels of barley, and some wine.

God's reasoning: "For the LORD still loves Israel even though the people have turned to other gods" (Hosea 3:1).

Though both Jewish nations—Israel in the north and Judah in the south—would cease to exist, with their survivors dragged off like slaves, God would one day bring the Jews back home. "Then I will heal you of your idolatry and faithlessness, and my love will know no bounds" (Hosea 14:4).

HOSHEA
(ho SHE uh)
Hosea, Hebrew
"salvation"
Reigned 732–724 BC
First mention: 2 Kings 15:30

Though his name means "salvation," King Hoshea turned the lights out on the northern Jewish nation of Israel. His actions prodded Assyria to wipe Israel off the map by deporting the Jews and repopulating the land with Assyrian settlers.

Hoshea assassinated King Pekah in 732 BC to capture the kingdom, which by that time was a taxpaying servant of Assyria. When Assyria's leader died, Hoshea stopped paying taxes and sought an alliance with Egypt. Assyria's new ruler, Shalmaneser, overran Israel and imprisoned Hoshea.

IBLEAM

(IB lee uhm)
Yibleam, Hebrew
First mention: Joshua 17:11

Two Jewish kings died on the same day after a surprise attack near Ibleam, a town today called Belameh, which guards a mountain pass in northern Israel.

The attacker was Jehu, a military commander. The prophet Elijah told Jehu to kill King Joram, son of Ahab and Jezebel. At the time, the king had a visitor—his cousin, King Ahaziah, of the southern Jewish nation of Judah.

Jehu and his men got in chariots and drove frantically toward Jezreel. When a watchman on the tower recognized the frenzied driving style of Jehu and reported in, the two kings climbed in their chariots and rushed to meet him. Jehu shot Joram dead. Then Jehu and his men chased Ahaziah across the Jezreel valley for about five miles before getting close enough to shoot him. Wounded, the king drove another ten miles before dying at Megiddo.

ICONIUM

MAP 5
D2

(eye CONE ee uhm)
Ikonion, Greek
First mention: Acts 13:51

On their first missionary trip, Paul and Barnabas narrowly escaped getting stoned to death in Iconium, a city in what is now Turkey.

Their preaching about Jesus divided the citizens, and a mob decided to kill them. Fortunately, the two heard about it and headed to Lystra. Unfortunately, Jews from Iconium followed. They convinced people at Lystra to stone Paul and leave him for dead. He recovered. The persistent pair moved on to the next city before backtracking to check on their new converts—including those at Lystra and Iconium.

IDUMEA

MAP 4
A6

(id you ME uh)
Idoumaia, Greek
First mention: Mark 3:8

When Babylon wiped out the Jewish nation in 586 BC, some Arab neighbors in what is now Jordan started moving in. *Idumea* is the Greek name for Edom, a nation descended from Esau. By the time of Jesus, the migration was so complete that Idumea had become a strip of land from the Dead Sea to the Mediterranean Sea, encompassing cities such as Hebron, Gaza, and Arad. Herod the Great, king of the Jews, was an Idumean Arab. Jews considered him an outsider, though his family had converted to Judaism a century earlier.

ILLYRICUM

(ill LEER uh cum)
Illyrikon, Greek
First mention: Romans 15:19

MAP 5
A1

In his letter to Christians in Rome, Paul said he had preached "from Jerusalem clear over into Illyricum" (Romans 15:19). Illyricum was a Roman district between Italy and Greece, along the coastline of what is now the Balkans. Among several countries there now are Croatia and Yugoslavia. Other reports place Paul in neighboring Macedonia, but this is the only clue that he made a trip to Illyricum that wasn't reported elsewhere.

IMMANUEL

(em MAN u el)
Immanuel, Hebrew
"God is with us"
First mention: Isaiah 7:14

In a cave beneath Bethlehem's Church of the Nativity is this altar—marking the place where ancient tradition says Jesus was born.

"Look! The virgin will conceive a child! She will give birth to a son and will call him Immanuel—'God is with us' " (Isaiah 7:14).

The virgin wasn't Mary. And Immanuel wasn't Jesus. Not in the original story written seven hundred years before Jesus.

Isaiah was talking about a woman in his own time, perhaps his own wife or a new wife of Ahaz, king of the southern Jewish nation of Judah. The birth was a sign, intended to convince the king that God would help Judah. Ahaz was worried about being overrun by coalition forces from Syria and the northern Jewish nation of Israel. So he was planning to ask Assyria for help. Isaiah advised against it, insisting that before Immanuel was old enough to eat honey, the kings of Syria and Israel would be dead. Ahaz called on Assyria anyhow, costing Judah its independence.

Scholars debate whether the Hebrew term for the child's mother should be translated *young woman* or *virgin.* It can work either way. But Jewish scholars who translated the Hebrew Scriptures into Greek more than two hundred years before Jesus chose *virgin.* Perhaps they believed that in the original story, the mother-to-be was still a virgin when Isaiah spoke the prophecy.

New Testament writers clearly saw a double meaning to the prophecy. When Matthew told the story of how Jesus was born to an unmarried virgin, he quoted

Isaiah's prophecy and said it happened this way "to fulfill the Lord's message through his prophet" (Matthew 1:22).

ISAAC
(EYE. zack)
Yishaq, Hebrew
 he laughs
2000s BC
First mention: Genesis 17:19

Isaac was an unbuttered bagel kind of a guy. Plain. That's why we have the old saying: "An Abraham is usually followed by an Isaac."

Abraham was exciting. He ventured into unknown territory, chased down a raiding party to take back what they stole, and fathered a son at age one hundred. Isaac, however, stayed on familiar turf, backed away from shepherds who took control of his wells, and didn't get married until after his mother died—when he was forty.

As for his bride, who moved five hundred miles to marry him sight unseen, the Bible leaves the distinct impression that she married a momma's boy: "Isaac brought Rebekah into his mother's tent, and she became his wife. He loved her very much, and she was a special comfort to him after the death of his mother" (Genesis 24:67).

Yet he became part of the father, son, and grandson trio—Abraham, Isaac, and Jacob—famed for starting the Jewish nation.

HAPPY BIRTHDAY
God named the boy Isaac, which means "laughter." The question is: Why this name?

Was it because when God announced that Abraham would have a son, the one-hundred-year-old patriarch "laughed to himself in disbelief" (Genesis 17:17)? That's when God named Isaac. Or was it because when ninety-year-old Sarah overheard God repeating this to Abraham, "she laughed silently to herself" (Genesis 18:12)? Or perhaps it was because God knew that Isaac's birthday would be happy: "Sarah declared, 'God has brought me laughter! All who hear about this will laugh with me. For who would have dreamed that I would ever have a baby?'" (Genesis 21:6–7).

Sarah had given up hope of being a mother.

At the last moment, an angel stops Abraham from sacrificing his son Isaac.

In her midseventies, she persuaded Abraham to use her servant as a surrogate mother. Ishmael was born. But after she had Isaac, she convinced Abraham to send the servant and Ishmael away so Isaac wouldn't have to share his inheritance. God promised to take care of both sons.

Years later, God tested Abraham's faith by asking him to sacrifice the boy. Abraham agreed. Jewish legends say Isaac was thirty-seven at the time and that when 127-year-old Sarah found out about Abraham's intention, she died. Abraham didn't have to go through with the sacrifice; an angel stopped him at the last moment.

Many scholars see in this dramatic story a foreshadowing of the Crucifixion. What Abraham was willing to do —sacrifice his son—God did.

FAMILY MAN

Isaac mourned his mother for three years. That's when Abraham decided Isaac needed a wife. Abraham didn't want a Canaanite daughter-in-law. So he sent his most trusted servant on a wife-hunt to the family in Haran, a city in what is now Turkey. The servant came back with Rebekah.

Rebekah was so beautiful that Isaac found himself repeating a lie his father told. To wait out a famine, Isaac and Rebekah moved to the city of Gerar, on the southern coastal plain. He told everyone that Rebekah was his sister—so no one would kill him to get her. When the king learned the truth, he ordered that no one harm either of them.

Isaac's crops and herds grew so well that the neighbors got jealous and the king asked him to leave. Isaac moved to a valley outside of town and reopened a well his father had dug. But local shepherds said it was theirs. Isaac reopened another of his father's wells. The same thing happened. Isaac dug a third well and got to keep it.

After twenty years of marriage, when Isaac was sixty, Rebekah delivered twin boys, Esau and Jacob. God told Rebekah that the older twin would serve the younger. Perhaps that's why she preferred the younger, Jacob, who tended to stay close to camp. Isaac grew partial to Esau, a hunter who brought wild game for him to eat.

When Isaac grew old and blind and thought he was about to die, he asked Esau to get him some game to eat. Afterward, he would give Esau the irrevocable blessing that transferred family leadership to him. While Esau hunted, Rebekah apparently decided to help God put Jacob in charge. She cooked a meal, dressed Jacob in Esau's clothes, and tied goatskin on his arm to mimic Esau's hairy arms. Then Jacob pretended to be Esau. It worked. But when Esau found out, he vowed to kill Jacob.

Jacob left for Rebekah's homeland on the pretense of looking for a wife. By the time he came back, twenty years later, Esau's anger had faded. But Rebekah had died. Isaac, however, was still alive. He lived to age 180 and died at his camp near Hebron, where his sons buried him.

ISAIAH

(eye ZAY uh)
Yesayahu, Hebrew
"God is salvation"
About 740–700 BC
First mention: 2 Kings 19:2

More than seven hundred years before Jesus was born, a Jerusalem prophet named Isaiah wrote like he knew Jesus as well as any disciple ever would.

"The virgin will conceive a child! She will give birth to a son and will call him Immanuel—'God is with us'" (Isaiah 7:14).

"For a child is born to us, a son is given to us. And the government will rest on his shoulders. These will be his royal titles: Wonderful Counselor, Mighty God, Everlasting Father, Prince of Peace" (Isaiah 9:6).

"Out of the stump of David's family will grow a shoot. . . . The Spirit of the LORD will rest on him. . . . He will never judge by appearance, false evidence, or hearsay. He will defend the poor and the exploited" (Isaiah 11:1–4).

"He was wounded and crushed for our sins. He was beaten that we might have peace. He was whipped, and we were healed! . . . He was led as a lamb to the slaughter. And as a sheep is silent before the shearers, he did not open his mouth. From prison and trial they led him away to his death. . . . He was buried like a criminal; he was put in a rich man's grave" (Isaiah 53:5, 7–9).

No wonder New Testament writers quoted Isaiah's book more than any other—about fifty times—or that scholars have nicknamed it "the Fifth Gospel."

A PROPHET IN THE ROYAL FAMILY?
The Bible says very little about Isaiah, but there are clues that he was at least an educated noble and perhaps a relative of the kings he served—four in all: Uzziah, Jotham, Ahaz, and Hezekiah.

For one thing, the eloquence of his language points to a privileged education. For another, he had easy access to the kings. In addition, Jewish tradition suggests that Isaiah's father, Amoz, was the brother of King Amaziah—Uzziah's father. If so, King Uzziah and

On the ceiling of the Sistine Chapel hovers one of Michelangelo's masterpieces—a portrait of the prophet Isaiah.

167

ISAIAH'S FAMILY

Isaiah was the father of at least two sons. Like some of the other prophets, Isaiah gave his children symbolic names.

Maher-shalal-hash-baz was one of Isaiah's boys. His name is the longest word in the Bible. More like a sentence, it means "swift to plunder and quick to spoil." It was Isaiah's way of assuring the king that he didn't need to worry about his enemies to the north: Syria and Israel. Assyria would invade and plunder them.

Shear-jashub was his second son. The name means "a remnant will return." This referred to Jewish survivors who would one day return to Israel and devote themselves to God.

Isaiah were first cousins.

Isaiah's forty-year ministry began in the southern Jewish nation of Judah about 740 BC, "in the year King Uzziah died" (Isaiah 6:1). That was about twenty years before Assyria destroyed the northern Jewish nation of Israel, and about 150 years before Babylon destroyed Isaiah's homeland of Judah.

Decimation of his homeland was exactly where Isaiah's ministry pointed. He knew that from the beginning, because of a dramatic vision. Isaiah had apparently gone to the Jerusalem temple to worship. While he was there he saw God sitting on a throne and surrounded by heavenly beings. God asked who would carry his message to the people. Isaiah volunteered. That's when God gave young Isaiah the discouraging news: The people would reject his message.

Isaiah asked how long he had to preach doom.

"Until their cities are destroyed, with no one left in them," God replied (Isaiah 6:11).

If Isaiah had any hope of helping turn the Jews back to God, he was to abandon all hope.

WATCHING ISRAEL FALL

Knowing where the Jewish nations were headed, Isaiah generally advised the kings to keep a low profile when it came to dealing with the superpowers. For example, he wasted his breath trying to talk King Ahaz out of asking for Assyria's help in fighting off the combined armies of Syria and Israel. Those two nations were trying to break free of Assyrian domination, and Ahaz refused to join the rebellion. So they vowed to overthrow Ahaz.

Isaiah advised Ahaz not to worry about them, and he offered a sign that New Testament writers later saw as having a second meaning, pointing to Jesus. "The virgin will conceive a child! She will give birth to a son and will call him Immanuel—'God is with us'" (Isaiah 7:14). By the time this child is weaned from milk, Isaiah promised, the kings of Syria and Israel will be dead.

Ahaz ignored the advice. Assyria overpowered the northern nations, eliminating Israel from the world map in 722 BC, but at tremendous cost to Judah: the nation's independence. Assyria forced the Jews to start paying heavy annual taxes.

NAKED IN JERUSALEM

Isaiah often used signs and symbolism to get his point across. Once, he spent three years walking around Jerusalem naked, or perhaps in a loincloth like a slave. He was trying to talk King Hezekiah out of signing a treaty with Egypt. Hezekiah wanted protection against Assyria. Isaiah's point was that God would allow Assyria to take the Egyptians captive. So there was no point in depending on them. Instead, the Jews were to have faith in God. Hezekiah followed the prophet's advice.

That advice was tested when Assyrian soldiers surrounded Jerusalem in 701 BC and warned that God couldn't protect the people. Isaiah assured Hezekiah that the enemy wouldn't get inside the city. "That night the angel of the LORD went out to the Assyrian camp and killed 185,000 Assyrian troops" (Isaiah 37:36). An Assyrian document from the time confirms that soldiers surrounded the city, but it stops short of saying they got inside. (See *Hezekiah*.)

DID ISAIAH WRITE THE ENTIRE BOOK?

Many scholars say Isaiah didn't write all sixty-six chapters. Instead, some experts suggest, there were at least two writers, and perhaps three.

The problem is that only the first thirty-nine chapters seem set in Isaiah's lifetime. Chapters 40 through 55 seem set 150 years later, after Babylon wiped out Judah and took the survivors captive to the Babylonian homeland in what is now Iraq. Chapters 56 through 66 seem set even further in the future, after Persia overran Babylon and freed the Jews to go home. In an unprecedented prophecy, Isaiah even named the Persian leader who would free the Jews—Cyrus (Isaiah 45:13). And that leads some to think the material was written as history instead of prophecy.

Other Bible experts, however, say God could have allowed Isaiah to see these future events. And they argue that the writing style is similar throughout. In addition, they note that the oldest copy of Isaiah—found among the Dead Sea Scrolls and written about 100 BC—shows no break that would suggest two or three books instead of one.

GOOD NEWS AHEAD

Though Isaiah contains plenty of bad news for the Jews as well as their enemies, that's not the end of the story.

The Jewish nation would be dismantled. And so would the empires that waged war against it. In addition, there would be global devastation: "Look! The LORD is about to destroy the earth and make it a vast wasteland" (Isaiah 24:1). Bible experts call chapters 24 through 27 the Apocalypse of

A B C D E F G H I J K L M N O P Q R S T U V W X Y Z

Isaiah, and they wonder if this is talking about end times ahead rather than Israel's ancient history.

The good news is that God's people will return to Jerusalem, free from slavery.

This prophecy seems to work on several levels. It could refer to Israel's Old Testament history, because they did return in the early 500s BC. It could also refer to freedom from slavery to sin because of the "Suffering Servant" passage that New Testament writers said pointed to Jesus: "He was wounded and crushed for our sins" (Isaiah 53:5). It might also refer to events described in Revelation, at the end of human history, when the people of God make their eternal home with the Lord in a new and improved Jerusalem: "I will rebuild you [Jerusalem] on a foundation of sapphires and make the walls of your houses from precious jewels" (Isaiah 54:11).

ISAIAH SAWED IN TWO

The Bible doesn't say how Isaiah died. But another ancient Jewish book does. It is known as the *Martyrdom and Ascension of Isaiah*. Many scholars say a Jew living in what is now Israel probably wrote this book no later than the first Christian century and perhaps much earlier.

According to this book, Isaiah was arrested during the reign of Hezekiah's son Manasseh, the most notorious king of Judah. Isaiah was charged with falsely predicting the destruction of Judah, and he was ordered to repeat these words: "Everything I said has been lies, and Manasseh is good."

He refused, and an executioner used a wooden saw to cut him in two. Absorbed in a vision, Isaiah's eyes stayed open and he didn't cry out in pain. But his lips moved as though he was talking with God.

The Jewish Talmud, a collection of sacred laws, history, and commentaries, preserves this story. Hebrews 11:37 seems to refer to this execution, as well. Speaking of Old Testament heroes, the writer says, "Some were sawed in half."

ISHBOSHETH

(ish BO sheth)
Isboset, Hebrew
"man of shame"
Ruled about 1010–1008 BC
First mention: 1 Samuel 14:49

With King Saul and three of his sons dead on the battlefield, killed by the Philistines, Saul's general appointed the next king, Ishbosheth, one of Saul's surviving sons. Jews in the south, however, crowned their own king, David the giant killer.

Ishbosheth was a nervous king, afraid of his military. He had a right to be. Two years into his shaky reign, two of his commanders sneaked into his house during his afternoon nap. They cut off his head and carried it as a trophy to David. They thought David would be pleased to have revenge on the family of

Saul, who had tried to kill him. Instead, David responded the same way he did earlier when a man claimed to have finished off Saul. He ordered the confessed king killers executed.

ISHMAEL
(ISH mail)
Yismael, Hebrew
"God hears"
2000s BC
First mention: Genesis 16:11

In the green of early spring, a shepherd watches his sheep graze in pastures of the Jordan River valley.

Ishmael, Abraham's first son, is considered the father of the Arab people. God had promised to make Abraham's family into a vast nation. But when Abraham's wife, Sarah, reached her midseventies without children, she resorted to an ancient Middle Eastern custom. She used her slave maid, Hagar, as a surrogate mother. Ishmael was born. About fourteen years later, Sarah gave birth to Isaac and convinced Abraham to send Hagar and Ishmael away.

God promised to make nations of both sons. Hagar and Ishmael moved south, near the Sinai, where Ishmael became an expert archer and married an Egyptian. He apparently stayed in touch with his brother, since they both buried Abraham. Ishmael lived to age 137 and became the father of twelve sons, who founded twelve tribes scattered from Egypt to Arabia.

ISRAEL
(IS ray uhl)
Yisrael, Hebrew
Israel, Greek
Possibly "God struggles" or "one who struggles with God"
First mention: Genesis 32:28

MAP 1, MAP 2

Israel began in violence some thirty-four hundred years ago when the walls of Jericho came tumbling down. After all this time, Jews are still fighting for the Promised Land and for the right to exist as a nation.

Even the name of the country comes from violence—an all-night fight between Jacob and a mysterious heavenly being that many scholars say was God in human form. Jacob wanted a blessing, and he wouldn't let go of the man until he got it. " 'Your name will no longer be Jacob,' the man told him. 'It is now Israel, because you have struggled with both God and men and have won' " (Genesis 32:28).

When Joshua led Jacob's descendants in conquering what was then

BIBLE EVENTS:

- God promises the land to Abraham's descendants
- Jacob takes his family to Egypt to escape drought
- Moses brings the Hebrews home from Egyptian slavery
- Joshua conquers much of the central highlands
- Saul becomes first king of Israel
- Israel splits, with Judah in the south, Israel in the north
- Israel wiped out by the Assyrians, and Judah by the Babylonians
- Jews rebuild Israel
- Rome invades and occupies
- Jesus ministers
- Christian church is born

HOLY SITES:

- Bethlehem, birthplace of Jesus
- Nazareth, where Jesus grew up
- Jerusalem, where Jesus was crucified, buried, and resurrected

STATISTICS:

- Modern Exodus—Zionist movement in late 1800s urges Jews to settle in Palestine
- Modern Israel formed—1948
- Size of land—About 250 miles north to south and 70 miles at its widest, roughly the size of New Jersey
- Population—6.5 million
- Immigrants since 1948—3 million
- Location—East coast of Mediterranean Sea, surrounded by four Arab nations: Lebanon, Syria, Jordan, Egypt

called Canaan, he divided the land among the twelve tribes—extended families descended from Jacob's twelve sons. Each tribe was assigned some territory, and the coalition took the name of their shared ancestor—Israel.

IN BIBLE TIMES

From chaos to kings. Joshua's generation didn't capture all the land, or even the best land. They were confined mostly to the stretch of hills that ran alongside the Jordan River and to a barren tract of land beside the Dead Sea. Yet unconquered were Canaan's rich pasturage in the sprawling Jezreel valley up north and fertile plains along the seacoast that had been taken over by other new arrivals, the Philistines.

Rather than unite to finish the job, each tribe had to conquer its own territory. It didn't happen. The tiny tribe of Dan, assigned mainly to Philistine territory, packed up and moved a hundred miles north, to the fringes of Canaan beyond the Sea of Galilee.

Moses had warned the Israelites to get rid of all the Canaanites: "This will keep the people of the land from teaching you their detestable customs in the worship of their gods, which would cause you to sin deeply against the LORD your God" (Deuteronomy 20:18).

Instead, the Israelites learned to live with the Canaanites and began picking up bad habits—like worshiping idols.

A violent cycle followed:

- God punished Israel by allowing a Canaanite neighbor to oppress certain tribes.
- The Israelites prayed for deliverance.
- God sent heroes such as Gideon and Samson.
- The Israelites went back to sinning.

This happened over and over, as reported in Judges. The last word in that report is chaos: "In those days Israel had no king, so the people did whatever seemed right in their own eyes" (Judges 21:25).

Actually, God considered himself Israel's king. So when tribal leaders asked for a king, God's elderly prophet and spokesman—Samuel—took it personally. But God consoled him: "It is me they are rejecting, not you. They don't want me to be their king any longer" (1 Samuel 8:7).

Israel crowned Saul their first king in about 1050 BC. He died in battle against the Philistines. The two kings who followed are the most acclaimed in Jewish history. David united the tribes, overpowered the Philistines, and established Jerusalem as the nation's capital. He also stretched Israel's boundaries deep into what is now Syria and Jordan. David's son, Solomon, lived off the

Father and daughter wait for customers at their street-side market in Jerusalem. In Bible times, as today, Jerusalem's streets bustled with trade.

prosperity of those conquered cities, along with income from trade routes he controlled and heavy taxes he imposed on his people. With these resources, he built Israel's first temple, along with a palace and fortresses.

One nation becomes two. Solomon's people weren't impressed. They paid the bills—in taxes and forced labor. When Solomon's son and successor threatened more of the same, ten northern tribes broke from the union, chose their own king, and started their own nation—which they called Israel. The two southern tribes took their name from the larger tribe, Judah. David's descendants ruled them in Jerusalem.

Two nations become none. Israel in the north not only broke from the union; they broke from God. Their king set up idols so his people wouldn't go back to the Jerusalem temple. He didn't want any chance of reunification. Rulers who followed him were generally godless people such as Ahab and Jezebel. Many of David's descendants were just as bad. Godly Hezekiah's son, Manasseh, was perhaps the most notorious of all Jewish kings. Obsessed with idolatry and the occult, he burned his own son in sacrifice to a Canaanite god.

God had an agreement with the Jews. If they followed his rules—summed up nicely in the Ten Commandments—"The LORD will conquer your enemies when they attack you" (Deuteronomy 28:7). But for disobedience, "The LORD will exile you" (Deuteronomy 28:36).

God tried to win the people back. He sent prophets with warnings. He even sent plagues and disease—a bit like warning shots over a ship's bow. Finally, in 722 BC, he allowed the Assyrians to overrun Israel, deport all but the poorest citizens, and repopulate the land with Assyrian settlers. Nearly the same thing happened to Judah more than a century later. Babylon leveled Jerusalem and exiled the people in 586 BC.

There was no Jewish nation left on the map.

About fifty years later, Persia defeated Babylon and freed the exiles to go home. The Jews rebuilt Jerusalem and the temple, along with other cities. But they remained under the authority of the Persians, then the Greeks led by Alexander the Great. In 142 BC, the Jews won a war of independence from Alexander's successors. The Jewish nation was free for the first time in nearly 450 years.

Roman Israel. Freedom lasted about eighty years. The Romans arrived in 63 BC, annexed the land, and forced the people to pay taxes to support the empire.

A century later, the Jews were weary of mistreatment and occupation. In AD 66, they drove the Romans out of Judea, as the Romans called the region. Four years later, the Romans were back in force, destroying Jerusalem and leveling what became the last Jewish temple. It was never rebuilt.

AFTER BIBLE TIMES

Banned from Jerusalem. After a second Jewish revolt in AD 131, Rome banned Jews from Jerusalem and renamed the region *Palestine,* after similar-sounding *Philistine.* Without a Jerusalem temple to attract them, Jews began scattering abroad.

It would take them two thousand years to regain the national sovereignty that the Romans took away.

In the meantime, Arabs invaded in the 600s and built a Muslim shrine—the Dome of the Rock—on Jerusalem's sacred temple site. From the large rock inside this temple, the Muslim founder Muhammad is said to have ascended to heaven.

For most of the next thirteen hundred years, Arabs ruled the land.

TODAY

Canaan conquest, part two. Work on reestablishing Israel as the Jewish homeland began in 1897. That's when a Jewish Hungarian journalist named Theodor Herzl convened the First Zionist Congress.

About two hundred representatives agreed on a goal: "The aim of Zionism is to create for the Jewish people a home in Eretz-Israel [the land of Israel] secured by law."

Jews began returning to Palestine and in 1909 founded the first Jewish city, Tel Aviv. Arab rule ended in 1919 when the British captured Palestine from the Ottoman Turks and promised independence both to the local Arabs and to the Jews. The British couldn't deliver on the promise, though, because of disputes between Arabs and Jews.

The death of six million Jews in the Holocaust generated support for creating a Jewish nation. And in 1947 the United Nations proposed a division of land, which the Jews accepted but the Arabs rejected. Israel declared its independence on May 14, 1948.

War broke out, with six hundred thousand well-prepared Jews against 1.3

AN EXAGGERATED BRAG

Israelites never conquered the Promised Land. Egypt wiped them out before they got the chance. That's the brag—chiseled in black granite—of Egyptian king Merneptah in about 1210 BC.

There's more than a little irony in the fact that this first-known mention of Israel outside the Bible says it doesn't exist. "Israel is laid waste, his seed [people] is not."

The king erected the seven-foot brag slab in Thebes, Egypt, to commemorate his military victories in Canaan after the Exodus. Though exaggerated, the king's brag supports the Bible story about the Israelites leaving Egypt in the mid-1400s BC or perhaps in the mid-1200s BC and settling in Canaan.

Israeli soldiers check identity papers of men coming into Jerusalem. With Palestinians and Jews each claiming the region as their ancient homeland, violence occasionally erupts.

ISSACHAR

(IS a car)
Yissakar, Hebrew
"reward" or "hired man"
1800s BC
First mention: Genesis 30:18

In the emotionally fierce battle over which of Jacob's two wives could produce more children—Rachel or her sister, Leah—the early score was Leah four, Rachel nothing. Rachel resorted to folk medicine. When she learned that one of Leah's sons found mandrake roots, shaped like humans and used for infertility, she cut a deal. Rachel let Leah sleep with Jacob that night in trade for the roots. In a way, the roots worked. But it was Leah who got pregnant, and she gave birth to Issachar, her fifth son. Years later, Rachel had two sons.

ISSACHAR

(IS uh car)
Yissakar, Hebrew
First mention: Numbers 2:3

MAP 1
C3

There's good reason archaeologists haven't found many ruins in the territory assigned to descendants of Jacob's fifth son, Issachar. The small strip of land—twenty miles wide and ten miles north to south—was mostly rugged slopes just below the Sea of Galilee. The tribal boundary stretched westward from the Jordan River, up and over rocky hills and into part of the Jezreel valley.

million Palestinians who were quickly reinforced by five Arab armies. The Jews won more territory than the UN had designated. In a Jewish-Arab rematch, the Six-Day War of 1967, Israel captured from Jordan the West Bank—a chunk of land about a fourth the size of what ancient Israel had been. Israel also captured the Gaza Strip from Egypt and the Golan Heights from Syria.

Looking for peace. Today, Palestinians and Israelis struggle for ways to coexist. Hardliners on both sides reject coexistence, and each wants all the land. Palestinians, without a conventional army, press their demands by using terrorism tactics such as suicide bombers on public buses. Israelis retaliate in force, attacking Palestinian leaders and property and blowing up homes in the bomber's extended family.

Yet both sides make the same request of tourists visiting the Holy Land: "Pray for the peace of Jerusalem" (Psalm 122:6). It's the symbol and soul of the land they both love.

JABBOK RIVER
(JAB bahk)
Yabboq, Hebrew
First mention: Genesis 32:22

MAP 1
D4

Israel got its name in the Arab country of Jordan, along the banks of the Jabbok River. That's where Jacob wrestled a mysterious man that some Bible experts say was God. Jacob wanted a blessing and wouldn't let go of the man until he got it.

"Your name will no longer be Jacob," the man told him at dawn. "It is now Israel, because you have struggled with both God and men and have won" (Genesis 32:28). Jacob's twelve sons became fathers of twelve Hebrew tribes who united and took the name of their shared ancestor, Israel.

The Jabbok River sheds water from the Jordan highlands and carries it some sixty miles before emptying it into the Jordan River, about twenty miles north of the Dead Sea. The river served as a boundary between the tribes of Gad in the north and Reuben in the south.

JABIN
(JAY bin)
Yabin, Hebrew
1400s BC
First mention: Joshua 11:1

After Joshua's army swept through much of what is now southern Israel, King Jabin in the north figured the Hebrews would be coming to him soon. He ruled the city of Hazor in northern Galilee. Jabin assembled a vast coalition force representing perhaps dozens of kingdoms and equipped with cavalry and chariots. Joshua, however, launched a surprise attack, crippling the horses, burning the chariots, and wiping out the coalition force.

JACOB
(JAY cub)
Yaaqob, Hebrew
Perhaps "heel grabber" or "God protects"
1900s BC
First mention: Genesis 25:26

Jews trace their birth as a nation to this man whose twelve sons produced the twelve tribes of Israel.

The man was a crook. He cheated his older twin brother, Esau, out of two priceless family treasures: the birthright and the father's deathbed blessing—both of which belonged to the oldest son. That's low enough. Lower still, stealing the deathbed blessing meant cheating his blind father, Isaac, out of Isaac's last request.

What could God have possibly seen in a man like Jacob—a man his own brother vowed to kill?

With his mother's help and goatskin on his arm, Jacob tricks his nearly blind father into thinking he is hairy Esau, the older brother who gets a double share of inheritance.

RIVALS IN UTERO AND BEYOND

Siblings fight from time to time, but Jacob and Esau—Abraham's grandsons—got an early start. They pushed and shoved each other so much before they were born that their mother, who had been infertile for twenty years, asked God, "Why is this happening to me?" (Genesis 25:22). God told Rebekah, Isaac's wife, that the two boys would become rival nations and that descendants of the older son would serve the younger.

Esau arrived first, with Jacob clinging to his heel. That may be how Jacob got his name, since it sounds like the Hebrew word for heel. Yet the name shows up in other Middle Eastern languages as "God protects," and Rebekah may have intended this, given what God had told her.

Perhaps understandably, Jacob grew up as his mother's favorite. He preferred to stay close to camp. Esau, on the other hand, loved hunting. He often brought home fresh meat, endearing himself to Isaac.

Once, however, Esau came home meatless, exhausted, and famished. And there stood Jacob by the fire, cooking a savory red stew. It looked like a trap Jacob had been waiting to spring after just the right futile hunt. Esau asked for a bowl, and Jacob replied, "All right, but trade me your birthright for it" (Genesis 25:31).

A birthright gave the oldest son special privileges, including a double share of the inheritance. That means when Isaac died, Esau and Jacob would divide the property three ways, and Esau would get two-thirds. Esau traded his birthright for the stew. God later prohibited younger sons from taking the birthright (Deuteronomy 21:16).

When Isaac was over one hundred years old and blind, he called for Esau, who was already over forty and married. Isaac mistakenly thought he was dying, and he wanted to give Esau his blessing. This was both a prayer and an irrevocable transfer of power to the next family leader. Isaac asked Esau to fix him some wild game first.

Rebekah overheard and convinced Jacob to snatch the blessing—perhaps intending to help God fulfill his promise of making Jacob the more powerful son. Rebekah cooked Isaac's favorite meal, and Jacob served it, claiming to be Esau and wearing Esau's clothes. Jacob even wore goatskin on his arms and neck, since Esau was hairy.

Isaac may have been blind, but he recognized Jacob's voice. Even so, the hairy arms and the smell of Esau apparently convinced him that his hearing wasn't what it used to be. So he gave the blessing, including this prayer: "May all your mother's sons bow low before you" (Genesis 27:29).

When Esau got home and found out what had happened, he quickly hatched a plot of his own: "My father will soon be dead and gone. Then I will kill Jacob" (Genesis 27:41).

Rebekah heard about it and got Isaac's permission to send Jacob to her homeland near Haran, a city in what is now southern Turkey. Her excuse was so he could find a wife there among her brother Laban's family, instead of marrying pagan Canaanites like Esau's two wives.

ON THE RUN

From his home in Beersheba, in what is now the Negev desert in southern Israel, Jacob headed north and made camp near a village some seventy miles away—about twelve miles north of Jerusalem. Using a stone for a pillow, he dreamed about a stairway to heaven. God stood at the top and made Jacob the same promise he once made to Abraham—a strange promise, given what Jacob had just done. The descendants of this conniving swindler would one day fill Canaan and would become a blessing to the world.

Jacob named the place Bethel, "house of God." And in what sounds like one part deal and one part conversion, Jacob promised that if God would take care of him and someday bring him home, "I will make the LORD my God" (Genesis 28:21).

In Jacob's long story, there's only one character more brutally dishonest than he: his uncle Laban. Laban agreed to let Jacob marry his beautiful daughter, Rachel, but only after Jacob worked for him seven years. Beneath the veil on the wedding night, however, was Rachel's older sister, Leah. It was classic bait and switch. Horrified the next morning, Jacob stormed off to Laban, who justified the deception: "It's not our custom to marry off a younger daughter ahead of the firstborn" (Genesis 29:26).

After the traditional weeklong wedding celebration, which could not have been anything but awkward and painful for Jacob, Leah, and Rachel, the groom was allowed to marry Rachel as well—in exchange for another seven years of labor.

Leah and Rachel were constantly competing for Jacob's affection. Each woman wanted to give him lots of sons. With the help of their two maids as supplemental, surrogate mothers, the four women gave Jacob a dozen sons and a daughter: six sons and a daughter by Leah, two sons by Leah's maid Zilpah, two sons by Rachel, and two sons by Rachel's maid Bilhah.

With fourteen years served, Jacob wanted to go home. But Laban didn't want him to go because the flocks had grown so much under Jacob's care that Laban got rich. And he wanted to get richer. So Laban agreed to pay Jacob by giving him all the sheep and goats that weren't white. Then Laban promptly cut those animals from his flocks and gave them to his sons to take care of. A cheat cheating a cheater.

Jacob retaliated with a trick of his own. Some shepherds thought that if their animals mated in front of streaked tree bark, their offspring would be dark or spotted. So whenever the best of Laban's flock were ready to mate, Jacob set up partly peeled branches at the water trough in front of them.

Jacob got rich. Laban's sons got jealous. And God told Jacob to go home.

Bound for Canaan land

So twenty years after arriving in Haran, Jacob gathered his family, servants, and flocks and sneaked out while Laban was away shearing sheep.

A week later, Laban caught up with Jacob's caravan. The tense reunion ended in a peace treaty.

But there was another tense reunion ahead. Jacob's brother, Esau, was waiting. Jacob sent messengers ahead with gifts for Esau, who was living in Edom, now Jordan. The messengers returned with news that Esau was coming—with four hundred men.

Jacob sent more messengers with wave after wave of gifts. Then he sent everyone in his caravan across the Jabbok River toward Edom territory. He alone stayed behind. A mysterious man came and wrestled him all night. Some scholars speculate this was God in human form or perhaps an angel. Jacob seemed to think the man was God because he wouldn't let go until he got a blessing, then he named the place Peniel, meaning "face of God," saying, "I have seen God face to face, yet my life has been spared" (Genesis 32:30).

The man gave Jacob a new name: "It is now Israel [which may mean 'one who struggles with God'], because you have struggled with both God and men and have won" (Genesis 32:28).

Jacob was never the same after that night. No more do we read of him exploiting people. Greed and selfishness gave way to generosity and compassion. Perhaps that is what God saw in him many years earlier.

Esau forgave his brother and invited him to live in Edom. But Jacob settled for a time near Shechem, in Canaan's heartland, before returning to his father, who was still alive and living near Hebron. Along the way, on the road to Bethlehem, Rachel died giving birth to Benjamin. When Isaac died, at age 180, Jacob and Esau buried him with their mother and their grandparents, Abraham and Sarah.

Decades later, when Jacob was 130 years old, a drought struck Canaan. Jacob moved his entire extended family southwest to Egypt at the invitation of his son Joseph. Jacob had so favored Joseph—his first son with Rachel—that some of the other brothers grew insanely jealous. They ended up selling him to slave traders and telling their father that a wild animal had eaten him. Joseph, however, was gifted at interpreting dreams, and he rose to become Egypt's second highest official, after the pharaoh.

Jael, a nomad's wife, invites a military commander running from a lost battle to rest in her tent. When he falls asleep, she drives a tent peg into his head.

Jacob died in Egypt, but not before blessing each of his sons and asking Joseph to bury him with his father and grandfather in Hebron. Joseph had Jacob embalmed, then took his body home for burial.

JAEL
(JAY el)
Yael, Hebrew
"wild goat"
1100s BC
First mention: Judges 4:17

With a tent peg and a hammer, a nomadic woman named Jael killed one of Israel's most feared enemies, Sisera. He commanded the powerful army and chariot corps of Hazor, a city in northern Galilee. His army ruthlessly oppressed northern Israel for twenty years until an Israelite leader named Deborah organized a militia to fight back. A rainstorm bogged Sisera's chariots in mud, and the Israelite militia rushed in on foot. Sisera jumped off his chariot and ran until he came to the tent of Jael and her husband, Heber. They were Kenites, a clan originally from the northern Sinai.

Jael invited the exhausted Sisera inside her tent, gave him milk, and covered him. When he fell asleep, she drove a tent peg through his temple and into the ground. Why, the Bible doesn't say. But Kenites, known for metalworking, relied on good relations with their neighbors—in this case, the Israelites.

JAIRUS
(jay EYE russ)
Iairos, Greek
"he enlightens"
First century AD
First mention: Mark 5:22

While Jesus was teaching in Galilee, a synagogue leader by the name of Jairus dropped on his knees in front of Jesus and begged Him to come and heal his only child—a twelve-year-old daughter who was dying. As Jesus accompanied him, a messenger arrived with tragic news: The girl had died. "Just trust me," Jesus said, "and she will be all right" (Luke 8:50).

The house was filled with mourners. When Jesus assured them that the girl was just sleeping, they laughed at him. Jesus ordered everyone out. Then, accompanied by only the girl's parents and disciples Peter, James, and John, Jesus took the girl's hand and said, "Get up, my child!" (Luke 8:54). She got up. In similar miracles, Jesus raised Lazarus and a widow's son at Nain.

JAMES
Iakobos, Greek
From *Yaaqob,* Hebrew for Jacob
1. Executed about AD 44
2. Executed in late AD 60s
First mention: 1. Matthew 4:21
2. Matthew 13:55

1. **Disciple of Jesus.** Two of the first disciples Jesus invited to join him were sons of a Galilean fisherman named Zebedee—James and John. Jesus called them "sons of thunder," perhaps a description of their bold temperament. When a Samaritan village refused to welcome Jesus, the brothers asked, "Should we order down fire from heaven to burn them up?" (Luke 9:54). Jesus declined. Another time, the brothers had the nerve to ask if they could sit beside Jesus on his throne. That upset the other disciples.

Even so, James and John along with Peter became Jesus' most trusted disciples. They accompanied him when the others were left behind. Only they joined him when his body was transfigured into a glowing spiritual form. And only they were invited to slip away with him for private prayer on the night of his arrest.

Early Christian writers reported that most of the disciples were martyred. The Bible reports only the execution of James, the first disciple martyred. King Herod Agrippa had him killed by the sword during persecution of the church, a campaign intended to boost Agrippa's popularity with the Jews. Later Christian stories say that before James died, he preached in Spain, where he is now the patron saint.

2. **Brother of Jesus.** Jesus had brothers and sisters who, at one point in his ministry, didn't believe he was the Messiah. Yet his brother James later became the church's top leader—with authority over the apostles.

When Jesus preached in his hometown, some wondered where he got his wisdom and power to do miracles: "He's just a carpenter's son, and we know Mary, his mother, and his brothers—James, Joseph, Simon, and Judas" (Matthew 13:55). Exactly what kind of brothers and sisters these were remains debatable. Some Christian traditions teach that Mary remained a virgin all her life and that James and the others were Joseph's children by a previous marriage or perhaps cousins of Jesus.

Whatever the relationship, Mary and the others in Jesus' family once tried to interrupt him while he was teaching a crowd. They may have wanted to silence him. One clue: "Even his brothers didn't believe in him" (John 7:5).

After Jesus died, the top Jerusalem official was "James, our Lord's brother" (Galatians 1:19). He chaired the first Christian council meeting, in which church leaders debated the controversial issue of whether or not Gentiles should obey Jewish laws. James ruled in favor of a compromise: "We should stop troubling the Gentiles who turn to God, except that we should write to them and tell them to abstain from eating meat sacrificed to idols, from sexual immorality, and from consuming blood or eating the meat of strangled animals" (Acts 15:19–20).

Initially, the apostles seemed to agree. But in time, Paul eliminated the Jewish dietary rules.

Some early Christian writers said James the brother of Jesus wrote the book of James—a letter that speaks highly of Jewish traditions. Many scholars today disagree, arguing that the writer's expertise in Greek is far above what they would expect from a carpenter's son. Yet that sounds similar to what the hometown people said after hearing Jesus.

The Jewish historian Josephus, writing in the first Christian century, said Jewish leaders condemned James for breaking the law. Then they pushed him from a high spot in the temple complex and finished him off with clubs and stones.

JEHOAHAZ

(juh HO uh has)
Yehoahaz, Hebrew
"God grabs hold"
Reigned about 815–802 BC
First mention: 2 Kings 10:35

Three Jewish kings owned this name, including two from the southern nation of Judah. But the better-known king ruled the northern nation of Israel. He inherited the throne from his father, Jehu, who ended the dynasty of Ahab and Jezebel with a deadly coup. Jehoahaz ruled a nation weakened by prolonged war with Syria, leaving Israel with only "fifty mounted troops, ten chariots, and ten thousand foot soldiers" (2 Kings 13:7). Worse, Assyria's power was on the rise, and its empire would eventually crush Israel and Syria.

JEHOIACHIN

(juh HOY uh kin)
Yehoyakin, Hebrew
"God establishes"
Reigned in 597 BC
First mention: 2 Kings 24:6

Jehoiachin was only eighteen years old
when he inherited Judah's throne from
his father, Jehoiakim, who had died. It
was horrible timing. The Babylonian
king, Nebuchadnezzar, was already on
his way to surround Jerusalem for
refusing to pay its taxes.

Jehoiachin reigned only three
months. He and his officials were taken
captive to Babylon, along with treasures
from the palace and temple. This probably included the nation's most sacred
relic, the Ark of the Covenant—a gold-
plated chest containing the Ten
Commandments.

Babylonian records speak of
Jehoiachin several times, once reporting his monthly oil ration (five quarts).
Babylonian records indicate he was
treated well, supporting the Bible's
claim that he received "preferential
treatment over all the other exiled
kings in Babylon" and was allowed to
"dine at the king's table for the rest of
his life" (2 Kings 25:28–29).

JEHOIAKIM

(juh HOY uh kim)
Yehoyaqim, Hebrew
"God raises up"
Reigned 609–598 BC
First mention: 2 Kings 23:34

Eight years before Babylon surrounded
Jerusalem, the prophet Jeremiah warned
the Judean king, Jehoiakim, it would
happen as punishment for the king's
godless leadership. Jeremiah's prophecy
was written in a first draft of the Old
Testament book named after him. It was
a first draft because, as the scroll was
read, the king cut off pieces and tossed
them in a fire "until the whole scroll was
burned up" (Jeremiah 36:23).

Jehoiakim's name was originally
Eliakim. But Egypt dominated the region, and Pharaoh Neco made the name
change when he installed the twenty-
five-year-old as king. Jehoiakim replaced
his younger brother Jehoahaz.

After Babylon defeated Egypt,
Jehoiakim paid taxes to Babylon for
three years. Then he stopped. Nebuchadnezzar came to collect, but Jehoiakim died just before the army arrived—
perhaps assassinated. His son, Jehoiachin, surrendered the city and was taken
captive.

JEHOSHAPHAT

(juh HO shuh fat)
Yehosapat, Hebrew
"The Lord has judged"
Reigned 873–849 BC
First mention: 1 Kings 15:24

While Ahab and Jezebel ruled the
northern Jewish nation of Israel,
Jehoshaphat led Judah in the south.
Both nations united to recapture
Ramoth-gilead, a city east of the
Jordan River that the Syrians had
taken. Since a prophet predicted Ahab
wouldn't return alive, he disguised
himself. Jehoshaphat, however, wore
royal robes. Syrian charioteers charged

at Jehoshaphat until he screamed and they realized it was the wrong man. A stray arrow killed Ahab.

JEHU
(JAY hue)
Yehu, Hebrew
"he is the Lord"
Reigned 842–814 BC
First mention: 1 Kings 19:16

God promised to wipe out the family of Israel's king Ahab and Jezebel, so he ordered the prophet Elisha to anoint a new king. That man was Jehu. He commanded troops in what is now Jordan and controlled a major trade route south of Damascus. Ahab had already died, but his son, Joram, led the nation.

Freshly anointed, Jehu led his chariot corps some forty miles west to Jezreel, where King Joram was recovering from battle wounds. As Jehu's contingent approached at high speed, the king rode out to get what looked like urgent news. Jehu shot him through the heart with an arrow.

Then Jehu rode into Jezreel and executed Jezebel. Next he sent word to the people in Samaria, the capital, to bring him the heads of Ahab's seventy sons. The heads arrived the next day, and Jehu piled them outside the city gate.

Afterward, Jehu went to Samaria and finished killing Ahab's extended family. Finally, he invited all Baal worshipers to join him at the Baal temple. Jehu executed all of them and converted the temple into a public toilet.

JEPHTHAH
(JEFF thuh)
Yiptah, Hebrew
"God opens" or "God frees"
1100s BC
First mention: Judges 11:1

Jephthah—one of Israel's military heroes—grew up despised. His family ran him off because his mother was a prostitute, and they didn't want to split the inheritance with him. Jephthah moved away and gathered an army. At the same time Ammonites, in what is now Jordan, started trying to recapture land they lost when the Israelites invaded after their exodus from Egypt. Jephthah's family lived on the contested land, and they convinced him to help. He became one of Israel's famed leaders known as the judges.

After driving off the Ammonites, Jephthah rashly vowed to sacrifice the first thing that greeted him when he got home. Out came his daughter—his only child.

JEREMIAH
(jerr uh MY uh)
Yirmeyah, Hebrew
Possibly "may the Lord exalt"
Born 640 BC; prophesied 627–586 BC
First mention: 2 Chronicles 35:25

God assigned a boy perhaps no older than thirteen to deliver the worst news in Israel's history—then to watch the horrifying prediction come true.

The boy was Jeremiah. The bad news was the end of the Jewish nation. What the Assyrians did to the northern Jewish nation of Israel more than a century earlier, Babylon would do to the southern Jewish nation of Judah.

Babylonians from what is now Iraq would invade, overrun Jewish cities, and level Jerusalem—including the holiest Jewish site on the planet, a place Jews considered God's earthly home and the only worship center where they were allowed to offer sacrifices: the temple.

A PROPHET TOO YOUNG

Jeremiah was the son of a priest, Hilkiah, who lived about three miles north of Jerusalem in the village of Anathoth.

God called Jeremiah to become a prophet during a nationwide revival in which King Josiah ordered all pagan shrines destroyed. That was in year twelve of Josiah's reign. Jeremiah got the

Rembrandt's portrait of a pensive Jeremiah reflects the bleak mood of the prophet's writings. His message: Jerusalem is doomed.

divine call a year later, in about 627 BC.

Scholars used to say Jeremiah was a young adult at the time, perhaps eighteen or so. But scholars today say the Hebrew word describing his young age is more accurately translated "boy." In the context of Jeremiah's story, that would fit a child of about twelve or thirteen.

As if that wasn't young enough, God pushed the numbers back even further: "I knew you before I formed you in your mother's womb. Before you were born I set you apart and appointed you as my spokesman to the world" (Jeremiah 1:5).

Jeremiah delivered many messages during his forty-year ministry, criticizing evil international leaders and warning proud nations. But his bombshell message was for his own people: "Listen! I am calling the armies of the kingdoms of the north to come to Jerusalem. They will set their thrones at the gates of the city. They will attack its walls and all the other towns of Judah. I will pronounce judgment on my people for all their evil—for deserting me and worshiping other gods" (Jeremiah 1:15–16).

This is why God told Jeremiah not to get married and have children. In the near future, God said, Jewish children would die from war and starvation: "Their bodies will be food for the vultures and wild animals" (Jeremiah 16:4). The prophet's bachelorhood—

uncommon in a day when large families ruled—served as a constant reminder of the coming disaster.

GOD THE POTTER

King Josiah's reform lasted only as long as he did. When his son Jehoiakim became king in about 609 BC, pagan worship bounced back. Even then, some twenty years before Babylon wiped the Jewish nation off the world map, it wasn't too late for the Jews to change their ways.

God illustrated his point. He sent Jeremiah to watch a potter at work. The potter didn't like how his clay jar turned out, so he squashed the soft clay and started over. God said he could do the same for Judah and turn them into something beautiful.

Regardless of Judah's response, God announced a new plan for humanity—one that would retire the old Jewish laws and sacrificial system he delivered through Moses. "The day will come," God said, "when I will make a new covenant with the people of Israel and Judah. This covenant will not be like the one I made with their ancestors. . . . They broke that covenant. . . . I will put my laws in their minds, and I will write them on their hearts. I will be their God, and they will be my people" (Jeremiah 31:31–33).

Jesus later described his sacrifice on the cross as the beginning of this new agreement: "This wine is the token of God's new covenant to save you—an agreement sealed with the blood I will pour out for you" (Luke 22:20).

A CHILD WILL LEAD THEM

It's intriguing that God called a "boy," Jeremiah, to become the prophet who would grow up to turn the lights out on the Jewish nation. He foretold the destruction and witnessed it.

What makes this especially fascinating is that centuries earlier God had called a boy named Samuel to do just the opposite. Samuel grew up to become the prophet who turned the lights on. He anointed Israel's first king.

And it was yet another boy, Jesus, who came to inaugurate a new Israel not of this world. He turned the lights on forever.

THE FIRST BIBLE BURNING

God told Jeremiah to write down all the prophecies he had ever delivered. The project became a first draft of what we now call the Old Testament book of Jeremiah. It was a first draft because King Jehoiakim didn't approve of it, so he burned it.

The king's disapproval may have had something to do with excerpts like this: " 'Destruction is certain for Jehoiakim. . . . You are full of selfish greed and dishonesty! You murder the innocent, oppress the poor, and reign ruthlessly.' Therefore, this is the LORD's decree. . . . 'His family will not weep for

PROPHETS WHO DIDN'T WANT THE JOB

Jeremiah. When asked to become a prophet, Jeremiah politely told God no. "I'm too young!" Jeremiah argued (Jeremiah 1:6).

Moses. Prophets had been trying to turn God down since day one, when God called His first spokesman on record—Moses. God asked Moses to go to Egypt and demand that Pharaoh release the Hebrew slaves. "O Lord, I'm just not a good speaker. I never have been, and I'm not now, even after you have spoken to me. I'm clumsy with words" (Exodus 4:10).

Jonah. The most explicit rejection of all came from Jonah. Ordered to go to Assyria—in what is now Iraq—and tell the people that their capital would be destroyed in forty days, he didn't say a word. "Jonah got up and went in the opposite direction" (Jonah 1:3). But one seafaring storm and a large fish later, he was on his way to Assyria.

Many scholars speculate that Jeremiah wrote only the prophecy sections of the book and that his secretary, Baruch, and perhaps some other writers added the biographical sections later.

JERUSALEM FALLS

On January 15, 588 BC, King Nebuchadnezzar of Babylon arrived with his armies outside the walled city of Jerusalem. He had already overrun the other Jewish cities, and now he surrounded the capital. Jeremiah advised King Zedekiah to surrender, explaining that Babylon was doing God's work of punishing the nation. For that, Jeremiah got imprisoned on the charge of treason.

The siege lasted two and a half years, long enough to starve Jewish mothers into killing their children for food.

On July 18, 586 BC, Babylon broke through the walls. A month later, on August 17, Babylonian wrecking teams began dismantling the city walls and tearing down the temple and other major buildings.

King Zedekiah—the last king of the sovereign Jewish nation—ran away. He tried to escape with his army. The Babylonian army chased him down twenty miles away in the plains of Jericho, forced him to watch the execution of his sons, blinded him, and took him captive to Babylon.

As for Jeremiah, the Babylonians freed him apparently because they learned he had advised the leaders to surrender. It may have been during

him when he dies. His subjects will not even care that he is dead. He will be buried like a dead donkey—dragged out of Jerusalem and dumped outside the gate!' " (Jeremiah 22:13, 17–19).

Jeremiah wrote a new and improved edition, with added prophecies.

this lonely time in his decimated homeland that he wrote the book of Lamentations, traditionally attributed to him. Known as the saddest book in the Bible, it's an eyewitness report of the siege and fall of Jerusalem, followed by the grief of a people with no nation.

Nebuchadnezzar assigned a governor to oversee the region, populated mainly with the poor and returning refugees who had fled the war. By midautumn, a surviving member of the royal family led a group of ten other Jewish men in assassinating the governor. Fearing reprisal, many Jews planned an escape to Egypt. The irony is that the Jews had escaped *from* Egypt to start their nation, and now they were planning to escape *to* Egypt after the death of their nation. "If you insist on going to Egypt," Jeremiah warned, "you will die there" (Jeremiah 42:15–16).

They went anyhow and forced the prophet to go with them. As far as history scholars can tell, Jeremiah was never heard from again.

JERICHO
(JERR ee ko)
Yeriho, Hebrew
First mention: Numbers 22:1

MAP 1
C5

There's nothing subtle about the message God sent when he dropped the walls of Jericho for the Israelite

An Arab boy at a fruit stand in Palestinian-controlled Jericho, an oasis town famed for citrus fruit, dates, and vegetables.

invaders: God is unstoppable. God's subtlety, however, may be peeking through in the choice of Jericho.

This wasn't just any strategically located oasis town in a valley rich with springs and fruit. Certainly, the location was important, six miles from a popular ford across the Jordan River. By destroying Jericho first, Israelites controlled access to their future homeland. But Jericho is also the oldest settlement discovered on the planet—established at least seven thousand years before Joshua.

Squatter's rights in the court of common sense would have brushed off any Israelite claim to the land. But nothing we have is ours to keep. Creation belongs to the Creator. Joshua acknowledged this by refusing to let his people take anything for themselves from Jericho. Some scholars say this

BIBLE EVENTS:

- Walls come tumbling down
- Babylonians catch Israel's runaway king
- King Herod builds a winter palace
- The tax collector Zacchaeus watches Jesus from a tree
- Jesus heals a blind man

JERICHO

STATISTICS:

- Founded—About 9000 BC
- Size—Ten acres
- Destroyed—Perhaps 1400 BC (hotly debated)
- Exploration of ruins begins—1868
- Location—Near the Jordan River, about twenty miles east of Jerusalem

might explain why archaeologists found Jericho pottery filled with grain.

IN BIBLE TIMES

A walk around Jericho. At God's instruction, Joshua's army marched around Jericho once a day for six days. On day seven, they circled seven times, priests blew ram's horns, and the soldiers screamed. "Suddenly, the walls of Jericho collapsed" (Joshua 6:20). Perhaps an earthquake brought them down. A four-thousand-mile-long fault runs right along the Jordan River, as the Sinai Peninsula plate pushes south and the Arabian plate plows north.

Runaway king. After a six-month siege of Jerusalem, the Babylonian army broke through part of the wall. The Jewish king, Zedekiah, apparently knew Babylon would attack at first light, so he and the soldiers decided to run for it. They made a nighttime dash for the Jordan valley, perhaps hoping to cross the river at the shallow ford. The Babylonians caught Zedekiah on the Jericho plain, abandoned by his men just as he had abandoned the people of Jerusalem. Israel's last king was forced to watch his sons executed, then he was blinded and led away to Babylon as a war trophy.

Herod's winter palace. Winters in Jericho are mild, partly because it's one of the lowest cities on earth, about eight hundred feet below sea level. King Herod the Great built an elegant winter palace there, overlooking a new Jericho. Ruins of Old Testament Jericho rested nearly two miles away.

Tax man up a tree. When Jesus passed through Jericho on his way to

Jerusalem, crowds were so thick that a short but curious tax collector named Zacchaeus climbed a sycamore tree to catch a glimpse of him. Bulky, gnarled sycamores still shade the city to the delight of tourists. Jesus called Zacchaeus down and invited himself to spend the night. The crowd criticized Jesus for keeping company with a notorious sinner, but the experience changed Zacchaeus. He vowed to give half his money to the poor and repay four times what he had swindled.

Blind Bartimaeus. As crowds tried to shut him up, a blind beggar named Bartimaeus cried out to Jesus for mercy. Jesus called the man up and asked what he could do for him. "I want to see!" (Mark 10:51). Jesus healed him, and Bartimaeus followed him down the road.

TODAY

Digging in Jericho. All that remains of Joshua's Jericho is a ten-acre mound of dirt and ruins about seventy feet high. The height comes from settlements built one on top of the other. This mound, called Tell es-Sultan, stretches roughly 350 yards long and 150 yards wide.

Trenches and holes litter the mound—scars of exploration left by more than a century of archaeologists.

Arab Jericho. Modern Jericho surrounds the ancient ruins. This is a Palestinian town on the eastern edge of a massive tract of land called the West Bank—twenty-two hundred square miles of land that Israel captured from Jordan in a 1967 war.

NO WALLS AT JERICHO?

There were no walls when Joshua arrived. That was the conclusion of Oxford archaeologist Kathleen Kenyon in the 1950s. She said the walls fell in about 1550 BC, a century or more before Joshua got there.

Before Kenyon, archaeologist John Garstang in the 1930s had dated the collapsed mudbrick walls to Joshua's time, about 1400 BC. More recently, archaeologist Bryant Wood agreed, saying Kenyon misidentified the pottery styles. Like cars today, ancient pottery came in different styles during different eras. Archaeologists use that to help date various levels of a ruin.

Experts continue to debate what kind of city, if any, Joshua saw when he arrived at Jericho.

When Israel began transferring authority back to the Palestinians in 1994, Jericho became the first city returned, probably because it was isolated from trouble spots like the Gaza Strip, where Israelis and Palestinians clashed.

Some twenty-five hundred people live in and around Jericho, many of them making their living from crops such as dates, bananas, citrus fruit, flowers, and winter vegetables.

JEROBOAM

(jair uh BO uhm)
Yarobam, Hebrew
"may the people be great"
1. Reigned about 922–901 BC
2. Reigned about 786–746 BC
First mention: 1. 1 Kings 11:26
2. 2 Kings 13:13

1. Jeroboam I. He split Israel into two nations and became king of the northern nation of Israel—leaving Judah in the south for David's descendants.

This was God's doing. While Solomon was alive, a prophet tore off ten pieces of his own new cloak and gave it to Jeroboam, one of Solomon's building foremen. The pieces represented Israel's ten northern tribes, which the prophet said God would give him because Solomon worshiped idols. When Solomon found out and tried to kill Jeroboam, the foreman escaped to Egypt and stayed there until Solomon died.

Solomon's son Rehoboam refused to ease taxes and the forced labor for building projects. So the northern tribes rallied around Jeroboam and started a new nation. Rehoboam mustered his army to fight, but a prophet convinced him that God was behind the split.

Jeroboam turned out badly. To keep Jews from worshiping at the temple in Judah, he set up golden calves at two cities on his northern and southern borders. He told the people, "These are the gods who brought you out of Egypt!" (1 Kings 12:28).

The prophet Ahijah, who earlier predicted Jeroboam's rise to power, now said dogs and vultures would eat the king and his family. Jeroboam's son reigned only two years before being assassinated in a coup.

2. Jeroboam II. More than a century after Israel's split, the northern nation was ruled by the family of Jehu, who led a coup against Ahab's family. Jehu's great-grandson, Jeroboam, was an evil man (2 Kings 14:24), ruling at the peak of Israel's prosperity. It was a greedy time. As one prophet described it, rich people exploited the needy, cheated customers with dishonest scales, and sold the poor as slaves to recoup debts as small as "a pair of sandals" (Amos 8:6).

JERUSALEM

MAP 1
C5

(jah ROO sah lem)
yerusalayim, Hebrew
Perhaps "founded by Salem," a Canaanite god
First mention: Joshua 10:1

There's one prophecy about Israel's capital that hasn't been fulfilled. Some wonder if it ever will be. "Peace and prosperity will overflow Jerusalem like a river. . . . The wealth of the nations will flow to her" (Isaiah 66:12).

Not today.

Consider this quote from Jerusalem's Web site: "The employment base is problematic and the city suffers from a relatively high poverty level." That's because tourism is the main source of income, and folks don't want to visit a city where innocent people occasionally get blown up by terrorists.

Ancient words that describe

BIBLE EVENTS:

- David makes it his capital
- Solomon builds the temple
- Babylon destroys the city
- Jesus is crucified and resurrected
- Holy Spirit descends on disciples; church is born

HOLY SITES:

- Garden of Gethsemane, commemorating Jesus' prayer and arrest
- Church of the Holy Sepulchre, said to be where Jesus was crucified and buried
- Garden Tomb, another ancient burial site
- Western (Wailing) Wall, where temple once stood
- Dome of the Rock, where the Jewish temple once stood

STATISTICS:

- Population—670,000
- Elevation—About 2,500 feet
- Location—Near the center of Israel on a rocky ridge in the Judean hills, some forty miles east of the Mediterranean Sea and twenty miles west of Israel's border with Jordan.

Jerusalem twenty-five hundred years ago seem just as fitting today: "We hoped for peace, but no peace came. We hoped for a time of healing but found only terror" (Jeremiah 14:19).

Perhaps no city on the entire planet has witnessed as much violence over such a long period as Jerusalem, conquered dozens of times, reduced to rubble no less than five times, and in recent years a frequent target for Palestinian terrorists trying to reclaim their land.

IN BIBLE TIMES

David takes Jerusalem. One of the world's oldest continually occupied cities, Jerusalem was already twenty-five hundred years old by the time King David arrived to capture it and make it his capital.

There's a reason for the city's old age and why the Israelites hadn't been able to capture it. The location was easy to defend. Walls around the city were built on the crest of a steep ridge surrounded by hills. And there was

The gold-painted Dome of the Rock dominates Jerusalem's skyline. This thirteen-hundred-year-old Muslim shrine marks the hilltop location where the Jewish temple stood before Romans destroyed it in AD 70.

plenty of water from Gihon Spring hidden in a small cave.

David knew his army didn't have a chance using conventional strategies. So he sent some warriors into the cave of Gihon Spring and up a fifty-foot-high vertical shaft that functioned like a city well. People inside the hilltop city could drop a bucket into the cave spring at the base of the hill, which was just outside the walls. Once inside, the soldiers opened the city gates.

Solomon's cosmopolitan capital. With Israel's borders secure, thanks to King David's military prowess, the king's son and successor focused on building a world-class nation. Solomon more than doubled the size of Jerusalem. And he began a lavish building program that caught the eye of the international community and transformed Jerusalem from an isolated fortress into a cosmopolitan capital.

First up was the temple—the only place in the world where Jews were permitted to offer formal sacrifices to God. Like a spiritual magnet, this shimmering white limestone building that dominated the Jerusalem hilltop drew worshipers from across the nation and beyond.

The city decimated. Jerusalem also attracted powerful enemies, eager to siphon the wealth. Because of the nation's habitual sins, God allowed Israel's enemies to do just that and more.

Babylonian soldiers forced Jerusalem to pay huge annual taxes. When Jerusalem tried to rebel, Babylonian soldiers dismantled cities throughout the nation, including Jerusalem. Then they took most of the survivors captive and left Jerusalem a decimated ghost town. For about fifty years, beginning in 586 BC, the Jewish nation was nothing but a memory. Persians, however, defeated Babylon and freed the captives. Some Jews returned to Jerusalem and rebuilt it.

City where Jesus was killed. Jesus often traveled to Jerusalem to worship at the temple on religious holidays. The biggest holiday was Passover. So many Jews came to Jerusalem during Passover that Roman governors, fearing a spontaneous revolt, brought in extra troops.

As Jesus walked to Jerusalem for

one final Passover, he told the crowds, "It wouldn't do for a prophet of God to be killed except in Jerusalem! O Jerusalem, Jerusalem, the city that kills the prophets and stones God's messengers! How often I have wanted to gather your children together as a hen protects her chicks beneath her wings, but you wouldn't let me" (Luke 13:33–34).

Condemned for claiming to be God's Son, Jesus was executed. The Crucifixion took place outside the city walls because, under Jewish law, coming too close to a corpse would make a person ritually unclean and unfit for worship that day. Jesus was buried nearby in a garden tomb.

The church is born. After his resurrection and just before ascending to heaven, Jesus told the disciples, "Do not leave Jerusalem. . . . In just a few days you will be baptized with the Holy Spirit" (Acts 1:4–5).

This took place during the Pentecost early-harvest festival, fifty days after Passover. Crowds again filled the city and saw the evidence of God's Spirit at work. The disciples healed the sick and preached about Jesus in native languages of the international pilgrims. About three thousand Jews believed, and the Christian church was born.

Jerusalem's Jewish leaders who had

GROWING JERUSALEM

Over the past three thousand years, Jerusalem has gobbled up land to make room for the people moving there.

From a city not much larger than a shopping mall, it has grown into a rambling metropolis the size of Disney World in Florida, or San Francisco, or two Manhattan islands.

In Charge	Date	Land Size	Population
Jebusites (a group of Canaanites)	1050 BC	11 acres	1,000
King David	1000 BC	15 acres	2,000
King Solomon	950 BC	32 acres	5,000
King Hezekiah	700 BC	125 acres	25,000
King Herod	4 BC	230 acres	40,000
Israelis/Palestinians	1948	10,000 acres	165,000
Israelis	2004	30,000 acres (47 square miles)	670,000

A B C D E F G H I J K L M N O P Q R S T U V W X Y Z

JERUSALEM'S VIOLENT HISTORY

This isn't a complete list of the battles over Jerusalem,
just some of the more famous ones.

BC

1000	David captures city
586	Babylon destroys it*
332	Alexander the Great captures it
320	Egypt captures it
198	Seleucids of Syria take control
168	Seleucids destroy the walls*
165	Jews win independence
63	Rome conquers it and destroys the walls*

* *Major destruction of the city*

AD

66	Jewish rebels liberate it
70	Rome takes it back, destroying the temple and city walls*
132	Jewish rebels recapture it, decimating it in the process*
135	Rome takes it back, rebuilds it, and bans Jews from the city
638	Muslim Arabs capture the city, later building the Dome of the Rock shrine where the Jewish temple had been
1071	Seljuk Turks take control
1099	Crusaders capture the city
1187	Muslims retake it
1517	Turkey's Ottoman Empire controls it
1917	British take control in WW I
1949	City is divided after war between Jews and Palestinians
1967	Israel takes control of entire city after Six-Day War

A Jerusalem boy with a toy gun pretends to shoot the photographer who's shooting him. Tensions between Palestinians and Israelis sometimes erupt into violence.

objected to Jesus launched attacks that drove many Jewish Christians out of Jerusalem. But this helped spread the message throughout the Roman Empire.

AFTER BIBLE TIMES

Jews banned from Jerusalem. New Testament writers said Jesus' death was a sacrifice that made the Jewish sacrificial system obsolete. Roman soldiers made that teaching a reality in AD 70 by ending the sacrificial system once and for all. Jewish rebels had ousted the Romans several years earlier, but the Romans came back with a vengeance—leveling Jerusalem and destroying the temple, which has never been rebuilt.

When Emperor Hadrian built a Roman city on the site a generation later, Jews again rebelled. Fighting destroyed the city, and the Jews lost again. In AD 135, Hadrian banned Jews from even visiting Jerusalem.

Jerusalem's first church. About two hundred years later, Emperor Constantine legalized Christianity and started building churches on revered sites in the Holy Land. In 335, he consecrated the Church of the Holy Sepulchre. It was built outside Jerusalem's first-century walls on land where Emperor Hadrian in the early 100s had built a temple to Venus—an apparent attempt to erase the memory of Jesus.

Fighting for the Holy City. Though Jerusalem enjoyed long stretches of peace, religious groups fought for the right to control it. For Jews, it was their holy city. For Christians, it was where Jesus died and rose from the dead. And for Muslims, it was where Muhammad ascended to heaven.

Muslims held it longest. Beginning with their invasion in the AD 600s, they controlled Jerusalem for twelve of the next thirteen centuries. Crusaders temporarily won it back for Christianity in 1099.

Jews were only bit players until the 1800s, when they began returning and buying property from Palestinian locals. By the late 1800s, they made up a majority of Jerusalem's citizens. War broke out in 1948, when they declared themselves a nation. In the battles that followed, they won control of West Jerusalem, but not the Old City that includes their holiest site, the Western Wall. But in a 1967 war, they took control of the entire city.

TODAY

Jerusalem in recent years has been a city on edge. Two out of three people there are Jewish. And they never know when a Palestinian bomber will show up at a café or on a bus. The other one in three is a Palestinian usually living in cramped and shrinking territory on Jerusalem's poor-looking east side. These people wonder if their neighborhood will be the next one evicted by the courts to make way for a Jewish community.

Both groups want this city. And they haven't yet agreed to share.

Despite the violence, between one and two million tourists continue to visit each year.

Garden of Gethsemane. Early Christian pilgrims said the olive grove where Jesus prayed on the night of his arrest was on the lower slopes of the Mount of Olives. Rome built a church there in the 300s, but an earthquake destroyed it. In its place stands the Church of All Nations, built in 1924 with donations from sixteen nations. In the courtyard is a small garden with some old olive trees. (See *Gethsemane.*)

Church of the Holy Sepulchre. Jesus was probably crucified and buried on this site. Other sites make that claim, but this one has the oldest tradition—dating to at least the early 300s. That's when Rome built the first Jerusalem church.

Tourists can't visit that church. Persians destroyed it in 614, and later a Muslim caliph hacked the tomb down to level bedrock. What tourists can visit is the church that the Crusaders built on the same site in the 1100s.

Garden tomb. A few blocks north of the church is what appears to be the image of a skull eroded onto the face of a cliff. A short walk away sits a small garden cemetery with an ancient tomb. General Charles Gordon noticed them in 1883. He speculated that the cliff was the crucifixion site: "Golgotha (which means Skull Hill)" (Matthew 27:33). And he figured the tomb once held Jesus. But experts say this tomb was cut in Old Testament times, while Jesus was buried in a "new tomb" (Matthew 27:60).

Western Wall. This is all that remains of the Jewish temple from Jesus' day. It's part of a retaining wall that held the hilltop in place. Jews gained access to this their holiest site after capturing all of Jerusalem in a 1967 war. Today, the wall functions as a synagogue, where Jews pray and conduct rituals such as bar mitzvahs.

Dome of the Rock. One reason the Jews haven't rebuilt their temple is because sitting on the temple hilltop is the oldest surviving Muslim shrine, the Dome of the Rock, completed in 691. It was built to protect a huge rock inside. According to legend, it was on this rock that Abraham nearly sacrificed his son, David built the Jerusalem altar, and Muhammad ascended to heaven.

JESSE
(JESS ee)
Yisay, Hebrew
1000s BC
First mention: Ruth 4:17

Father of Israel's most famous king—David—Jesse was a Bethlehem shepherd with seven older sons, as well. He thought these sons were better suited to meet the visiting prophet Samuel, so Jesse left David in the field taking care of the sheep.

Samuel, however, didn't go to Bethlehem just to meet Jesse's family. He was there to secretly anoint Israel's future king. But God didn't select any of Jesse's seven sons. Only after Samuel pressed Jesse did the elder shepherd acknowledge that he had another son. When David arrived, Samuel somehow knew he was the one destined to lead Israel.

JESUS
(GEEZ us)
Iesous, Greek
Yesua, Hebrew and Aramaic
"the Lord is salvation"
Born about 6 BC, died about AD 30
First mention: Matthew 1:1

There are more than 180,000 words in the New Testament. Boil them down to a single sentence, and Jesus is there. "For God so loved the world that he gave his only Son, so that everyone who believes in him will not perish but have eternal life" (John 3:16).

That shocked the Jews. They didn't know God had a Son. And when they heard about it, most didn't believe it. They couldn't set aside their traditional way of believing in "one God" long enough to consider Jesus' explanation: "The Father and I are one" (John 10:30).

For most devout Jews, nothing could break through the tradition and convince them. Not Jesus healing the sick, calming the storm, or raising the dead. Not prophecies of the Messiah, which are astonishingly accurate in their portrait of Jesus' birth, ministry, and death. Not the radical change in Jesus' disciples—cowardly at the Crucifixion and lionhearted after the Resurrection.

Yet, a few believed. They convinced others. And Christianity was born.

STRANGE FAMILY TREE
Four writers tell the story of Jesus. Their books—written thirty to sixty years after Jesus' death—are called Gospels, from a Greek word that means "Good News."

Each writer had a unique take on the story. Matthew is the most Jewish. As the first book in the New Testament, it's a fine transition from the Jewish Bible that Christians call the Old Testament. Mark is the shortest, most action-packed, and probably the first Gospel written. Luke, tradition says, was written by a non-Jewish physician. He documented details like a historian. John is the work of a deep thinker, intent on proving that Jesus was and is divine.

For the most Jewish of the Gospels, Matthew had an odd way of starting the story. There's nothing odd about an introductory genealogy, especially since the writer

Mary kisses her son, Jesus, in Joseph's carpentry shop.

JESUS' FAMILY

Jesus had brothers and sisters, it seems, though not all Christians agree.

Matthew and Mark both report that when Jesus returned home to Nazareth, the people couldn't understand his sudden fame. "He's just a carpenter's son," they said, "and we know Mary, his mother, and his brothers—James, Joseph, Simon, and Judas. All his sisters live right here among us" (Matthew 13:55–56).

These brothers and sisters weren't Mary's children—so says a church tradition taught among Roman Catholics and traced to at least the late AD 200s.

This tradition says Mary wasn't just a virgin at the birth of Jesus; she stayed a virgin all of her life. Many who believe this speculate that the children may have been Joseph's sons and daughters by an earlier marriage. The New Testament, however, says nothing about this.

wanted to show that Jesus was the promised Messiah, descended from King David.

What is odd are the four women he spotlighted on the family tree. They weren't the four Jewish founder wives: Sarah, Rebekah, Leah, and Rachel. At least three of the four weren't even Jews. They were Tamar the Canaanite, Rahab the Canaanite prostitute of Jericho, Ruth of Moab (now Jordan), and Bathsheba, the wife of a Hittite warrior and later of David. Why Matthew listed them is anyone's guess, but some scholars say the point was this: Gentiles were not God's afterthought. They were family to Israel's greatest kings, David and Solomon, and they were family to Jesus. The Good News was for them, too.

That's also apparent in the story of Jesus' birth. It wasn't rabbis who came with gifts but "wise men from eastern lands" (Matthew 2:1)—probably astrologers from what is now Iran or Iraq. They followed a new star, believing it marked the birthplace of a future king. When they arrived in Jerusalem, they told King Herod about it and asked for directions. Herod consulted the leading Jewish scholars, asking them where the Messiah would be born.

Just six miles south in Bethlehem, they replied, quoting the prophet Micah: "O Bethlehem of Judah, you are not just a lowly village in Judah, for a ruler will come from you who will be the shepherd for my people Israel" (Matthew 2:6).

Herod died in 4 BC, so the wise men arrived some time before then. They told Herod they first saw the star two years earlier, which is why Herod ordered the execution of all Bethlehem boys age two and under. That means Jesus was probably born no later than 6 BC, or perhaps 7 BC. The star that the astrologers followed could have been any number of things, including a comet, the temporary light of a supernova, or perhaps the alignment of Jupiter and Saturn in 6 BC.

Only Matthew and Luke tell about Jesus' birth. But it's a miraculous event in both versions. Matthew tells it from Joseph's point of view, recording Joseph's dreams advising him to go ahead with the marriage and later to take his family to Egypt to escape the Bethlehem slaughter. Luke preserves the now-famous Christmastime reading from Mary's perspective, reporting her visit from the angel Gabriel and her pensive reaction to the shepherds. Both versions describe Jesus as the world's Savior sent from God.

Growing Up

If Mary would have written a Gospel, we might know what kind of child Jesus was. But she didn't, so we don't. Only one scene in the Bible tells of Jesus as a youngster. If it's any indication, he was a gifted child with perhaps a bit of a strong-willed attitude.

When he was twelve, his family made what was perhaps a four-day walk from their home in Nazareth to the temple in Jerusalem. They did this every spring to celebrate one of the most important Jewish holidays, Passover. Pilgrims from all over the

PROPHETS PREDICTING JESUS

Jews were a hard sell when it came to convincing them that their promised Messiah had already come—and He wasn't anything like they expected.

After Jesus ascended into the heavens, the disciples used Jewish Scriptures to make their case, pointing out the many prophecies Jesus fulfilled.

None is more dramatic than one particular chapter about a Suffering Servant. By the time of Jesus, Jews had been studying it for centuries. "He was wounded and crushed for our sins. He was beaten that we might have peace. He was whipped, and we were healed! All of us have strayed away like sheep. We have left God's paths to follow our own. Yet the LORD laid on him the guilt and sins of us all. He was oppressed and treated harshly, yet he never said a word. He was led as a lamb to the slaughter. And as a sheep is silent before the shearers, he did not open his mouth. From prison and trial they led him away to his death. But who among the people realized that he was dying for their sins—that he was suffering their punishment? He had done no wrong, and he never deceived anyone. But he was buried like a criminal; he was put in a rich man's grave" (Isaiah 53:5–9).

Jesus blesses children in a crowd after his disciples tried to shoo the youngsters away.

sounded more like a young man already in touch with his purpose in life than a twelve-year-old boy trying to shift blame: " 'But why did you need to search?' he asked. 'You should have known that I would be in my Father's house' " (Luke 2:49).

Nothing more is known of Jesus' childhood, though Christian writers in later centuries tried to satisfy people's curiosity by writing stories about him. Some stories are bizarre. The *Infancy Gospel of Thomas,* for example, says five-year-old Jesus was playing in the mud, making pools of water, when another boy took a stick to the pools and drained them. "Even now you will be dried up," Jesus said. The boy instantly withered up and died.

Roman Empire poured into the city.

Joseph and Mary couldn't find Jesus when it came time for the Nazareth group to head home. But they assumed he was with some of his friends. When they couldn't find him that evening, they hurried back to Jerusalem and began searching the crowded city. After three days, they found him at the temple, amazing religious scholars with his insights.

His parents weren't impressed. "Why have you done this to us?" Mary said. "Your father and I have been frantic, searching for you everywhere" (Luke 2:48).

In his first recorded words, Jesus

More likely, Jesus experienced a relatively normal childhood. He learned to read, write, and memorize scripture at the synagogue school. His father taught him carpentry—how to make and repair farming implements and household furnishings such as wooden plows, yokes, carts, pitchforks, tables, and beds.

TRAVELING RABBI

"Jesus was about thirty years old when he began his public ministry" (Luke 3:23).

More likely in his midthirties.

202

Jesus launched his ministry after getting baptized by John the Baptist. Based on the names of the Roman rulers Luke identified, John started his ministry sometime between the winter of AD 27 and the summer of AD 29. Since Jesus was born before Herod died in 4 BC, this means he was at least thirty-two years old, and perhaps thirty-six or more when he started teaching others. Luke gave an approximate age—one that's connected to beginnings for other Jewish leaders. Thirty was the age for becoming a priest. It was also the age of Ezekiel when God called him to ministry and of David when he became king. Luke's point was that Jesus was ready.

Jesus didn't find his disciples in the usual way. Typically, students picked the rabbi they wanted as mentor. But Jesus did the picking. And the team he put together is reminiscent of Gideon's tiny army—a group that didn't seem adequate for the job. Gideon had three hundred volunteers against more than one hundred thousand invaders. Jesus had a dozen uneducated men, mostly fishermen, who were to take God's message to the world.

Both stories seem intent on showing how much God can do with so little.

At first, Jesus resisted performing miracles. In Cana, a village near his hometown, Jesus performed his first known miracle: turning water into wine. He did it only at his mother's insistence. Jesus may have hesitated because he knew that once people discovered his power, it wouldn't take long before he'd be hanging from a cross.

Jesus' ministry lasted about three years—an estimate based on the number of times he seems to have gone to Jerusalem for festivals. During those years, he traveled no farther than about seventy miles from his home—as far south as Jerusalem and as far north as Tyre, in what is now Lebanon. He spent most of that time in his hometown

CHRIST, THE TITLE

"Jesus Christ" isn't a name. It's a name and a title together, a bit like "Jesus, Ph.D." The difference is that the title, "Christ," identifies Jesus as the promised Messiah—David's descendant who would save Israel. "Christ" comes from the Greek word *Christos* which translates the Hebrew term *Masiah*, meaning "Anointed One."

Jewish kings were known as messiahs, "anointed ones" chosen by God. For example, when David was on the run from King Saul, David scolded his men for wanting to kill Saul. "It is a serious thing to attack the LORD's anointed one [Messiah], for the LORD himself has chosen him" (1 Samuel 24:6).

It was Peter's brother, Andrew, who first recognized Jesus as the Christ. Andrew told his brother, "We have found the Messiah" (John 1:41).

A ROMAN'S VIEW OF JESUS

Josephus was a Jewish historian and Roman citizen born in AD 37, just a few years after Jesus died. He had this to say about Jesus:

At this time there was a wise man who was called Jesus, and his conduct was good, and he was known to be virtuous. And many people from among the Jews and the other nations became his disciples. Pilate condemned him to be crucified and to die. And those who had become his disciples did not abandon their loyalty to him. They reported that he had appeared to them three days after his crucifixion, and that he was alive. Accordingly they believed that he was the Messiah, concerning whom the Prophets have recounted wonders.

region of Galilee, in northern Israel. The fishing village of Capernaum, where Peter and four other disciples lived, became his base of ministry. Wherever he went, crowds followed.

HIS MESSAGE AND MIRACLES

"At last the time has come!" Jesus announced in his first known sermon. "The Kingdom of God is near! Turn from your sins and believe this Good News!" (Mark 1:15).

Jesus spent much of his time helping people understand what he meant by the "Kingdom of God" and how citizens of that Kingdom should behave. God's Kingdom, as Jesus portrayed it, isn't just heaven somewhere in the believer's future. It's God in charge—past, present, and future. The Kingdom of God was "near" for Jesus' audience because they were about to learn how to become citizens: turn from their sins and pledge allegiance to God.

A masterful teacher, Jesus often used colorful stories—parables—to make an abstract point easier to understand.

"What is the Kingdom of God like?" Jesus once asked. "How can I illustrate it? It is like a tiny mustard seed planted in a garden; it grows and becomes a tree, and the birds come and find shelter among its branches" (Luke 13:18–19). That's a fine description of how the Christian faith blossomed in the following centuries.

There's probably no parable more famous than the one Jesus told about a good Samaritan. Jesus told it to a religious scholar who said he knew he should love his neighbor as himself, but he didn't know who qualified as his neighbor.

Jesus answered with a parable that essentially says all of humanity is our neighbor. As the story goes, bandits attacked a lone Jewish man traveling on the rugged mountain trail between Jerusalem and Jericho. They robbed him, beat him, and left him nearly dead. A priest walked by, saw him, and kept walking. So did a temple assistant. The traveler who finally helped was a man from Samaria, in central Israel. Back then, Samaritans and Jews got along about as well as Palestinians and Jews in recent years. They were racially related but bitter enemies. Jesus asked which of the three was a neighbor.

"The one who showed him mercy," the scholar replied (Luke 10:37).

"Yes," Jesus replied, "now go and do the same" (Luke 10:37).

There was power in the simple, elegant truth of his words. Yet his miracles, for many, added the stamp of God's approval. Jesus healed the sick, exorcised demons, raised the dead, calmed storms, and fed thousands with a little boy's lunch.

HIS LAST DAYS

Even so, the Jewish religious leaders didn't see him as the Messiah or God's Son. They saw him as a troublemaker and a heretic.

Jesus opposed many of their revered interpretations of Jewish law. For example, he healed people on the Sabbath. Healing is work, and it shouldn't be done on the Sabbath, most Jewish scholars insisted. But Jesus said God made the Sabbath to help people, not hurt them. Jesus also associated with disreputable people like prostitutes and crooked tax men, and he justified it by arguing, "Healthy people don't need a doctor—sick people do" (Matthew 9:12).

Jewish scholars could never win a debate with him, so they decided to shut him up. Permanently. They started looking for an opportunity to kill him. They convinced themselves it would be in the best interest of national security, since it would spare the Jewish people from following a fraud messiah into a disastrous war of independence.

"Why should the whole nation be destroyed?" the high priest asked. "Let this one man die for the people" (John 11:50).

Judas, one of Jesus' disciples, provided the opportunity. He told the Jewish leaders where they could arrest Jesus privately, without starting a riot. The Bible doesn't say why Judas did it. Perhaps he thought he could force Jesus into a showdown that would lead to a free Jewish nation.

But as Jesus explained to the Roman governor, Pilate, after an all-night trial by the Jewish leaders, "I am not an earthly king. If I were, my followers would have fought when I was arrested by the Jewish leaders. But my Kingdom is not of this world" (John 18:36).

Instead of fighting, Jesus' followers hid. Only a few women and one of his twelve disciples, presumed to be John, stood at the foot of his cross that Friday and watched him die. Judas committed suicide.

ALIVE AGAIN

Because Jesus died shortly before

Sabbath began at sundown on Friday, the first chance anyone had to prepare his body adequately for burial was on Sunday morning. That's when some women walked to his tomb in a garden cemetery outside of Jerusalem.

Jesus was waiting for them.

He later appeared to his disciples at various times and once even ate with them along the shores of the Sea of Galilee. In addition, "he was seen by more than five hundred of his followers at one time" (1 Corinthians 15:6).

His resurrection did for the disciples what no amount of his teaching and wonder-working had been able to do. It convinced them once and for all that he was who he said he was—God's Son—and that "eternal life" meant just that.

Once cowards, the disciples became courageous preachers who risked their lives to continue Jesus' ministry—in defiance of the same Jewish leaders who had him executed. Christians writing in the next century reported that most of the disciples died martyrs. But by then, the Kingdom of God was sprouting like mustard seeds all over the Roman Empire. And believers were singing songs of prophecy fulfilled: "Death is swallowed up in victory. O death, where is your victory? O death, where is your sting?" (1 Corinthians 15:54–55).

JETHRO
(JETH row)
Yitro, Hebrew
1400s BC
First mention: Exodus 3:1

On the run after killing an Egyptian foreman for mistreating a Hebrew slave, Moses fled east into the Sinai Peninsula. When he stopped running, he found himself near the camp of Jethro, also known as Reuel, a shepherd and priest of Midian. The nation was descended from Midian, one of Abraham's six sons with his second wife, Keturah (Genesis 25:1–2).

Jethro hired Moses as a shepherd and let him marry one of his daughters, Zipporah. Decades later, when Moses led the Hebrews through the Sinai region, Jethro advised the overworked Moses to delegate some duties, such as settling disputes.

Experts aren't certain which god Jethro served as a priest. Midianites generally worshiped idols. But after hearing how God saved the Hebrews from Egypt, Jethro declared, "I know now that the LORD is greater than all other gods" (Exodus 18:11).

JEZEBEL
(JEZZ uh bell)
Izebel, Hebrew
"where is the prince?"
Reigned about 875–854 BC
First mention: 1 Kings 16:31

The "queen of mean" among Jews was no Jew. Not by race and certainly not by religion. In fact, if Jezebel had finished what she started, there would have been no Jewish religion left in her kingdom, the northern Jewish nation of Israel.

Jezebel's father was King Ethbaal of Sidon, a Phoenician city in what is now Lebanon, about twenty miles south of Beirut. Israel's king Omri arranged the marriage to his son Ahab to strengthen ties between the two countries. Omri had no idea that this strong-minded woman would almost single-handedly wipe out Judaism in Israel.

Jezebel worshiped the Canaanite gods of Baal and Asherah and proved herself an effective promoter of the religion. Her strategy was simple: Elevate the status of preferred religious leaders, and kill the others. With money from the royal treasury, she supported a kind of religious congress: 450 Baal prophets and 400 Asherah prophets— even feeding them. She tried to wipe out God's prophets, how-

Carved from ivory, this regal woman peering out of a window is reminiscent of the wicked queen Jezebel. Servants threw her from a palace window.

ever, in a bloody holocaust. One hundred survived by hiding in caves.

The prophet Elijah boldly challenged all 850 of Jezebel's prophets to a showdown on Mount Carmel. The challenge was to call down fire from the sky to light a sacrificial offering— right up Baal's alley as a weather god, since he was often pictured holding lightning bolts. Yet Jezebel's prophets lost, and at Elijah's command the crowd killed them.

Jezebel wasn't intimidated. Remarkably self-confident, she intimidated Elijah with nothing but a one-sentence message: "May the gods also kill me if by this time tomorrow I have failed to take your life like those whom you killed" (1 Kings 19:2). Elijah fled into the desert.

MURDERING FOR VEGETABLES

Absolute power had made it hard for Jezebel to understand Ahab's depression when a farmer refused to sell him a piece of land. Ahab wanted a man named Naboth's vineyard for a vegetable garden.

"Are you the king of Israel or not?" she asked (1 Kings 21:7). She arranged to have two men testify that Naboth had cursed God and the king. Found guilty, Naboth was stoned to death, and Ahab happily confiscated his land.

God sent Elijah with a message for Ahab. The king and his family would die violently, and dogs would eat the body of Jezebel. Ahab died later from a battle wound, but Jezebel lived on as queen mother during the reigns of two sons, Ahaziah and Joram. She died in a coup that ended Ahab's dynasty. But she died with mean-spirited style. Hearing that the coup leader, Jehu, was coming and had killed her son, "she painted her eyelids and fixed her hair and sat at a window." Then she yelled down at Jehu, "Have you come in peace, you murderer?" (2 Kings 9:30–31).

Jehu called up to the harem eunuchs: "Throw her down!" (2 Kings 9:33). They did, Jehu ran over her with his horse-drawn chariot, and dogs ate her body. By the time Jehu gave the order to bury her, all that was left was her skull, feet, and hands.

JEZREEL
(jez REEL)
Yizre el, Hebrew
"God plants"
700s BC
First mention: Hosea 1:4

God told the prophet Hosea what to name his first son.

"Name the child Jezreel, for I am about to punish King Jehu's dynasty to avenge the murders he committed at Jezreel" (Hosea 1:4). Jehu's dynasty began with Israel's bloodiest coup at the city of Jezreel. It ended four generations after him with the assassination of his great-great-grandson, Zechariah.

JEZREEL
(jez REEL)
Yizre el, Hebrew
"God plants"
First mention: Joshua 15:56

MAP 2
C3

Once upon a time, the heads of seventy princes were piled up at the entrance of a city. That city was Jezreel, and the head stack was a grisly monument to a murdered grape farmer.

Ahab and Jezebel, rulers of Israel, often lived at their second palace in this hilltop city, which had a stunning view of the vast Jezreel valley. Jezebel orchestrated the farmer's murder after he refused to sell his family vineyard to the king, who wanted to rip up the vines and plant vegetables.

The prophet Elijah vowed Ahab's family would die for this. Later, Ahab died in battle, and one of the Israelite commanders led a coup to wipe out the rest of the family. He murdered Ahab's son, the new king. And he ordered the queen mother, Jezebel, thrown from her palace window. He crushed her beneath his chariot. Then he ordered Ahab's sons killed, with their heads stacked at the front gate.

Archaeologists started excavating the city in 1990, two years after a construction worker on a bulldozer accidentally discovered the ruins while leveling ground for a visitors' center parking lot.

A patchwork of crops covers the largest and richest plain of Israel—the Jezreel valley. On the distant horizon lies the rounded hill of Mount Tabor, where Deborah's forces defeated an invading chariot corps.

JEZREEL VALLEY
First mention: Joshua 17:16

MAP 4
B3

Israel's largest valley is a vast and fertile plain known by various names: Jezreel valley, Plain of Esdraelon, and Valley of Armageddon. Roughly shaped like a triangle about twenty miles by twenty miles by twelve miles, the valley lies at the foot of the Mount Carmel mountain range in northern Israel.

Dozens of battles have been fought in this valley throughout the centuries, including several mentioned in the Bible (Joshua, Deborah, Gideon, King Josiah). Some scholars say that John in the book of Revelation tells of a future battle there in which God's army will defeat world forces allied with an evil leader. Others say the battle isn't literal, but a symbol of God defeating evil once and for all.

Today, the valley is home to productive farms, bustling cities such as Afula, and highways leading to the busy coastal town of Haifa. (See also *Armageddon.*)

JOAB
(JOE ab)
Yoab, Hebrew
"the Lord is father"
1000s BC
First mention:
2 Samuel 2:13

Joab was the military man behind Israel's most successful warrior king, David—the ruler who put Israel on the map and secured its borders. In spite of that, just before the elderly uncle David died—Joab was a son of David's sister—David ordered Joab executed. Character traits that built Joab into a huge commander also, in time, eroded him into a small person.

KILLER INSTINCT
All three sons of David's sister, Zeruiah, fought in David's army even before he was king. But the job of commander went to Joab after he rose to David's challenge to lead the attack on Jerusalem. Joab rose literally. He and some men went into the hidden cave of Gihon Spring under the hilltop city and climbed up a fifty-foot-high vertical shaft that served as a well to the spring.

Cunning and courageous though he was, Joab was also driven by revenge and power. When Abner, the general of King Saul's successor, wanted to

Skilled and ruthless, Joab commanded David's army. But for murdering David's rebel son and others, Joab was eventually executed.

switch sides to David—bringing the army with him—Joab murdered Abner. He did it because Abner had killed one of Joab's brothers in a battle. David was livid.

Joab later killed David's son Absalom, who led a coup—even though David had asked his soldiers to spare the prince. For this, David replaced Joab with another commander—Amasa. But Joab murdered him, too, and got his job back.

As the elderly David lay dying, Joab backed David's oldest son, Adonijah, as the future king. But David chose Solomon. And as a last request, David asked Solomon to remember Joab's murders and "don't let him die in peace" (1 Kings 2:6). Joab was executed as he held on to the altar at Jerusalem's worship center, perhaps hoping to receive what he never seemed ready to give—mercy.

JOASH

(JOE ash)
Yoas, Hebrew
"The Lord gives"
Reigned 832–803 BC
First mention: 2 Kings 11:2

Joash was just a one-year-old baby when his grandmother, Athaliah, ordered him executed. Her son, King Ahaziah of Judah, had just been murdered, and she wanted to become queen. So she ordered the entire royal family killed. Only Joash survived. He was spirited away by an aunt to the Jerusalem temple. Six years later, a priest, Jehoiada, orchestrated a coup. The queen was executed and seven-year-old Joash became king.

Jehoiada initially ran the country and later served as Joash's main adviser. So it's not surprising that Joash ordered an extensive repair of the temple.

JOB

(JOHB)
Iyob, Hebrew
Possibly "where is the divine father?"
Perhaps about 2000 BC
First mention: Job 1:1

Famed for his patience in suffering, Job wasn't that patient.

Who would have been, under

those horrifying circumstances? A rich man, Job suddenly lost his flocks of thousands, all ten of his children, and eventually his health.

Then, as he sat scraping his oozing boils, his wife told him to curse God and die. If that wasn't enough to depress him, Zophar, one of his best friends who came to comfort him, offered this critique: "God is doubtless punishing you far less than you deserve!" (Job 11:6).

With stress like that, pursuing patience wasn't at the top of Job's list. He wanted justice, and he had a few choice words for God about it. "Why won't you leave me alone—even for a moment? . . . What have I done to you, O watcher of all humanity? Why have you made me your target?" (Job 7:19–20).

What unfolds is a remarkable, insightful debate about human suffering.

SEARCHING FOR JOB
It's so hard to place Job in history that some scholars suggest he doesn't belong there—that he was a fictional character in a story intended only to teach people to trust God even in difficult times.

Others see clues that Job lived in the times of the patriarchs Abraham, Isaac, and Jacob.

- A man with a similar name, Iob, is listed as Jacob's grandson (Genesis 46:13 NASB).

- The story mentions Sabean and Chaldean raiders, who lived in those times.
- Job survived 140 years after his tragedies, which fits the long life span of the Jewish fathers.
- Job's wealth was measured by the size of his flocks, as was common in those times.
- The type of money mentioned in Job 42:11, a *kesitah,* is from those times.
- Job served as a household priest, apparently before the formal priesthood.
- Job's story has more rare words than any other book in the Bible—a testament to its age.

Job uses a broken piece of pottery to scratch his oozing sores. Perplexed by his suffering, he asks God to explain himself.

Job lived in the land of Uz, which doesn't help much in pinpointing his location. Uz is mentioned elsewhere in the Bible, but it's unclear exactly where Uz was. Bible lists connect it with territory now occupied by Syria and Jordan. And one of Job's friends came from Edom, in what is now Jordan. So Job may have lived in that general area.

Those were fine grazing lands, which Job would have needed. The richest man in the region, he owned seven thousand sheep, three thousand camels, five hundred teams of oxen, and five hundred donkeys. He also had seven sons and three daughters. By ancient standards, Job was a man extraordinarily blessed of God.

ANOTHER SUFFERING JOB

There are other ancient stories of unjust suffering, including one from the world's first known civilization—Sumer, a kingdom in what is now southern Iraq.

Written before 2000 BC, the story is called "A Man and His God," but it is more commonly known as the Sumerian Job.

Like the Bible's Job, the Sumerian Job insisted he had done nothing wrong and was suffering unjustly.

The Bible Job lamented his suffering: "Cursed be the night when I was conceived" (Job 3:3). So did the Sumerian Job: "Let my mother who bore me not stop lamenting for me."

In the end, both declare faith in their God. The Sumerian Job says it with poetry: "I have set my sights on you as on the rising sun."

TOTAL LOSS

As the story goes, God tells Satan that Job is the finest man on earth. Satan says it's no wonder, given how God has blessed him with prosperity. "Take away everything he has," Satan says, "and he will surely curse you to your face!" (Job 1:11). So God allowed Satan to test Job's faith.

Suddenly, messengers started arriving at Job's home—all with tragic news. Raiders stole the oxen and donkeys, then killed the workers. Fire killed the sheep and shepherds. Other raiders stole the camels and killed the herders. A wind toppled the house, crushing all of his children. "The LORD gave me everything I had, and the LORD has taken it away," Job said. "Praise the name of the LORD!" (Job 1:21).

Satan got permission to extend the suffering, and he struck Job with boils from head to toe.

LOUSY COMFORTERS

Three of Job's friends—Eliphaz, Bildad, and Zophar—arrived to console him. For a full week, they sat with him in silence—which was the only smart thing they did.

Once they started talking, they

only inflated Job's misery with their hot air.

The problem was that in ancient times people tended to think that the gods rewarded good people with prosperity and punished bad people with disasters, poverty, and sickness. So it was clear to Job's friends that he had done something to deserve his suffering.

Eliphaz: "My experience shows that those who plant trouble and cultivate evil will harvest the same" (Job 4:8).

Bildad: "Does the Almighty twist what is right? Your children obviously sinned against him, so their punishment was well deserved" (Job 8:3–4).

Zophar: "If only you would prepare your heart and lift up your hands to him in prayer! Get rid of your sins" (Job 11:13–14).

Job's response: "What miserable comforters you are!" (Job 16:2).

GOD THE DEBATER

God has a few choice words of his own for everyone who thinks they know so much. That includes Job's comforters, a latecomer named Elihu, and especially Job himself.

Speaking from a whirlwind, the Lord asked a long string of questions that humans couldn't possibly answer. Questions like these:

- "Where were you when I laid the foundations of the earth? Tell me, if you know so much" (Job 38:4).
- "Can you hold back the movements of the stars?" (Job 38:31).

QUOTABLE JOB

Many old sayings that people still use come from the Bible. Three come from Job:

- I escaped by the skin of my teeth (from Job 19:20).
- Naked I came into this world, and naked I'll leave (from Job 1:21).
- The LORD gives and the LORD takes away (from Job 1:21).

Job got the point: There's a limit to human understanding. But the end of understanding can be the beginning of faith in God.

Job replied, "I take back everything I said, and I sit in dust and ashes to show my repentance" (Job 42:6).

God blessed Job with ten more children and larger flocks: fourteen thousand sheep, six thousand camels, one thousand teams of oxen, and one thousand donkeys.

JOCHEBED
(JOCK uh bed)
Yokebed, Hebrew
1500s BC
First mention: Exodus 6:20

If Moses' mother—Jochebed—had lived by the laws her son later gave the Hebrews, Moses wouldn't have been born. Moses' father, Amram, married his aunt. That was forbidden under the laws God gave Moses.

Jochebed was born during the 430 years the Hebrews lived in Egypt. She was in the extended family of Levi, the tribe later entrusted with running Israel's worship system. By the time Moses was born, Pharaoh had become so worried about the Hebrews overrunning his country that he ordered all newborn Hebrew boys thrown into the Nile River.

Locusts swarm onto an Israeli farm. Joel used this common natural disaster to warn of an invasion force that would wipe out the Jewish nation.

In a way, Jochebed obeyed. She just made sure her son floated.

She nursed Moses for three months, then put him in a papyrus reed basket waterproofed with tar. Then she set the basket near the riverbank, among tall reeds that blocked the current from pushing it downstream. Jochebed chose the very spot and time of day that Pharaoh's daughter bathed.

When the princess found Moses, her heart melted. Jochebed's daughter, Miriam, was on hand, asking the princess if she should find a Hebrew to nurse the baby. Jochebed took Moses home, nursed him, and got paid for it.

JOEL
Yoel, Hebrew
"the Lord is God"
First mention: Joel 1:1

There are more than a dozen men in the Bible named Joel. Unfortunately, the most famous of them is a man we know almost nothing about. Scholars can't even place him within four hundred years of when he lived.

The Bible identifies him as the son of Pethuel. He's also the prophet who wrote the book named after him. With only three chapters, it's one of the shortest books in the Bible. But it paints graphic word pictures: "A vast army of locusts has invaded my land. It is a terrible army, too numerous to count! Its teeth are as sharp as the teeth of lions!" (Joel 1:6).

Joel used this natural disaster that was all too common in the ancient Middle East to illustrate the horror of a coming invasion. But which invasion? Assyrians in the 700s BC, Babylonians in the 500s BC, or perhaps Alexander the Great in the 300s BC? Joel didn't say.

JOHN

Ioannes, Greek
From *Johanan,* Hebrew
"the Lord has been gracious"
First century AD
First mention: Matthew 4:21

"Sons of thunder" is what Jesus nick-named two of his closest disciples, John and his brother, James. We can only guess why because the Bible doesn't say. Actually, they were sons of Zebedee, a Galilean fisherman successful enough to hire a crew. The family lived near the fishing village of Capernaum, Jesus' ministry headquarters.

Scholars say the brothers probably earned their nickname because of their bold and impetuous style. When Samaritans refused to welcome Jesus and his entourage into their city, the brothers sounded a bit like they had a hotline to lightning: "Should we order down fire from heaven to burn them up?" (Luke 9:54). Another time, John ordered a man exorcising demons in Jesus' name to stop because he wasn't one of the twelve disciples.

But the boldest request they made —one that upset the other ten disciples—was asking if they could sit beside Jesus on his throne. Jesus didn't give them satisfaction in any of these cases, declining their requests and telling them not to stop miracle workers.

Even so, Jesus had a special connection to the brothers and Peter. They were his best friends, invited to witness events the other disciples would only hear about: the raising of Jairus'

Ruins of a first-century boat, retrieved from the Sea of Galilee during a drought.

daughter, the Transfiguration when Jesus met with Elijah and Moses, and Jesus' private prayer in the Garden of Gethsemane. John and Peter were entrusted with preparing the Last Supper.

CHURCH PILLAR

After Jesus returned to heaven, his three best friends continued the ministry and became what the apostle Paul described as "pillars of the church" (Galatians 2:9).

John's brother, James, became the first disciple martyred. Later, Peter and the other disciples followed, with John alone living a long life and dying a natural death. At least that's what some church leaders reported a century or more later.

Church tradition says John wrote the Gospel of John, apparently referring to himself only as "the disciple he [Jesus] loved." Though the Gospel names the other disciples, it never mentions John by name. Church tradition also says John moved to Ephesus, along the Turkish coast, and wrote the three letters of John. In addition, church leaders said he was "God's servant John" (Revelation 1:1) who wrote the last book in the Bible, while exiled on Patmos Island near Ephesus.

Many scholars, however, doubt that a fisherman could write much of anything, let alone some of the finest Greek

prose in the New Testament. But at least one fisherman—Peter—produced refined Greek with the help of a friend: "I have written this short letter to you with the help of Silas" (1 Peter 5:12).

JOHN THE BAPTIST
Born about 6 BC, died about AD 28
First mention: Matthew 3:1

If God wanted to draw a crowd before introducing his Son to the world, John the Baptist was a great choice. Crowd appeal was guaranteed, given John's creative blend of qualities.

- **Bizarre.** Other Jewish spiritual leaders dressed for success in imported robes draped with over-

JOHN IN OLD TESTAMENT PROPHECY

Jews were expecting a Messiah—a hero to lead Israel back to God and back to international glory like King David did a thousand years earlier. But before the Messiah came, they expected a prophet to prepare the way.

Old Testament prophecies like these led the Jews to that correct assumption.

- "Look! I am sending my messenger, and he will prepare the way before me. Then the Lord you are seeking will suddenly come to his Temple. The messenger of the covenant, whom

you look for so eagerly, is surely coming" (Malachi 3:1).
- "Listen! I hear the voice of someone shouting, 'Make a highway for the LORD through the wilderness. Make a straight, smooth road through the desert for our God' " (Isaiah 40:3).

John saw himself as that advance man. When Jewish priests asked him who he was, he paraphrased Isaiah, "I am a voice shouting in the wilderness, 'Prepare a straight pathway for the Lord's coming!' " (John 1:23)

sized prayer shawls, and they dined on rich food. But John wore scratchy camel-hair clothes strapped on with a leather belt. His balanced meal was grasshopper-like locusts and wild honey.

- **Innovative.** He started baptizing people who repented of their sins. He apparently adapted the idea from the Jewish practice of taking a ritual bath to purify oneself for worship.

- **Retro.** He was a living, breathing prophet in a day when prophets were little more than nostalgic characters from Jewish history.

- **Genuine.** His words and actions rang true, tracking with the old-time religion when prophets called Israel to repent of their sins. Crowds loved him, as both the Bible and ancient Roman history confirms.

MIRACLE BABY

Like several bigger-than-life characters in Jewish history, John was born to elderly parents who hadn't been able to have children. In the same crowd are Isaac, Samson, and Samuel.

His parents, Zechariah and Elizabeth, were both from priest families. And his father worked at the temple as a priest, back when sons usually followed in their father's footsteps. In fact, it was while Zechariah was in the temple that the angel Gabriel announced John's birth: "He will precede the

JOHN THE BAPTIST IN ROMAN HISTORY

The Bible isn't the only first-century record we have of John the Baptist.

His story shows up in a Jewish history book written by Josephus, a Roman Jew who was born about ten years after the Galilean ruler Herod Antipas ordered John's head cut off.

Names of key Bible characters such as John the Baptist, Jesus, and James are why Josephus' history survived. Jews ignored his work because they considered him a traitor. It was Christian writers who preserved it because it supported the New Testament.

Josephus confirmed the story of John's execution and added some interesting background. Josephus said that after executing John, Herod lost a battle to the Arabians, and the Jews concluded this was "punishment for what he did to John, who was called the Baptist. Herod killed him, a good man who commanded the Jews to exercise virtue, both in righteousness to one another and in piety to God, and in this spirit to be baptized."

After Herod Antipas promises his stepdaughter anything she wants for the pleasing dance she performed, she asks for the head of John the Baptist.

coming of the Lord, preparing the people for his arrival" (Luke 1:17).

Six months later, Gabriel told Mary that Jesus would be born and that John was already on his way. Mary and Elizabeth were related, though the Bible doesn't say how, so Mary paid a visit to Elizabeth. Gabriel may have been talking to Elizabeth, as well, given how Elizabeth greeted Mary: "What an honor this is, that the mother of my Lord should visit me! When you came in and greeted me, my baby jumped for joy the instant I heard your voice!" (Luke 1:43–44).

PROPHET INSTEAD OF PRIEST

John became a monklike prophet living in the wilderness, perhaps in the Judean desert along the Dead Sea. Why he chose this lifestyle over the more affluent one of a priest remains a mystery. Perhaps God led him, or he chose a lifestyle in keeping with prophecies he believed he would fulfill.

Some scholars wonder if John joined the Essenes, an isolationist branch of Jews who lived in the Qumran settlement that produced the Dead Sea Scrolls. But many say it's unlikely because Essenes didn't mix with crowds the way John did.

When John started his ministry, he preached along both sides of the Jordan River. It was after such a baptism service that Jesus started his own ministry, surrounded by John's crowds.

When John saw Jesus coming, he declared, "Look! There is the Lamb of God who takes away the sin of the world! He is the one I was talking about when I said, 'Soon a man is coming who is far greater than I am, for he existed long before I did.' I didn't know he was the one, but I have been baptizing with water in order to point him out to Israel" (John 1:29–31).

With John's assignment complete, many of his disciples started following Jesus. Some time later, John was beheaded at the order of the Galilean ruler Herod Antipas. John had publicly criticized Herod's marriage to Herodias, the ex-wife of Herod's brother. This was an incestuous marriage forbidden by Jewish law. When Herodias' daughter danced at Herod's birthday party, he was so delighted that he offered her anything. She consulted her mother, then requested John's head on a platter.

When Jesus heard the news, "he went off by himself in a boat to a remote area to be alone" (Matthew 14:13).

JONAH

(JOE. nuh)
Yona, Hebrew
"dove"
700s BC
First mention: 2 Kings 14:25

Best known for getting swallowed by a huge fish, Jonah bears yet another incredible distinction among God's prophets. He gave only one prophecy in the book named after him. And it didn't come true.

PROPHET ON THE RUN

If Jonah had gotten his way, there would have been no humiliating book named after him. He lived in the small Galilean village of Gath-hepher, near Nazareth, in the northern Jewish nation of Israel. And he lived there just a few decades before Israel got erased from the world map by one of history's most vicious empires—Assyria.

God told Jonah to go to Assyria's capital—Nineveh—near what is now Mosul in northern Iraq. Jonah's mission was to deliver bad news: "Forty days from now Nineveh will be destroyed!" (Jonah 3:4).

That was a bit like asking a Jew in the early 1940s to deliver similar news to Hitler in Berlin.

Jonah did what he thought was prudent. He caught a ship headed in the opposite direction.

A fierce storm erupted, forcing the crew to toss cargo overboard so the ship would ride higher in the water. In desperation, they cast lots—which may have been a bit like throwing dice. Jonah lost the toss, indicating he was the one who got the gods angry enough to churn up the storm. He admitted he was running away from God's assignment, and he told the crew to throw him overboard.

A large fish swallowed him. Jonah remained in the fish's stomach for three days. Jesus later said this foreshadowed his time in the grave: "For as Jonah was in the belly of the great fish for three days and three nights, so I, the Son of Man, will be in the heart of the earth for three days and three nights" (Matthew 12:40).

Tossed overboard as a sacrifice to calm a storm, Jonah is swallowed by a big fish.

NOT NECESSARILY A WHALE STORY

The Bible doesn't say a whale swallowed Jonah.

The original Hebrew language simply calls it a *dag gadol*, literally translated "fish great" (as in "big fish").

The writer could have used this general "fish" term for any number of reasons. Perhaps no one got a good look at the fish.

Another possibility may be related to the fact that Israelites weren't known for their seafaring savvy. They didn't have one good seaport until New Testament times, when King Herod built a harbor at Caesarea. So they may not have distinguished one fish from another, except to identify them as kosher and nonkosher.

DEPRESSED ABOUT SUCCESS

God ordered the fish to spit Jonah onto the shore. From there, Jonah traveled to Nineveh—a four-hundred-mile walk from the nearest beach. There, he delivered the message and became one of the few prophets who actually convinced people to repent. Because of Jonah's success, God didn't destroy Nineveh.

"I knew that you were a gracious and compassionate God," Jonah complained, furious about God's decision to show mercy. "Just kill me now, LORD! I'd rather be dead than alive because nothing I predicted is going to happen" (Jonah 4:2–3).

"Nineveh has more than 120,000 people," God answered. "Shouldn't I feel sorry for such a great city?" (Jonah 4:11).

That's how the story ends, almost like a make-believe parable to show that God cares for everyone—Jews and non-Jews alike. Many scholars say the story is just that. Others insist Jonah was a real prophet who was mentioned elsewhere during the reign of Jeroboam II (2 Kings 14:25).

JONATHAN
(JOHN uh thun)
Yonatan, Hebrew
"The Lord has given"
Died about 1010 BC
First mention: 1 Samuel 13:2

King Saul's oldest son, Jonathan, might have become one of Israel's greatest kings—had he survived his father. Brave and modest, with common sense and uncommon faith in God, Jonathan may have enjoyed the glory that went to his best friend, David. But Jonathan chose to die alongside his father in a hopeless battle.

Prince Jonathan first shows up in the Bible as commander of one thousand elite soldiers, defeating a Philistine garrison near Saul's capital at Gibeah. In response, the Philistines massed an army so huge that Israelite soldiers deserted by the thousands, until only a few hundred remained. Jonathan saved his nation. He and the man who carried his armor sneaked out of camp and attacked the Philistine outpost at a mountain pass. He knew the odds were against him, yet he assured his comrade that God would give them victory. They killed about twenty men. This, followed by an earthquake, panicked the Philistines, who fled.

PROTECTING HIS BEST FRIEND

After David killed Goliath, David was invited to move into the palace, where he met Jonathan. "There was an immediate bond of love between them, and they became the best of friends" (1 Samuel 18:1).

King Saul, however, grew insanely jealous of David and began plotting ways to kill him. He even asked Jonathan to assassinate David. Jonathan warned David instead and told him to hide. Afterward, Jonathan changed his father's mind. But Saul's jealousy returned, and he sent soldiers to kill David. David escaped and told Jonathan, who couldn't believe it. Again Jonathan advised David to hide. Saul got so angry at Jonathan's support of David that Saul tried to kill his own son with a spear.

Jonathan knew his best friend had to leave—and stay away as long as Saul lived. "Both of them were in tears as they embraced each other and said good-bye" (1 Samuel 20:41).

Loyal in life to his friend, Jonathan also proved himself loyal in death to his father. Jonathan stayed at Saul's side in the doomed battle, when the Philistine army overran the Israelites at Mount Gilboa. Saul died, along with three of his sons: Jonathan, Abinadab, and Malkishua.

JOPPA

(JOP uh)
Yapo, Hebrew
"beautiful"
First mention: Joshua 19:46

MAP 4
A4

Joppa is the seaside city where Jonah sailed away on a ship and made the unexpected voyage back inside a large fish. It's also where the king of Tyre sent rafts of cedar logs from Lebanon so Solomon's men could haul them thirty miles to Jerusalem for construction of the temple. Joppa was also where the apostle Peter raised from the dead a woman named Tabitha and where he later had a vision of God telling him to eat nonkosher food—prompting him to accept Gentiles into the church.

Today, Joppa is the southern half of the twin cities of Tel Aviv-Yafo, Israel's second largest metropolitan area after Jerusalem.

JORAM

(JOE ram)
Yoram, Hebrew
"God is exalted"
Reigned 850–843 BC
First mention: 2 Kings 1:17

A deadly coup that started with the murder of King Joram—son of Ahab and Jezebel—ended the three-generation dynasty that started with Ahab's father, Omri.

The prophet Elisha instigated the coup by anointing a military commander named Jehu as Israel's next king. Jehu got into a chariot and rode with some of his men to the city of Jezreel, where Joram was recovering from a battle wound. When Joram rode out to meet the commander, Jehu shot him through the heart with an arrow, then went inside the city and killed Jezebel. Next he ordered seventy princes beheaded and piled their heads at the city gate.

JORDAN RIVER
(JOR dun)
Yarden, Hebrew
Perhaps "the descender" or "water of Dan"
First mention: Genesis 50:10

MAP 1
C4

Compared to world-class rivers, the Jordan flowing south out of the Sea of Galilee is just a small stream. But with the floods of spring—when the Israelites arrived—it often became too swift and deep to cross.

The Jordan may be a "mighty river" in the desert Middle East, but it's a disappointment to tourists. At roughly thirty yards across and only two to ten feet deep, it seems barely fit for a canoe.

Yet it's the biggest and most important river in Israel—one that has carved and nourished a fertile river valley stretching from the Sea of Galilee to the Dead Sea—about seventy miles as a bird flies, but twice as long as the river winds.

The Jordan actually starts north of there. It gets much of its water from four streams fed by the melting snow on Mount Hermon in Lebanon, along the borders with Syria and Israel. These streams merge north of the Sea of Galilee to become what is sometimes called the Upper Jordan.

Farmers make good use of the narrow river valley, which averages only about six miles wide. But in the plain of Jericho, near the Dead Sea, the valley spreads out fifteen miles wide into orchards, vineyards, and gardens.

When Joshua and the Israelites crossed the Jordan, they did so on dry ground because "the water began piling up at a town upstream called Adam" (Joshua 3:16). Adam is near one of at least sixty fords across the river—shallow land caused by silt buildup or crumbled dirt cliffs. In 1927, an earthquake shook loose part of the 150-foot dirt cliffs at Adam, dropping them into the Jordan and damming up the river for almost a full day.

JOSEPH

(JOE zuhf)

Yosep, Hebrew

"may the Lord add more sons"

1. About 1800s BC

2, 3. Died first century AD

First mention: 1. Genesis 30:24

2. Matthew 1:16

3. Matthew 27:57

1. **Son of Jacob.** There are sixteen Josephs in the Bible, but the first is the one we know best. That's because his life's story consumes about a fourth of Genesis, the first book in the Bible. Chapter for chapter, that nearly puts him on equal footing with his great-grandfather, Abraham, founding father of the Jews.

Joseph may not seem as important as Abraham, but he was certainly the man of his century. Joseph is the reason the Jews spent 430 years in Egypt and had to be led home by Moses. It was on that trip home that God forged a ragtag bunch of refugees into the Jewish nation.

PAMPERED SON

Joseph's problems likely started the day he was born.

He was the first son of Jacob's favorite wife, Rachel, who had been infertile for so long that Jacob was an old man by the time Joseph arrived. Jacob had a dozen sons by his two wives and their two maids who served as surrogate mothers. But from Joseph's birthday onward, he was daddy's boy.

In a family of mothers and children fiercely competing for Jacob's affection, that made Joseph the primary target. He didn't help himself. In a way, Joseph was a target sticking out his tongue; he flaunted his favorite-son status and stoked the fire of jealousy.

At age seventeen, he dressed the part, wearing a beautiful one-of-a-kind robe his father gave him. He talked the part, reporting a dream he had about bundles of grain owned by his brothers bowing to his bundle of grain. And he talked the part some more, telling of another dream about eleven stars along with the sun and moon bowing before him—a dream everyone clearly saw as representing his family, with the sun and moon as his father and mother.

These dreams were a prophecy of what would happen decades later in Egypt. But Joseph's brothers thought they were just another way of rubbing it in. So they decided to rub him out.

They got their chance while grazing sheep about a three-day walk from their home in Hebron. They had taken the flocks some sixty miles north to Dothan, searching for good pasture. Jacob sent Joseph to check on them.

"Here comes that dreamer!" one of his brothers said. "Come on, let's kill him and throw him into a deep pit. We can tell our father that a wild animal has eaten him. Then we'll see what becomes of all his dreams!" (Genesis 37:19–20).

Instead, a caravan of Egyptian-bound traders came along and bought him as a slave for eight ounces of silver—$27.00 at today's price when silver sells for $4.50 an ounce. The brothers killed a goat, dipped Joseph's robe in it, then took it home to their father. They told him an animal had eaten Joseph.

FROM SLAVE TO RULER

It looked like Joseph would live a cushy life in Egypt because Potiphar, captain of the palace guard, bought him. Even better, Potiphar liked him and eventually made him the household business manager in charge of crops, livestock, and everything else involving his investments.

Unfortunately, Potiphar's wife had an eye for Joseph, a young man who was handsome and well built. Day after day she sexually harassed him, but he refused to have sex with her. One day, when no one else was around, she grabbed him by the shirt and made her demand: "Sleep with me!" (Genesis 39:12).

Joseph took off running, leaving her holding his ripped shirt. She retaliated by screaming rape—which rallied the servants. When her husband came home, she told him a twisted tale of fighting off the handsome slave who wanted her body.

Potiphar probably didn't buy her story. If he had, he would have executed Joseph on the spot. Instead, he put Joseph in prison—token punishment for such a violent crime committed by a slave.

Joseph flourished in prison, as well, with the jailer putting him in charge of running the facility. Prison is where Joseph first showed his ability to interpret dreams. He correctly predicted that a dream by Pharaoh's chief wine steward meant that the steward would get his old job back at the palace. Joseph also gave Pharaoh's baker the tragic news that the baker would be executed in three days.

The wine steward, restored to his job, quickly forgot about Joseph. But two years later, Pharaoh had a pair of troubling dreams. The steward suggested consulting Joseph.

In his dreams, Pharaoh saw seven gaunt cows eat seven fat cows and seven dried-up heads of grain swallow seven plump heads of grain. Joseph said the dreams warned that seven years of prosperity in Egypt would be wiped out by seven years of drought. Joseph advised the king to appoint the wisest man in Egypt to implement a nationwide program to stockpile grain so it could be rationed and sold during the drought.

Joseph got the job. Suddenly, an imprisoned slave became Egypt's second in command. Joseph was thirty years old. Pharaoh renamed him Zaphenath-paneah, which means "God speaks and lives." Then Pharaoh gave him an Egyptian wife, Asenath, daughter of a priest.

SURPRISE FAMILY REUNION

As predicted, there were bumper crops for seven years. Even Joseph's family grew. He had two sons, Manasseh and Ephraim. Drought came next. During that first or second dry year, Jacob heard about stored grain in Egypt and sent his ten oldest sons down to buy some. He kept his youngest son, Benjamin, with him since Benjamin was the only other child he had with Rachel, and he didn't want to risk losing him as he had lost Joseph.

Arriving in Egypt, Jacob's sons bowed before the man in charge of grain distribution—their brother— just as Joseph had dreamed some twenty years earlier. They didn't recognize him, but he recognized them. He quickly hatched a clever scheme to find out if they regretted what they did to him and to compel them to bring Benjamin down to Egypt so all the brothers could meet.

Joseph accused them of being spies, imprisoned them, and secretly listened to them talk. When they complained that this was happening because of what they had done to their little brother years ago, Joseph wept.

Joseph released all but Simeon, keeping him as a hostage while the others went home to bring back Benjamin. When Benjamin arrived, Joseph set up his little brother. It was a test to see how the older brothers would react. Joseph threw a banquet and fed Benjamin five times what he gave the others—special treatment, like Joseph had once received. Then Joseph had money and a silver cup stuffed in Benjamin's bags, as though Benjamin stole them. Joseph then arrested Benjamin.

Instead of abandoning their little brother, the others stood by him. Judah offered to take Benjamin's place and die.

Joseph began sobbing. " 'I am Joseph!' he said to his brothers. 'Is my father still alive?' " (Genesis 45:3).

FORGIVENESS

"God has sent me here to keep you and your families alive so that you will become a great nation," Joseph told them. "Yes, it was God who sent me here, not you!" (Genesis 45:7–8).

There were five more years of drought, so Joseph told his brothers to bring the entire family down to Egypt. He would let them graze their flocks in the lush Goshen region near where the Nile River fans out into streams that empty into the Mediterranean Sea.

When Jacob and his family arrived, Joseph rode out on his chariot to meet them, then he fell on his father's shoulder and wept for a long time. Jacob eventually died in Egypt, perhaps during the drought. Joseph took him home for burial. The family, however, stayed in Egypt, survived the drought, and prospered.

Joseph died at age 110. The Hebrews grew so numerous over the decades that a later pharaoh feared they might overrun the nation. So he enslaved them. When and for how long is unknown. But they remained in Egypt 430 years before Moses led them out (Exodus 12:41).

2. **Husband of Mary.** Some people are a bit squeamish about calling Joseph the father of Jesus, since the Bible teaches he wasn't the biological father—this was a virgin birth. Yet the

Bible repeatedly calls Jesus "the son of Joseph from Nazareth" (John 1:45). That's because Joseph was his legal father and the husband who helped Mary raise him.

The New Testament says remarkably little about Joseph—or Mary, for that matter. He was certainly kind-hearted, given his willingness to divorce Mary quietly when he learned of her pregnancy. He could have asked for her execution on grounds of adultery. Joseph also knew about God, since God told him in dreams to go ahead with the marriage, then to flee to Egypt until King Herod died.

It's also clear that Joseph was a carpenter living in Nazareth, a small hilltop village in what is now northern Israel. He would have spent his days making household and farming implements such as wooden plows, doors, and tables—and teaching his sons the trade.

There were other children in his family. Nazarenes who were surprised by Jesus' teachings and miracles said, "He's just a carpenter's son, and we know Mary, his mother, and his brothers—James, Joseph, Simon, and Judas. All his sisters live right here among us" (Matthew 13:55–56). It's unclear if these were Joseph's children with Mary, from a previous marriage, or perhaps members of his extended family such as nephews and nieces.

Joseph's last appearance in the Bible is when he and Mary took twelve-year-old Jesus to Jerusalem for Passover. Joseph apparently died before Jesus began his ministry more than twenty years later.

3. **Joseph of Arimathea.** This rich Jewish leader who worked up the courage to ask Pilate for Jesus' body, then buried it in his own newly cut tomb, probably took no pride in what he did. More likely, he thought himself a coward.

Joseph, from a nearby village of Arimathea, was an honored member of the highest Jewish governing body in the land—the Sanhedrin, which a few hours earlier had condemned Jesus to die. This council had about seventy members, led by the high priest. It functioned a bit like the Supreme Court and Congress rolled into one, though subject to Roman authorities.

As a respected member, Joseph was perfectly placed to defend Jesus. But he apparently didn't. "A secret disciple of Jesus," he also "feared the Jewish leaders" (John 19:38).

Only after the Crucifixion did Joseph come out publicly for Jesus. He "gathered his courage and went to Pilate to ask for Jesus' body" (Mark 15:43). *Courage a few hours too late,* he must have thought. Yet in requesting the body, Joseph risked his reputation and career. And by touching the body, he rendered himself ritually unclean—making him unfit to participate in Passover, the most beloved Jewish holiday.

Later Christian writers said angry Jews threw Joseph in prison, but the resurrected Jesus rescued him. Another

Removing the body of Jesus from the cross, Joseph of Arimathea takes charge of the burial—jeopardizing his career as a Jewish leader.

JOSHUA
(JOSH oo wuh)
Yehosua, Hebrew
"the Lord is salvation"
1400s BC
First mention: Exodus 17:9

"Vicious" might be an unfair tag to hang on Joshua, the Hebrew warrior who followed God's advice on how to conquer what is now Israel. But Canaanites living there at the time would have called that word a bit too mild.

Consider excerpts from Joshua's story, in the book named after him:

"Joshua kept holding out his spear until everyone who had lived in Ai was completely destroyed" (Joshua 8:26).

"Joshua told the captains of his army, 'Come and put your feet on the kings' necks. . . . Be strong and courageous, for the LORD is going to do this to all of your enemies.' Then Joshua killed each of the five kings" (Joshua 10:24–26).

The story sounds like a Canaanite holocaust—ethnic cleansing on a national scale. But the Bible portrays it as a spiritual cleansing not unlike the Flood, intended to rid the land of idolatry and sinful traditions. This job—one of the most gruesome in Jewish history—fell to Joshua.

legend, traced to medieval times, said Joseph took Christianity to England and brought with him the Holy Grail—the cup Jesus used at the Last Supper. Joseph supposedly collected some of Jesus' blood in this cup, and legendary King Arthur tried to find it, thinking it had power to perform miracles.

STRATEGY OF A CONQUEST

Jewish conquest of what is now Israel turned into a four-stage campaign, launched from what is now Jordan and Syria.

Capture Jordan. Refused permission to pass through eastern nations in peace, the Hebrews overpowered armies sent against them. Then they took possession of the fine grazing lands. Two and a half tribes settled in Jordan and Syria: Reuben in the south, along the Dead Sea and eastward; Gad in the center, along the Jordan River; and half the tribe of Manasseh in the north, stretching from well below the Sea of Galilee to Mount Hermon some forty miles farther north.

Invade Canaan's southland. Crossing the Jordan River into the Promised Land of Canaan, the Hebrews destroyed the border town of Jericho. Then they swept through southern Canaan, sticking mostly to the highlands, where their foot militia had the edge over armies with chariots and cavalry. Surprise was a favorite Hebrew tactic. Once they marched all night and managed to shock and destroy five combined armies at Gibeon.

Push north to Galilee. The Hebrews pushed north into Galilee, where they faced a massive coalition army drawn from perhaps dozens of kingdoms. There were too many enemy horses and chariots to count—let alone soldiers. But Joshua led a surprise attack, crippling the horses, burning the chariots, and wiping out the enemy.

Mopping up. With major forces defeated, Joshua considered the rest of the conquest a mopping-up action. He assigned each tribe to finish the job in its own territory.

A TIME TO KILL

He was a slave in Egypt when Moses arrived, bringing ten plagues that compelled Pharaoh to let the Hebrews return to their homeland after 430 years. Joshua's name then was Hoshea, meaning "salvation." Somewhere on the trip home, Moses changed his name to Joshua, meaning "the Lord is salvation"—a reminder of who would do the saving.

Joshua was a warrior from the beginning of his story. The first time the Bible mentions him, soldiers from Amalek in what is now southern Israel had marched south to intercept the advancing Hebrews. Joshua commanded the Hebrew army, which gained the upper hand as long as Moses held his staff up. Moses' brother, Aaron, helped support Moses' arms. Joshua won the battle.

When the Hebrews reached the southern border of Canaan, Joshua was among the twelve scouts whom Moses sent ahead. Ten recommended against invading, warning of giants and heavily fortified cities. Only Joshua and Caleb urged the people to press on, saying God would give them victory. The masses chose the majority opinion, and God sentenced them to forty years in the desert—one year for each day the scouts explored the land. Of the adults alive at the time, only Joshua and Caleb would live to set foot on the Promised Land.

When the forty years ended, Moses led his people to the eastern side of the Jordan River, in what is now Jordan. It was there he died, but not before installing Joshua as his successor. In miracles similar to some in Moses' story, God confirmed that Joshua was his choice.

- God stopped the Jordan River so the Hebrews could cross into Canaan, just as he parted the Red Sea a generation earlier.
- The commander of God's spirit army met with Joshua on the eve of the invasion in an encounter similar to Moses' at the burning bush before setting out on his mission to free the Hebrews.

More than a military man, Joshua served as a kind of prophet, as well, for he delivered God's messages to the people. And he demanded strict obedience.

After one man, Achan, stole a robe along with some gold and silver from Jericho against God's instructions, the Hebrews lost their next battle. Joshua ordered Achan and his entire family executed—a graphic reminder that one

CANAANITE HOLOCAUST

Many people have trouble understanding why God would order the Hebrews to slaughter everyone in Canaan—men, women, and children. It sounds unnecessary and barbaric.

Moses delivered the order and added a short explanation: "This will keep the people of the land from teaching you their detestable customs in the worship of their gods" (Deuteronomy 20:18).

The Hebrews didn't do as they were told. Many Canaanite cities survived and later rose to oppress the Israelites. Worse, the Canaanites did exactly what Moses warned they would do. They lured God's people into idolatry.

For breaking their vow to serve God alone, the Israelites would eventually become people without a land. The Babylonians overran the nation and exiled the Jews about eight hundred years later, in 586 BC.

person's sin affects more than the sinner.

From that point on, the Bible records nothing but victories for the Hebrews—first in the central and southern highlands, then north into what is now the Galilean hills of Israel.

With several of the largest Canaanite cities defeated, Joshua declared an end to joint military action. He divided the land among the twelve tribes and ordered each tribe to finish wiping out the Canaanites in their territories.

A TIME TO HEAL

In his final act, Joshua assembled the people at Shechem in central Israel to renew their vows to God. He traced their history from the time God promised the land to Abraham's descendants up to the time God delivered on that promise—even giving the Hebrews cities they didn't build and olive groves and vineyards they didn't plant.

"Choose today whom you will serve," Joshua challenged the crowd. "But as for me and my family, we will serve the LORD" (Joshua 24:15).

The people vowed they would never forsake God or worship idols.

Joshua and the people returned to their lands. A short time later, Joshua the son of Nun died at age 110. He was buried on land God gave him in the hill country of his tribal territory, Ephraim, in central Israel.

JOSIAH
(joe SIGH uh)
Yosiyyah, Hebrew
Reigned 640–609 BC
First mention: 1 Kings 13:2

One of the best kings in Jewish history, Josiah waited eight years into his reign to get religion. But, then, he was only eight years old when he came to the throne. And he had a long family tradition of pagan worship to overcome.

Josiah's grandfather, Manasseh, was possibly the worst king in Jewish history—building pagan altars throughout the country and even sacrificing one of his sons. Josiah's father, Amon, wasn't much better. Also a pagan worshiper, he was so hated that his own servants murdered him after he had ruled just two years. That murder is why Josiah became king so young.

At age sixteen, "Josiah began to seek the God of his ancestor David" (2 Chronicles 34:3). Four years later, he launched a religious reform, destroying pagan shrines and even crossing Judah's border into Assyrian-controlled land that had once been the northern Jewish nation of Israel. There, in the city of Bethel, Josiah destroyed the calf idol worship center built centuries earlier to keep northern Jews from worshiping at the temple in the southern Jewish nation of Judah.

SHOCKING DISCOVERY

When Josiah was about twenty-six years old, he ordered the temple renovated. In the process, the high priest found something that may have been lost for more than seventy years: "the Book of the Law" (2 Chronicles 34:15). This was probably the book of Deuteronomy, which summarizes Jewish laws and concludes with God's blessings on the Jews for obedience and curses for disobedience.

The curses may be why Josiah "tore his clothes in despair" (2 Chronicles 34:19). There were curses like this one: "The LORD will scatter you among all the nations from one end of the earth to the other" (Deuteronomy 28:64).

The prophetess Huldah confirmed this would happen. But she added that God would delay until after Josiah died, since the king was genuinely sorry for the state of the nation.

Josiah died from a battle wound at age thirty-nine, after a thirty-one-year reign. It happened when he tried to block Pharaoh Neco's Egyptian army from driving north to reinforce the Assyrians—a crumbling empire that had already lost its capital city of Nineveh to a coalition force of Babylonians and Medes.

A little more than two decades later, Josiah's nation suffered the full wrath of God's curses. Judah ceased to exist when the Babylonian army overran it.

JUDAH
(JEW duh)
Yehuda, Hebrew
Possibly "give thanks"
1800s BC
First mention: Genesis 29:35

Jacob's fourth son was father of the tribe of Judah, Israel's most powerful and longest-lasting extended family— the family that produced David and Jesus. But Judah was no saint.

As a widower, he had sex with a woman he thought was a prostitute but who was actually his disgruntled daughter-in-law, Tamar. She was upset because, after her husband died, Judah didn't honor his promise to give her to his young son, which would have kept her in the family. Tamar got pregnant and delivered twins, including Perez, an ancestor of David and Jesus.

Judah did, however, have redeeming qualities. When his brothers agreed to kill their teenaged brother Joseph, Judah talked them into selling him to slave traders instead—which at least kept Joseph alive. Years later, Judah showed his remorse by offering to take Benjamin's place as a slave in Egypt rather than allow his father, Jacob, to suffer the loss of Joseph's only full brother, born to Rachel.

In Jacob's deathbed blessing, he called Judah a young lion, saying, "All your relatives will bow before you" (Genesis 49:8). In fact, the tribe of Judah's main city became Jerusalem, where Jews from every tribe came to bow at the temple.

JUDAH

MAP 2 C6

(JEW duh)
Yehuda, Hebrew
Possibly "give thanks"
First mention:
Deuteronomy 34:2

The tribe of Judah—the extended family of the patriarch Jacob's fourth son—was assigned most of the land in what is now southern Israel. King David was born in Bethlehem of

Judas guarantees his legacy of betrayal by kissing Jesus. This signal identifies Jesus for arresting officers from Jerusalem's temple.

Judah, which is why Jesus was born there, too. Joseph, a descendant of David and the fiancé of Mary, had to go back to his family's ancestral home for a census.

When Israel split in two about forty years after David died, the ten northern tribes kept the name Israel. The tribes of Judah and Simeon in the south took the larger tribe's name, Judah.

JUDAS ISCARIOT

(JEW duhss is CARE ee uht)
Ioudas Iskariotes, Greek
Possibly "Judas from Kerioth"
Died about AD 30
First mention: Matthew 10:4

One of the most puzzling mysteries of the Bible is why Jesus—if he knew so much—chose Judas Iscariot as one of his disciples.

It seems Jesus knew what he was getting himself into, for he once told the men, "I chose the twelve of you,

but one is a devil" (John 6:70).

The Bible reveals almost nothing about its chief villain. Judas' first name is the Greek version of Judah. *Iscariot* is perplexing. It sounds a bit like Sicarii, a group of militant Jews who wanted to free Israel. The name also sounds related to the Hebrew word *saqar,* which means "fraud."

But it's more common for a second name to refer to a hometown—as in Mary from Magdala. And it seems likely that Judas' second name referred to a town, as well, since his father had the identical second name, Simon Iscariot. The hometown, some speculate, could have been the similar-sounding Kerioth (Joshua 15:25). If so, Judas would have been the only disciple from outside Galilee. Kerioth was somewhere in Judah, in southern Israel.

CONSISTENTLY THE BAD GUY

If Judas contributed anything

meaningful to Jesus' ministry, nobody said so.

John's Gospel talks about Judas' attraction to money: "He was a thief who was in charge of the disciples' funds, and he often took some for his own use" (John 12:6). John adds that Judas criticized Mary for pouring twelve ounces of expensive perfume on Jesus' feet: "That perfume was worth a small fortune," Judas said. "It should have been sold and the money given to the poor" (John 12:5).

Some say money is why Judas betrayed Jesus. Judas agreed to lead Jewish officials to Jesus for thirty silver coins—the price of a slave (Exodus 21:32). Yet when Judas learned that the Jews condemned Jesus to die, he took the money back to the priests and threw it on the temple floor. Priests bought a potter's field with the money and turned it into a cemetery.

New Testament writers saw this fulfilling prophecy: "So I took the thirty coins and threw them to the potters in the Temple of the LORD" (Zechariah 11:13).

Judas' remorse, many say, hints that his motive may have been political—that he wanted to force Jesus to declare himself the Messiah, in hopes of sparking a grassroots revolt.

Whatever the motive, Judas plunged immediately into depression and killed himself. Matthew says Judas hung himself (Matthew 27:5), while Acts says he fell and his intestines splattered out (Acts 1:18). Perhaps both happened, if the rope or a tree branch broke.

JUDE
(JOOD)
Ioudas, Greek (short for Judas)
First century AD
First mention: Jude 1:1

Jude was one of Jesus' brothers, and according to some early Christian leaders, he also wrote the New Testament letter of Jude.

His full name was Judas—Jude was just a nickname. He's listed among the four brothers of Jesus: "James, Joseph, Simon, and Judas" (Matthew 13:55). Early in Jesus' ministry, "even his brothers didn't believe in him" (John 7:5). After the Resurrection, it seems James and Judas became church leaders.

JUDEA
(jew DEE uh)
Yehuda, Hebrew
First mention: Ezekiel 24:21

MAP 4
B4

The Romans didn't call the Jewish homeland Israel. They divided the land into regions and called part of the southern area Judea, a Greek-Roman variation on the Hebrew name Yehuda, or Judah.

Judea was roughly the same area as the tribe of Judah, though it stretched farther north and met up with Samaria, a territory in what is now central Israel. Above that was yet another territory, Galilee, where Jesus grew up. The English word *Jew* comes from Rome's Latin word *Judaeus,* which means a person from Judea.

KADESH-BARNEA

MAP 2
B7

(KAY daysh bar NEE yuh)
Qades barnea, Hebrew
First mention: Genesis 14:7

On their exodus out of Egypt, the Hebrews spent most of their forty years in the desert camped at the spring-fed oasis of Kadesh-barnea, about ninety miles south of Jerusalem. It was just south of Canaan's border. Today the site, Ein el-Qudeirat, lies about five miles inside Egypt's territory in the Sinai.

From there, at the largest oasis in the northern Sinai—with a spring producing a quarter of a million gallons of water a day—Moses sent out scouts to explore Canaan. Their report of giants and walled cities so terrified the people that they refused to go farther. God punished them for their lack of faith in him. The only two from that generation of adults who lived to see Canaan were Joshua and Caleb, two scouts who insisted that giants and walls were no match for God.

Miriam, sister of Moses, died and was buried at Kadesh, as it was sometimes called. This was also where Moses and Aaron somehow offended God when they struck a rock to provide water for the grumbling Hebrews. For this, God said they would never set foot in the Promised Land.

KIDRON VALLEY

See Jerusalem

(KID run)
Qidron, Hebrew
"dark" or "not clear,"
 describing the creek
First mention: 2 Samuel 15:23

MAP 4
B5

Between a ridge of hills called the Mount of Olives and the hilltop city of ancient Jerusalem there runs a deep ravine called the Kidron valley.

On the night of Jesus' arrest, after the Last Supper, the disciples and Jesus maneuvered down the steep slopes of eastern Jerusalem and climbed partway up the slopes of the Mount of Olives. There, in an olive grove, Jesus prayed until

A stretch of green in the desert, the Kadesh-barnea oasis is where Moses and the Israelites spent most of their forty years in the wilderness. The valley is fed by a spring that pumps a quarter of a million gallons of water a day.

A British artist visiting Jerusalem in the early 1800s painted this quiet scene of the Kidron valley slicing between two hilltops: Jerusalem off the picture to the left and the Mount of Olives to the right.

The caravan route stretched some three hundred miles, from Damascus, Syria, in the north, southward through Jordan, and on to the Red Sea's Gulf of Aqaba in Egypt.

The Romans upgraded the trail and renamed it Trajan's Road, after the emperor at the time. Today the road is a high-speed desert highway from Damascus to Jordan's capital of Amman. From there it continues south along a scenic, secondary road that runs past ancient ruins.

Jewish officials came and arrested him.

Many Jerusalem tourists waken early to watch the sunrise. To see it, they have to look toward the Kidron valley and above the Mount of Olives. When it rains hard, the dry valley floor becomes a muddy brook. This stream merges with other normally dry creek beds called wadis, then drains into the Dead Sea about fifteen miles east.

KING'S HIGHWAY

MAP 2
D6

Derek hammelek, Hebrew
First mention: Numbers 20:17

In steady use for more than three thousand years now, the King's Highway was the caravan route that Moses asked permission to travel on when he led the Hebrews on the last leg of their journey to the Promised Land. The king of Edom, in what is today southern Jordan, denied the request. That forced Moses to take a long and dangerous detour around Edom.

KIRIATH-JEARIM

MAP 1
C5

(KIR *ee* ath JEE uh rim)
Qiryat yearim, Hebrew
"city of woods"
First mention: Joshua 9:17

Israel's most sacred object—a chest holding the Ten Commandments—spent twenty years in a man's house in the tiny, hillside village of Kiriath-jearim.

Philistines captured it in battle, but they kept it only seven months because it caused an outbreak of tumors and a rat infestation—in three different cities. So they sent it back to Israel. The leaders appointed a man named Eleazar to take care of it. King David later moved the chest about ten miles south to his worship center in Jerusalem.

Usually a dry riverbed at the foot of round-top Mount Tabor (right), the Kishon can become a raging river during a rainstorm—as an invading chariot corps found out the hard way.

KISHON RIVER
(KI shawn)
Qison, Hebrew
First mention: Judges 4:7

MAP 1
B3

In the Valley of Armageddon, better known in Israel as the Jezreel valley, there's a dry riverbed that can turn into a rushing river during spring rains. It's called the Kishon River, and it flows westward, into the Mediterranean Sea. This river once saved an Israelite militia from getting wiped out by a chariot corps.

Deborah, one of Israel's famous leaders, assembled Israelite fighters on Mount Tabor. A king who had been oppressing the Israelites sent nine hundred charioteers to engage them. The invaders advanced along the valley, perhaps in the dry riverbed, when a sudden downpour swept many away and trapped others in mud. Charioteers ran for their lives, but the Israelites killed them.

KORAZIN
(koh RAY zin)
Korazin, Greek
First mention: Matthew 11:21

MAP 4
C2

"What horrors await you, Korazin," Jesus warned. "For if the miracles I did in you had been done in wicked Tyre and Sidon, their people would have sat in deep repentance" (Luke 10:13). Korazin—a Galilean town once famed for its wheat—has the distinction of being one of three towns Jesus condemned for its unbelief, along with Capernaum and Bethsaida. Ruins are all that's left of this eighty-acre site two miles north of Capernaum. Ancient coins tossed in the synagogue ruins may have come from Christian pilgrims bearing witness to Jesus' fulfilled prophecy.

LABAN
(LAY bun)
Laban, Hebrew
"white"
2000s BC
First mention: Genesis 24:29

Greedy and conniving, Laban outmaneuvered even the likes of his nephew Jacob. That was no small feat, since Jacob had tricked his own blind father, Isaac, into giving him the deathbed blessing that belonged to his older brother, Esau. Laban tricked the trickster, and Jacob ended up married to the wrong woman.

Laban was the brother of Jacob's mother, Rebekah—Uncle Laban to Jacob. Laban was a herdsman living near Haran, a village in southern Turkey. After Esau vowed to kill Jacob for stealing the blessing, Rebekah sent Jacob north to Laban. Jacob fell in love with Laban's youngest daughter, Rachel. But Jacob didn't have any money to pay the traditional bride fee. So he agreed to work seven years for Laban. Blessed of God, Jacob made Laban rich. But Laban repaid him with a substitute bride—Leah,

Rachel's older sister. Apparently married at night, Jacob didn't discover the switch until dawn.

Jacob stormed off to Laban, who casually replied, "It's not our custom to marry off a younger daughter ahead of the firstborn" (Genesis 29:26). Jacob agreed to work another seven years for Rachel, whom he married the next week—after the traditional weeklong wedding celebration for Leah.

When Jacob's fourteen-year obligation was fulfilled, Laban agreed to pay Jacob by letting him have all the spotted sheep and goats from his herd. But that same day, Laban cut those spotted animals from the flock and had his sons hide them in a field three days away. In

Jacob's skill as a shepherd makes his father-in-law, Laban, a rich man. Laban agrees to let Jacob marry his beautiful daughter, Rachel, but switches brides at the last moment.

spite of this, God blessed Jacob and gave him a vast flock.

Twenty years after arriving in Haran, Jacob and his family left for Canaan while Laban was away shearing sheep. Laban chased him down, but God warned him in a dream not to harm Jacob. The two men made a peace treaty. Then Laban kissed his daughters and grandchildren goodbye and went back home.

LACHISH

(LAY kish)
Lakis, Hebrew
First mention: Joshua 10:3

After conquering the Jewish city of Lachish, Assyrian invaders impale many survivors. This stone relief once decorated Assyria's palace walls in Nineveh.

Among green and gently rolling hills about thirty miles southwest of Jerusalem sat the eighteen-acre city of Lachish, fortified by double walls and a mote. Invaders had to take this city before advancing on Jerusalem if their army traveled on the main caravan route—along the seacoast.

Building a dirt ramp to the top of the wall, Assyria captured Lachish in 701 BC and commemorated the battle in a famous stone relief they put in their capital palace. It's now at the British Museum.

Babylonians also took the city in 586 BC, before leveling Jerusalem. A lookout sent to Jerusalem a warning written on a piece of broken pottery, which has survived. The note says, "We were watching for the smoke signals of Lachish. . .because we do not see Azekah." This confirms the Bible account: "At this time the Babylonian army was besieging Jerusalem, Lachish, and Azekah—the only cities of Judah with their walls still standing" (Jeremiah 34:7).

LAODICEA

(LAY uh duh SEE uh)
Laodikeia, Greek
First mention: Colossians 2:1

Jesus had stern words for Christians in Laodicea, a city on a main travel route in what is now western Turkey. His message, delivered in a vision to the writer of the Bible's last book was: "You are neither hot nor cold. I wish you were one or the other! But since you are like lukewarm water, I will spit you out of my mouth!" (Revelation 3:15–16). Jesus added that the people thought they were rich, but they were spiritually bankrupt, and they thought they could see, but they needed eye salve.

These three criticisms used tailor-made images. Laodicea's water, piped in from six miles away, was luke-warm—not like the cold spring water of neighboring Colosse or the hot springs of nearby Hierapolis. The city was also rich enough to rebuild without Rome's help after an earthquake in AD 60. Laodicea also operated a medical school.

LAZARUS

(LAZ uh russ)
Lazaros, Greek
Abbreviation of *Elazar,* Hebrew
"God helps"
First century AD
First mention: John 11:1

Only once does the Bible say Jesus cried. It was in a crowd mourning the death of Lazarus. The mystery is why Jesus cried. He could have prevented the death in the first place, and he had come specifically to raise Lazarus from the grave.

Lazarus was probably his friend. That's a fair assumption since Lazarus was the brother of Mary and Martha, who often hosted Jesus in their home. Lazarus and his sisters lived together in Bethany, a tiny village on the outskirts of Jerusalem.

When Lazarus grew deathly ill, his sisters sent word for the Healer to come right away. But instead of hurrying to Bethany, apparently at least a two-day walk away, Jesus waited. He assured his disciples, "Lazarus' sickness will not end in death. No, it is for the glory of God" (John 11.4).

By the time Jesus arrived, Lazarus had been dead four days. Martha heard Jesus was approaching, and she rushed outside the village to meet him. There, she complained that Jesus could have prevented this. Jesus simply answered that Lazarus would rise again. Martha said she knew he would—on resurrection day.

Waiting for tourists, souvenir hawkers and beggars stand at the entrance of "Lazarus' Tomb," in Bethany. The entrance leads down a winding flight of twenty-two stairs, to a vestibule and a small crypt.

"I am the resurrection and the life," Jesus replied. "Those who believe in me, even though they die like everyone else, will live again" (John 11:25).

Martha went and got Mary, who arrived weeping and with a crowd in tow. That's when Jesus cried, perhaps troubled by the heartbreak of a follower he dearly loved. He and Mary had enjoyed long talks.

"LAZARUS, COME OUT!"

Jesus ordered the gravestone rolled from the tomb's opening, though Martha protested. She said Lazarus' corpse would smell bad.

Jesus shouted three words to wake the dead: "Lazarus, come out!" (John 11:43). Lazarus did.

Ironically, when Jewish leaders heard Jesus had raised the dead, they decided to kill him. They feared he would pass himself off as the Messiah and lead Jews in a revolution that would end with Rome destroying the nation.

A few days later, on the Saturday before the Crucifixion, Lazarus hosted a banquet for Jesus. Martha served the food. And Mary anointed Jesus —a tender gesture of devotion that he described as preparing him for burial.

One week later, Jesus lay in a tomb. But like Lazarus, he walked out again.

LEAH
(LEE uh)
Lea, Hebrew
Probably "cow"
1900s BC
First mention: Genesis 29:16

Leah was the woman Jacob got tricked into marrying. Jacob worked seven years to marry Leah's younger sister, Rachel, but the father of the bride switched women at the ceremony. Jacob didn't realize it until daybreak. A week later, Jacob was allowed to marry Rachel for another seven years of labor.

Jacob's two wives spent their lives competing for his affection. In that culture, the more children a woman delivered, the better—especially if the children were sons. "Because Leah was unloved, the LORD let her have a child, while Rachel was childless" (Genesis 29:31).

Leah had six sons—ancestors of half the tribes of Israel: Reuben, Simeon, Levi, Judah, Issachar, and Zebulun.

Jacob meets his future wives, Rachel and Leah. He wanted just Rachel but got tricked into marrying Leah first.

In time, Rachel had two sons. The maids of the two wives served as surrogate mothers in the childbearing rivalry, providing four more sons.

LEBANON

(LEB uh none)
Lebanon, Hebrew
"white"
First mention: Deuteronomy 1:7

On Israel's northern border, in ancient times as well as today, lies the nation of Lebanon, once famed for its mountain forests—the cedars of Lebanon. Rot-resistant and bug-repelling, this premium lumber was preferred by builders. Solomon had cedar logs lashed together and floated down the coast to use in building the Jerusalem temple and a palace he named the Palace of the Forest of Lebanon. Most of Lebanon's forests disappeared in the 1500s under the rule of the Ottomans of Turkey. Little remains today.

Israel had a notorious queen from Sidon, Lebanon, about twenty-five miles south of Beirut—Jezebel.

LEHI

See *Philistia*

(LEE hi)
Lehi, Hebrew
First mention: Judges 15:9

Samson killed a thousand Philistine soldiers with a donkey's jawbone. He did this at Lehi, an Israelite village probably somewhere near the Philistine border in southern Israel.

The famous one-man massacre started after Samson found out that the Philistine bride he abandoned in anger had quickly married his best man. Samson torched Philistine fields, vineyards, and olive groves. The Philistines retaliated by killing Samson's ex-wife and raiding the Israelite village of Lehi. Some Israelites convinced Samson to turn himself in at Lehi, where he broke free of his ropes and slaughtered the Philistine raiders.

LEVI

(LEAVE eye)
Lewi, Hebrew
"attached"
1800s BC
First mention: Genesis 29:34

Israel's father of the priestly tribe—Levi, third son of Jacob and Leah—was a vicious and vengeful man.

When Levi's sister Dinah was raped by an overzealous prince who later asked for permission to marry her, Levi and his brothers insisted that all men of the village get circumcised first. While the men were still nursing their wounds, Levi and his brother Simeon killed them.

LOT

Lot, Hebrew
"hidden"
2100s BC
First mention: Genesis 11:27

Abraham's nephew, Lot, is best known for his incredibly poor choice in real estate. When his uncle gave him first pick of all the land in what is now Israel, Lot ended up in Sodom.

There, raiders once kidnapped

Running from Sodom's blaze, Lot's wife lingers behind and turns into a pillar of salt—perhaps caught in the explosive spray of superheated minerals.

him, though his uncle came to the rescue. Then angels nearly dragged him out of town and sent him running for his life moments before a fiery cataclysm burned Sodom and neighboring cities off the map.

Lot was the son of Haran, one of Abraham's younger brothers. Haran died a young man, while Abraham's extended family, led by his father, Terah, was still living in Ur, a thriving city on the Euphrates River in what is now southern Iraq. Abraham apparently took Lot under his wing—a good match since Lot had no father and Abraham and his wife, Sarah, had no children.

Terah moved the family upriver, intent on following the main caravan route to Canaan, now called Israel. Terah stopped halfway and settled in Haran. But when he died, seventy-five-year-old Abraham continued to Canaan, accompanied by Lot.

GOOD-BYE, UNCLE ABRAHAM

When drought struck Canaan, the two moved their families and flocks to Egypt—as Egyptian records confirm many herdsmen from neighboring regions did. There was nearly always good grazing along the Nile River. By the time the men were able to return to Canaan, their flocks had grown so large that their herdsmen argued over available pastures and wells.

"Take your choice of any section of the land you want, and we will separate," Abraham said (Genesis 13:9).

Lot chose the fertile Jordan River valley and pitched his tent in the plains near Sodom. In time, Lot moved his family into the city.

Evil was so rampant in the cities on the plain that God decided to purge their sin from creation, much as he did with the Flood in Noah's day. But this time, God sent fire. Lot escaped with his two daughters, but his wife was lost when she lingered to look at the destruction and perhaps got caught in the superheated spray of minerals: "She became a pillar of salt" (Genesis 19:26).

Lot's daughters thought there wasn't a man alive in the entire region, so they got their father drunk and became pregnant by him. Their two sons became ancestors of two nations later pitted against Israel—Moab and Ammon—in what is now Jordan.

LUKE

Loukas, Greek
First century AD
First mention: Colossians 4:14

If early church tradition is right, Luke was the only non-Jew to write any books of the Bible. Church leaders credit this man—whom the apostle Paul identified as a physician and a fellow worker—with writing an anonymous two-part history. The first is a history of Jesus, known as the Gospel of Luke. And the second is a history of the early church, known as the Acts of the Apostles. Together, these books make up nearly a fourth of the New Testament.

The Bible says almost nothing about Luke, other than describing him as an uncircumcised (non-Jewish) physician who traveled with Paul and stayed with him when Paul awaited execution: "Only Luke is with me" (2 Timothy 4:11).

One reason scholars have long suspected Luke wrote the two-part history is because of a shift in Acts from third person to first when reporting Paul's later travels. The writer includes himself with Paul's entourage: "We decided to leave for Macedonia at once" (Acts 16:10).

Luke paints a portrait of Mary and Child. Though legend says he was a painter, scholars doubt he painted anything but wonderful word pictures in the Gospel of Luke and the Acts of the Apostles.

LUKE'S MYSTERIOUS READER

Luke addressed both of his books—the Gospel of Luke and Acts of the Apostles—to a mysterious reader known only as "most honorable Theophilus" (Luke 1:1).

Theophilus may have been a wealthy Christian who paid Luke to write this history for him. Or he could have been an influential leader Luke was trying to convert. Another possibility is that he may have represented all believers everywhere, since Theophilus means "lover of God."

Also, there's a lot of detail that would catch the eye of a physician. The Gospel of Luke reports more healing miracles than any other Gospel, and it provides the most dramatic account of Jesus' birth.

LYDIA

(LID ee uh)
Lydia, Greek
First century AD
First mention: Acts 16:14

Paul's first reported convert in Europe was a rich businesswoman named Lydia, who sold expensive purple cloth.

Originally from Thyatira, Turkey, Lydia moved to Philippi, a Greek city near the seacoast. Paul met her on the Sabbath when he gathered with Jewish believers at their regular worship place —a riverbank. Lydia invited Paul and his associate, Silas, to use her home as a base of operation in town. Lydia's home became Europe's first known church.

Throughout Paul's ministry, the Philippian Christians had sent him money. Paul's New Testament letter of Philippians was a note of appreciation for such gifts.

LYSTRA

MAP 5
D2

(LIE struh)
Lystra, Greek
First mention: Acts 14:6

Paul and Barnabas started their missionary journeys in familiar territory. First they sailed to the island of Cyprus, where Barnabas grew up; then they moved on to southern Turkey, near where Paul was born. Lystra was one of four cities they visited in Turkey. There, Paul healed a cripple. The people reacted by calling Paul and Barnabas gods. But angry Jews from two previous towns they had visited arrived and turned the crowd into a mob that stoned Paul and left him for dead. When Paul came to, he got up and went back into the city.

The next day, he and Barnabas walked to the neighboring city of Derbe, the only Turkish town that didn't run them off. Then they backtracked to the three towns that did to check on their new converts.

MACEDONIA

(MASS uh DOE nee yuh)
Makedonia, Hebrew
First mention: Acts 16:9

**MAP 5
A1**

It was a vision of a man from Macedonia that convinced Paul to bring Christianity to Europe. "Come over here and help us," the man pleaded (Acts 16:9). So Paul and his associates sailed from Turkey to what is now northern Greece, where he started Europe's first known church in the city of Philippi.

In Paul's day, Macedonia wasn't the small, landlocked former Yugoslav Republic of Macedonia that we know of today. Then, the Roman province covered most of Greece, north of Athens.

MACHPELAH

(mahk P.F.F. lah)
Makpela, Hebrew
First mention: Genesis 23:9

See Hebron

**MAP 1
C5**

In what is now Hebron, a Palestinian town about twenty miles south of Jerusalem, Abraham bought a field to serve as his family cemetery. His wife, Sarah, had died, and Abraham buried her on this property in a cave called Machpelah. Later, Abraham was buried there, too, along with his son Isaac and wife Rebekah, Jacob and Leah, and

later Jacob's son Joseph.

Herod the Great enshrined the cave in a massive building that's still standing and visited by tourists. In 1119, during Crusader-Muslim wars, an expedition into the chambers below the building reportedly turned up bones. A brief search after the Six-Day War of 1967 revealed three tombstones and an Arabic inscription about Allah, but no bones.

MAGDALA

(MAG duh luh)
Magdala, Aramaic
"tower"
First mention: (Magdalene) Matthew 27:56

**MAP 4
C3**

Mary Magdalene apparently got her second name from her hometown of Magdala. A fishing village on the western shore of the Sea of Galilee, Magdala was just a few miles from Jesus' ministry headquarters in Capernaum.

Jesus may have visited the village after feeding four thousand people with seven loaves of bread and a few fish. Matthew 15:39 says that after the miracle, Jesus retreated "to the region of Magadan," which may have been the Magdala area.

MAHER-SHALAL-HASH-BAZ

(MAY ur SHALL uhl HASH bahs)
Maher-salal-has-baz, Hebrew
"swift to plunder and quick to spoil"
700s BC
First mention: Isaiah 8:1

Isaiah's son ended up with the longest name in the Bible—and hopefully an upbeat nickname like "Swifty" (*Maher*).

As the prophet Hosea did with his children about the same time, Isaiah gave his son a symbolic name to make a point. For Isaiah, the point was that King Ahaz of Judah didn't need Assyria's help to fight off coalition forces of Syria and the northern Jewish nation of Israel. The invaders themselves would be plundered and spoiled before Isaiah's son could talk.

Ahaz called Assyria anyhow. Their forces crushed the coalition but took Judah's sacred temple treasures as payment.

MALACHI

(MAL uhk eye)
Malaki, Hebrew
"my messenger"
Early 400s BC
First mention: Malachi 1:1

The last book in the Old Testament, Malachi may have been written by a prophet whose name coincidentally described his job. Or it may not have been a name at all. Malachi means "my messenger" and could refer to any prophet.

So the book's introduction could read either way: "The oracle of the word of the LORD to Israel through Malachi" [or "through my messenger"] (Malachi 1:1 NASB).

Whether Malachi is a name or a title, the man behind the book remains a mystery. About the only safe conclusion scholars can draw about him is that he wrote sometime after 450 BC. That's clear because of his message. He urged Jews who returned from exile in Babylon (now Iraq) to follow God's law by giving a tenth of their income to the Jerusalem temple, which had been rebuilt in about 515 BC. He also addressed some of the problems covered by Ezra and Nehemiah in the mid-400s BC—problems such as divorce and the dangers of intermarriage with non-Jews.

Many Christians consider the book of Malachi an excellent place to end the Old Testament. That's because it predicts the coming of the Messiah with images that seem to describe the ministry of Jesus:

"The messenger of the covenant, whom you look for so eagerly, is surely coming," the Lord says through his messenger. "At that time I will put you on trial. . . . I will speak against those who cheat employees of their wages, who oppress widows and orphans, or who deprive the foreigners living among you of justice" (Malachi 3:1, 5).

Jesus spoke those words in many different ways, but perhaps no more eloquently than this: "Do for others what you would like them to do for you. This is a summary of all that is taught in the law and the prophets" (Matthew 7:12).

MAMRE

(MAM rah)
Mamre, Hebrew
First mention: Genesis 23:17

MAP 1
C5

After Abraham and Lot parted company in Canaan because their flocks had grown too large to graze together, Abraham set up camp in an oak grove called Mamre. The area took its name from the owner, an Amorite king and ally of Abraham.

Mamre was near Hebron, a town about twenty miles south of Jerusalem. Near this grove is where Abraham bought a plot of ground with a cave that he used as his family tomb.

MANASSEH

(MUH nass uh)
Menasseh, Hebrew
"God has made me forget," perhaps referring to the death of a son
Reigned 687–642 BC
First mention: 2 Kings 20:21

At the bottom of the barrel of Jewish kings rots the smelliest apple of all—Manasseh, son of saintly King Hezekiah.

Thirteenth king of the southern Jewish nation of Judah, Manasseh was one unlucky number for his people—and he stuck around fifty-five years, longer than any other Jewish king in history. That's partly because he didn't get to finish growing up before taking the throne. He was only twelve at the time.

Following in the footsteps of his evil grandfather, King Ahaz, Manasseh built pagan shrines throughout the country, and he even put one of them in the temple. Also like his grandfather, "Manasseh even sacrificed his own son in the fire" (2 Kings 21:6). In addition, he practiced sorcery and consulted with psychics. God's laws strictly prohibited all of this.

MANASSEH ASKS FORGIVENESS

Manasseh's prayer of repentance is supposedly preserved in fifteen verses that scholars say were probably written about five hundred years after the king lived.

The Prayer of Manasseh, as it's called, is included in Bibles of Eastern Orthodox churches. Here's verse 13: "I earnestly implore you, forgive me, O Lord, forgive me! Do not destroy me with my transgressions! Do not be angry with me forever or store up evil for me; do not condemn me to the depths of the earth. For you, O Lord, are the God of those who repent."

A different account of Manasseh's life adds that he eventually repented and "finally realized that the LORD alone is God!" (2 Chronicles 33:13). Afterward, he removed all the pagan shrines and idols.

Some scholars speculate that the happy ending was added to justify Manasseh's long reign. Others say Manasseh's story was too well known for the writer of Chronicles to tinker with.

MANASSEH

MAP 1
C4, D2

(muh NASS uh)
Menasseh, Hebrew
"God has made me forget," perhaps referring
to the death of a son
First mention: Genesis 48:6

Descendants of Manasseh, Joseph's
older son, became one of Israel's twelve
tribes. Manasseh was the only tribe, or
extended family, to split in two. Half
the tribe settled east of the Sea of
Galilee, on an eighty-mile-long plot of
land stretching southward from Mount
Hermon, taking up parts of what are
now Syria and Jordan. The other half
continued into Canaan and settled in
the north-central highlands that
extended north to the Jezreel valley.

MARAH

See Sinai

MAP 3
C4

(MAH rah)
Mara, Hebrew
"bitter"
First mention: Exodus 15:23

After crossing the Red Sea, the
Hebrews traveled three days into the
barren Sinai Peninsula. They camped
at a place they called Marah, after the
undrinkable, bitter water they found
there. Fearing the people would die of
thirst, Moses cried out to God for
help. The Lord showed Moses a
branch, which Moses threw into the
water, making it good to drink.

MARK

Markos, Greek
Marcus, Latin
First century AD
First mention: Acts 12:12

He may have written the Gospel of
Mark, if early church historians are
right, but to the apostle Paul he was a
lousy traveling companion.

Mark often went by two names—
John Mark—blending his Hebrew
name with his Roman name. He lived
with his mother, Mary, in Jerusalem,
the house Peter went to after an angel
freed him from prison one night.

Mark's run-in with Paul happened
during the first missionary trip. Mark
came along with his cousin, Barnabas.
But for some reason, Mark went home
before the trip was over—turning back
after they hit Turkey's swamps. When
it came time for the follow-up trip,
Barnabas insisted on taking Mark, but
Paul refused. He took Silas and went in
another direction.

The relationship was eventually
restored because Paul asked Timothy to
come to him and bring Mark "for he
will be helpful to me" (2 Timothy 4:11).
Even more endearingly, Peter described
Mark as "my son" (1 Peter 5:13).

Papias, a church leader in the AD
100s, said Mark wrote the shortest and
most action-packed Gospel by drawing from Peter's memories. Mark's
Gospel, many scholars say, was a main
source for the other Gospel writers.

MARTHA

(MARR thuh)
Martha, Greek
"lady"
First century AD
First mention: Luke 10:38

People who know the story of Martha and her sister, Mary, tend to remember Martha as the one who would rather cook than talk with Jesus. But she proved herself a devoted follower.

The sisters lived with their brother, Lazarus, in the village of Bethany, on the outskirts of Jerusalem. When Jesus came to Jerusalem, he ate with the family. Once, Martha complained that Mary was just sitting around talking with Jesus while Martha did all the work, fixing a big meal.

"My dear Martha," Jesus answered, "you are so upset over all these details! There is really only one thing worth being concerned about. Mary has discovered it— and I won't take it away from her" (Luke 10:41–42).

In a later story, moments before Jesus raised Lazarus from the dead, Martha showed that she cared deeply about spiritual matters, too. When Jesus asked her if she believed that he was the source of eternal life, she answered, "Yes, Lord" (John 11:27). And she said that though her brother was dead, she believed God would give Jesus whatever he asked. Martha was right.

MARY

Maria/Mariam, Greek
From *Miryam,* Hebrew for Miriam
"rebellious" or "bitter"
First century AD
First mention: 1. Matthew 1:16
2. Matthew 27:56
3. Luke 10:39

Mary was a popular name in Jesus' time—there are at least half a dozen in the New Testament. That seems odd since the name comes from Miriam, the big sister of Moses. Miriam was the woman God turned white with leprosy because of her bitter jealousy toward Moses.

Perhaps parents simply liked the sound of her name or didn't associate it

A Middle Eastern girl in her early teens—about the age that girls in Bible times married.

249

FOREVER A VIRGIN

Roman Catholics teach more than the Virgin Birth. They teach that Mary remained forever a virgin.

They draw these conclusions from early Christian writings, such as the Protoevangelium of James, and from early church leaders such as Origen and Athanasius who referred to the "ever-virgin Mary."

Here are two of the main counterpoints many Protestants make and responses by Catholics.

• "While she was still a virgin, she became pregnant by the Holy Spirit" (Matthew 1:18). That first phrase implies Mary later had sexual relations. Some Catholic scholars translate the first phrase, "before they came together," and they say it means before Mary and Joseph lived together.

• "He's just a carpenter's son, and we know Mary, his mother, and his brothers—James, Joseph, Simon, and Judas. All his sisters live right here among us" (Matthew 13:55–56). Many Catholics say these children were Jesus' cousins or perhaps Joseph's children by a previous marriage.

with Miriam's rebellious anger. In any case, none of the three best-known Marys in the Bible was anything like her ancient namesake. These were selfless women.

1. **Mother of Jesus.** Surprisingly, the Bible says very little about this woman held in such high esteem by many Christian groups, especially the Roman Catholic Church.

She's mentioned in the birth of Jesus, the story of finding twelve-year-old Jesus talking with scholars at the temple, prodding Jesus to perform his first public miracle, and in a few brief references during Jesus' ministry, the Crucifixion, and at the Holy Spirit's arrival at Pentecost. But once the church was born, after Peter's sermon at Pentecost, Mary disappears from the Bible.

If Mary followed ancient Middle Eastern custom, she was in her early to middle teens when she delivered Jesus—by today's standards, a junior high or high school student. Young women typically got engaged shortly after they started having monthly periods. Mary was engaged to Joseph, a carpenter.

Though Mary and Joseph each lived in Nazareth, a hilltop village in the Galilean territory of northern Israel, Jesus was born in Bethlehem. That's because Mary accompanied

Joseph to his ancestral hometown for the Roman census. Engagement was that legally binding.

If Mary had been as young as many scholars claim, she was an incredibly mature teenager. When shepherds arrived and astonished the Bethlehem residents by saying angels told them to come and see the new-born Messiah, "Mary quietly treasured these things in her heart" (Luke 2:19).

Twelve years later, Mary was a little more vocal. She scolded Jesus for staying at the Jerusalem temple when the rest of the Nazareth Jews had headed home from the festival. "Son!" she said. "Why have you done this to us? Your father and I have been frantic, searching for you everywhere" (Luke 2:48).

Jesus calmly replied that they should have known where to look.

Mary was the reason Jesus performed his first recorded miracle. The wine was all gone at a wedding feast in Cana, and Mary told Jesus to take care of it. He initially refused. But Mary, seeming not to hear, told the servants, "Do whatever he tells you" (John 2:5). Jesus made great wine.

During Jesus' ministry, Mary and her other children showed up a time or two, wanting to talk with Jesus. Once, after Jesus exorcised demons, they came to take him home, saying, "He's out of his mind" (Mark 3:21).

When it came time for Jesus to die on the cross, Mary was there with him. Joseph had apparently long since died. Jesus entrusted Mary to the care of a disciple, probably John. Several early church writers say John moved to Ephesus, in what is now western Turkey, and took Mary with him. Here she lived out her final years.

2. **Mary Magdalene.** Mary, the first person to see Jesus after his resurrection, was not a former prostitute, insist many scholars.

They say the case of mistaken identity happened about five hundred years later, when Bible students started speculating that Mary was the unnamed "immoral woman" who washed Jesus' feet with her tears and hair (Luke 7:37). The trouble with that theory is this: Luke told the story, which would have been the perfect place to introduce Mary if she had been that person, but he introduced her in the very next story instead. Also, it seems unlikely that the wife of a top Roman official—one of Mary's traveling companions—would have associated with a prostitute. The official was a business manager for Herod, ruler of Galilee.

Mary was apparently a well-to-do woman from Magdala, a town on the shores of the Sea of Galilee, a few miles from Jesus' ministry headquarters in Capernaum. She was also part of a group of Galilean women Jesus had healed and who were "contributing from their own resources to support Jesus and his disciples" (Luke 8:3). Jesus had exorcized Mary of "seven demons."

Mary and the other women followed Jesus on his final walk to Jerusalem, in a day when rabbis typically refused to let women follow them. Mary stayed close. She was there at the foot of his cross. She followed his body to the grave. And before sunrise on the first day she was allowed to finish preparing his body for burial, she was at the tomb.

But Jesus wasn't.

Mary began to cry, thinking someone had stolen his body.

" 'Mary!' Jesus said. She turned toward him and exclaimed, 'Teacher!' " (John 20:16).

Of all the people Jesus could have chosen as the first person to deliver his Good News, he chose someone who wasn't even allowed to speak in public worship services—a woman. "Mary Magdalene found the disciples and told them, 'I have seen the Lord!' " (John 20:18).

3. **Sister of Martha.** Apparently a single woman, Mary lived with her sister and brother, Martha and Lazarus, in the small village of Bethany. That was just outside Jerusalem, hidden from view on the opposite slopes of a ridge called the Mount of Olives.

Mary appears in three stories about Jesus, two involving meals and the most famous involving Jesus raising Lazarus from the dead.

In the first story, Mary is the one talking with Jesus instead of helping to fix dinner. Martha appealed to Jesus, "Lord, doesn't it seem unfair to you that my sister just sits here while I do all the work? Tell her to come and help me" (Luke 10:40). Jesus politely answered *no,* implying that if Martha

knew what was best for her, she would sit down and talk with him, too.

When Lazarus grew deathly ill, Mary and Martha sent for Jesus, but he arrived four days after Lazarus died. Jesus stopped outside the village, where Martha came to meet him. Then he sent Martha back to get her sister. Only then, when Mary arrived crying and surrounded by mourners, did Jesus do something reported nowhere else: "Jesus wept" (John 11:35).

Mary's last scene with Jesus is the most tender. Less than a week before Jesus died, Mary and her sister prepared a meal in his honor—a thank-you for raising Lazarus. There, Mary took a twelve-ounce jar of expensive perfume, poured it on his feet, and wiped it with her hair. Judas, the group's treasurer, objected. He said the perfume valued at a year's salary could have helped the poor.

"Leave her alone," Jesus replied. "She did it in preparation for my burial. You will always have the poor among you, but I will not be here with you much longer" (John 12:7–8).

MASADA

(mah SAH dah)
Mesada, Hebrew
"mountain fortress"

MAP 4
C6

Masada isn't mentioned in the Bible. But since the first century, Jews have cherished the ruins of this fortress that sits on top of an 820-foot mesa near the Dead Sea. That's because more than nine hundred Jews—men, women, and

Masada's sheer cliffs made the ancient Jewish fortress on top seem invincible. Roman invaders, however, built a massive ramp up the side (right). The defenders committed suicide.

one of the winding trails, such as one that snakes alongside the Roman ramp. On top are ruins of a retreat center built by Herod the Great, with a massive cistern to hold water, a bathhouse, and a palace. With its steep cliffs, crowned in walls, the fortress seemed impregnable. But the relentless Romans knew better.

MATTHEW

(MATH you)
Maththaios, Greek
"gift of God"
First century AD
First mention: Matthew 9:9

children—committed suicide there in AD 73 rather than surrender to the Roman army.

Jews had rebelled against their Roman occupiers in AD 66. Masada became the last holdout. Roman soldiers stormed the walled fortress after building a massive dirt ramp up the mesa. But what they found were bodies laid out in rows.

Israeli soldiers inducted into the armed forces today take their oath of allegiance at this mesa, some thirty-five miles south of Jerusalem. There, they pledge, "Masada shall not fall again!"

Today, tourists visit the site, riding a cable car to the top or walking up

If we listed the twelve disciples according to what society thought of them, at the very bottom—lower than a fisherman—would be the man church leaders in the AD 100s said wrote the Gospel of Matthew.

Matthew ran a tollbooth at the fishing village of Capernaum, collecting taxes from people transporting fish and other goods to and from the area. He probably agreed to pay Roman officials a fee for the right to do this, and he got to keep any money above that fee. Tax collectors were so corrupt that many Jews treated them as ritually unclean, like lepers.

Jesus walked up to Matthew's booth and invited him to become a disciple. Matthew agreed and invited Jesus to supper—with Matthew's tax collector friends.

"Why does your teacher eat with such scum?" Jewish leaders asked the disciples (Matthew 9:11).

"Healthy people don't need a doctor—sick people do," Jesus replied. "I have come to call sinners, not those who think they are already good enough" (Matthew 9:12–13).

Mark and Luke identify the tax collector as Levi, leading scholars to guess that Jesus changed Matthew's name to or from Levi.

MATTHIAS
(muh THI us)
Maththias, Greek
"gift of God"
First century AD
First mention: Acts 1:23

After Jesus ascended to heaven, the disciples went back to Jerusalem to wait for the Holy Spirit—as Jesus instructed.

While they waited with a group of about 120, Peter decided to replace Judas Iscariot, who had committed suicide. The new disciple, Peter said, should be someone who had been with the group since the beginning. Two were nominated—Joseph and Matthias. Instead of voting, the disciples asked God to decide. They used lots, perhaps stones with names on them, pulled from a jar. Matthias was chosen.

MEDIA
(ME de uh)
Maday, Hebrew
First mention: Ezra 6:2

In the 500s BC, when the Jewish nation got erased from the world map and its citizens were exiled to Babylon in what is now Iraq, four kingdoms competed for world domination: Media, Babylon in Iraq, Egypt, and Lydia in western Turkey. The largest was Media, covering most of what is now Iran, but stretching into parts of Iraq and Turkey. Allied with its tiny neighbor of Persia, in what is now southern Iran, the Medes and Persians defeated Babylon and produced the world's next dominator, the Persian Empire, which swallowed all the other kingdoms.

MEDITERRANEAN SEA
(MED uh tur RAIN ee uhn)
Yam, Hebrew
"the sea"
Medius terra, Latin
"midland"
First mention: Exodus 23:31

Israelites weren't seafaring people—even though their nearly two-hundred-mile-long western border stopped at the Mediterranean Sea. They were sea-*fearing.*

Part of the reason they remained landlubbers is because they didn't have a natural harbor—or even a good man-made harbor until Herod the Great built one at Caesarea a few decades before Rome dismantled the Jewish nation. Also, Israelite heritage was one of nomadic shepherding. They preferred the desert to the sea. And stories like Jonah getting swallowed by a large fish worked a bit like the 1975 *Jaws* movie about a hungry shark. People who knew the stories avoided the ocean.

The Mediterranean Sea did,

Herod the Great built Israel's first harbor here in Caesarea, though most of it washed away. Israel doesn't have a natural harbor, but it does have several artificial ones now.

MEGIDDO MAP 1 C3

(muh GID oh)
Megiddo, Hebrew
perhaps "place of troops"
First mention: Joshua 12:21

Invading armies or caravans on their way through ancient Israel usually had to get past one well-placed city perched on top of a one-hundred-foot hill. From this vantage point, beside the easiest pass through the Mount Carmel range, lookouts at Megiddo could see for miles. That's because below them stretched the Jezreel valley, sometimes called the Valley of Armageddon.

Archaeologists say this site was occupied as early as 3000 BC. In Bible times, the hilltop fort city covered thirteen acres surrounded by walls.

Perhaps just a few decades before the Hebrews began their exodus, the Egyptian ruler Thutmose III in 1479 BC captured Megiddo after a seven-month siege. His records quote him explaining why he bothered: "Capturing Megiddo is as good as capturing a thousand cities." Because of its strategic location, Solomon strengthened the fortifications to protect Israel and monitor the key north-south trade route along the Mediterranean coast.

Megiddo was permanently abandoned about the time Alexander the Great conquered Palestine in 322 BC. The most recent battle in the region was

however, deliver one of Israel's most persistent enemies: the Philistines, who were apparently part of a migration of "sea people" from somewhere around Greece. They invaded Canaan and Egypt about the time the Israelites arrived in Canaan.

The Mediterranean is an inland sea about twenty-two hundred miles long—roughly the distance from New York City to Spokane or Phoenix. It's almost completely surrounded by land. The only natural opening is in the west, at the Rock of Gibraltar, where the southern tip of Spain comes within a few miles of touching Morocco in northern Africa. Through the Strait of Gibraltar, ships sail to and from the Atlantic Ocean. The Suez Canal in Egypt is a man-made opening that leads into the Red Sea.

To cross the mountains in the background, armies marching south along the seacoast trail first had to pass the fortress on this hilltop: Megiddo.

during the Arab-Israeli war of 1948, when Israeli soldiers defended the land against Syrian and Iraqi forces.

Today Megiddo is a popular tourist attraction where visitors explore the layered remains of about two dozen civilizations. (See *Armageddon*.)

MELCHIZEDEK
(mel KIZ uh deck)
Malkisedeq, Hebrew
"king of righteousness"
2100s BC
First mention: Genesis 14:18

On his way home from rescuing Lot from a raiding party, Abraham was met by the king of Jerusalem, then called Salem. This king was a mysterious figure called Melchizedek, "a priest of God Most High" (Genesis 14:18). This was some seven hundred years before God appointed Aaron as Israel's first priest.

Abraham gave Melchizedek a tenth of all the goods he recovered—a fiscal predecessor of tithing, which God later required of the people, to provide funds for Israel's temple and priesthood.

In what early Christians considered a prophecy about the Messiah, Jesus, a psalm writer said the coming ruler would be "a priest forever in the line of Melchizedek" (Psalm 110:4).

The New Testament writer of Hebrews picked up on this and said that because Israel's priesthood became useless, God replaced it. Instead of a line of flawed and mortal priests, God anointed Jesus as the perfect priest in the line of Melchizedek—a priesthood that will never end. "Therefore he [Jesus] is able, once and forever, to save everyone who comes to God through him" (Hebrews 7:25).

MEMPHIS
(MEM fuss)
Menophreos, Greek
First mention: Isaiah 19:13

MAP 3
B4

About fifteen miles south of Cairo on the banks of the Nile River rests the ruins of an ancient Egyptian capital—Memphis. There's not much left testifying to the city's former glory. Best known is a colossal limestone statue of Rameses II—forty feet long even with its legs missing. Founded nearly a

Statue of Rameses II in Memphis, former capital of Egypt.

thousand years before Abraham, Memphis was where most of Egypt's kings lived—just a two- or three-day walk from where Joseph's Hebrew family grazed their flocks in the Goshen region, before a pharaoh enslaved their descendants.

MEPHIBOSHETH

(muh FIB uh sheth)
Mephiboset, Hebrew
Perhaps "from the mouth of the Lord"
1000s BC
First mention: 2 Samuel 4:4

Trembling in terror as he bowed before King David, the crippled Mephibosheth must have thought he was about to die.

He was King Saul's grandson, and it was customary for new kings to lock in their power by wiping out the previous king's male heirs—to keep them from later proclaiming themselves the rightful ruler.

But Mephibosheth wasn't just any royal grandson. He was the son of Jonathan, David's dearest and most loyal friend. Mephibosheth was only five years old when his father and grandfather died in battle. When news of the lost battle reached Saul's capital, Mephibosheth's nurse grabbed the boy to run from the Philistine invaders, but she dropped him, crippling both feet.

"Don't be afraid!" King David told him. "I've asked you to come so that I can be kind to you because of my vow to your father, Jonathan. I will give you all the land that once belonged to your grandfather Saul, and you may live here with me at the palace!" (2 Samuel 9:7).

ACCUSED OF TREASON

Years later, when David's son Absalom led a coup and marched on Jerusalem, David fled. Mephibosheth was supposed to join him, but he didn't show up. When David asked Mephibosheth's servant, Ziba, about it, the servant said his master was staying: "He said, 'Today I will get back the kingdom of my grandfather Saul'" (2 Samuel 16:3). David promptly gave all Mephibosheth's land to Ziba.

David returned after his forces crushed the rebels. There to greet him was Mephibosheth, unwashed since the day David left. Mephibosheth said he planned to go with the king, but that Ziba stole his donkeys. Unable to determine who was telling the truth, David split the land between the two.

Later, citizens of a town Saul once tried to exterminate asked David to execute seven of Saul's sons or grandsons—as a way of getting justice. David complied, but he spared Mephibosheth.

MESHACH

(ME shek)
Mesak, Hebrew
Misaaku, Akkadian
"who is what Aku [moon god] is"
About 600 BC
First mention: Daniel 1:7

Thrown into a furnace for refusing to worship a statue of the Babylonian king, Nebuchadnezzar, Meshach survived to become a Jewish hero—with his friends Shadrach and Abednego. His Hebrew name was Mishael, meaning "who is what God is." (See *Shadrach.*)

MESOPOTAMIA

(MESS oh poh TAY me uh)
Mesopotamia, Greek
"between the rivers"
First mention: Acts 2:9

MAP 3
D3

Human civilization got its start on a fertile, eight-hundred-mile-long stretch of land extending from the Persian Gulf north through Iraq and into parts of Syria and Turkey. Greeks called it Mesopotamia because most of this land

fell "between the rivers" of the Tigris in the east and the Euphrates in the west.

Abraham came from there—from Ur, a city on the west bank of the Euphrates in southern Iraq, just across the river from the modern town of Nasiriya. Assyrians built their capital of Nineveh in Mesopotamia, near the Iraqi city of Mosul. Babylonians built Babylon there, some fifty miles south of Baghdad. And Persians built Susa there, about 150 miles north of the Persian Gulf.

MICAH

(MY kuh)
Mika, Hebrew
"Who is like the Lord?"
Ministered 742–687 BC
First mention: Jeremiah 26:18

Micah was a small-town prophet who took a stand against some of the most powerful leaders of his day in a ministry spanning the reigns of three kings: Jotham, Ahaz, and Hezekiah.

Micah lived in Moresheth, a village some twenty miles southwest of Jerusalem—about a day's walk. He must have made that walk many times because the kings knew him well. Once, when he predicted that Jerusalem would be reduced to rubble and the temple hilltop to a plowed field, King Hezekiah led the people in prayer, and "the LORD held back the terrible disaster he had pronounced against them" (Jeremiah 26:19).

In both Jewish nations—Israel in the north and Judah in the south,

PREDICTING JESUS' BIRTHPLACE

Wise men asked King Herod for directions to the newborn king of Israel. Herod turned to religious scholars, who said Micah had predicted the Messiah's birthplace.

"But you, O Bethlehem Ephrathah, are only a small village in Judah. Yet a ruler of Israel will come from you, one whose origins are from the distant past. . . . He will be highly honored all around the world. And he will be the source of our peace" (Micah 5:2, 4–5).

Jesus was born there about seven hundred years later.

where Micah lived—judges took bribes, false prophets told the future for money, nobles took advantage of the poor, and the poor prayed to idols for help.

Both nations would fall, Micah warned, but God would later restore the Jewish people. Micah lived to see Assyria wipe Israel off the map in 722 BC. Babylon overran Judah in 586 BC, but about fifty years later, Persia defeated Babylon and released Jewish exiles to go home.

Micah's prophecies are preserved in the seven-chapter book named after him.

MICHAL
(MY kuhl)
Mikal, Hebrew
"Who is like God?"
1000s BC
First mention: 1 Samuel 14:49

To win the girl of his dreams—Saul's daughter Michal—David had to come up with foreskins from one hundred Philistines; he came up with two hundred.

To keep this lady's love, however, proved impossible.

The gruesome bride price was Saul's idea. Insanely jealous of the giant killer's popularity, Saul hoped David would die fighting the Philistines.

Sometime after the marriage, Michal found out that her father planned to kill David. She helped David escape and bought him time by stalling the assassins.

Since David became a fugitive, Saul married Michal to another man. Years later, after Saul died, David demanded Michal back. She apparently didn't want to come. Her second husband followed, weeping, until he was ordered home.

The Bible's last scene about Michal reports her contempt for David. He danced as priests brought into Jerusalem the sacred chest containing the Ten Commandments. But Michal said in disgust, "How glorious the king of Israel looked today! He exposed himself to the servant girls like any indecent person might do!" (2 Samuel 6.20).

Michal died childless.

MICMASH

(MICK mash)
Mikmas, Hebrew
First mention: 1 Samuel 13:2

MAP 2
C5

King Saul's army started deserting in droves when they saw the force that the Philistines had mustered against them: countless infantry, six thousand cavalry, and three thousand chariots—the ancient battlefield fear-factor equivalent of today's tank. This invasion force, arriving to crush Israel's uprising led by their new Hebrew king, camped at Micmash, just a few miles north of Saul's capital in Gibeah.

Saul's son, Jonathan, saved the day. In a kind of special forces operation, he and his armor bearer killed about twenty Philistines who were guarding a key mountain pass. This attack, followed by an earthquake, panicked the Philistines. They ran for their lives, even fighting each other in the confusion.

MIDIAN

(MID ee un)
Midyan, Hebrew
First mention: Genesis 25:2

MAP 3
C4

Suddenly a fugitive, after murdering an Egyptian for beating a Hebrew slave, Moses ran to the land of Midian—a place hard to pinpoint.

The country is named after the son Abraham had with Keturah, a second wife. Midian moved east of Canaan. Later, Midianite traders bought Joseph and sold him as a slave in Egypt. They operated a caravan from Gilead in Jordan southward to Egypt. So at one time, Midian may have been in Jordan. But in Moses' time, Midian seems to have shifted south, perhaps into Arabia on the east bank of the Red Sea. The boundary may have drifted even into the Sinai Peninsula, because that's where Moses grazed the sheep of his Midianite father-in-law at Mount Sinai when God appeared to him in a burning bush.

MIRIAM

(MEAR ee uhm)
Miryam, Hebrew
About 1525–1400s BC
First mention: Exodus 15:20

Long before Moses' big sister became Israel's first female prophet, she was just another little girl looking out for her baby brother.

In her first dramatic scene recorded in the Bible, Miriam stood on the bank of the Nile River, waiting to see what the Egyptian princess would do when she came to bathe and found three-month-old Moses floating in a basket among the reeds.

Miriam was the unnamed girl who offered to find a Hebrew woman to take care of the baby—a woman who turned out to be Moses' mother, Jochebed.

Miriam is mentioned just two more times in the Bible. After crossing the Red Sea, she led the Hebrew women in a song that scholars say is among the oldest poems in the Bible.

Later, Miriam grew jealous of Moses, arguing that she was a prophet as worthy as he was. She also got angry that Moses married a "Cushite," perhaps referring to his wife, Zipporah, or to a second wife from somewhere in the North African or Arabian region.

God set Miriam straight. He said that though he spoke to her and other prophets in dreams and visions, he spoke to Moses face-to-face. And in what seems a fitting punishment for Miriam's comment about the dark-skinned Cushite, God turned Miriam lily white with a skin disease that lasted a week.

Miriam died sometime during those forty years the Hebrews camped at the wilderness oasis of Kadesh, south of Canaan.

MIZPAH

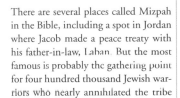

(MIZ puh)
mispa, Hebrew
"watchtower"
First mention: Genesis 31:49

There are several places called Mizpah in the Bible, including a spot in Jordan where Jacob made a peace treaty with his father-in-law, Laban. But the most famous is probably the gathering point for four hundred thousand Jewish warriors who nearly annihilated the tribe of Benjamin.

The location of that Mizpah is unknown, but Jews from all Israel met there, intent on bringing justice to the tribe that refused to punish men who gang-raped the wife of a Jewish traveler. When the battles were over, everyone from Benjamin was dead, except for "six hundred men who escaped" (Judges 20:47).

Israel regretted the massacre. So they kidnapped Jewish women and gave them as wives to the surviving men of Benjamin.

MOAB

(MOW ab)
Moab, Hebrew
"from father"
2100s BC
First mention: Genesis 19:37

Like his cousin, Ben-ammi, Moab was a child of incest.

Lot was their father. He was also their grandfather.

After Lot and his two daughters escaped the fiery cataclysm that destroyed Sodom and killed Lot's wife, the daughters figured there weren't any men left in the region. So they got their father drunk and had sex with him to preserve their family line.

Moab and Ben-ammi became ancestors of two nations that later fought Israel—Moab and Ammon—both in what is now Jordan.

MOAB

(MO ab)
Moab, Hebrew
"from father"
First mention: Genesis 36:35

Descendants of Moab, a son the drunken Lot had with his daughter, settled east of Israel in what is now part of Jordan. There weren't many livable places in that region. The western side is a rugged wall of steep slopes and cliffs that drop thousands of feet into the Dead Sea. In the east lies the Arabian

Desert. So most people lived on a narrow strip of fertile land, where they could graze their flocks and grow crops.

Moab and Israel often fought. One Bible story says that when Israel was about to defeat Moab, King Mesha of Moab sacrificed his oldest son "as a burnt offering on the wall" (2 Kings 3:27). Israelites soldiers saw it and retreated.

An inscription called the Moabite Stone, discovered in 1868, reports Mesha's accomplishments, which included winning back Moab's independence from Israel.

MORDECAI

(MORE duh khi)
Mordekay, Hebrew
Perhaps "the most excellent man"
400s BC
First mention: Esther 2:5

Mordecai is a Jewish hero who helped save his race from a holocaust throughout the vast Persian Empire, which stretched from India to Egypt.

On the other hand, he's the fellow who got the Persians angry in the first place—one Persian in particular, the prime minister named Haman.

Mordecai refused to bow when Haman walked by. The Bible doesn't say why. Perhaps it was because Mordecai knew Haman's family history. Haman was an Amalekite, from the nomadic tribe that tried to stop the Hebrew exodus out of Egypt.

In classic overkill, Haman decided to get even by wiping out Mordecai's race. March 7 was set for the genocide.

Jewish property would go to anyone who killed the property owners.

Haman managed to get the king's irrevocable authorization, without even identifying the race. What neither Haman nor the king knew was that this order hung a bull's-eye on Queen Esther. She was not only a Jew; she was Mordecai's cousin, whom he had raised after her parents died.

Mordecai convinced Esther to ask for a meeting with the king, though Persian law said that anyone who requested a meeting with him would be executed if the king turned the person down. At Esther's request, Mordecai mobilized the Jews in the capital to fast for three days, praying that the king would accept Esther's request.

When the king found out what Haman had done, he ordered him hanged on the gallows intended for Mordecai. Then he ordered his soldiers to protect the Jews against any citizens who attacked. Many did attack, but the Jews came out ahead, killing some seventy-five thousand.

Mordecai came out ahead, too. He took Haman's job as prime minister. So the empire headquartered in what is now Iran had both a Jewish queen and a Jewish prime minister.

MOREH

See Shechem

(MOH rah)
Moreh, Hebrew
First mention: Genesis 12:6

MAP 1
C4

Abraham was seventy-five years old when he arrived in what is now Israel.

With his wife, flocks, and servants, he continued south until he reached the heartland—about midway between the Sea of Galilee in the north and the Dead Sea in the south. There, near the village of Shechem and beside an oak tree at a place called Moreh, Abraham set up his first camp in what was then called Canaan. God appeared to him there and said, "I am going to give this land to your offspring" (Genesis 12:7).

MORIAH

(mo RYE uh)
Moriyya, Hebrew
First mention:
Genesis 22:2

See Jerusalem

MAP 1
C5

A Muslim shrine, the Dome of the Rock, now rests on Mount Moriah where the Jewish temple once stood. In the distant background is the higher Mount of Olives, across the narrow Kidron valley.

There are two places named Moriah mentioned in the Bible, but many believe they are one and the same. The first is where Abraham nearly sacrificed his son, and the other is Mount Moriah, where Solomon built a temple as the only place Israelites could offer sacrifices to God.

Abraham took Isaac to Moriah. The only clues about its location are that there were hills, and it was a three-day journey from their home in Beersheba. Though some scholars say three days may simply refer to a short journey, Beersheba is an easy three-day walk from Jerusalem—about forty-five miles. Most travelers covered about twenty miles a day.

Inside Jerusalem's most prominent building—a thirteen-hundred-year-old Muslim shrine called the Dome of the Rock—there's a huge stone on which tradition says Abraham prepared to sacrifice Isaac until an angel stopped him at the last moment.

MOSES

(MOW zuhs)
Mosheh, Hebrew
"draw out," of the water
About 1520–1400 BC
First mention: Exodus 2:10

No man is more famous in Jewish history than Moses. But no man argued harder with God to avoid fame.

At eighty years of age, the last thing Moses wanted to do was go back to the country where he was wanted for murder.

If he had to go back, the last person he wanted to visit was Pharaoh, the king who could order him killed in a heartbeat.

And if he had to go to Pharaoh, who thought himself a god, the last thing he wanted to do was tell Pharaoh that the real God said to release the Hebrew slaves used as cheap labor on pet projects.

Moses was an old shepherd. He wanted to get older.

MOSES FLOATS

Moses was born in Egypt about 350 years after his ancestor Jacob arrived there with an extended family of seventy children and grandchildren. They had come to escape a drought in Canaan—now Israel—and they stayed.

Too long.

They grew. *Swarmed* is closer to the Hebrew word. Worried that they would take over the nation, the Egyptian king identified only by his title of Pharaoh, ordered them all enslaved. At first, Pharaoh tried to slow their birthrate by working them to exhaustion, building entire cities. When that proved ineffective, he tried a new approach: "Throw all the newborn Israelite boys into the Nile River" (Exodus 1:22).

In a way, Moses' parents complied. They just arranged for Moses to float.

BABIES IN A BASKET

Moses wasn't the only baby floating in a basket pulled from a river. There are more than thirty such stories from ancient history.

That's not surprising, given that cities often sprang up alongside rivers. People back then apparently abandoned babies in floating baskets the way modern folks do by setting them at the doorstep of a home or a church. The hope was that someone along the busy riverbank would find the child and raise it.

One Assyrian story, nearly a thousand years older than Moses, tells about a priestess who wasn't supposed to have sex. But she got pregnant, delivered a son, and put him adrift on the Euphrates River in a waterproof basket. A farmer found the boy and raised him. That child grew up to become Sargon, an emperor in the 2300s BC.

His father was Amram from the extended family, or tribe, descended from Jacob's third son, Levi—the family that would later serve as Israel's worship leaders. Moses' mother was Jochebed. The couple had two other children—Miriam, the oldest, and Aaron, who was about three years old at the time.

Jochebed managed to keep her

baby hidden for three months. Then she put him in a reed basket waterproofed with tar and carefully set the basket among river reeds where the princess in Pharaoh's court bathed. Little Miriam kept an eye on her brother, and when the princess found him, Miriam volunteered to find a Hebrew woman to nurse the boy. Jochebed got the job—a mother paid to take care of her own baby.

FUGITIVE AND FAMILY MAN

Raised a prince in Egypt, Moses knew he was a Hebrew. At age forty, he saw an Egyptian foreman beating a Hebrew slave. When Moses thought no one was looking, he killed the foreman. But the next day, when he tried to break up a fight between two Hebrews, one of the angry men said, "Do you plan to kill me as you killed that Egyptian yesterday?" (Exodus 2:14).

Pharaoh soon heard about the murder, and he ordered Moses caught and executed. Moses ran for his life, east to the Sinai Peninsula in the same direction he would later take the Hebrews. He stopped running when he reached the flocks of a Midian shepherd and priest named Jethro, also called Reuel. Midian was a nation along the northeastern banks of the Red Sea, in what is now Saudi Arabia. Moses came to a well at the same time Jethro's daughters were being driven away by other shepherds. Moses stood up for the women and helped water their sheep.

That earned him a job and eventually a wife and family. Jethro hired him as a shepherd and gave him one of his daughters, Zipporah, as a wife. The couple had a son that Moses named Gershom, meaning "stranger," since Moses considered himself a stranger in Midian.

DEBATING GOD

Forty years later, when Moses was eighty and grazing his father-in-law's sheep at the foot of Mount Sinai, God caught his attention with a fiery bush that didn't burn up. As Moses approached, God spoke, ordering Moses

Forced to build an Egyptian city, enslaved Israelites transport a lion statue. God sent Moses to free the Israelites and take them home.

MOSES, THE NAME

Moses was a Hebrew with a common Egyptian name—but a name perfectly fitting for a Hebrew.

Moses sounds like the Hebrew word masa, meaning "draw out." The princess who ordered the baby Moses drawn from the Nile probably knew that and realized how appropriate this name was. But the name is actually from the Egyptian word Mose—the noun version meaning "boy" and the verb version meaning "to give birth." So, working the Egyptian and Hebrew angles together, Moses was the "boy drawn from the Nile."

Many Egyptian kings had this name, usually tacked to the name of a god. The more famous kings were Rameses (Ra is born) and Tuthmosis I through IV (Toth is born).

to take off his sandals before walking on holy ground. God told Moses he heard the prayers of the Hebrews suffering in Egypt.

"I am sending you to Pharaoh," God said. "You will lead my people, the Israelites, out of Egypt" (Exodus 3:10).

That began a debate.

"Who am I to appear before Pharaoh?" Moses asked.

God replied, "I will be with you."

"They won't believe me," Moses said, referring to the Hebrews. "They will ask, 'Which god are you talking about? What is his name?' "

God replied, "I AM THE ONE WHO ALWAYS IS. Just tell them, 'I AM has sent me to you.' "

"Look," Moses replied, "they won't believe me! They won't do what I tell them. They'll just say, 'The LORD never appeared to you' " (Exodus 3:11–4:1).

God showed Moses several miracles he could perform as proof, such as turning his shepherd staff into a snake.

Moses persisted. "I'm just not a good speaker. I never have been, and I'm not now, even after you have spoken to me. I'm clumsy with words."

"Who makes mouths?" the Lord asked.

"Lord, please! Send someone else" (Exodus 4:10–11, 13).

God agreed to let Moses' older brother, Aaron, serve as spokesman.

Double-teamed by these brothers, Pharaoh was unimpressed by the words or the miracles. It took ten plagues and the life of his oldest son to convince him to let God's people go.

THE EXODUS BEGINS

What follows is the most famous event in the four-thousand-year history of the Jews—a long walk home called the Exodus. It was on this journey that God took an unorganized, loosely connected race of refugees and forged them into a nation united in faith and guided by a new and unique set of laws.

The reported number of refugees creates a world of doubt: six hundred thousand men. Adding women and children, the number easily inflates to 2.5 million—enough to fill thirty large football stadiums. The Hebrews wouldn't need to stop at a well for water; they would need a lake—in the desert. And if they crossed the Red Sea on a one-hundred-yard-wide swath of dry ground, the line of humanity would stretch twenty miles.

Some scholars suggest that the word translated "thousand" may mean "group," such as an extended family. If so, there may have been six hundred groups of men—with each group being a father and his married sons, for a total crowd of maybe fifteen thousand or more.

LAWGIVER

However many people there were, Moses led them to Mount Sinai, where they heard God speak the Ten Commandments even before they were

NATURALLY OCCURRING PLAGUES IN EGYPT

It took ten plagues for Moses to arm-twist Pharaoh into freeing the slaves. Most of the plagues could have been naturally occurring events that God used.

1. Nile turns red. Perhaps a form of red tide algae stirred up by a flood. An Egyptian story from the 1300s BC reports: "The river is blood. People refuse to drink it, and thirst for water."

2. Frogs. They may have fled the flooded and polluted river.

3. Insects. Possibly mosquitoes, gnats, or other insects bred in pools from the receding flood.

4. Flies. This could have been the stable fly, which lays eggs in decaying substances such as wet hay or dead frogs.

5. Diseased livestock. Anthrax, or possibly African Horse Sickness or Bluetongue Virus, carried by insects.

6. Boils. Anthrax and the stable fly can produce blisters and boils.

7. Hail. Common in Egypt.

8. Locusts. Common.

9. Darkness for three days. Possibly from the hot Khamsin winds blowing in from the Sahara Desert.

10. Death of firstborn. Oldest children often got special treatment and may have eaten more food than others—food contaminated by insects and disease. But that wouldn't explain how the oldest animals died, too.

written on stone. The people were so traumatized that they didn't want to go through it again. So they told Moses, "You tell us what God says, and we will listen. But don't let God speak directly to us" (Exodus 20:19).

Over the years that followed, Moses delivered the hundreds of laws now preserved in the first five books of the Bible and still observed by religious Jews—laws that determined not only how the nation of Israel would worship, but how it would govern. The laws read a bit like a church manual, Bill of Rights, and federal law code rolled into one.

FORTY YEARS IN THE DESERT

After camping at Mount Sinai for more than a year, the people left for Canaan, following a pillar of cloud that had guided them.

They complained as they walked—about food, water, and the harsh conditions. Though Moses had earlier interceded for them and urged God not to wipe them out after they worshiped the golden calf at Mount Sinai, Moses repeatedly got frustrated with them. Like the time they grew tired of the mysterious honey-flavored manna God sent and wanted fresh meat.

"What did I do to deserve the burden of a people like this?" he asked the Lord (Numbers 11:11). God sent a flock of exhausted quail, perhaps those that migrate each year between Africa and Europe.

When the Hebrews approached Canaan's southern border, Moses sent in a dozen scouts. After ten of the twelve reported seeing giants and fortified cities, the Hebrews refused to go any farther. For this lack of faith, God sentenced the nation to forty years in the desert. Of the entire adult generation on the Exodus, only the two scouts who gave the good report—Joshua and Caleb—would enter the Promised Land.

Even Moses was forbidden entrance because of some mysterious sin. After angrily striking a rock to release water, God criticized him: "Because you did not trust me enough to demonstrate my holiness to the people of Israel, you will not lead them into the land I am giving them!" (Numbers 20:12). How Moses failed God is unclear.

Moses got as far as the country of Jordan—close enough to see Canaan from Mount Nebo east of the Jordan River. There, at age 120, he died. He was buried in a valley, and the nation mourned for a month. His story concludes with this testimonial: "There has never been another prophet like Moses, whom the LORD knew face to face" (Deuteronomy 34:10).

More than a thousand years later, however, Moses reappeared. He stood with Elijah and Jesus at the Transfiguration, when "Jesus' appearance changed so that his face shone like the sun, and his clothing became dazzling white" (Matthew 17:2).

What Moses had done—helped forge Israel into the nation—Jesus would take to the next level, fulfilling prophecy that Israel would become "a

One ridge of many in the Mount Carmel range.

blessing to the nations of the world" (Jeremiah 4:2). Jesus, a Jew from Israel, did this by spreading the news that salvation was available to everyone—not just the Jews.

MOUNT CARMEL

(CAR muhl)
Har Hakkarmel, Hebrew
"garden"
First mention: 1 Kings 18.19

Mount Carmel, where the prophet Elijah challenged 850 pagan prophets to a battle of the gods, isn't a single mountain. It's a mountain range about thirteen miles long in northern Israel. This range forms a massive wall on the south side of the Valley of Armageddon, better known by locals as Jezreel valley or the Valley of Esdraelon.

Caravans and armies traveling to or from Egypt along the popular coastline route had to travel through one of several Carmel mountain passes.

Early Jewish stories say that it was on a hilltop near the sea where Elijah challenged the prophets of Baal and Asherah to meet him and to call down

fire from heaven to consume a sacrifice. After hours of pleading from the pagan prophets, Baal—the fertility god who was thought to control rain and lightning—did nothing. God, however, promptly answered Elijah's short prayer. Elijah then ordered the pagan prophets taken into the valley near the Kishon River and executed.

Today, Carmel's hills are among the most lush and beautiful in Israel, partly because of the moist winds from the Mediterranean Sea. Forests, grain fields, vineyards, and orchards still blanket many of the hillsides.

MOUNT EBAL

(E bull)
Har Ebal, Hebrew
First mention: Deuteronomy 11:29

Mount Ebal and Mount Gerizim stand like a couple of three-thousand-foot-high sentinels guarding the narrow valley below, where Palestinians live in the city of Nablus. The ruins of ancient Shechem in the center of Canaan lie nearby, at the east entrance of the valley.

When Joshua led the Israelites into

Canaan, he followed the instructions of Moses and assembled the people in this valley along with the sacred chest that held the Ten Commandments. The Israelites then listened as leaders read the blessings for obeying God's laws and the curses for disobeying—blessings and curses preserved in Deuteronomy 28 and 29. Curses were read from Mount Ebal, and after each curse, the people responded with an "Amen." Blessings were read from Mount Gerizim.

MOUNT GERIZIM

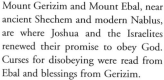

(GARE uh zim)
Har Gerizzim, Hebrew
First mention: Deuteronomy 11:29

Mount Gerizim and Mount Ebal, near ancient Shechem and modern Nablus, are where Joshua and the Israelites renewed their promise to obey God. Curses for disobeying were read from Ebal and blessings from Gerizim.

Ironically, in AD 70, nearly twelve thousand Samaritans—people who revere the teachings of Moses—were slaughtered on the Mount of Blessing, as Gerizim became known. Romans, reestablishing control in the region after Jews rebelled in AD 66, surrounded this mountain sacred to the Samaritans and attacked. Today, just a few hundred Samaritans live in the Samaritan Quarter of Nablus. (See *Mount Ebal.*)

MOUNT GILBOA

(gill BOW uh)
Gilboa, Hebrew
First mention: 1 Samuel 28:4

Israel's first king—Saul—and three of his sons died in a battle at Mount Gilboa after the Philistines assembled such a vast army that Israel's terrified king resorted to consulting a psychic for advice.

Saul had apparently planned to capture a nearby city that would have given him control of a key trade route in the Jezreel valley of northern Israel, but he was surprised by the staggering Philistine response. Since the prophet Samuel was dead and God wasn't talking to Saul, the king asked a psychic to call up Samuel's spirit. To the horror of everyone, psychic included, Samuel appeared and said that Saul would be joining him the next day.

MOUNT HERMON

Har Hermon, Hebrew
First mention: Deuteronomy 3:8

There's just one place in Israel where a person can see snow on a mountain peak most of the year. That's Mount Hermon—the highest spot in Israel and the source of the Jordan River.

Some say this mountain is where Jesus met with Moses and Elijah, when his body was transfigured into a glowing celestial form. Others say this happened fifty miles south, at Mount Tabor. But it was at the foot of Mount Hermon, near Caesarea Philippi, where Jesus told his disciples he was going to Jerusalem to "suffer at the hands of the leaders and the leading priests and the teachers of religious law. He would be killed, and he would be raised on the third day" (Matthew 16:21).

Mount Hermon is a three-summit cluster of mountains at the southern tip of the Anti-Lebanon Range on the border of Lebanon and Syria. Since the 1967 Six-Day War, Israel has controlled about forty square miles of the southern and western regions that produce snowmelt for the Jordan River.

MOUNT NEBO

(NEE bo)
Nebo, Hebrew
First mention: Numbers 32:3

MAP 1
D5

It was the closest Moses got to the Promised Land—ten miles away and twenty-seven hundred feet high. He stood on a mountain beside where the Jordan River pours into the Dead Sea, just a little south of Jericho. People of Jordan, where the mountain rests, call it Jabal Naba. It's part of the Mount Pisgah range that runs alongside the Jordan River and the Dead Sea.

Moses climbed to one of its peaks and looked in wonder at what would become Israel—from Mount Hermon some one hundred miles north, to the Mediterranean Sea sixty miles west, to the Negev desert across the Dead Sea and south. Then he died on the mountain and was buried at a secret location in the valley.

MOUNT OF BEATITUDES

See Sea of Galilee

Beati, Latin "blessed" or "happy"

MAP 4
C3

"One day as the crowds were gathering, Jesus went up the mountainside with his disciples and sat down to teach them" (Matthew 5:1).

What followed was the most famous sermon in history—a concise summary of Jesus' most important teachings.

Since at least the AD 300s, people have called it the Sermon on the Mount. Jesus began with a list of ways to find enduring happiness—scholars

A Moses'-eye-view of the Promised Land, from Mount Nebo.

title that list the Beatitudes. That's where Christians came up with "Mount of the Beatitudes," which isn't mentioned by name in the Bible.

All that the Gospel of Matthew says about the location is that Jesus preached on a hillside. Luke, on the other hand, says Jesus preached a similar sermon on a plain. Exactly where Jesus preached those sermons is unknown. But there are both large hillsides and sprawling plains along the Sea of Galilee's shoreline. And some gently sloping hillsides are flat enough to be considered a plain.

The most persistent tradition about where Jesus preached—a tradition dating back to at least the AD 300s—points to a gentle hillside about a mile's walk from Jesus' Galilean headquarters, which

From the Chapel of the Beatitudes, built to commemorate Jesus' Sermon on the Mount, a green hillside slopes into the Sea of Galilee.

was the fishing village of Capernaum. The vast hillside lies about midway between Capernaum and Tabga, a place where Jesus is said to have fed thousands with a few fish and loaves of bread. This hillside, called Mount Eremos in ancient times, could seat tens of thousands and it carries sound like an amphitheater. Early Christian pilgrims said several early churches existed in the area, but were probably destroyed during the Persian invasion of the AD 600s and again during the Crusader-Muslim wars several hundred years later.

Tourist groups often gather on these slopes to read the Beatitudes, sing, and pray.

At the top of the hill is a small, beautiful chapel designed as an octagon—one side for each of the Beatitudes. This chapel was built in the late 1930s for the Franciscan Sisters, a group of Catholic nuns. Money for the project, oddly enough, came from the World War II Italian dictator Benito Mussolini.

Nearby is the Plain of Gennesaret, where Jesus may have preached the similar sermon that's at least partly preserved in Luke.

MOUNT OF OLIVES

See Jerusalem
MAP 4
B5

Har hazzetim, Hebrew
First mention:
2 Samuel 15:30

Rising above the Kidron valley is a two-mile-long ridge, the Mount of Olives where Jesus prayed before his arrest.

In Israel, no hills are better known than these—just a few minutes' walk down Jerusalem's east slope and across the narrow Kidron valley. Jesus prayed on the Mount of Olives the night Jewish officials arrested him. And he later ascended to heaven from there.

By many standards, the Mount of Olives is no mountain at all—just a two-mile ridge of hills with three peaks. The highest peak rises about twenty-nine hundred feet above sea level, but it doesn't seem that high because the entire area is hilly; and Jerusalem's main hilltop, where the temple once stood, is only about three hundred feet lower.

In Jesus' day, the Mount of Olives hillside facing Jerusalem was "an olive grove called Gethsemane" (Matthew 26:36). Jesus often prayed there, as he did the night before his crucifixion. A few old olive trees are preserved there in the courtyard of the Church of All Nations, though these are probably not trees from Jesus' day. Roman soldiers cut them down to use in the siege of Jerusalem forty years after Jesus' death and resurrection.

Several weeks after his resurrection, Jesus gathered his disciples on the Mount of Olives and told them to tell people about him. "It was not long after he said this that he was taken up into the sky while they were watching, and he disappeared into a cloud" (Acts 1:9).

The Church of the Holy Ascension commemorates the site. The Arab invader Saladin converted the church into a mosque in 1187, and it remains one today. Inside is a stone with an imprint that legend says was the ascending footprint of Jesus.

A Jewish graveyard from before the time of Christ fills the southern slope. Since ancient times, Jews have buried their loved ones beside the Holy City. Many believe the tradition that says when the Messiah comes, he will walk through Jerusalem's eastern gate toward the Mount of Olives and raise the dead. Risen, they believe, they will find themselves standing in his presence.

Mount Sinai. The monastery below is said to have been built at the place where Moses talked with God at the burning bush.

MOUNT SINAI

MAP 3
B4

(SIGH nigh)
Har Sinay, Hebrew
First mention: Exodus 3:1

Israel was born 250 miles south of Jerusalem, an ancient tradition says—in Egypt, at the base of a granite mountain today called by its Arabic name, Jebel Musa—"Mountain of Moses."

In the Bible, it's known as Sinai or Horeb—the place where Moses encountered the burning bush and where he later received the Ten Commandments and many of the other laws that define what it means to be a Jew.

The Bible never says exactly where Mount Sinai is located. But Jewish evidence from the AD 100s seems to place it where a monastery was built some two hundred years later, soon after Rome legalized Christianity. That would be at Jebel Musa, near the southern tip of Egypt's Sinai Peninsula. The peninsula is a Martian badlands shaped like a giant wedge of stone pie shoved into the northern top of the Red Sea, parting the sea in two. West of Mount Sinai lies the Gulf of Suez, and to the east is the Gulf of Aqaba.

If Jebel Musa is the right mountain, Moses had a long climb to the top to meet with God. And he had a long climb back down carrying those heavy, stone tablets inscribed with Israel's ten bedrock laws on which all the other laws are built. Following the most common path, it takes about three hours to climb the seventy-five-hundred-foot-high mountain.

At the base of Mount Sinai today lies the monastery of Saint Catherine, built in the AD 500s on what is said to have been the site of the burning bush.

274

Oddly, one of the oldest surviving copies of the Bible was discovered in that monastery—in a trash heap in 1844. Called the *Codex Sinaiticus,* it was written about three hundred years after Jesus' earthly ministry.

MOUNT TABOR
(TAY bore)
Har Tabor, Hebrew
First mention: Joshua 19:22

MAP 4
C3

The mountain where Israel's only woman leader in the time of the judges—Deborah—chose to assemble her army stands out as much as she did. It's a single, isolated dome rising from the flat plains of the Jezreel valley. There are no other hills nearby, so it stands out for miles in northern Israel and climbs to about fourteen hundred feet above the plains.

It was the perfect place for Deborah to muster her troops because the Israelite militia faced an enemy noted for its chariot corps. But chariots would have been useless on Tabor's steep slopes. As it turns out, before the invaders reached Tabor, God drenched them in a rainstorm that flooded their route in the frequently dry Kishon River valley. Many of the charioteers were swept away. Others abandoned their chariots stuck in mud and ran for their lives.

Early Christian writers said Tabor was the mountain of the Transfiguration, where Jesus met with Elijah and Moses and his body glowed with celestial glory. The mountain is only about a two-hour walk from Jesus' hometown of Nazareth, approximately six miles away.

"I'll make three shrines," the astonished Peter told Jesus, "one for you, one for Moses, and one for Elijah" (Matthew 17:4). Though Jesus declined the offer, there are now three sacred buildings on the hilltop: two churches and a monastery. To see them, it's about a two-mile drive to the top, on a narrow road with sharp switchback turns.

NAAMAN
(NAY uh muhn)
Naaman, Hebrew
"pleasant"
800s BC
First mention: 2 Kings 5:1

As commander of Syria's army, Naaman was a powerful man—but with a problem he couldn't fix. He had a skin disease that terrified people because they thought it was leprosy. Actually, it could have been any number of diseases.

The only person who offered him any hope at all was his wife's maid, a Jewish slave girl captured in a raid on Israel. She said the prophet Elisha could heal him.

Naaman loaded up gifts for the healer: 750 pounds of silver, 150 pounds of gold, and ten sets of clothing.

Elisha refused the gifts and didn't even come out to greet Naaman. He just sent a messenger to tell him to take a bath. "Go and wash yourself seven times in the Jordan River" (2 Kings 5:10).

Naaman was furious. No greeting. No mysterious ritual. Just a bath.

His officers convinced him to do as he was told, and the skin disease disappeared.

Naaman promised to sacrifice only to God from then on, and he loaded two mules with dirt so he could worship God on Israel's soil.

NABOTH
(NAY buhth)
Nabot, Hebrew
800s BC
First mention:
1 Kings 21:1

Vegetables killed Naboth.

King Ahab wanted to plant a vegetable garden outside his getaway palace in Jezreel, but Naboth owned a vineyard there. It had been in his family for generations, so he rejected Ahab's offer to buy it or trade it for a better one.

A springtime job in Israel is pruning grape vines. Naboth lost his entire vineyard—and his life—because King Ahab wanted the land for a vegetable garden.

Ahab pouted and refused to eat. Queen Jezebel didn't understand. Her father ruled a kingdom in Lebanon, and he apparently did as he pleased. So Jezebel ordered the city elders to arrange for "two scoundrels" to accuse Naboth of cursing God and the king and to stone Naboth to death. The moment Ahab got word that Naboth was dead, he confiscated the vineyard.

Abuse of the poor eventually became common in Israel. The prophet Micah cried foul and declared, "The only example you follow is that of wicked King Ahab!" (Micah 6:16).

The Assyrian cavalry is depicted in a relief from King Sennacherib's palace.

NAHUM

(NAY uhm)
Nahum, Hebrew
"comfort"
Perhaps 600s BC
First mention: Nahum 1:1

"Comfort" was Nahum's name in Hebrew. But comfort wasn't his message—not for the Assyrians. They attacked the northern Jewish nation of Israel and erased it from the map. Only the southern Jewish nation of Judah was left.

"I am preparing a grave for you," Nahum told the Assyrians, delivering God's message, "because you are despicable and don't deserve to live!" (Nahum 1:14).

Scholars have turned up nothing about this mysterious prophet from Elkosh—not even the location of Elkosh. When Nahum lived is unknown, too. It's presumed he delivered this prophecy shortly before Babylonian forces overran Assyria in 612 BC.

NAIN

MAP 4 C3

Nain, Greek
First mention: Luke 7:11

About ten miles from his hometown of Nazareth, Jesus and his disciples arrived at the village of Nain while a funeral procession was leaving. A widow was burying her only son. Filled with compassion for the mother, Jesus walked over to the boy's body.

"Young man," Jesus said, "get up" (Luke 7:14). The boy did, and Jesus gave the child to his astonished mother. A Christian traveler in the AD 300s said a church was built there, over the widow's house. Today, the site is a ruins once surrounded by a circular wall.

NAOMI

(nay OH me)
Noomi, Hebrew
"pleasant"
Perhaps 1100s BC
First mention: Ruth 1:2

To escape a famine, Naomi and her husband took their two sons and left Bethlehem in search of greener pastures. They ended up in Moab, in what is now Jordan. There the two sons married Moabite women, and all three men died.

Naomi decided to go home, hoping a family member would take her in. She urged her daughters-in-law to go back to their fathers, but Ruth refused to leave the elderly woman. When the two arrived in Bethlehem, Naomi told people to call her Mara, "bitter," because she said God had made life bitter for her.

But life took a turn for the better when young Ruth met Boaz, a member of Naomi's extended family. Under Jewish law, the deceased husband's closest male relative was supposed to marry the man's widow—ancient Social Security. Naomi realized this and set up the plan that united the two.

Boaz and Ruth had a son, who became King David's grandfather. That made Naomi the great-great-grandmother of Israel's most revered king.

NAPHTALI

(NAF tuh lie)
Naptali, Hebrew
"my struggle"
First mention: Deuteronomy 34:2

MAP 1
C2

Descendants of Jacob's sixth son grew into the extended family, or tribe, named after their forefather, Naphtali. They settled in northern Israel, along the Sea of Galilee's west shore, then up toward the hills and forests near Mount Hermon. Jesus made his ministry headquarters in this region, in the fishing village of Capernaum.

NATHAN

(NAY thun)
Natan, Hebrew
"gift"
Ministered about
1010–970 BC
First mention: 2 Samuel 7:2

Nathan was a prophet who knew how to look a king in the eye and call him an adulterer. And a murderer. He did this to King David, with force and style.

David—already married to at least seven wives—had an affair with a soldier's wife, Bathsheba. He got her pregnant. To cover it up, he killed her husband by sending him to the front lines and ordering the support troops to withdraw. David married Bathsheba.

Sly Nathan told David's own story to him, with a few character changes. A rich man with vast herds stole the only lamb a poor man owned—a pet lamb who drank from the man's own cup. The rich man took it, killed it, and served it at a meal.

David was livid. He said a man like that deserved to die.

"You are that man!" Nathan declared (2 Samuel 12:7).

David immediately confessed. God forgave him, but the tragic consequences were unstoppable. The baby boy died, and in time, David's family became the definition of dysfunctional—with one of his own sons attempting a coup.

The Bible tells of two other encounters between Nathan and David.

Once, David hoped to build a worship center in Jerusalem, and Nathan

The prophet Nathan accuses King David of adultery and murder.

NATHANAEL
(nuh THAN ee uhl)
Nathanael, Greek
First century AD
First mention: John 1:45

One of the twelve disciples of Jesus, Nathanael didn't think much of Jesus at first. "Nazareth!" exclaimed Nathanael, after the disciple Philip told him where Jesus came from. "Can anything good come from there?" (John 1:46). His opinion changed when he met Jesus because Jesus said he saw Nathanael sitting under a fig tree before Philip arrived. Astonished, Nathanael declared that Jesus was God's Son. But Jesus promised that Nathanael would see even greater evidence. Some scholars say Nathanael and Bartholomew were the same person. (See *Bartholomew.*)

NAZARETH
(NAZ er eth)
Nazaret, Greek
"branch" or "shoot"
First mention: Matthew 2:23

MAP 4
B3

"Can anything good come from there?" (John 1:46). That's what the disciple Nathanael said when he heard that Jesus came from Nazareth.

It's not that Nazareth was a bad town. It's that it was hardly a town at all—just a dip of a town, literally. Nazareth was hidden in a large dip eroded into a ridge off the beaten trail. In Jesus' day, it didn't measure more

said to go ahead. But that night God appeared to Nathan in a dream and said otherwise. David's son Solomon would build the temple. In the meantime, God promised to build a house for David—a dynasty of kings.

Nathan's last scene with David took place as the king was dying and David's oldest son was throwing a party to declare himself king. Nathan and Bathsheba reminded David of his promise to transfer leadership to Bathsheba's son, Solomon. David quickly honored that promise. He ordered Nathan and a chief priest to take Solomon out to the city spring and anoint him king.

A shepherd drives his flock through fields below the hilltop village of Nazareth. Angry villagers once tried to throw Jesus from this hilltop.

away, some twenty miles, to the fishing village of Capernaum along the Sea of Galilee. Leaving seemed a good idea given the response when he came home, a miracle worker proclaimed as Messiah: "Jumping up, they mobbed him and took him to the edge of the hill on which the city was built. They intended to push him over the cliff, but he slipped away through the crowd and left them" (Luke 4:29–30).

ARAB TOWN TODAY

Nazareth is no small town today. It's the largest Arab city in Israel, with sixty thousand residents. Most people are Israeli Arabs—Palestinians with Israeli citizenship. Many are Christians, and others are Muslims. There are also thousands of Jews living in a newer, expanded section called Upper Nazareth.

Among the tourist attractions is the well where Jesus probably drew water. Known today as Mary's Well, it was Nazareth's original water source. It's enshrined within a Greek Orthodox Church built over the remains of a Crusader church from the 1100s—Muslim invaders destroyed it in the 1200s. Outside the Greek church, built in 1750, are water fountains that allow visitors to drink from the same spring that fed the ancient well.

Nearby is the Church of the Annunciation, a Catholic church built over what tradition says was Mary's home—where the angel Gabriel is said

than nine hundred by two hundred yards—and most of that was empty fields for farming or grazing. There couldn't have been more than five hundred people there at the most, and more likely about one hundred.

The closest the Old Testament comes to mentioning Nazareth is in a prophecy that must have seemed absolutely unrelated to Jesus' hometown: "Out of the stump of David's family will grow a shoot—yes, a new Branch bearing fruit from the old root" (Isaiah 11:1).

Nazareth seems to come from the Hebrew word that means branch or shoot: *neser*. A play on words, perhaps —the Branch from a branch.

When Jesus left home to start his ministry, he moved about a day's walk

to have appeared to her and announced the coming birth of Jesus. Beneath the church are the remains of what appears to have been a Christian worship center—with a cross designed into the mosaic floor. This church was built in the AD 300s, when Rome first legalized Christianity.

NEBUCHADNEZZAR
(neb uh cud NEZ ur)
Nebukadnessar, Hebrew
Reigned 605–562 BC
First mention: 2 Kings 24:1

After destroying Jerusalem, Babylonian king Nebuchadnezzar slips into insanity. His hair grows long and he eats grass. When his sanity returns, Nebuchadnezzar praises God.

This is the Babylonian king, from what is now Iraq, who beat the life out of Jerusalem.

He wiped Israel off the map, destroying Jewish cities one by one until he came to the capital, Jerusalem, and leveled it—temple and all.

The Jewish nation was gone.

WARRIOR KING
Even before becoming the Babylonian Empire's second and greatest king, the crown prince Nebuchadnezzar had already made a name for himself as a savvy battlefield commander. In fact, he had just defeated the Egyptians in the pivotal battle of Carchemish, along Syria's northern border with Turkey. That's when his father got sick. The prince rushed home in time to claim the throne, then went back to fighting his way throughout the Middle East, expanding his empire.

Nebuchadnezzar paid three notable visits to the southern Jewish nation of Judah—the northern Jewish nation was already gone, wiped out by Assyrians in 722 BC.

- 604 BC. He reduced King Jehoiakim to a servant ruler who was forced to pay taxes to Babylon.
- 597 BC. He put down Judah's rebellion, took the king captive, installed a new king, and took "ten thousand captives from Jerusalem, including all the princes and the best of the soldiers, craftsmen, and smiths. So only the poorest people were left in the land" (2 Kings 24:14). The prophets Daniel and Ezekiel were among the captives.
- 586 BC. He crushed one last Jewish rebellion. His final solution was to put an end to the Jewish nation. Many survivors were exiled to Babylon.

BUILDER KING

Oddly, this warrior king famed for his skill in destroying cities and nations is also well known for his skills as a builder.

Funded by taxes wrenched from conquered kingdoms, he launched a massive building program. It was under his watch that one of the Seven Wonders of the World was built: the Hanging Gardens of Babylon. (See *Babylon,* featuring "The Hanging Gardens," page 45.)

He also built and repaired dozens of temples in religious centers throughout the region, including the great stair step temple (ziggurat) of Babylon, on the outskirts of what is now Baghdad. He paved streets, dug canals, and reinforced defensive walls.

Surprisingly, the Bible and Jewish tradition treat Nebuchadnezzar kindly —as an instrument God used to punish the Jews for idolatry.

Twice, the Bible reports Nebuchadnezzar praising God. The first time was after he witnessed the prophet Daniel's three friends—Shadrach, Meshach, and Abednego—survive inside a furnace. And the second time was after God punished him for sin by turning him temporarily insane. The king actually "ate grass like a cow" (Daniel 4:33). But after he regained his senses, he composed a beautiful poem praising "the King of heaven."

NECO
(NEE koh)
Nekoh, Hebrew
Reigned 609–595 BC
First mention: 2 Kings 23:29

The Egyptian king Neco raced north to reinforce his Assyrian allies from the attacking Babylonians. But King Josiah of Judah—no friend of Egypt or Assyria —set up a blockade at the mountain pass in the Mount Carmel range. Neco's forces overran the Jews and killed Josiah. But by the time Neco arrived at Carchemish on the Syrian-Turkish border, Assyria was defeated. Egypt alone fought Babylon and lost.

On Neco's retreat home, he installed a new king in Judah and forced the nation to pay a heavy fine for interfering. The Babylonians tried to invade Egypt several years later, but Neco fought them to a standstill on the Egyptian frontier.

NEGEV
(nuh GEHV)
Negeb, Hebrew
"dry southland"
First mention: Genesis 12:9

MAP 2
C6

Half of Israel lies well south of Jerusalem in a dry wasteland called the Negev, or Negeb. Some call it a desert—and it is part of the bridge between the Arabian Desert in the east and the Sahara Desert in the west. But it doesn't have many rolling sand dunes—it's more like the forbidding Dakota Badlands or perhaps a shrunken Grand Canyon, with lots of rocks, dirt, and canyons.

On a map, it looks like an arrowhead pointed to the Red Sea. The fat part of the triangle starts at Beersheba, where Abraham spent much of his life, forty miles south of Jerusalem. The tip ends at Elat. This is Israel's southernmost town, a port city on the Gulf of Aqaba in the Red Sea.

In Bible times, the Negev was nowhere near this large. The southern regions were too hot and inhospitable for humans. When the Bible talks about the Negev, it's talking about just the more temperate northern section. There, herders grazed flocks, and cities were born. This is the region where Abraham lived when Isaac was born. It's also where the king of Arad, a city about twenty miles east of Beersheba, gathered his troops in a futile attempt to stop Moses and the Hebrews from entering the area.

After Babylon dismantled the Jewish nation in 586 BC, the people of Edom, a nation east of the Negev in what is now Jordan, migrated across the border and settled in the Negev. Herod the Great came from this relocated nation.

Today, cities throughout the Negev —north to south—continue to grow as Israel absorbs a continuing flow of Jewish immigrants.

NEHEMIAH
(nee uh MY uh)
Nehemeyah, Hebrew
Arrived in Jerusalem 445 BC
First mention: Nehemiah 1:1

Nehemiah, a royal wine taster from what is now Iran, managed to get himself put in charge of rebuilding Jerusalem's walls—the walls Babylonian soldiers knocked down when they demolished the Jewish capital in 586 BC.

Tourists visit a model of Jerusalem, while a worker makes repairs. More than a century after Babylon destroyed Jerusalem, Nehemiah led the job of rebuilding the city walls.

Nearly a century and a half later— long after Jews exiled by the Babylonians started returning to their homeland—Jerusalem's walls were still in a heap. Nehemiah got that news when his brother came for a visit at the Persian palace.

Nehemiah couldn't believe it. He started mourning, fasting, and praying. King Artaxerxes eventually took notice and asked Nehemiah what was bothering him. When Nehemiah explained, the king asked if he could help. By that time, Nehemiah had been thinking about the problem throughout the winter months. He knew exactly how the king could help.

Nehemiah asked for:

- a leave of absence to rebuild the walls
- a letter granting him safe travel to Jerusalem
- a letter to the manager of the king's forests, instructing him to provide timber for the project

The king agreed to everything, and Nehemiah left for Jerusalem.

ANGRY NEIGHBORS

Arab and Samaritan leaders who had settled in the region while the Jews were exiled got angry about the building project. They probably figured that rebuilding Jerusalem's walls was just the first step. In the end, perhaps the Jews would try to take back all their land.

Nehemiah knew about the opposition. And he knew it was essential to finish the wall as quickly as possible. So he pushed the workers from sunrise to sunset. He posted armed guards around the wall and told workers to carry their weapons.

As the walls rose quickly, opposition leaders hatched a plan. They would offer to meet Nehemiah, then kill him. They gave five invitations, but Nehemiah wisely refused each one and kept working.

In an astonishing fifty-two days, the walls were reassembled.

The sheer speed of the project terrified the non-Jewish opposition to it, because, as Nehemiah put it in his memoirs: "They realized that this work had been done with the help of our God" (Nehemiah 6:16).

NICODEMUS
(nick oh DEE muhs)
Nikodemos, Greek
"conqueror of the people"
First century AD
First mention: John 3:1

Under the cover of darkness, a Jewish leader named Nicodemus came secretly to Jesus with a question.

It's strange that Nicodemus came in secret, because Jesus' answer became the best-known Bible verse of all—one that

Apparently afraid of being seen with Jesus, Jewish leader Nicodemus meets with him at night. Oddly enough, that secret talk produced the most famous quote in the Bible, preserved in John 3:16.

often shows up on posters at ballgames.

Nicodemus wanted to know exactly what message Jesus had from God.

Jesus answered with what Protestant reformer Martin Luther called the gospel in a sentence: "For God so loved the world that he gave his only Son, so that everyone who believes in him will not perish but have eternal life" (John 3:16).

Nicodemus apparently didn't believe enough to publicly support Jesus. But he did defend Jesus once. When Jewish scholars criticized Jesus, Nicodemus asked, "Is it legal to convict a man before he is given a hearing?" (John 7:51).

It was the Crucifixion, however, that brought out the boldness in Nicodemus. He helped another top Jewish leader, Joseph of Arimathea, bury Jesus.

It seems ironic—Nicodemus risked his reputation and career by burying someone who had promised believers eternal life. Even so, Nicodemus decided to stand with those believers. He must have been happy with his choice, come Sunday morning.

NILE RIVER

(NI uhl)
Yeor, Hebrew
First mention: Genesis 41:1

MAP 3
B4

RAMESES FACELIFT

Construction of the Aswan Dam in Egypt created an archaeological crisis. It would bury four gigantic statues of Rameses II. A team of international engineers worked four years cutting the statues into more than a thousand pieces, then reassembling them high above what became Lake Nasser.

the way back again. It starts in the tiny nation of Burundi in central Africa and flows 4,145 miles north, cutting a fertile river basin through ten nations before emptying into the Mediterranean Sea along the north shores of Egypt.

Egypt is the reason the Bible talks about the Nile. But the Nile is the reason Egypt existed.

The only land Egyptians could live on was the ten-mile-wide strip of fertile "black land" along the riverbanks and the fan-shaped delta in the north, where the river splits into streams before flowing into the sea. The east side of this delta region was the land of Goshen, where Jacob and his extended family migrated during a drought, then grazed their flocks before Pharaoh enslaved their descendants and Moses had to free them.

Annual floods used to spread a fresh layer of fertile soil in Egypt's river valley. But with construction of the Aswan Dam in southern Egypt

Longest river in the world—nearly twice as long as the Mississippi—the Nile River could stretch from New York City to Los Angeles and most of

during the 1970s, the water flow is now controlled and much of the fertile sediment stays above the dam in Lake Nasser.

NIMROD

(NIM rod)
Nimrod, Hebrew
Before 2500 BC
First mention: Genesis 10:8

Painting of Assyria's Nineveh, based on ruins of the city.

Noah's great-grandson, Nimrod, became a hunter and a warrior who founded several ancient cities, including two in Iraq that later became world famous:

- Babel, the Hebrew name for Babylon, capital of the Babylonian Empire (near modern Baghdad)
- Nineveh, capital of the Assyrian Empire (near Mosul)

Nimrod was the son of Cush and the grandson of Noah's second son, Ham.

NINEVEH

(NIN uh vuh)
Nineweh, Hebrew
First mention: Genesis 10:11

MAP 3
D2

If any prophet deserved hazard pay, it was Jonah. God told him to take at least a four-hundred-mile, monthlong walk to a city near modern-day Mosul, Iraq, along the Turkish border.

He wasn't headed to just any city. It was Nineveh, capital of Israel's fiercest enemy at the time—the Assyrian Empire. Jonah was supposed to tell the citizens that their city—which had a palace decorated in battle scenes with impaled enemies—was about to fall. He took a boat headed the other way. But God, using a large fish, convinced him to reconsider.

The Bible says a warrior descendant of Noah—Nimrod—built Nineveh, which rested along the banks of the Tigris River. King Sennacherib selected it for his capital around 700 BC and began a massive building program. Afterward, a walk around the city walls took nearly half a day—eight miles. That's more than enough room for the number of people God said were saved when they repented after Jonah's prophecy: "more than 120,000" (Jonah 4:11).

Coalition forces of Babylonians from what is southern Iraq and Medes from Iran defeated the Assyrian Empire in 612 BC, demolishing the capital. Excavations of Nineveh, which was buried beneath heaping mounds of dirt, have turned up the five-acre palace with stone artwork showing battle scenes in Israel. Archaeologists also found an ancient library of twenty thousand tablets—which provide incredible insights into Assyria's ancient culture.

NOAH
(NO uh)
Noah, Hebrew
Perhaps "to rest"
Before 2500 BC
First mention: Genesis 5:28

If Noah lived in the Persian Gulf area where human civilization is thought to have started—in what is now Iraq—the ark he built would have made a great dam for the largest river in the region, the Euphrates, but not a particularly good boat for cruising.

The winding river is fit for only small boats, since it averages about 450 to 500 feet wide and can drop to as shallow as two feet deep during the dry season. Though the ark was 75 feet wide—small enough to fit in the river—it was 450 feet long. So one wrong twist around a river bend, and the ark would have spun sideways, parking each tip on opposite riverbanks.

A boat of that size, even among the river community, would have raised a few questions about the sanity of the shipbuilder, Noah.

He was somewhere between the ages of five hundred and six hundred when he built the ark. The Bible says

he was five hundred when he started having sons—Shem, Ham, and Japheth—and he was six hundred when the Flood came.

Noah releases a dove from the ark, hoping it will find dry land.

ADAM'S GREAT- (TIMES SEVEN) GRANDSON

Descended from Adam's third son—Seth—Noah was born to humanity's tenth generation. That made him the great (times seven) grandson of Adam. Noah was grandson of Methuselah, whose death at age 969 makes him the longest-living human in Bible history. Human ages reported from before the Flood are much higher than afterward.

Noah's family tree appears in Genesis chapter 5. But Bible scholars

How Big Was the Ark?

Noah's ark was a little longer than a football field (end zones included) and half as wide. Surprisingly, the space inside the ark equaled the storage space of about 370 railroad boxcars.

Ark dimensions: 150 yards long, 25 yards wide, and 15 yards high.

A typical cruise ship today would dwarf it, since the ark was only about half the size.

Parked on a football field, the ark would stretch the full one hundred yards, extend through both ten-yard-long end zones, and push another fifteen yards into the stands on each end of the field. Since the ark needed only about half the width of the playing field, you could park two side-by-side. The ark's roof reached more than twice the height of the goalposts (twenty feet, with the crossbar at ten feet).

Space inside the ark: about 1.5 million cubic feet.

Actually, the ark would have had less storage space because of walls, floors, and support beams.

Was there enough room to store pairs of all the world's land animals along with food for a year—since the creatures stayed onboard that long? Perhaps, if the Flood covered just the civilized world at the time—which was the Persian Gulf region.

Beyond that, it would have been a tight pack. There are roughly twenty-five thousand species of land animals, not to mention a million or more species of bugs (we keep discovering new ones).

say the tree may represent only the bigger branches, skipping many generations. That means Bible students who use the Bible's family trees to calculate humanity's birthday at about 4000 BC could be way off.

As humans began to populate, God made two decisions:

- "My Spirit will not put up with humans for such a long time, for they are only mortal flesh. In the future, they will live no more than 120 years" (Genesis 6:3).

- "I have decided to destroy all living creatures, for the earth is filled with violence because of them" (Genesis 6:13).

God made an exception for Noah, "a righteous man, the only blameless man living on earth at the time" (Genesis 6:9).

God warned Noah about the coming flood and gave him instructions for building a massive boat that looked like a huge barge topped with a warehouse. A week before the deluge, God told Noah to get in the boat, taking his wife, three sons, and their wives, along with pairs of animals and the food they would all need.

FLOODED

"Underground waters burst forth on the earth, and the rain fell in mighty torrents from the sky" (Genesis 7:11). Forty days later, the rain stopped. But by then, the Bible says, water covered the mountain peaks and had wiped out all humanity and animal life outside the boat.

Slowly the water receded. Five months later, the boat came to a rest on the mountains of Ararat in what is now Turkey. In all, Noah and his cargo remained on the ark a little over a year.

God made a promise to Noah and to all of humanity: "Never again will there be a flood that will destroy all life. When I see the rainbow in the clouds, I will remember the eternal covenant between God and every living creature on earth" (Genesis 9:15–16).

FARMER NOAH

Noah became a farmer, planted a vineyard, and became the first human on record to get drunk, though there must have been others before him.

Ham found his father lying naked in a drunken stupor. Instead of covering him, Ham called his brothers to have a look. They refused, grabbing a robe and backing up to cover their father.

When Noah woke up and found

ANCIENT FLOOD STORIES

Even if there wasn't a worldwide flood, there are worldwide stories of one—stories about a flood that killed everyone but a fortunate few.

About seventy cultures have them, from American Indians, to the Irish, to the Chinese. The Greeks and Romans heard stories about a couple who saved their children and some animals by sailing in a boat shaped like a box—very much the way the Bible describes Noah's ark.

One story was written in about 2700 BC—more than a thousand years before Moses could have written Genesis, as tradition says he did. The story tells of a Babylonian man, Utnapishtim, preparing for a flood in what is now Iraq. He built a cube-shaped boat after a god warned him of a coming weeklong flood. This Babylonian Noah, as he's sometimes called, loaded the boat with family and animals. The story has many similarities with Noah's, including the following excerpts, accompanied by the related Bible references: "When the seventh day arrived, I sent out a dove. The dove went out, but it came back. There was no resting place" (Epic of Gilgamesh). "Then he sent out a dove to see if it could find dry ground. But the dove found no place to land because the water was still too high. So it returned to the boat" (Genesis 8:8–9).

WAS THERE A WORLDWIDE FLOOD?

No, say most geologists. Seashells on mountaintops prove only what geologists already know: Mountains are gradually pushed up from land that was once flat.

There is, however, evidence of ancient floods that decimated the world where civilization began in the Middle East.

In 1929, an archaeologist named C. Leonard Woolley claimed to have found evidence of the Flood. This evidence was an eight-foot layer of silt in the major world city of the time—Ur, hometown of Abraham built along the Euphrates River in what is now southern Iraq. That flood dated to about 4000 to 5500 BC. But there wasn't similar silt in neighboring cities.

In the 1990s, geologists Walter Pitman and William Ryan suggested they may have found evidence of an ancient flood that produced a bevy of ancient flood stories. This flood was in the Black Sea, the coastline of which is about two hundred miles north of the Ararat mountains, where the Bible says Noah's ark came to a rest.

About 5500 BC, as the theory goes, the Black Sea was a smaller freshwater lake with people living along the shoreline. Melting ice from the Ice Age poured into the Mediterranean Sea, which eventually rose so high that it rushed through the narrow Bosporus Strait with the force of two hundred Niagara Falls. Underwater explorations in the Black Sea confirm a flood. Researchers found freshwater mollusks, along with an ancient shoreline and evidence of human occupation. The flood, it seems, caused the lake to rise 450 feet—pushing back the shoreline twenty miles.

out what had happened, he put a curse on Ham's son, Canaan. Why Canaan instead of Ham is unclear. "A curse on the Canaanites! May they be the lowest of servants to the descendants of Shem and Japheth" (Genesis 9:25). Many scholars see this curse fulfilled when the Israelites, descended from Shem, invaded Canaan at the time of Joshua.

Noah lived another 350 years after the Flood, making him 950 years old when he died—humanity's number three man for longevity, after his grandfather, Methuselah, and his great-great-grandfather, Jared (962).

NOB

Nob, Hebrew
First mention: 1 Samuel 21:1

MAP 2
C5

King Saul's insane jealousy toward the popular young David, his son-in-law, turned David into a fugitive. Running south from Gibeah, Saul's capital near Jerusalem, David and some men with him stopped at Nob, which was probably a neighboring village. Israel's worship center had apparently moved there after the Philistines destroyed the one at Shiloh.

Without telling the priest that he was on the run, David got some bread and took the sword of Goliath that had been kept there. Saul's chief shepherd, Doeg, saw this and reported it to the king. Furious, Saul called the priest and all his associates, wrongly accused them of treason, and ordered his bodyguards to kill them. The guards refused, so Doeg killed them—eighty-five priests in all. Then the shepherd went to Nob and killed their families. Only one son—Abiathar—survived. He joined David and later became Israel's high priest.

OBADIAH

(oh buh DIE uh)
Obadyahu, Hebrew
"the Lord's servant"
Sometime after 586 BC
First mention: Obadiah 1:1

The prophet Obadiah wrote the Old Testament book of Obadiah—without saying a thing about Obadiah.

In the Bible's shortest book—only twenty-one verses—the writer reveals only one historical fact about himself. He wrote the prophecy sometime after Babylon overran the southern Jewish nation of Judah, destroyed the cities, and exiled the survivors. This is obvious because of what Obadiah said about Judah's neighbor, Edom, people living in what is now Jordan and descended from Abraham, Isaac, and Esau. That made the Edomites relatives of the Jews. But when Jewish fugitives fled to Edom during the Babylonian invasion, the people of Edom arrested them, turned them over to Babylon, then looted Jerusalem for anything left behind.

"I will cut you down to size," Obadiah said, quoting God. "Every nook and cranny of Edom will be searched and looted" (Obadiah 1:2, 6).

OG
(AHG)
Og, Hebrew
1400s BC
First mention: Numbers 21:33

King Og is the perfect example of why the first generation of Hebrews on the Exodus refused to go into the Promised Land. Og was a giant. He ruled a kingdom of sixty cities fortified with high walls. "His iron bed was more than thirteen feet long and six feet wide" (Deuteronomy 3:11). The Hebrews kept it on display as a war trophy after killing him and conquering his kingdom of Bashan, in what is now southern Syria.

OMRI
(OHM ree)
Omri, Hebrew
886–875 BC
First mention: 1 Kings 16:16

Omri is best known as King Ahab's father and the man who sealed a peace treaty with what is now Lebanon by arranging the marriage of his son to the Phoenician princess Jezebel. But Omri was also the politically savvy founder of a forty-year dynasty that whipped Israel into a strong nation—as attested to on an ancient engraving called the Moabite Stone that belonged to neighboring King Mesha.

Assassination and the chariot corps launched Omri's dynasty and ended it. A chariot corps commander assassinated King Elah. Soldiers led by Omri declared their own leader the new king, and they defended him against opposing factions in the civil war that followed. Omri's dynasty ended when an arrow fired from an Israelite chariot struck the heart of his grandson, Joram, in another assassination.

Omri, written in stone. King Mesha of Moab reports that after a long oppression by Israel's King Omri, Moab broke free.

ONESIMUS
(oh NESS uh muhs)
Onesimos, Greek
First century AD
First mention: Colossians 4:9

Onesimus was a runaway slave owned by a church leader in Colosse, a city in western Turkey.

Remarkably, Onesimus converted to the faith of his slave owner after meeting the apostle Paul. The apostle convinced Onesimus to go home—and probably would have gone with him if he could. But Paul was a prisoner, perhaps when he was under house arrest in

Rome. Paul did send an associate named Tychicus with Onesimus. The two delivered Paul's letters to churches in Ephesus and Colosse. Onesimus had one more letter from Paul—addressed to his slave owner Philemon. That letter is now part of the New Testament.

Though Paul didn't order Philemon to free Onesimus, he certainly hinted at this possibility.

"I think of him as my own son because he became a believer as a result of my ministry here in prison," Paul said. "I really wanted to keep him here with me. . .he would have helped me on your behalf. But I didn't want to do anything without your consent" (Philemon 10, 13–14).

About fifty years later, a church leader named Ignatius wrote a letter to the church leader at Ephesus—Bishop Onesimus. Onesimus the former slave? Possibly.

OPHIR

(OH fear)
Opir, Hebrew
First mention: 1 Kings 9:28

MAP 3
D5

In a joint trading venture, King Solomon built a fleet of ships and King Hiram, from what is now Lebanon, provided experienced crews. The fleet sailed south from the Gulf of Aqaba in the Red Sea to a mysterious destination—Ophir.

There they picked up sixteen tons of gold and later brought back other valuable cargo, including silver, jewels, and rare wood. Scholars don't know

where Ophir was. Some trade items sound like they came from East Africa, perhaps at the south end of the Red Sea near the likely Arabian homeland of the queen of Sheba. But speculation includes South Africa and even India.

OPHRAH

(AHF ruh)
Oprah, Hebrew
First mention: Judges 6:11

MAP 1
C4

Israel's reluctant warrior, Gideon, lived in the village of Ophrah. That was somewhere in what is now central Israel, where Gideon's extended family of Manasseh settled. It's unclear exactly where Ophrah was. But wherever it was within the tribal area, that's where an angel delivered God's message: Gideon would put a stop to the Midianite raiders who kept arriving at harvest time.

ORPAH

(OR puh)
Orpa, Hebrew
Perhaps 1100s BC
First mention: Ruth 1:4

If Orpah had agreed to go to Bethlehem with her mother-in-law, Naomi, instead of letting Ruth go, Orpah might have become the mother of Israel's greatest line of kings: David, Solomon, and Jesus. Instead, that honor went to Ruth.

Naomi and her husband moved to Moab, in what is now Jordan, to escape a famine in Israel. Their two sons married Moabite women, Ruth and Orpah.

But by about a decade later, all three men were dead. So Naomi decided to go home to her relatives in Bethlehem. She urged Ruth and Orpah to return to their fathers and try to get married again. Orpah reluctantly agreed and was never heard from again. Ruth went with Naomi, married one of Naomi's relatives—Boaz—and became the mother of Obed, King David's grandfather.

OTHNIEL
(AHTH nee el)
Otniel, Hebrew
About 1300s BC
First mention: Judges 3:9

For perhaps two hundred years or so—between the time of Joshua and of Israel's first king, Saul—the nation didn't have a central leader. When raiders attacked, God raised up military leaders or judges to defend the nation. Othniel was the first of twelve. He was the son of Caleb's brother—Caleb the scout who helped Joshua and ten others explore Canaan. A Syrian king oppressed the Israelites for eight years, so Othniel raised an army and won the war. Israel enjoyed peace for a generation.

PADDAN-ARAM
(PAD dan AY ram)
Paddan-aram, Hebrew
First mention: Genesis 25:20

See Haran

MAP 3
D2

Abraham's hometown—after leaving Ur in southern Iraq, but before moving to what is now Israel—was an area in Turkey near the Syrian border.

The Bible calls the village Haran, but also associates it with a place called Padan-aram. Some scholars say *Paddan-aram* means "field of Aram [Syria]" and was probably the region that included Haran. Others say *Paddan* and *Haran* both mean "road" and that both names refer to the village.

Village or region, Abraham once lived there. His son, Isaac, married a woman from there—Rebekah. And Isaac's son, Jacob, married two women from there—Leah and Rachel.

PALESTINE
(PAL less tine)
Palaistine, Greek, from
Pelishtim, "Philistines"
First mention: Exodus 15:14, as Philistia

MAP 4

The once-powerful Philistine nation that seemed destined to assimilate Israel into its culture is gone—its power broken by Israel's greatest warrior king, David. But their name lingers on. It evolved into our modern word Palestine.

The Bible uses that name just a few times—as *Palestinia*. But each time, the name refers to only the coastal land once controlled by the Philistines, land from what is now the Palestinian Authority's Gaza Strip northward to near Tel Aviv. Only later, when the Greeks arrived, did *Palestine* come to mean the entire region. (See *Canaan; Israel*.)

PAMPHYLIA

(pam FILL ee uh)
Pamphylia, Greek
First mention: Acts 2:10

On the first missionary trip, when Paul, Barnabas, and Barnabas' cousin John Mark reached port in the steamy, marshy, and malaria prone territory of Pamphylia on Turkey's southern coast, John Mark bailed. He abandoned the two and sailed home.

When it came time for the second missionary trip and John Mark wanted to go along, Paul objected. Barnabas decided to go one direction with John Mark—not to Pamphylia. And Paul chose Silas to go with him in another direction—also bypassing Pamphylia.

PAPHOS

MAP 5 D3

(PAY fuss)
Paphos, Greek
First mention: Acts 13:6

Rome's first known politician to become a Christian was the governor of the island of Cyprus, living in the capital, Paphos. His name was Sergius Paulus. When Paul and Barnabas arrived, he asked them to teach him about God. A sorcerer in town tried to change the governor's mind, but Paul struck the sorcerer blind. That show of power apparently helped convince Sergius Paulus to believe Paul's message.

PARAN

(PAY ran)
Paran, Hebrew
First mention: Genesis 21:20

As Moses led the Hebrews out of Egypt, they camped for about a year in the Sinai Peninsula, then moved on to the wilderness of Paran—part of the harsh and barren badlands between the Sinai Peninsula and the southern border of Canaan, in what is now Israel's large Negev desert.

It was from the oasis at Kadesh-barnea in Paran that Moses sent a dozen tribal leaders to scout out the Promised Land. And it was there the Hebrews spent most of their forty years in the wilderness after the scouting report of giants and walled cities caused them to lose faith in God.

PATMOS

(PAT mohs)
Patmos, Greek
First mention: Revelation 1:9

"I was exiled to the island of Patmos for preaching the word of God and speaking about Jesus" (Revelation 1:9). Patmos is a tiny island about ten miles long and six miles at its widest, some

Patmos island, seen from the hilltop Monastery of St. John. The monastery was built where tradition says John wrote the end-time book of Revelation.

forty miles off Turkey's west coast. There a writer named John—some early church leaders identified him as the apostle John—had a vision of the end times. He recorded it all in what became the last book of the Bible—Revelation.

If the writer was the apostle John, he may not have had far to go for the exile. Christian tradition said he had moved to Ephesus, a port city about sixty miles north of Patmos.

PAUL

Paulos, Greek
Saul, Hebrew
"the one asked for"
About AD 5–64
First mention: Acts 7:58

"His speeches are really bad!" (2 Corinthians 10:10). That's what critics had to say about Paul, who more than any person other than Jesus is responsible for starting Christianity.

At least one person in Paul's audience might have agreed—Eutychus, the young man who made the mistake of sitting on a high windowsill during one of Paul's all-night sermons. As lamplights flickered to the midnight hour, poor Eutychus "became very drowsy. Finally, he sank into a deep sleep and fell three stories to his death below" (Acts 20:9).

Paul raised him from the dead, then preached till dawn.

He was like that. Not easily sidetracked.

That's the kind of man God chose to carry the Good News about Jesus an estimated ten thousand miles from one end of the Roman Empire to the other. A man who lumbered on for some thirty years, refusing to give up even after three shipwrecks, five beatings of thirty-nine lashes each, three beatings with a Roman rod, a public stoning that nearly killed him, and no less than five imprisonments—probably more.

God didn't need an eloquent talker.

He needed a relentless doer—someone who could stand up to intolerant Jewish traditionalists.

He chose an intolerant Jewish traditionalist.

FIERY PHARISEE

Paul was born on the green plains of Tarsus, a Rome-blessed city near Turkey's southern coast. Citizens of this town that once welcomed Julius Caesar and hosted Mark Antony and Cleopatra were declared free Romans several decades before Paul was born. So Paul was not only a Jew; he was a Roman citizen, as well.

At some point Paul moved to Jerusalem, perhaps with others in his family, since his married sister and her son lived there. In this Holy City Paul followed the career path of a Jewish scholar. He was educated by a leading teacher named Gamaliel, who tradition says was the grandson of the century's top Jewish scholar, Hillel. Paul, like his mentor, was a Pharisee—a Jewish group so obsessed with obeying the laws of Moses that they created extra laws to build a protective fence around the main ones. For example, to make sure they didn't break the Sabbath by working, they defined what they considered work. Plucking grain fresh from the field for a snack was harvest, as far as they were concerned. Jesus disagreed, insisting that God made the Sabbath to help people, not hurt them.

"I was one of the most religious Jews of my own age," Paul wrote, "and I tried as hard as possible to follow all the old traditions of my religion" (Galatians 1:14).

Not only did he follow them; like many people convinced that their way is the only way, Paul forced his beliefs on others. He did that in his first appearance in the Bible, serving as an official witness for Jews who stoned to death the first Christian martyr, Stephen.

"I became very zealous to honor God in everything I did, just as all of you are today," he once told a crowd of

The apostle Paul.

Jerusalem Jews. "I persecuted the followers of the Way, hounding some to death, binding and delivering both men and women to prison. The high priest and the whole council of leaders can testify that this is so. For I received letters from them to our Jewish brothers in Damascus, authorizing me to bring the Christians from there to Jerusalem, in chains, to be punished" (Acts 22:3–5).

SEEING THE LIGHT

It was a weeklong trip of about 150 miles to Damascus, which is now

WHAT DID PAUL LOOK LIKE?

He was not a pretty sight. That's if the only known description of him is true.

Paul was a bald-headed, bow-legged, short man with a hooked and honking big nose that stuck out below one long eyebrow that lay on his forehead like a dead caterpillar. That's according to a description paraphrased from a book called *Acts of Paul and Thecla,* written by a church leader in the late AD 100s. A more literal translation would be: "A man of small stature, with a bald head and crooked legs, in a good state of body, with eyebrows meeting and a nose somewhat large and hooked."

The writer got fired. It probably wasn't because of Paul's unflattering portrait. More likely, the writer lost his job because the story is about an eighteen-year-old woman, Thecla, who broke off her engagement after hearing Paul preach about celibacy. Early church leaders argued that Paul was a friend of marriage.

capital of Syria. Paul probably followed the trail out of Jerusalem, across the Jordan River at Jericho, and continuing east to near what is now Jordan's capital of Amman. There Paul would have linked up with the King's Highway, a main caravan route that took him north into Damascus.

A little ways outside the city, Paul was hit by a light so intense that it pushed the noontime desert sun into the shadows. He fell to the ground and heard a voice.

"Saul, Saul, why are you persecuting me?"

"Who are you, sir?" Paul answered.

"I am Jesus of Nazareth, the one you are persecuting."

"What shall I do, Lord?"

"Get up and go into Damascus, and there you will be told all that you are to do" (Acts 22:7–10).

That encounter with Jesus, whom Paul had apparently never met during his studies in Jerusalem, made such an impression that Paul later insisted it qualified him as an apostle—the highest office in the church and one reserved for disciples who had personally known Jesus.

Blinded by the light, Paul had to be led into Damascus by traveling companions. There, God sent a man named Ananias to restore Paul's sight.

Convinced, converted, and eager to tell his story, "Immediately he began preaching about Jesus in the synagogues, saying, 'He is indeed the Son of God!' " (Acts 9:20).

Damascus Jews reacted the way Paul would have done a week earlier. They decided to kill him. They put men at the city gate to ambush him. Paul got word of it, so he had colleagues smuggle him out of town by lowering him over the walls in a basket.

That was in roughly AD 35, when Paul was probably about thirty years old. What he did during the next dozen years or so, for the most part, remains a mystery. For the first three years, he retreated to Arabia. There, he probably studied the Jewish scriptures that Christians now call the Old Testament. He would have looked for prophecies about Jesus.

Many scholars speculate that while Paul was in Arabia, he preached to non-Jews in a ministry started by Damascus believers. Scholars base this guess on the fact that, afterward, Paul reported back to Damascus.

Paul then spent a couple of weeks in Jerusalem, perhaps staying with his sister. He met the apostle Peter along with James, the brother of Jesus, who emerged as leader of the Jerusalem Christians. From there, Paul returned to his hometown region, where he probably earned a living by following the tentmaking trade he learned as a youngster. It seems a good guess that he also continued to speak his mind.

About half a dozen years later, Paul was invited to serve as Barnabas' associate minister of a non-Jewish group in Antioch, Syria, about 150 miles southeast of his hometown. This is where believers of the Way, as they had been called, got the nickname "Christians." Originally this may have been an insult, much like the nickname for followers of Sun Myung Moon's Unification Church —Moonies. If so, believers soon grew to like the name.

ON THE ROAD

One day while Paul and Barnabas were worshiping God and eating with several church leaders, the Holy Spirit spoke up: "Dedicate Barnabas and

WHAT WAS PAUL'S THORN IN THE SIDE?

He never said, but he offered one tantalizing clue: "To keep me from getting puffed up, I was given a thorn in my flesh" (2 Corinthians 12:7).

Whatever it was, it humbled him.

Many scholars guess it was a physical problem, such as recurring malaria, since he traveled through some swampy lands. Or perhaps it was epilepsy.

Others think his thorn was the troublesome Corinthian church he started. The word thorn doesn't show up anywhere else in the New Testament, but it's in the Jewish Bible that Paul used—the Old Testament. There, it describes what the Canaanites would become to the Jews—"thorns in your sides" (Numbers 33:55).

HOW MUCH OF THE NEW TESTAMENT DID PAUL WRITE?

If early Christians had salvaged one more letter Paul wrote—some letters were lost—his signature would appear on half the New Testament. Thirteen of the New Testament's twenty-seven books claim him as writer.

But many Bible scholars aren't convinced.

For one thing, scholars argue, it was common for students and later disciples of a teacher to write in their mentor's name. Sometimes this was to honor the teacher, and other times it was to apply the dead teacher's ideas to new problems.

For another thing, scholars add, some of the letters supposedly written by Paul don't sound like him. Word choice, writing style, and sometimes even the theological teachings seem out of sync with other letters Paul wrote. On the other hand, people mature as the years pass, and writing styles can change.

Churches used to pass around collections of Paul's letters. The earliest known collections, from the AD 100s, usually included just ten or eleven books, excluding 1 and 2 Timothy along with Titus.

Many scholars trim the list of Paul's authentic letters a bit more to seven: Romans, 1 and 2 Corinthians, Galatians, Philippians, 1 Thessalonians, and Philemon.

Considered questionable, in the minds of these researchers, are Ephesians, 2 Thessalonians, 1 and 2 Timothy, Titus, and the anonymous book of Hebrews often attributed to Paul.

Saul for the special work I have for them" (Acts 13:2).

That was in about AD 43. For the next twenty years or more, Paul would spend his time preaching and starting churches. His work began in Syria on the Roman Empire's eastern edge and worked its way west, perhaps even to Spain on the far western edge. Scholars estimate he may have spent half his time in jail because of controversies he stirred up. Jewish traditionalists didn't like anyone messing with their traditions. And they drove their point home with stones, whips, riots, and lawsuits.

Paul, however, made good use of his downtime in jail. He wrote several letters of instruction and encouragement to congregations and individuals: Ephesians, Philippians, Colossians, 2 Timothy, Philemon.

Paul took at least three missionary trips, possibly four. On his first trip, he and Barnabas visited their home-lands—the island of Cyprus, where Barnabas came from, then southern Turkey. It was on this trip that the Bible stopped referring to Paul by his Hebrew name, Saul, and started using only his Greek name. This may have been to emphasize Paul's new focus on Gentiles instead of Jews.

In a heated moment, Paul made this bold announcement to a crowd of Jews who rejected his message: "It was necessary that this Good News from God be given first to you Jews. But since you have rejected it and judged yourselves unworthy of eternal life—well, we will offer it to Gentiles. For this is as the Lord commanded us when he said, 'I have made you a light to the Gentiles, to bring salvation to the farthest corners of the earth' " (Acts 13:46–47).

On his second and third trips, Paul traveled with other associates and expanded his circuit to western Turkey and into Europe, as far west as Greece. There, he started new churches, then backtracked to revisit many of them.

the temple. Roman soldiers stationed nearby saved him but took him under arrest to Rome's Judean headquarters in the oceanside city of Caesarea. Paul remained a prisoner for two years before finally appealing his stalled case to Caesar's high court.

Half a year and one shipwreck later, he arrived in Rome. Surprisingly, the book of Acts—the Bible's early church history—ends there.

Paul is decapitated after his trial in Rome. So wrote early Christian leaders, though the Bible is silent about how Paul died.

IN SEARCH OF PAUL'S DEATH

On his third trip, Paul collected an offering for believers suffering in Jerusalem. Then after delivering it, he got arrested. Jews upset with his "heretical" teachings mobbed him at

Perhaps the writer felt that readers knew the ending all too well. Some scholars speculate that in about AD 62, Paul was convicted and beheaded—the quick method of executing Roman citizens. Other scholars, supported by snippets of writing from early Christian leaders, suggest Paul was released, ministered in Spain, and only later was executed in Rome, perhaps during the emperor Nero's persecution of Christians in AD 64.

"I will come to see you on my way to Spain," Paul wrote the Roman Christians (Romans 15:28). The Roman bishop Clement, writing about thirty years after Paul, confirmed that Paul "went to the limit of the West," which was Spain.

Whether or not Paul reached Spain in person, his words certainly got there.

PENIEL

(puh NI ul)
Penuel, Hebrew
"face of God"
First mention: Genesis 32:30

After twenty years away from home, Jacob headed back to Canaan in what is now Israel. He was terrified. He knew his brother, Esau, had promised to kill him for stealing their father's deathbed blessing.

Jacob sent his family and servants across a shallow part of the Jabbok River that flows west into the Jordan River. But he stayed behind, perhaps to think. A mysterious stranger arrived. Jacob apparently thought the stranger was an angel or God, so he insisted on a blessing. He grabbed the stranger, and they wrestled until dawn, when Jacob finally got his blessing. Jacob named the spot Peniel, meaning "face of God" because as he put it: "I have seen God face to face, yet my life has been spared" (Genesis 32:30).

PERGA

(PUR guh)
Perge, Greek
First mention: Acts 13:13

After preaching on the island of Cyprus, Paul and Barnabas continued their first missionary journey by sailing for the southern coast of Turkey with Barnabas' cousin, John Mark. They landed at the port town of Perga, in the Roman province of Pamphylia. That's where John Mark promptly decided to go home.

The Bible doesn't say why John left, but it might have been because of the steamy heat and malaria there. Paul was angry with John Mark for abandoning them, but Paul and Barnabas left quickly, too, heading for towns in the Turkish highlands.

PERGAMUM

(PUR guh mum)
Pergamos, Greek
First mention: Revelation 1:11

Jesus had a message for each of the seven churches in western Turkey—a message that John delivered in a letter that became the last book in the Bible, Revelation. One of those cities was Pergamum, located near the northern coast and famed for its massive library of two hundred thousand works and for its medical center. A group of heretics known as Nicolaitans had

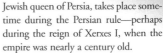

infiltrated the church and apparently convinced many to mix Christianity with pagan religions by worshiping idols and taking part in religious orgies. Jesus ordered them to stop.

PERSIA
(PURR zhuh)
Persis, Greek
First mention: 2 Chronicles 36:20

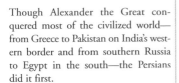

MAP 3
F4

Though Alexander the Great conquered most of the civilized world—from Greece to Pakistan on India's western border and from southern Russia to Egypt in the south—the Persians did it first.

They started as a small kingdom along the Persian Gulf's east shore, in southern Iran. The Babylonian Empire controlled lands to the west, including Israel and Egypt. And the Medes, a kingdom in northern Iran, dominated the eastern region, including Persia.

All of that began to change when Cyrus the Great came to the Persian throne in 559 BC. Nine years later, he conquered the Medes. Eleven years after that, in 539 BC, he conquered Babylon. Then he freed Babylon's captives, including the Jews—many of whom returned to Israel to rebuild Jerusalem and their nation.

The fascinating story of Esther, the Jewish queen of Persia, takes place sometime during the Persian rule—perhaps during the reign of Xerxes I, when the empire was nearly a century old.

Persia survived only another century, until Alexander's Greek army defeated them in a series of battles between 334 and 331 BC. Then he marched from east to west and north to south, claiming the Persian Empire as his own.

PETER
Petros, Greek
"rock"
Died in about AD 64
First mention: Matthew 4:18

One of Jesus' three best friends, Peter was the fisherman who stepped out of a boat to walk on the water with Jesus. And he was the disciple who hacked off an official's ear during the arrest of Jesus in the Garden of Gethsemane. He was also the first of the twelve

In the early 1900s, fishermen mend their nets at dawn beside the Sea of Galilee.

PETER'S TWO LETTERS

Perhaps shortly before he died, Peter wrote a letter—1 Peter—to believers he had visited in what is now western Turkey. He warned believers to expect suffering.

Peter wrote from "Babylon," a code name for Rome because both empires were rich, powerful, evil, and had conquered Jerusalem. Rome is where Peter died, according to Christian tradition—a victim of Nero's persecution of Christians.

Some scholars doubt Peter wrote 1 Peter because the language is polished Greek—not what you would expect from a fisherman. But Peter said, "I have written this short letter to you with the help of Silas" (1 Peter 5:12).

Some scholars also doubt that Peter wrote 2 Peter. This letter, directed to all believers, is about rejecting false teachers and patiently waiting for Christ's return. The problem is that the writer refers to Paul's letters as scripture. This suggests that 2 Peter was written long after Peter by someone wanting to honor his memory. Yet by the time Peter wrote this letter, some of Paul's letters had been circulating among the churches for over a decade.

disciples to declare that Jesus was divine.

Yet Peter is most famous not for his devotion to Jesus, but for the opposite.

While Jesus was being tried for blasphemy, Peter waited outside and denied even knowing him. Apparently Peter didn't want to die alongside Jesus.

Perhaps that's why when it came time for Peter to die, some thirty years later, tradition says he felt unworthy to die as Jesus did, and he asked to be crucified upside down.

PETER'S CAREER CHANGE

Peter was a commercial fisherman, born in the fishing village of Bethsaida along the north shore of a large lake called the Sea of Galilee. His name was Simon son of Jonah, but Jesus later renamed him, saying, "You are Peter, and upon this rock I will build my church" (Matthew 16:18).

As an adult, Peter lived in the neighboring village of Capernaum, where he and his brother, Andrew, worked with their partners James and John, sons of Zebedee. All four became Jesus' disciples, which may explain why Jesus chose Capernaum as his ministry headquarters. (See *Capernaum,* "Peter's house.")

One day while Jesus was teaching in the area, he spotted an empty boat and asked the owner to take him out a short way so he could talk to the crowd. Peter was the owner, and he agreed. After Jesus had finished speaking, he told Peter to go out a little farther and drop his net in the water.

"We worked hard all last night and didn't catch a thing," Peter answered. "But if you say so, we'll try again" (Luke 5:5). The net filled and began to rip, so Peter yelled to shore for his partners to jump in the other boat and row out from the shore.

Fish secured, Peter asked Jesus to leave, saying, "I'm too much of a sinner to be around you." Jesus replied, "Don't be afraid! From now on you'll be fishing for people!" (Luke 5:8, 10).

As soon as they landed, the fishermen left their boats—fish still flapping—and followed Jesus.

WALKING ON WATER

Peter, along with James and John, became Jesus' three best friends. They alone witnessed some of his greatest miracles, such as the resurrection of a little girl and the Transfiguration, when Elijah and Moses appeared and Jesus' body took on a celestial glow.

It wasn't long before Peter emerged as the leading disciple and a spokesman for the others. His name appears first in every New Testament list of the apostles.

Peter demonstrated his leadership most remarkably during a storm on the lake at about three in the morning. Jesus had sent the disciples across the lake, and when they got caught in a storm, he walked to them—on the water. The disciples thought he was a ghost, but Jesus told them not to be afraid.

"Lord, if it's really you," Peter said, "tell me to come to you by walking on water" (Matthew 14:28). Peter walked on the water, too. He started to sink only when he took his eyes off Jesus, who grabbed his hand and pulled him up.

TRYING TO STOP THE CRUCIFIXION

Peter tried at least twice to stop the crucifixion of Jesus. His first attempt came shortly after he declared that Jesus was the promised Messiah, the Son of the living God. Jesus started talking plainly about his coming execution—no longer hiding it in parables. Peter, like most Jews of his time, apparently couldn't conceive of the Messiah dying before Israel was restored to the glory it enjoyed in King David's time.

"Heaven forbid, Lord," he said. "This will never happen to you!"

"Get away from me, Satan!" Jesus replied. "You are a dangerous trap to me. You are seeing things merely from a human point of view, and not from God's" (Matthew 16:22–23).

Peter's second attempt was a violent one. When temple officials arrested Jesus in Gethsemane, "Simon Peter drew a sword and slashed off the right ear of Malchus, the high priest's servant" (John 18:10). Jesus ordered Peter to put the sword away, then he reattached the severed ear.

Courage failed Peter hours later, however, when someone noticed him among the group waiting outside

POPE PETER

Roman Catholics teach that Peter was the first pope, a title originally known as "bishop of Rome." That's why the Vatican is still in Rome.

As pope, Peter had the authority to speak for God, Catholics teach. They base this on something Jesus told Peter: "I will give you the keys of the Kingdom of Heaven. Whatever you lock on earth will be locked in heaven, and whatever you open on earth will be opened in heaven" (Matthew 16:19).

during Jesus' all-night trial. Three times someone asked if he was Jesus' disciple. He denied it every time. With the third denial, a rooster crowed. Jesus had predicted this at the Last Supper, earlier in the evening. And as Peter suddenly realized the prophecy had been fulfilled, he ran off crying.

CHURCH FOUNDER

Jesus' resurrection gave Peter absolute assurance that death wasn't the end. So during the springtime festival of Pentecost, some fifty days after the Crucifixion, he preached a bold sermon about Jesus. And he preached it in the very heart of Jerusalem—where the people who crucified Jesus could hear. Some three thousand Jews believed Peter when he said Jesus had risen from the dead.

Perhaps that's what Jesus was referring to earlier when he said he would build his church on Peter, the rock.

With this core of believers, the Christian church began as a kind of messianic branch of the Jewish faith—a bit like a new denomination of Jews. There were Pharisee Jews who emphasized keeping laws. There were Sadducee Jews who didn't believe in an afterlife. And now there were Christian Jews who believed Jesus was the Messiah. So the first Christians were Jews.

It took a vision to convince Peter that non-Jews deserved to hear the Good News about Jesus, too. He saw nonkosher animals and heard God telling him to kill and eat them. Then the Holy Spirit told him to go with messengers who were coming. Peter went to the house of a Roman soldier named Cornelius—a Gentile who was as ritually unclean as nonkosher food. Putting two and two together, Peter realized that God was reminding him of what Jesus had said—take the gospel to the whole world—not just to the Jews. Cornelius and his family joined the Christian movement.

Church leaders argued about whether or not Gentiles needed to observe Jewish laws, such as circumcision. In a Jerusalem conference led by Jesus' brother James, Peter helped convince the council not to impose those traditions on non-Jews. But it remained a hotly debated topic. The earliest Jewish Christians worshiped in the synagogue on Saturday and in house churches on Sunday. But later in the century, Jews who believed in Jesus were banned from Jerusalem synagogues.

PETER'S DEATH

The Bible doesn't say exactly how or when Peter died. But it hints.

How. Jesus told Peter, " 'When you are old, you will stretch out your hands.'. . . Jesus said this to let him know what kind of death he would die to glorify God" (John 21:18–19).

When. First Peter places the apostle in Rome. Several Christian writers from early centuries say he died there—crucified.

Some writers, such as the church historian Eusebius, who lived in the late 200s, said Peter and Paul died in the mid-60s, about the same time the Jews killed James, the brother of Jesus who led the Jerusalem church.

A key event in history may have prompted these executions. On July 19, AD 64, fire broke out in Rome, a city of two million people—many of whom lived in slums. The fire raged for six days, then reignited and burned another three. By then, two-thirds of the city was destroyed.

Many historians blame Nero, who was away at a resort and who may have ordered the fire as a way to sidestep the Roman Senate, since he wanted to renovate Rome.

Nero, however, blamed the new, troublesome Jewish sect known as Christians. He began crucifying them and forcing them to face lions and gladiators in the arenas. For some nighttime shows, he tied them to stakes around the arena and set them on fire as torches.

Origen, a theologian in the early 200s, offered this report of Peter's execution: "Peter was crucified at Rome with his head downward, as he himself had desired to suffer."

Archaeologists found an early shrine in Rome, built in Peter's memory. It lies under St. Peter's Church on Vatican Hill—the very church from which the pope often addresses massive crowds.

PETRA

(PET ruh)
Petra, Greek
Sela, Hebrew
"rock"

First mention: Judges 1:36

MAP 2
D7

More than two thousand years before "See Rock City" signs pointed people to Lookout Mountain, near Chattanooga, Tennessee, there was a rock city worth seeing about fifty miles south of the Dead Sea, on Jordan's side of the border with Israel.

It was the capital and treasure city of Nabataean Arabs. Its hidden entrance was through a mile-long, 250-foot-high crack in a rock mountain. Inside were homes, massive monuments, and a theater—all of which were chiseled into the cliffs of a rock valley. The treasury, with its towering columns, served as an outside temple shot for *Indiana Jones and the Last Crusade,* a movie in which an archaeologist raced Nazis to find the Holy Grail, the cup

The end of a narrow, mile-long crevice in a Jordanian mountain opens to the city of Petra, carved into rock cliffs.

Jesus used at the Last Supper. Petra is now uninhabited, except for tourists flocking there to see the other "Rock City."

PHILADELPHIA

MAP 5
C2

(fill uh DEL fee uh)
Philadelpheia, Greek
"love of brother"
First mention: Revelation 1:11

Jesus had messages for each of the seven churches in western Turkey, and John preserved them in the book of Revelation. Of those churches, only two escaped the Lord's criticism—Smyrna, on the coast, and its neighbor seventy-five miles inland, Philadelphia.

An agricultural city renowned for its vineyards, Philadelphia sat on a fertile plateau in a river valley. About the time Revelation was written, the Roman emperor Domitian, in AD 92, ordered half the vineyards in the entire region destroyed—perhaps to boost income for Italian vine growers. He also persecuted Christians.

"Because you have obeyed my command to persevere," Jesus promised, "I will protect you from the great time of testing that will come upon the whole world" (Revelation 3:10).

PHILEMON

(fi LEE muhn)
Philemon, Greek
First century AD
First mention: Philemon 1

Philemon was a slave owner and a church leader. The famous church in Colosse in western Turkey met in his home. Paul wrote him a letter from prison, perhaps in Rome.

What's most shocking about the letter is who Paul asked to deliver it—one of Philemon's runaway slaves, Onesimus. Paul had converted the slave to Christianity, then sent him back to his owner.

Runaway slaves were often beaten or killed. But Paul hinted strongly that Philemon should free Onesimus: "I really wanted to keep him here with me. . . . He would have helped me on your behalf. But I didn't want to do anything without your consent. . . . I won't mention that you owe me your very soul!" (Philemon 13–14, 19).

Paul closed the letter with a

promise—or perhaps a warning. After his release, he was coming to visit.

PHILIP

Philippos, Greek
First century AD
First mention: 1. Matthew 10:3
2. Acts 6:5

1. **Disciple of Jesus.** When Jesus started his ministry, one of the first men he invited to become a disciple was Philip. Like the brothers Andrew and Peter, Philip came from the fishing village of Bethsaida beside the Sea of Galilee.

The first thing Philip did was to rush off and tell a friend—Nathanael—who also joined the group. "We have found the very person Moses and the prophets wrote about!" Philip said. "His name is Jesus, the son of Joseph from Nazareth" (John 1:45).

2. **Church leader.** After Jesus returned to heaven, the apostles got swarmed with ministry duties. They appointed seven assistants to help administer a charitable food program—Stephen and Philip among them.

The job description apparently grew. Philip traveled north to Samaria, where he converted many through his teaching and miracles of healing. He even converted a sorcerer named Simon and later an Ethiopian treasurer who was trying to understand a prophecy of Isaiah: "He was led as a sheep to the slaughter" (Acts 8:32). Philip explained how Jesus fulfilled this prophecy, now known as the Suffering Servant passage.

PHILIPPI

MAP 5 B1

(FILL uh pie)
Philippoi, Greek
First mention: Acts 16:12

Europe's first known church started in a rich woman's house in a Greek town named after Alexander the Great's father. King Philip II of Macedonia conquered the gold-mining town of Krenides, located about ten miles from the coast, and it soon became Philippi.

Paul went there after experiencing a vision calling him to Macedonia, a Roman province in what is now northern Greece. There he met Lydia, a businesswoman who sold expensive purple cloth. She believed what Paul had to say about Jesus and invited him to use her home to start a church. Of the many churches Paul planted, Philippi is the only one from which the Bible says he accepted contributions for himself. In appreciation for one such gift, he wrote them the New Testament letter of Philippians.

PHILISTIA

MAP 2 B5

(fill ess TEE uh)
Peleset, Hebrew
First mention: Exodus 15:14

About the time the Hebrews invaded Canaan from the east, a group of seafaring people known as the Philistines invaded from the west and settled along the southern coast of what is now Israel. They probably came from around Greece. Their new land, Philistia, extended from what is now the Palestinian Authority's Gaza Strip

Philistine coffins. Now a dead race, only their name survives, in its Greek form—Palestine.

northward to near Tel Aviv. They had five key cities: Ashdod, Ashkelon, Ekron, Gath, and Gaza.

The Greek word for Philistines—*Palaistine*—evolved into what is now a familiar name in the region—Palestine.

PHINEHAS
(FIN ee us)
Pinehas, Hebrew
Probably "the southerner"
1400s BC
First mention: Exodus 6:25

A warrior priest, Aaron's grandson Phinehas is famed for running a spear through a man and woman having sex.

At the time, Moses and the Hebrews were approaching Israel but had camped in Moab, part of what is now Jordan. There, local women lured Hebrew men into sex rituals for the native gods. God struck the Hebrews with a plague, and Moses ordered all Hebrew ringleaders executed. In blatant defiance, one Hebrew took a local woman right past Moses and into a nearby tent. The appalled Phinehas grabbed a spear and followed.

"Phinehas thrust the spear all the way through the man's body and into the woman's stomach. So the plague against the Israelites was stopped, but not before 24,000 people had died" (Numbers 25:8–9).

Sometime later, Phinehas led twelve thousand men into battle to punish the Midianites for luring Hebrews into idolatry.

PHOEBE
(FEE bee)
Phoibe, Greek
First century AD
First mention: Romans 16:1

In some churches Paul ordered women not to take leadership roles—perhaps because it caused problems there. Phoebe is evidence this wasn't a universal policy.

Paul identified Phoebe as a deacon in the church at Cenchrea, near Corinth. That's a title Paul used elsewhere to refer to top church leaders. Paul once gave Timothy this advice: "Before they are appointed as deacons, they should be given other responsibilities in the church as a test of their character and ability. If they do well, then they may serve as deacons" (1 Timothy 3:10).

PHOENICIA

(foe NEE she uh)
Phoinike, Greek
"dark red"
First mention: Isaiah 23:11

Today's country of Lebanon, on Israel's northern border, was called Phoenicia in Bible times. This land between the Mediterranean Sea and the mountains that now separate Lebanon from Syria were heavily forested with huge cedar trees that resisted bugs and rotting. That made the lumber excellent for shipbuilding, and the Phoenicians became seafaring people. The king of Tyre, a city in southern Phoenicia, supplied crews for Solomon's fleet of trading ships that sailed the Red Sea.

PHOENIX

(FEE nix)
Phoinix, Greek
First mention: Acts 27:12

"I believe there is trouble ahead if we go on," Paul told officers in charge of the ship headed to Rome—"shipwreck, loss of cargo, injuries, and danger to our lives" (Acts 27:10).

Soldiers were taking Paul to Rome for trial, but the ship had gotten a late start. By the time they approached Crete—about halfway into the voyage—it was already late fall, well into the dangerous season for sailing. Paul wanted them to winter at Fair Havens, but the captain decided to try for the better-protected harbor at Phoenix, on the island's western tip.

They never made it. A gale swept them five hundred miles past Crete and ran them aground off the coast of Malta, a small island south of Italy and Sicily.

PHRYGIA

(FRIDGE ee uh)
Phrygia, Greek
First mention: Acts 2:10

Jews from the Roman province of Phrygia in what is now Turkey were among international pilgrims who came to Jerusalem to celebrate the Pentecost harvest festival—and ended up hearing Peter preach the sermon that launched the Christian church. Some three thousand Jews believed Peter's message about Jesus, and they started meeting together to learn more. During one of Rome's later persecutions of Christians, Phrygia was especially hard hit. One entire town was set ablaze—with the citizens inside.

PILATE

(PIE luht)
Pilatos, Greek
Pilatus, Latin
Governed about AD 26–37
First mention: Matthew 27:2

Saint Pilate. That's what some Christians call the man who ordered Jesus crucified.

Some Christians even pray to Pilate. They include members of the Coptic Church—the major church in Egypt—as well as the Ethiopian Church. After all, Pilate tried to save Jesus by offering to release him. And later church legends insist Pilate died a Christian martyr.

"Behold the man," Pilate says, pointing to the freshly bloodied Jesus.

Jewish historians from Pilate's day paint a different picture.

Philo, the Jewish writer and philosopher who grew up in Pilate's generation, said Pilate was "rigid and stubbornly harsh. . .of spiteful disposition and an incredibly vengeful man" with a tendency for "bribes, acts of pride, acts of violence. . .constant murders without trial, the ceaseless and most grievous brutality."

But that's a Jew talking about the leader of occupying forces in the Jewish homeland.

The truth about Pilate may lie somewhere between those two extremes.

GOVERNOR OF JUDEA

Pilate was appointed prefect, or governor, of Judea in about AD 26—perhaps just three or four years before Jesus stood before him. It wasn't a high-profile job, so far from Rome. But he commanded incredible power throughout his province, which covered much of what is now Israel.

Pilate was in charge of collecting taxes and sending a cut to Rome, while keeping some money to run the province. One Jewish historian of the century, Josephus, reported that Pilate once confiscated temple funds to build an aqueduct into Jerusalem. Pilate was also the top authority on legal matters, judging select cases.

And when some group wanted to execute a person—as the Jewish council did with Jesus—they had to get Pilate's approval.

Why Pilate agreed to execute Jesus remains unclear. He certainly didn't believe Jesus was a threat to the empire—he tried repeatedly to talk the Jews into releasing him. But the Jews replied, "If you release this man, you are not a friend of Caesar. Anyone who declares himself a king is a rebel against Caesar" (John 19:12).

Pilate may have taken this as a warning that the Jews might appeal to his superior, a Roman official named Vitellius, who commanded several legions in Syria.

That's exactly what happened several years later, after Pilate ordered a bloody attack on a crowd of unarmed Samaritans. They had gathered to hear a prophet who claimed he had found sacred objects once used by Moses. Vitellius ordered Pilate to Rome to answer the charges.

Pilate was never heard from again.

Some Christian writers reported that Caligula, the new and unpredictable emperor, found Pilate guilty. They say that after a brief exile in France, Pilate committed suicide—as was the custom among Roman officials convicted of crimes. Coptic Church legend says he was crucified on the very cross of Jesus.

PISGAH

See Mt.Nebo

MAP 1
D5

(PIZ guh)
Pisga, Hebrew
First mention: Numbers 21:20

When Moses and the Hebrews arrived on the doorstep of the Promised Land, they camped about ten miles from the Jordan River. "Moses went to Mount Nebo from the plains of Moab and climbed Pisgah Peak, which is across from Jericho" (Deuteronomy 34:1). From there he saw what is now Israel, from Mount Hermon in the north to the Negev in the south. Some scholars say Pisgah was a separate mountain from Nebo, but others say it was one of the peaks on Mount Nebo—or Jabal Naba as the Jordanians call it. (See *Mount Nebo*.)

PITHOM

MAP 3
B4

(PIE thum)
Pitom, Hebrew
"house of Atum," sun god
First mention: Exodus 1:11

Egypt had two cities made in Israel—built by Hebrew slaves from what is now Israel. The cities were Pithom and Rameses, and they became supply centers and defensive outposts for Egypt. Though Pithom certainly existed and was mentioned in an Egyptian report to the king, scholars don't agree on where it was. There are several theories, but all of them place the city somewhere in the Nile Delta region of Goshen, where the Bible says the Hebrews lived before Moses led them out of Egypt.

Joseph runs from Potiphar's wife as she tries to seduce him.

though he always refused her.

After she grabbed him one day, he ran out of the house, leaving her holding the shirt she ripped off him. Furious, she screamed rape. Potiphar probably didn't believe it. If he had, he would have executed Joseph. Instead, he put Joseph in the palace prison—minor punishment for such a violent crime committed by a slave.

PRISCILLA
(pruh SILL uh)
Priskilla, Greek
First century AD
First mention: Acts 18:2

In a male-dominated world, Priscilla was apparently a standout woman, evidenced by the fact that nearly every time she and her husband, Aquila, are mentioned in the Bible, her name comes first. Perhaps that's because she led in ministry, while her husband led in the family business of tent making. The apostle Paul, also trained as a tent maker, lived and worked with the couple while he founded the church in Corinth, Greece.

POTIPHAR
(POT uh fur)
Potipar, Hebrew
"he is given by Re," the sun god
About 1800s BC
First mention: Genesis 37:36

Potiphar was captain of the palace guard in Egypt and the man who bought Jacob's teenaged son, Joseph, from slave traders.

Young Joseph might have enjoyed a cushy life there, since Potiphar liked him and eventually put him in charge of all his business dealings. But Potiphar's wife sexually harassed Joseph day after day—

QUIRINIUS
(kwhy REN ee us)
Kyrenaios, Greek
50s BC–AD 21
First mention: Luke 2:2

Publius Sulpicius Quirinius was his full name in the Latin language of Rome. The Bible says Joseph and Mary went to Bethlehem to register for "the first census taken when Quirinius was governor of Syria" (Luke 2:2). That's puzzling because Quirinius, who was well known as a soldier and a friend of the emperor, Tiberius, wasn't governor until AD 6—about a decade after Jesus was born. Several ancient sources agree on this. Bible experts offer many theories about the contradiction, including the possibility that Quirinius served two terms, first when Jesus was born and again a decade later.

QUMRAN
(KOOM ron)
Qumran, Arabic

MAP 4
C5

Copies of Bible books a thousand years older than those used to translate the King James Version were found among the Dead Sea Scrolls at Qumran—a desert settlement that died violently in AD 68.

A monklike Jewish sect called Essenes, meaning "pious ones," withdrew from Jewish society about 150 years before Christ. They moved fourteen miles east of Jerusalem near the Dead Sea. There, on the flat top of a dry ridge, they built a settlement where they copied sacred Jewish writings and waited to join God's army in the apocalypse. The Roman army arrived first. They wiped out the settlement—part of a campaign to crush the Jewish rebellion that started two years earlier.

As Romans took up their attack positions, Qumran scribes apparently rushed part of their sacred library to nearby caves, storing some in clay jars. It wasn't until 1947 that a shepherd boy found the first jar, with three scrolls inside. Since then, scholars have found in eleven caves parts of about eight hundred manuscripts, some two hundred of which are copies of Old Testament books. Only a few manuscripts were complete, like the Isaiah Scroll. Most were a jigsaw puzzle of about twenty-five thousand scraps—many no bigger than a fingernail.

RACHEL

(RAY chuhl)
Rahel, Hebrew
"ewe" (female sheep)
1900s BC
First mention: Genesis 29:6

Rachel was the woman whom Jacob worked seven years to marry—only to get tricked by her father, Laban, into marrying the older sister first. Apparently married at night, Jacob didn't discover the switch until dawn, when he woke up next to Leah.

Laban explained it was the custom to marry off oldest daughters first. Then Laban offered to let Jacob marry Rachel the next week, if he agreed to work another seven years. Jacob agreed.

Rachel and Leah competed fiercely for Jacob's affection. Rachel was the woman he loved, but she felt inadequate because she couldn't have children. And Leah felt unloved even though she gave birth to six sons and another two by using her maid as a surrogate mother.

Rachel countered by offering her maid as a surrogate, as well, producing two sons. In time, Rachel had two boys of her own—Jacob's favorite sons, Joseph and Benjamin. Tragically, Rachel died on the road to Bethlehem during childbirth. With her last breath, she named her newborn son Ben-oni, "son of my sorrow." But Jacob renamed the boy Benjamin, "son of my right hand."

RAHAB

(RAY hab)
Rahab, Hebrew
1400s BC
First mention: Joshua 2:1

While the Hebrews of the Exodus were still camped in what is now Jordan, their leader, Joshua, sent two spies to scout the fortified border town of Jericho.

The spies went straight to the house of a prostitute, Rahab. And they spent the night.

Why they went there, the Bible doesn't really say. Perhaps they felt it would be a good place to get

The Bible's only reported kiss between a man and a woman. When Jacob meets Rachel, the woman who will become his wife, he kisses her. Sadly, he gets tricked into marrying her sister.

information while keeping a low profile, since strangers often spent the night there. If so, their strategy didn't work. Someone slipped out and told the king where the spies were and why they came.

Rahab got word of the leak. What she did next put her life in jeopardy. She hid the spies under layers of flax drying

All that's left of Rahab's hometown—Jericho—is this partly excavated mound. Invading Israelites approached from the fertile plain at the top, which extends to the Jordan River six miles eastward.

on her flat roof. When the soldiers arrived, she said the spies just left and if the soldiers hurried they could catch them. So the soldiers chased nothing into the night, five miles to the Jordan River and back again.

Rahab's house was built into the city wall, so she used a rope to let the spies escape from her window, but not before getting their promise to spare her extended family during the coming attack. The spies asked only that Rahab mark her home with a scarlet rope dangling from the window.

The spies kept their promise. Rahab and her relatives lived among the Israelites.

In a New Testament shocker, Rahab seems to show up in the family tree of Jesus. She's listed as the mother of Boaz. That would have made her the great-great-grandmother of King David. It's uncertain if this was the same Rahab, but Jesus' family tree does include other women of questionable background—Tamar, who slept with her father-in-law, and Bathsheba, who committed adultery with David.

RAMAH

(RAY mah)
Rama, Hebrew
"high place"
First mention: Joshua 18:25

MAP 1
C5

There are about half a dozen towns named Ramah in the Bible. Most familiar is the one about five miles north of Jerusalem, now called er Ram. Located in the tribe of Benjamin, Ramah sat along the border between the northern Jewish nation of Israel and the southern nation of Judah, so it often got caught in a tug of war.

One tradition says Rachel died in Ramah, giving birth to her second son, Benjamin, whose descendants became the tribe of Benjamin. This Ramah may also have been the hometown and birthplace of Samuel and where he judged court cases. Here, too, is where Babylon processed prisoners after leveling Jerusalem in 586 BC.

RAMESES
(RAM uh sees)
Raamses, Hebrew
First mention: Genesis 47:11

MAP 3
B3

Second in command of Egypt after the king, Joseph gave his father's extended family the land of Rameses, probably somewhere in the fertile delta where the Nile River splinters into streams that empty into the Mediterranean Sea. A later Egyptian king enslaved the Hebrews and forced them to build the supply cities of Rameses and Pithom. It's uncertain where Rameses was located, but it was probably somewhere in the delta. Rameses became the starting point for the Exodus. That was in the mid-1400s BC according to some scholars and in the 1200s BC according to others. Rameses served as the capital of Egypt during the nineteenth and twentieth dynasties, from roughly 1300 through 1100 BC.

RAMOTH-GILEAD
(RAY moth GIL ee add)
Ramot gilad, Hebrew
"heights of Gilead"
First mention: Deuteronomy 4:43

MAP 1
E3

This fortified city in the fertile grazing land of Gilead, in what is now Jordan, wasn't kind to King Ahab's family. The Syrians captured it from the Israelites, and Ahab died trying to take it back.

Ahab's son Joram also died because of what happened there—the prophet Elisha anointed the military commander Jehu as Israel's next king. Jehu promptly raced to Joram's palace and shot the king in the heart with an arrow.

Ramoth-gilead was designated one of Israel's six cities of refuge—a place where people accused of accidentally killing someone could get a trial and find protection from the dead person's vengeance-seeking family.

REBEKAH
(ruh BEC kuh)
Ribqa, Hebrew
2000s BC
First mention: Genesis 22:23

An ancient version of a mail-order bride, Rebekah traveled some five hundred miles from what is now south Turkey to marry a forty-year-old man she had never met—Isaac.

Isaac's father, Abraham, sent his most trusted servant to find a wife for Isaac. Abraham didn't want a Canaanite daughter-in-law, but a member of his extended family. Rebekah fit the bill. Her grandfather was Abraham's brother, Nahor, which meant that her father, Bethuel, was Isaac's cousin. So Rebekah was Isaac's second cousin.

Rebekah met Abraham's servant at a well and graciously answered his request for a drink by offering to water his camels, as well. That was the very response the servant was looking for. He had asked God to point out Isaac's wife by having the woman offer to water his camels.

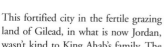

Just east of the Nile River, the Red Sea separates Egypt (left) from Saudi Arabia. The Sinai Peninsula, where Moses led the Israelites, sits like a pie wedge between two rabbit ears at the top of the Red Sea.

Rebekah agreed to the marriage proposal, which came with gifts of jewelry and clothing. Isaac fell deeply in love with her.

Rebekah remained infertile for twenty years but eventually had twin sons, Esau and Jacob. Isaac favored Esau, the outdoorsman, while Rebekah favored Jacob. When Isaac grew old and blind, Rebekah convinced Jacob to fool his father into giving him the blessing that transferred family leadership—which should have gone to Esau, as the oldest. Perhaps she was trying to help God fulfill the promise he made to her before the boys were born: "Your older son will serve the descendants of your younger son" (Genesis 25:23).

When Rebekah learned of Esau's plan to kill Jacob, she convinced Isaac to send Jacob to her homeland to find a wife. By the time Jacob returned, twenty years later, Rebekah had died. She was buried in Abraham's family tomb near Hebron.

RED SEA

MAP 3
C5

Yam sup, Hebrew
"sea of reeds" or "sea at the
end of the world"
First mention: Exodus 10:19

No sea is more famous to Bible students than the one God parted for Moses and the Hebrews as they fled Egypt.

Though this miracle has long been connected with the Red Sea, scholars aren't so sure. In the original Hebrew language, the body of water is called *yam sup. Yam* means "sea." But what's *sup?* Sometimes it means "end" or "far away." Other times it means "reeds." This second meaning leads some scholars to suggest the body of water God parted was actually a reed-filled marshland north of the Red Sea.

The Red Sea is a long and narrow ocean separating Africa and Arabia. On a map, the sea looks like it has a couple of rabbit ears sticking out on top, with

319

the triangle-shaped Sinai Peninsula wedged between. The left ear is the Gulf of Suez, connected to the Mediterranean Sea by the Suez Canal. The Exodus miracle took place somewhere in that area. The right ear is the Gulf of Aqaba. Solomon anchored his fleet of trading ships at the tip of that ear, in the port city of Ezion-geber, near today's Israeli port of Elat.

REHOBOAM
(REE huh BO uhm)
Rehabam, Hebrew
Reigned about 930–913 BC
First mention: 1 Kings 11:43

King Solomon's son and successor, Rehoboam, made the foolish decision that split Israel into two countries.

Solomon had been an insatiable builder, which required him to impose heavy taxes and to draft workers by the tens of thousands for seasonal duty. When Rehoboam came to power, tribal leaders asked if he would lighten up. Elderly advisers told Rehoboam to do as the people asked. Younger advisers said that would signal weakness. So Rehoboam told the tribal leaders, "My little finger is thicker than my father's waist—if you think he was hard on you, just wait and see what I'll be like!" (1 Kings 12:10).

They didn't wait to see.

Ten northern tribes seceded from the union and crowned their own king—oddly, one of Solomon's former building foremen—Jeroboam. They called their nation Israel. Rehoboam's nation became Judah, named after the larger of the two tribes loyal to him.

Five years later, Egypt's king—Shiskak—took advantage of the split by raiding both nations. This invasion recorded in the Bible is preserved on hieroglyphics from Shiskak's reign.

Rehoboam followed his father's practice of marrying foreign women as part of peace treaties. "In all, he had eighteen wives and sixty concubines, and they gave birth to twenty-eight sons and sixty daughters" (2 Chronicles 11:21).

An old well in Israel, perhaps much like the well Isaac named Rehoboth.

REHOBOTH
(REE ho bauth)
Rehobot, Hebrew
"room enough"
First mention: Genesis 26:22

See Beersheba

MAP 2
C6

Issac named his wells. Rehoboth was the third well he dug for his flocks. The first two wells were taken over by other shepherds. Rather than fight, Isaac simply named the wells "Argument" and "Opposition," then moved on to a third, uncontested well. He named it "Room Enough," *Rehoboth* in Hebrew, explaining, "At last the LORD has made room for us, and we will be able to thrive" (Genesis 26:22). This well was somewhere in the Negev desert in the area of Beersheba, about forty miles south of Jerusalem.

REUBEN

(RU ben)
Reuben, Hebrew
"look, a son!"
About 1800s BC
First mention: Genesis 29:32

Jacob's first son was Reuben, delivered by the wife Jacob was tricked into marrying.

Jacob's bride, Leah, tried to win his affection by producing sons—six of them. Reuben was the first. After Reuben's delivery, Leah declared in giddy delight, "The LORD has noticed my misery, and now my husband will love me" (Genesis 29:32).

Reuben lost his right as the oldest son to lead the extended family. That's because he had sex with his stepmother, Bilhah, Rachel's maid. Bilhah was a surrogate mother who gave Jacob two sons.

Reuben married and had four sons. His descendants became the tribe of Reuben.

REUBEN

(RU ben)
Reuben, Hebrew
"look, a son!"
First mention: Numbers 32:1

MAP 1
D5

The extended family, also called a tribe, descended from Jacob's oldest son didn't settle in what is now Israel. Like the tribes of Gad and half of Manasseh, they settled east of the Jordan River. They saw that the land in what is now Jordan looked ideal for grazing flocks, so they asked Moses for the land where they had set up camp along the Dead Sea's eastern shore.

RHODA

(ROW duh)
Rhode, Greek
First century AD
First mention: Acts 12:13

King Herod Agrippa executed James, a disciple of Jesus. When he saw how happy this made the Jews, he arrested Peter, as well. On the night before Peter's trial, Jerusalem Christians gathered in a home to pray, most certainly for Peter. An angel freed Peter during that prayer, and the apostle walked directly to that home. The servant girl who answered the door was Rhoda. She couldn't believe her eyes. She was so excited that she left Peter standing outside while she ran to tell the others.

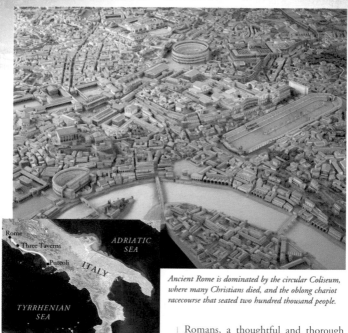

Ancient Rome is dominated by the circular Coliseum, where many Christians died, and the oblong chariot racecourse that seated two hundred thousand people.

ROME
Rhome, Greek
Roma, Latin
First mention: Acts 2:10

See Map Above

This is an Italian city that has certainly left its mark on the church—for better and worse.

For better: Paul wrote his most eloquent letter to believers in this town—the New Testament letter of Romans, a thoughtful and thorough explanation of what Christians believe.

For worse: This city executed Paul and Peter. So say early Christian writers. In addition, though Rome soon became the international capital of Christianity led by the bishop of Rome—a title later changed to pope—the arrogant opulence of churches that have dominated Rome's skyline for centuries stands in stark contrast to the Bethlehem cave where Christianity started. That simple cave, tradition says, was the birthplace of a Savior who said he came "to preach Good News to the poor" (Luke 4:18).

THE RISE AND FALL OF ROME

When King David, in about 1000 BC, was beating back Israel's neighboring nations to secure the borders of his new kingdom, European settlers were moving onto one of the seven hills that would later become capital of the Roman Empire and eventually of Italy.

And about the time Babylon wiped the Jewish nation off the map, in 586 BC, Rome was experiencing a makeover from rustic village to urban center, thanks to an invasion of people from northern Italy known as Etruscans. They drained marshes between the hills, paved the streets, and built a city wall.

By about a century before Jesus, Rome ruled a growing empire.

In New Testament times, when Roman emperors reigned, lavish architecture rested like jewels imbedded on the Seven Hills. Enough of the ruins remain that visitors to sites such as the Coliseum are astonished at what the ancients accomplished. And yet surrounding those awesome public buildings funded by tax money from conquered king-doms, much of the population lived in shacks. That's why Nero wanted to rebuild Rome. He was accused of starting the fire that destroyed two-thirds of the city—a fire he blamed on Christians before launching a wave of perse-cution said to have led to the exe-cution of Paul and Peter.

Rome fell in the AD 400s to tribal invaders from what is now Germany and later to Arabs. But the city started its comeback in about AD 1000, during the time of the Crusades. Rome became capital of Italy in 1871 and now has a population of more than three million.

RUTH

Rut, Hebrew
"companion, friend," or "satisfied"
1100s BC
First mention: Ruth 1:4

King David's great-grandmother got her husband by sneaking into his bed with him after he fell asleep.

But it wasn't her idea. It was her former mother-in-law's—Naomi.

Both were destitute widows at the

An Arab woman in the early 1900s, dressed in clothes much like Ruth would have worn. Also non-Jewish, the foremother of Israel's most famous kings came from what is now Jordan.

time. Naomi and her husband had taken their sons from Bethlehem during a drought, and they moved to Moab in what is now Jordan. There, the sons married Moabite women—Ruth and Orpah. But within about a decade, all three men were dead.

In that male-led culture, widows couldn't own property and were helpless unless they could remarry or find relatives to take them in. Naomi decided to go home, and she urged her daughters-in-law to go back to their parents. Orpah reluctantly agreed. Ruth refused: "I will go wherever you go and live wherever you live. Your people will be my people, and your God will be my God" (Ruth 1:16).

The two arrived in Bethlehem during barley harvest in early spring. Jewish law said the poor could follow behind harvesters and pick leftovers. Ruth did that, fortunately choosing the field of Boaz, one of Naomi's relatives. Boaz took an immediate liking to Ruth because of her devotion to Naomi. So he told his harvesters to leave extra grain for her.

RUTH UNDERCOVER

When Naomi saw the half bushel of barley that Ruth brought back and heard about Boaz's kindness, she hatched a plan.

Jewish law said that if a man died, the man's brother should take care of the widow by marrying her. That law apparently extended to include other relatives when there was no brother.

"Boaz is a close relative of ours," Naomi told Ruth. "Tonight he will be winnowing barley at the threshing floor. Now do as I tell you—take a bath and put on perfume and dress in your nicest clothes. Then go to the threshing floor, but don't let Boaz see you until he has finished his meal. Be sure to notice where he lies down; then go and uncover his feet and lie down there. He will tell you what to do" (Ruth 3:2–4).

It wasn't until midnight that Boaz realized Ruth was under the covers with him.

And that's when she proposed. "Spread the corner of your covering over me, for you are my family redeemer" (Ruth 3:9). The original word for covering is the same for "wing." She pointed Boaz to his own blessing of her earlier: "May the LORD, the God of Israel, under whose wings you have come to take refuge, reward you fully" (Ruth 2:12). Ruth was asking Boaz to become God's wing of refuge.

Flattered that she chose him over younger men, he agreed—but only after checking to make sure that a closer relative didn't want to marry her.

Boaz and Ruth married and had a son—Obed, grandfather of David. Naomi cared for the boy like he was her own son.

And so, a mixed marriage between an Israelite man and an Arab woman from Jordan produced Israel's most revered family of kings—including David, Solomon, and Jesus.

SALAMIS

(SAL uh muhs)
Salamis, Greek
First mention: Acts 13:5

The first stop in Paul's ten thousand miles of missionary journeys was Salamis, a port city on the eastern coast of Cyprus. This island was where Paul's traveling associate, Barnabas, grew up. There were apparently several synagogues in this city alone. Paul and Barnabas worked their way across the 138-mile-long island, preaching in one synagogue after another. About half a century later, Jews on Cyprus led a rebellion against Rome. When the Romans crushed the rebellion, they banned Jews from setting foot on Cyprus.

SALOME

(suh LOW me)
Salome, Greek
First century AD
First mention: Matthew 14:6, "Herodias' daughter"

There are two women named Salome in the Bible, and the one who is known best isn't even mentioned by name.

The lesser-known Salome was a follower of Jesus who saw the Crucifixion (Mark 15:40). The better-known Salome was a dancer who cost John the Baptist his head. The Bible refers to her only as Herodias' daughter, but the first-century historian Josephus said her name was Salome.

John criticized Herod Antipas' marriage to Herodias, divorced from Herod's brother. Jewish law considered the marriage incest. Later, when Salome danced at her stepfather's birthday party, he offered her anything. Her mother told her to ask for John's head on a tray.

Along a barren trail, midway between Jericho and Jerusalem, this Good Samaritan Inn commemorates Jesus' famous parable of a compassionate traveler.

SAMARIA

MAP 4
B4

(suh MAIR ee uh)
Somron, Hebrew
First mention: Luke 17:11

In Jesus' day, Jews hated people from Samaria—a forty-mile-long plug of land in the middle of the country. That's why Jews didn't take kindly to Jesus' parable of the good Samaritan—it made a villain out of a Jewish priest who walked right past a Jew beaten nearly to death, and it made a hero of the Samaritan who helped.

Before Samaria was a region, it was a city—near the modern village of Sebastiya, about forty miles north of Jerusalem. King Ahab's father, Omri, built Samaria on a hill in about 885 BC and turned it into the capital of the northern Jewish nation of Israel. Samaria flourished for about a century and a half, until the Assyrians conquered it in 722 BC.

After taking control of the nation, the Assyrians extended the name of Samaria to include the surrounding region, from the Jordan River to the Mediterranean Sea, and from the Jezreel valley in the north to the Aijalon valley in the south. Assyrian pioneers settled in the land and married Jewish survivors, mixing the races and religions into what became known as Samaritans.

The region formed a huge roadblock between Galilee in the north and Judea—with Jerusalem—in the south. Jews traveling between Galilee and Jerusalem generally avoided the shortest route, through Samaria. Instead, they followed the Jordan River. Jesus, however, sometimes traveled through the Samaritan hills and once taught a Samaritan woman at a well about "living water" that gives eternal life (John 4:10). Another time, when a Samaritan village refused to welcome Jesus, some of the disciples asked, "Lord, should we order down fire from heaven to burn them up?" (Luke 9:54). Jesus said no and moved on.

A few hundred Samaritans still live in the region and celebrate Passover by offering animal sacrifices. Jews haven't offered sacrifices since Romans destroyed the temple in AD 70.

SAMSON
(SAM son)
Simson, possibly "little sun," Hebrew
About 1100–1050 BC
First mention: Judges 13:24

It's hard to say anything good about Samson once you've read his story.

Especially perplexing is why God chose him to become a national hero. And why an unnamed writer in the New Testament put him on an elite list with David, Samuel, and Gideon as leaders whose "weakness was turned to strength" (Hebrews 11:34). Samson seemed exactly the opposite: a muscleman so driven by his animal appetites—especially sex and revenge—that his strength was turned to weakness.

He was at his weakest around unsavory women—three that we know of, each of whom got him into deep trouble. They were his bride, a prostitute, and Delilah. In fact, his entire life story spins around these three women, the trouble they got him into, and the violence that came of it.

A MIRACLE BABY
Samson was born to an Israelite couple

who thought they couldn't have children. That puts Samson in the company of several distinguished Hebrew leaders: Isaac, Joseph, Samuel, and John the Baptist. Samson's parents—Manoah and his unidentified wife—lived in the gently sloping hills of Judea, in the tiny village of Zorah. That's about fifteen miles west of Jerusalem and a few miles from several Philistine villages on the coastal plain farther west.

An angel appeared to Manoah's wife and told her she would have a son. Not just any son. "The boy is to be a Nazirite, set apart to God from birth, and he will begin the deliverance of Israel from the hands of the Philistines" (Judges 13:5 NIV).

Nazirites were Hebrews who lived by unique rules to show a devotion to God that was above and beyond the normal. There were three main rules:

- Don't eat grapes or drink wine made from them.
- Don't go near a corpse—not even a close relative.
- Don't cut your hair.

An angel told Samson's mother to live by these rules while she was pregnant and explained that Samson was supposed to live by them all his life.

A PHILISTINE WEDDING

Samson decided to marry a Philistine woman from the neighboring village five miles away. This angered his parents, who asked, "Why must you go to the pagan Philistines to find a wife?"

SAMSON THE JUDGE

Samson was one of twelve leaders called judges, chosen by God to save Israel from enemies in the years before they had a king. Most weren't legal experts who settled disputes. Instead, they were warriors who rallied the families in their region to fight off enemies.

Samson was an exception. He led no one. A lone maverick, he fought the Philistines by himself—a one-man army who killed thousands.

(Judges 14:3). There was no talking him out of it. This choice set him on a deadly collision course with the Philistines. Deadly for them. Deadly for him.

At the beginning of his seven-day wedding festival, Samson bet the thirty Philistine men who came as guests that they couldn't solve a riddle. If they did, Samson said, he would give each man a set of robes. If they didn't, they would each give him a set of robes.

Samson's riddle was about honey he found in the carcass of a lion: "From the one who eats came something to eat; out of the strong came something sweet" (Judges 14:14).

After four days, the guests threatened Samson's bride, "Get the answer to the riddle from your husband, or we will burn down your father's house with you in it" (Judges 14:15). She did as ordered.

Furious that his bride had betrayed him, Samson stormed off to Ashkelon, a Philistine city twenty-five miles away. There, he killed thirty men, stripped off their clothes, and paid his debt to the guests. Then he stomped home to his parents—without his bride. He calmed down eventually and went back to get her. But by that time, her father had given her to the best man, explaining that he thought Samson hated her.

"This time I cannot be blamed for everything I am going to do to you Philistines," Samson replied (Judges 15:3).

He caught three hundred foxes, tied their tails in pairs along with torches, and set them loose in Philistine grain fields, vineyards, and olive groves. A burnt field wipes out only a single harvest, but the damage to vineyards and olive groves is much more extensive. Newly planted grapevines take three to five years to produce a full crop. Olive trees in Bible times were most productive only after forty or fifty years.

The Philistines retaliated with fire of their own. They burned to death Samson's ex-wife and her father for starting the trouble. Samson lashed back, killing many Philistines before retreating into the Judean hills.

Philistine soldiers launched a manhunt into Jewish territory. Judeans saw this invasion as the start of potentially worse consequences ahead. So a contingent of three thousand asked Samson to give himself up. In a rare selfless gesture, Samson agreed.

Bound with new ropes, Samson was turned over to the Philistines. Once in custody, however, he promptly broke free, picked up a donkey's jawbone, and killed a thousand soldiers.

DATE WITH A PROSTITUTE

Another woman generated the next scene in Samson's story. She was a prostitute in the Philistine coastal city of Gaza. When Samson arrived at her place of business, word spread throughout the town.

On his way to propose to a Philistine, Samson is attacked by a lion, which he kills with his bare hands.

Men surrounded the place and lay in wait, planning to kill Samson when he left in the morning, exhausted from sex. But the surprise was on them. Samson left about midnight, energized. He tore off the city's massive front gate—posts and all—and hauled it away on his shoulders. He lugged it some forty miles before setting it up on a hilltop in front of the Israelite village of Hebron.

Philistines rush into Delilah's tent to arrest Samson. Awakened by the clamor, Samson is horrified to discover that Delilah has cut his hair—the source of his supernatural strength.

DELILAH, THE FATAL ATTRACTION

Samson's most famous story begins with a third woman, Delilah, a Philistine living in the Valley of Sorek just a couple of miles from his home. Samson fell in love with her. But Philistine leaders each promised to pay her twenty-eight pounds of silver if she coaxed out of him the secret of his strength.

For days, Delilah begged, nagged, and badgered Samson. Three times he tried to silence her with a lie.

Lie No. 1: He would get weak if tied up with seven new bowstrings. When he fell asleep at Delilah's place, she tied him up with seven new bowstrings and woke him. Instantly, he snapped the cords.

Lie No. 2: New ropes would do the trick. Delilah tried again while he slept. Same result.

Lie No. 3: Weaving together the seven braids of his hair would sap his strength. Next time he fell asleep, Delilah tested the theory. Negative.

With a question wrapped in guilt, Delilah tried once more. "How can you say you love me when you don't confide in me?" (Judges 16:15).

"My hair has never been cut," Samson finally admitted, "for I was dedicated to God as a Nazirite from birth. If my head were shaved, my strength would leave me, and I would become as weak as anyone else" (Judges 16:17).

Why Samson expected to fall asleep in Delilah's presence and wake up with hair is beyond comprehension.

Samson woke up—his clipped head on the lap of Delilah and his fate in the hands of the Philistine soldiers she called. They seized him, gouged out his eyes, and led him away to grind grain at a prison mill.

For twenty years, Samson had been on the Philistines' most wanted list. So they celebrated. With thousands of happy Philistines crowded into a temple—three thousand on the roof alone—Samson was paraded in front of them. By this time his hair was growing back.

Samson asked the attendant leading him to let him rest by the support pillars, which in many temples were blocks of wood or stone set on top of one another. Samson's last words were a prayer for revenge: "O God, please strengthen me one more time so that I may pay back the Philistines for the loss of my eyes" (Judges 16:28).

He pushed against the columns, the temple collapsed, and he was crushed to death with more Philistines than he had killed in all the years before. His family came to retrieve the body, then buried him with his father near their home.

SAMSON'S LEGACY

The Bible doesn't say that God was orchestrating Samson's bad decisions. But the story of Israel's history shows that God was able to put those bad decisions to good use.

Before Samson came along, Israel was in danger of becoming assimilated into the stronger Philistine nation. But Samson drove a wedge between the two nations, keeping them apart and suspicious of each other. What Samson started, King David finished about fifty years later—crushing the Philistine

army. David made Israel the leading nation in the region. In time, the Philistines vanished from history, assimilated into other Middle East nations.

SAMUEL

(SAM you uhl)
Semuel, Hebrew
"asked of God"
About 1100–1010 BC
First mention: 1 Samuel 1:20

If the prophet Samuel had his way, there would have been no King Saul or King David.

God agreed.

God was king, and Samuel delivered God's messages to the people.

The trouble was that Samuel had grown old, and his two sons were crooked. They took bribes and let money do the talking instead of God.

So the Israelites took a monumental step away from the Lord and toward self-reliance. Rather than trust God for the future, evidenced by the past, the Israelites decided to take care of themselves. They asked Samuel for a king.

Angrily, he complied.

GOD'S BOY

Samuel never really belonged to his parents. He was God's boy from the beginning. Samuel's mother, Hannah, saw to that.

Hannah was one of Elkanah's two wives. The family lived in the village of Ramah in the hills of Ephraim—tribal territory in what is now central Israel. Hannah couldn't have children, as

SAMUEL, THE LONG-HAIRED NAZIRITE

Samuel's mother, Hannah, made a deal with God.

Infertile, Hannah prayed, "O LORD Almighty, if you will look down upon my sorrow and answer my prayer and give me a son, then I will give him back to you. He will be yours for his entire lifetime, and as a sign that he has been dedicated to the LORD, his hair will never be cut" (1 Samuel 1:11).

Hannah was promising that her son would be a Nazirite for life, just as Samson had been.

People could take the Nazirite vow for a lifetime or for a short time, similar to fasting, as Paul once did. But in either case, they had to follow the rules in Numbers 6. No alcoholic drinks, grape juice, grapes, or raisins. No haircuts. No going near a corpse, even that of a close relative.

Any infraction—even unintentional, such as a person dropping dead beside the Nazirite—required purification rituals that involved shaving the "contaminated" hair.

Elkanah's other wife often cruelly reminded her. One day, when the family made their annual trip to the tent worship center in the nearby hill town of Shiloh, Hannah went alone to the tent. Weeping, she prayed for a son, vowing to give the boy back to God in full-time service.

Samuel was born within the year. Hannah kept him until he was weaned from breast milk—perhaps for several years in that culture. Then Hannah took him to the worship center and entrusted him to the care of Eli, the high priest. Each year, when the family came to worship, Hannah brought Samuel a new coat. In time, Hannah had three more sons and two daughters.

Samuel was still a young boy, sleeping in the tent worship center when God first spoke to him. God's message was for Eli, whose sons were abusing their privileges as priests by seducing women assistants and taking the best sacrificial meat for themselves.

"I am going to carry out all my threats against Eli and his family," God said. "I have warned him continually that judgment is coming for his family, because his sons are blaspheming God and he hasn't disciplined them" (1 Samuel 3:12–13).

"It is the LORD's will," Eli replied after young Samuel delivered the message. "Let him do what he thinks best" (1 Samuel 3:18).

Eli's sons died in battle, carrying the chest that held the Ten Commandments. When Eli got the news, he fell backward off his seat, breaking his neck.

A model of the Ark of the Covenant, the gold-plated chest that held the Ten Commandments.

JUDGE SAMUEL

After Samuel grew up, he became Israel's spiritual and political leader. He called the people together at Mizpah, a village about ten miles south of where the worship center had been before the Philistines likely destroyed it. There, he urged all Israelites to get rid of any idols they had and to worship only God.

The Philistines got word of the meeting and massed an army to attack. But Samuel prayed for help, and God responded with thunder so loud that the Philistines scattered.

To commemorate this miracle, Samuel erected a large stone and named it Ebenezer, meaning "the stone of help."

Samuel served Israel not only as a prophet, but also as a circuit-walking judge who settled disputes. His circuit formed a triangle of three cities in central Israel—Mizpah, Bethel, and Gilgal. The complete circuit covered only about thirty-five miles, a two-day walk. After each trip, Samuel returned to the hometown of his parents, where he had moved. Unable to live near them as a child, he apparently chose to be near them as an adult.

ANOINTING KINGS
SAUL AND DAVID

When Samuel grew old and appointed his greedy sons as judges, Jewish leaders took a stand. They asked for a king, which hurt Samuel deeply.

But God consoled him: "It is me they are rejecting, not you. They don't want me to be their king any longer. Ever since I brought them from Egypt they have continually forsaken me and followed other gods. And now they are giving you the same treatment. Do as they ask, but solemnly warn them about how a king will treat them" (1 Samuel 8:7–9).

So Samuel warned of:

- High taxes—a tenth of all harvest and flocks.
- Sons drafted into the army. Others drafted for work detail such as plowing the king's fields and building his palaces—as unpaid slave labor.
- Daughters drafted to cook the king's meals and make his perfume.

- The best vineyards and olive groves confiscated for the royal family.

Still, the leaders wanted a king. The Lord chose Saul, a humble donkey herder, but a tall and handsome man whose very presence commanded attention. Saul's strength was in battle, and he led Israel to many victories. But he repeatedly disobeyed God on the battlefield, once offering a sacrifice that Samuel was supposed to offer and another time taking enemy plunder he was supposed to destroy.

So God rejected him as king, and Samuel refused to see Saul any longer.

"Go to Bethlehem," God told Samuel. "Find a man named Jesse who lives there, for I have selected one of his sons to be my new king" (1 Samuel 16:1).

One by one, Jesse presented each of his sons to the prophet—each one but the youngest, David, who was taking care of sheep.

At first, Samuel saw Eliab, a son who was apparently tall and handsome, like Saul. But God said, "Don't judge by his appearance or height, for I have rejected him. The LORD doesn't make decisions the way you do! People judge by outward appearance, but the LORD looks at a person's thoughts and intentions" (1 Samuel 16:7).

God rejected all seven of the sons before Jesse called David in from the field.

"This is the one," God said. "Anoint him" (1 Samuel 16:12).

Samuel never lived to see David become king—the most beloved king in Israel's history. When Samuel died an old man, people came from all over Israel to mourn him. He was buried near his home in Ramah.

SAMUEL IN THE SPIRIT WORLD

When kings went into battle in ancient times, it was common for them to consult the gods for advice. In Israel, kings got their advice from prophets or from God in dreams. But Saul got nothing. Samuel was gone, God was silent, and a massive Philistine army rattled their swords in a nearby camp, waiting eagerly for dawn.

Saul slipped behind enemy lines and visited a psychic at the village of Endor—though he himself had banned psychic practices.

"I have to talk to a man who has died," Saul said. "Call up Samuel" (1 Samuel 28:8, 11).

To the psychic's horror, Samuel appeared.

The dead prophet had shocking news for the king.

"The LORD has done just as he said he would. He has taken the kingdom from you and given it to your rival, David," Samuel said. "The LORD will hand you and the army of Israel over to the Philistines tomorrow, and you and your sons will be here with me" (1 Samuel 28:17, 19).

King Saul and three of his sons died in battle the next day

SAPPHIRA

(suh FI ruh)
Sapphira, Greek
"good" or "beautiful"
First century AD
First mention: Acts 5:1

Wanting to look holier than they really were, a married couple named Ananias and Sapphira committed the church's first recorded sin.

They saw the attention Barnabas got for selling some property and giving the disciples the money to help needy people in the Jerusalem church. So they did the same, but they secretly kept part of the money.

The apostle Peter accused the husband, Ananias, of lying to God. This apparently so shocked the benefactor that he died on the spot. Three hours later, his wife, Sapphira, showed up, not knowing what had happened. When she, too, lied about the sale price of the land, Peter told her what had happened to her husband. He added that the same thing would happen to her. She died instantly, and fear swept through the church.

SARAH

(SAIR uh)
Sara, Hebrew
"princess"
2100s BC
First mention: Genesis 17:15
(Genesis 11:29 for "Sarai")

Sarah became mother of the Jewish nation by marrying her half brother, Abraham.

They had the same father—Terah—but different mothers. Jewish law would later forbid such marriages. But this was nearly a millennium before Moses and the law. And there were probably fewer partners to choose from.

Sarah was infertile. By the time she reached her midseventies, she had given up on becoming the birth mother who would fulfill God's promise to make Abraham into a nation. So she gave Abraham her maid—an Egyptian woman named Hagar—to use as a surrogate mother. Ishmael was born.

But God did for Sarah what he had earlier done for Abraham. Before, God had made a covenant with Abraham—and confirmed it by changing the patriarch's name from Abram. Now God did that for Sarah. "Her name will no longer be Sarai," God told Abraham. "From now on you will call her Sarah. And I will bless her and give you a son from her!" (Genesis 17:15–16).

One-hundred-year-old Abraham laughed. So did ninety-year-old Sarah.

At Sarah's insistence, Abraham evicts his secondary wife, Hagar, and the son he had with her. Sarah wanted her own son to inherit the family wealth.

But God had the last laugh. Isaac was born within the year. Sarah gave her son an appropriate name that means "he laughs."

Sarah insisted that Abraham send Hagar and Ishmael away so Isaac would inherit all of his father's property, not just a third. The oldest son typically got twice as much as any other son. God told Abraham to do as Sarah said, vowing to make Ishmael into a great nation, as well. Many consider Ishmael the father of the Arab people.

Sarah died at age 127 and was buried in a cave called Machpelah, which Abraham bought near Hebron, a village about twenty miles south of Jerusalem. King Herod built a shrine over what was believed to be Abraham's family tomb, and it's still visited by local Palestinians, Jews, and tourists.

however, warned the church, "You have a reputation for being alive—but you are dead" (Revelation 3:1).

The archangel Michael defeats Satan, a victory described in the Bible's final book.

SARDIS
(SARR diss)
Sardeis, Hebrew
First mention: Revelation 1:11

MAP 5
C2

Revelation—the book that closes the Bible—is a collection of visions addressed to seven churches, Sardis among them. Located in Turkey sixty miles inland from the ruins of Ephesus, Sardis was a leading city in New Testament times. It had a huge temple to the hunter goddess Artemis that was more than double the size of the Parthenon in Athens. It also has one of the largest ancient synagogues excavated. Jesus,

SATAN
(SAY ton)
Satan, Hebrew
"enemy," "accuser"
First mention: 1 Chronicles 21:1

It seems like heresy to present God as Satan, but the Bible does just that in one story told in two places:

- "Satan rose up against Israel and caused David to take a census" (1 Chronicles 21:1).

- "The anger of the LORD burned against Israel, and he caused David to harm them by taking a census" (2 Samuel 24:1).

It's not that God is bipolar or a split personality. It's that the term *satan* didn't originally mean the devil. In fact, it didn't refer to one particular person at all. *Satan* is a Hebrew word that works as a noun or a verb, and it can refer to anyone who's an enemy.

This enemy might be a celestial being, as when an angel told the prophet Balaam, "I have come to block [satan] your way" (Numbers 22:32). Or it can refer to a human: "God also raised up Rezon son of Eliada to be an enemy [satan] against Solomon" (1 Kings 11:23).

That doesn't mean there's no such creature as the devil—the New Testament has plenty to say about him. It just means that it took a long time for people to discover him.

TEMPTING JESUS

The story of Jesus' temptation in the desert leaves little doubt that Satan is a being. He walked and talked with Jesus, once taking Jesus to the peak of a mountain to show him the kingdoms of earth.

"I will give you the glory of these kingdoms and authority over them," Satan said, "because they are mine to give to anyone I please. I will give it all to you if you will bow down and worship me" (Luke 4:6–7).

"Get out of here, Satan," Jesus replied. "For the Scriptures say, 'You must worship the Lord your God; serve only him' " (Matthew 4:10).

Normally, New Testament writers referred to Satan as the devil. That's because they used the Greek language, which translated the Hebrew word *satan* as *diabolos*, which is "devil" in English.

INVISIBLE WARRIOR

The devil is an all-too-real, evil spirit being—and the leader of an army of evil spirits. That's what the apostle Paul wrote in a letter to Christians at Ephesus, a city in what is now Turkey.

"Put on all of God's armor so that

DEVIL IN THE GARDEN

In the beginning, it wasn't Satan who tempted Eve to eat the forbidden fruit. It was a serpent, "the shrewdest of all the creatures the LORD God had made" (Genesis 3:1).

Clearly, this creature was anti-God, because it lobbied the first couple to do the one and only thing God told them not to do.

But it took centuries before a biblical writer connected the serpent to Satan: "the ancient serpent called the Devil, or Satan, the one deceiving the whole world" (Revelation 12:9).

you will be able to stand firm against all strategies and tricks of the Devil. For we are not fighting against people made of flesh and blood, but against the evil rulers and authorities of the unseen world, against those mighty powers of darkness who rule this world, and against wicked spirits in the heavenly realms" (Ephesians 6:11–12).

The prince of demons sets traps for people. Paul warned his close friend Timothy to avoid choosing a new Christian as a church leader: "He might be proud of being chosen so soon, and the Devil will use that pride to make him fall" (1 Timothy 3:6).

Another biblical writer offered a strategy for defeating this invisible warrior: "Resist the Devil, and he will flee from you. Draw close to God, and God will draw close to you" (James 4:7–8).

LOST CAUSE
Though the New Testament talks at length about humanity's ongoing warfare with Satan, it leaves no doubt about how the war will end.

Satan loses.

After seeing a dramatic vision of the future, a New Testament writer named John reported what happened after Satan led the nations of the world against God's people. Fire from the sky wiped out the attacking armies. "Then the Devil, who betrayed them, was thrown into the lake of fire that burns

with sulfur, joining the beast and the false prophet. There they will be tormented day and night forever and ever" (Revelation 20:10).

This report sounds like news from a time traveler in the future to humanity struggling for spiritual survival in a pitched battle in the here and now. And it's reminiscent of news that the commander of God's army delivered to Joshua when the Israelites were getting ready to march on Jericho: "I have given you Jericho" (Joshua 6:2).

The battle lies in the future, but in God's reality, the victory has already been won.

Desperate to know the outcome of a battle, Saul asks a psychic to call the spirit of Samuel. In a few hours, Samuel warns Saul and his sons will be dead.

SAUL
Saul, Hebrew
"the one asked for"
About 1065–1010 BC
First mention: 1 Samuel 9:2

Israel's first king was a shy donkey man who preferred herding animals to people.

Saul raised donkeys for his father.

SAUL'S FAMILY

Saul had five sons and two daughters by his wife Ahinoam and another two sons by his secondary wife (concubine) Rizpah. Merab, a daughter, was his oldest. Jonathan was the oldest son and heir to the throne.

Saul chose his cousin, Abner, as military commander. When Saul died, Abner appointed as king one of Saul's surviving sons, Ishbosheth. But Ishbosheth's shaky reign lasted only two years, before a couple of his commanders cut his head off and took it to David—who executed them both.

In fact, he was out hunting strays when he met the prophet Samuel, who invited him to a meal, then anointed him king. When it came time for Samuel to introduce Saul to the people, the reluctant leader, who was about thirty, hid among a baggage train of pack animals, probably donkeys.

It must have been hard for Saul to hide there, or anywhere, since he was "the most handsome man in Israel—head and shoulders taller than anyone else in the land" (1 Samuel 9:2). Despite his good looks and height, he thought little of himself. When Samuel said Israel's hopes rested on Saul and his family, Saul replied, "But I'm only from Benjamin, the smallest tribe in Israel, and my family is the least important of all the families of that tribe! Why are you talking like this to me?" (1 Samuel 9:21).

FROM PLOWED FIELD TO BATTLEFIELD

Israelites didn't rally around him. Some in his hometown of Gibeah, a few miles north of Jerusalem, complained, " 'How can this man save us?' And they despised him and refused to bring him gifts" (1 Samuel 10:27).

The Bible's first scene of Saul as king describes him walking behind a team of oxen, plowing a field. Not a kingly endeavor. But what happened next certainly was.

Ammonites in what is now Jordan had been oppressing the two tribes east of the Jordan River—Gad and Reuben. Ammon's king ordered the right eyes of each Israelite gouged out—to humiliate the nation. Some Israelites escaped north to the city of Jabesh-gilead, but the Ammonites followed. When the Israelites offered to surrender, the merciless king said only if they agreed to lose their right eyes. With a week to think about whether or not depth perception was worth dying for, they sent messengers to Saul pleading for help.

"The Spirit of God came mightily upon Saul, and he became very angry" (1 Samuel 11:6). He cut his oxen to pieces and sent them with messengers throughout Israel. The message was essentially this: Anyone who didn't join Saul in battle would become like these lifeless hunks of meat.

More than three hundred thousand

came, and Saul led his militia on a surprise attack that slaughtered the Ammonites.

"Now where are those men who said Saul shouldn't rule over us?" the crowds cheered. "Bring them here, and we will kill them!" (1 Samuel 11:12). Saul vetoed the execution proposal and gave God credit for the victory.

BATTLEFIELD BLUNDERS

Saul was at his best in battle—and that's about the only good thing the Bible has to say about his performance. Two battlefield mistakes, however, doomed his dynasty.

After the Israelites captured a Philistine garrison, the Philistines mustered a massive army. Terrified, the Israelites started deserting. Samuel promised to come within seven days to offer a sacrifice so the battle could begin. But he didn't arrive in time. Saul thought if he waited any longer, Israel wouldn't have an army left. So he offered the sacrifice himself, as though he were a priest or a prophet. Samuel arrived a short time later.

"How foolish!" Samuel said. "You have disobeyed the command of the LORD your God. Had you obeyed, the LORD would have established your kingdom over Israel forever. But now your dynasty must end" (1 Samuel 13:13–14).

Saul won the battle, thanks to his oldest son, Jonathan, who led a surprise attack that panicked the Philistines. Saul also won a later battle against the Amalekites, nomadic herders in the Negev desert, but again he disobeyed God. Instead of wiping out all traces of the enemy, he brought back the king, and he brought some animals he said were for a sacrifice. "Obedience is far better than sacrifice," Samuel scolded (1 Samuel 15:22). Samuel killed the Amalekite king himself and never again met with Saul.

"The Spirit of the LORD had left Saul, and the LORD sent a tormenting spirit that filled him with depression and fear" (1 Samuel 16:14). Saul's servants recommended music therapy. They arranged for a shepherd boy named David to come and play a harp. Neither the king nor his servants knew that by this time Samuel had already anointed David as the future king.

After young David killed the Philistine champion, Goliath, the Israelites found a new hero. Saul grew increasingly jealous, trying twice to spear David while he played music. Saul plotted ways to kill him, giving him dangerous assignments in hopes David would get killed. But David's legend grew ever larger.

Finally, Saul sent troops to kill David at home. But David's wife, who was Saul's daughter Michal, helped him escape. Saul tried for years to capture David, wasting time and resources that could have been better spent securing Israel's borders.

ONE LAST BATTLE

Saul apparently decided to capture the

city of Beth-shan, to gain control of trade routes through the Jezreel valley. He assembled his army on a nearby hilltop, but the Philistines got word of it and mustered an army so massive that it terrified even Saul.

Samuel was dead, and God had stopped talking to Saul, so the king had no way of knowing what to do. He resorted to consulting a psychic—though he had ordered anyone practicing the occult to be executed. Under cover of night and in disguise, he made his way behind enemy lines and to the village of Endor.

Saul asked the psychic to call up Samuel's spirit. To the psychic's horror, Samuel appeared with a message for Saul: "The LORD will hand you and the army of Israel over to the Philistines tomorrow, and you and your sons will be here with me" (1 Samuel 28:19).

In the battle, the Philistines overran the Israelites. Three of Saul's sons died in the fierce fighting: Jonathan, Abinadab, and Malkishua. Wounded by archers, Saul asked his armor bearer to finish him off before the Philistines could capture him. The armor bearer was too afraid, so Saul fell on his own sword.

The Philistines took Saul's armor and displayed it as a trophy in one of their temples. Then they cut off Saul's head and tied the bodies of him and his sons to the walls of Beth-shan, the city he intended to defeat.

It's unclear how long Saul served as king—perhaps twenty-five years or more. However long it was, the people he saved in his first battle at Jabesh-gilead honored his memory. Some of their warriors made a nighttime, twenty-mile march to Beth-shan and took the bodies of Saul and his sons back to Jabesh-gilead, where they were cremated.

SEA OF GALILEE

MAP 4
C3

(GAL uh lee)
Galila, Hebrew
Galilaia, Greek
"circle"
First mention: Matthew 4:13

It's not a sea at all. It's a freshwater lake no more than 160 feet deep at its deepest.

But it can churn up deadly storms in an eye blink. That's because of where's it's located—at the bottom of a bowl, with hills and even the nearby ocean towering above it. The Sea of Galilee squats fifteen hundred feet below the Mediterranean Sea, thirty miles away. Hills and mountains surround the lake, with ravines on the west side channeling cool sea breezes toward it. When a burst of cool air crashes into hot air rising from the valley lake, the swirl of wind can churn up angry waves high enough to sink fishing boats.

Jesus and his disciples got caught in such a storm one day while crossing the lake. "On the way across, Jesus lay down for a nap, and while he was sleeping the wind began to rise. A fierce storm developed that threatened to swamp them, and they were in real danger" (Luke 8:23). The disciples woke Jesus, and he calmed the storm.

HARP LAKE

Locals don't generally call this lake the Sea of Galilee. Some call it Lake Tiberias, after a major city on the western shore. Others called it Harp Sea, as it would translate into English—or the Sea of Kinnereth, using the Hebrew word   for harp.

An Israeli tour guide holds up a fish named after a famous Galilean fisherman. Saint Peter's fish, as it's called, is a basslike creature caught in the Sea of Galilee and served with its head intact.

That's because the lake is shaped like a harp—a big harp about thirteen miles long and seven miles across at its widest point.

The lake functions like a reservoir along the Jordan River. The Jordan flows into the lake at the north and out of the lake at the southern tip. In Jesus' time, fishing villages dotted the northern shores. That's where he called most of his disciples, and that's where he set up his ministry headquarters, in Capernaum.

Fishermen like Peter, James, and John worked in the thriving industry. There was no other large lake in the country, and Jews weren't fond of ocean fishing. The lake held three main kinds of fish. There were sardines—perhaps the "few small fish" Jesus used to feed a crowd of thousands (Matthew 15:34). There were barbels, named after the barb-looking feelers on their upper lips. And there was a mild-tasting, basslike fish that lakeshore restaurants serve tourists and call St. Peter's fish.

Peter certainly caught plenty of them.

THE BOAT

When a 1986 drought shrunk the massive lake, widening the shoreline by several yards, two men on a walk noticed the outline of a boat in the mud.

It turned out to be a fishing boat from the time of Jesus—perhaps the same kind Jesus sailed on with his disciples.

Experts quickly decided to get it out before the lake rose. It's now on display near where it was discovered. At about eight yards long and two yards wide, it would have held fifteen men—enough for Jesus and all twelve of his disciples.

SENNACHERIB

(sin NACK ur rib)

Senherib, Hebrew

Sinahheeriba, Assyrian

The god "Sin has substituted the dead brothers," perhaps meaning Sennacherib was the first son in his family to survive

Reigned 704–681 BC

First mention: 2 Kings 18:13

Stories in the Bible paint one picture of what happened when the Assyrian king Sennacherib and his army surrounded Jerusalem. But Assyrian records from the king paint quite another.

He was a conquering hero in his version and a conquered coward in the Bible. Oddly enough, when the two versions are read together, the story makes sense.

The Assyrian king Sennacherib's report that he trapped Hezekiah inside Jerusalem.

Sennacherib invaded Judah in 701 BC, when Hezekiah was king. After capturing most fortified cities, Sennacherib surrounded Jerusalem. But the Bible says that before he could take the city, an angel killed 185,000 Assyrians and sent the others running for home. An Assyrian clay prism confirms the invasion, reports that Sennacherib conquered forty-six cities, but stops short of claiming victory over Jerusalem.

"As for Hezekiah," Sennacherib said for the record, "I made [him] a prisoner in Jerusalem, his royal residence, like a bird in a cage. I surrounded him."

Sennacherib was later murdered at home by two of his sons.

SEPPHORIS

(SEFF uh riss)

Sepphoris, Greek

Zippori, Hebrew

Not even mentioned in the Bible, Sepphoris was the capital of Galilee during most of Jesus' lifetime—and was only about four miles from his Nazareth home, to the northwest. A busy city on the crossroads of two ancient highways, it probably generated work for carpenters such as Joseph and Jesus. Since Sepphoris rested between Nazareth and Cana, Jesus may have passed through the town on his way to the wedding at Cana, where he performed his first miracle.

SETH
Set, Hebrew
Perhaps "granted"
Before 4000 BC
First mention: Genesis 4:25

Adam and Eve had a third son after they lost the first two. Cain killed Abel, then God banished Cain from the region. Eve named her third child Seth, which apparently means "granted," because "God has granted me another son" (Genesis 4:25). He looked very much like his father. Seth had a son named Enosh, along with other sons and daughters. An ancestor of Noah, Seth lived to be 912.

SHADRACH
(SHAD rack)
Sadrak, Hebrew
Sudur Aku, Akkadian
"at command of Aku," moon god
About 600 BC
First mention: Daniel 1:7

A few years before the Babylonian king Nebuchadnezzar wiped Israel off the map, he tried to force the Jewish nation in line by taking some leaders hostage. Among them were three princes: Shadrach, Meshach, and Abednego.

The king brought them to his capital. In time, officials recognized their wisdom and appointed them royal advisers. They each got Babylonian names to replace their Hebrew names of Hananiah, Mishael, and Azariah.

They're famous for surviving an

To the king's horror, Shadrach and his two companions survive inside a furnace intended to execute them.

attempted execution inside a blazing furnace. This was their punishment for refusing to worship a ninety-foot-tall, gold statue of the king. But when the king looked into the furnace, he saw the three walking around—with a fourth person. "Servants of the Most High God," the king yelled, "come out!" (Daniel 3:26). When they did, they didn't even smell like smoke.

SHALMANESER
(SHALL muh NEE zur)
Salmaneser, Hebrew
Reigned 726–722 BC
First mention: 2 Kings 17:3

Shalmaneser V was a relatively unimportant king in Assyrian history, but in

343

Jewish history, he was a heavyweight. The ten lost tribes of Israel are lost because of him. His army invaded the northern Jewish nation of Israel because Israel stopped sending him the taxes he demanded. He besieged the capital of Samaria for three years before overrunning it, exiling the survivors, and repopulating the nation with Assyrian settlers. Some of these settlers intermarried with the Jews left behind, producing a people of mixed race and faith called Samaritans.

SHARON

(SHARE on)
Saron, Hebrew
First mention: 1 Chronicles 5:16

MAP 2
C3

"I am the rose of Sharon, the lily of the valley," sang one young woman to her lover (Song of Songs 2:1). The Sharon Plain was a fertile tract of land along Israel's coast. It stretched about ten miles wide and thirty miles long—between the Mount Carmel mountains in the north and Tel Aviv. Though much of Sharon consists of sand dunes and marshland, parts of it are ideal for grazing sheep and cattle—which is how it was used in Bible times.

SHEBA

(SHE buh)
Seba, Hebrew
First mention: 1 Kings 10:1

MAP 3
E5

King Solomon welcomed the queen of Sheba, who came to test his wisdom and brought with her "a great caravan of camels loaded with spices, huge quantities of gold, and precious jewels" (2 Chronicles 9:1). Scholars speculate that the queen's real motive was to jump-start trade with Israel.

It's uncertain where Sheba was located. One persistent and plausible theory points to the southwest corner of Arabia, in what is now Yemen, below Saudi Arabia. The area had an advanced culture by Solomon's time. And African trading resources—gold, jewels, rare wood, and exotic animals—were a mere seventeen miles away, across the Red Sea's strait of Bab el Mandeb, Arabic for "gate of tears."

SHECHEM

(SHECK come)
Sekem, Hebrew
"shoulder of a mountain"
1800s BC
First mention: Genesis 33:19

Prince Shechem of Shechem is the reason the village bearing his name got wiped out. He raped Dinah, daughter of Jacob. And Dinah had twelve brothers.

Jacob's family camped near the village of Shechem about thirty miles north of Jerusalem, in the valley pass between two peaks—Mount Gerizim and Mount Ebal. When Dinah visited the village, the prince kidnapped her, raped her, then asked to marry her. Dinah's brothers, reeling with vengeful hate, insisted that all the men of the village honor the covenant that Jacob's ancestors had made with God—and they were to do this through circumcision.

Dinah's brothers got even while the

The village of Shechem, along the pass between two mountains: Gerizim (left) and Ebal.

men were still suffering from the painful surgery. Two of Dinah's full brothers—Simeon and Levi, who, like Dinah, were children of Leah—killed every man in the village. Then Jacob's other sons helped plunder the village, taking the women and children as slaves.

Jacob was horrified at what his sons had done. He told them, "You have made me stink among all the people of this land" (Genesis 34:30). The family moved south a day's walk, to Bethel.

SHECHEM

(SHECK come)
Sekem, Hebrew
"shoulder of a mountain"
First mention: Genesis 12:6

MAP 2
C4

Some of Israel's most important events took place in a valley in the middle of Israel. That's where the city of Shechem grew up, at the end of a narrow pass between two gently rolling hills—Mount Gerizim and Mount Ebal.

Shechem is why the Jews feel the land belongs to them. It was there God led Abraham, then told him, "I am going to give this land to your offspring" (Genesis 12:7). And it's where Joshua brought the invading Hebrews of the Exodus to renew God's agreement with Abraham's descendants.

Other key events at Shechem:

- Jacob's daughter, Dinah, was raped
- Dinah's brothers killed all the men and enslaved the others
- Designated a city for priestly workers, the Levites
- Designated one of six cities of refuge, where people who accidentally killed someone could get a trial
- Ten northern tribes seceded from the union and formed their own country
- Selected as capital of the northern Jewish nation of Israel

Ruins of ancient Shechem lie near the modern city of Nablus. The ruins are known by the Arab name Tell Balatah. That comes from the village of Balatah, built on part of the *tell,* a word that refers to a mound of ruins.

In Bible times, main caravan routes converged at Shechem, which had a reliable source of underground water.

SHEM
Sem, Hebrew
Before 2500 BC
First mention: Genesis 5:32

The oldest of Noah's three sons, Shem produced the line of descendants called Semites, which includes Jews and Arabs.

Shem and his youngest brother, Japheth, treated their father respectfully when the middle brother, Ham, reported that Noah was drunk and naked. Shem and Japheth backed into Noah's tent and covered him. Noah cursed Ham for his disrespect, saying that Ham's descendants should serve those of Ham's brothers. Japheth's descendants settled in what is now Turkey and Iran. Ham's descendants settled in Egypt and Canaan. Many consider Noah's curse fulfilled when Joshua and the Hebrews invaded Canaan.

SHILOH
(SHY low)
Siloh, Hebrew
First mention: Joshua 18:1

MAP 2
C4

Jerusalem was not Israel's first capital. Shiloh was—for at least a century.

A high plains village nearly half a mile above sea level and thirty miles north of Jerusalem, in Israel's hill country, Shiloh was where Joshua and the Israelites pitched the tent of God, or the worship center called the tabernacle. This is where the Israelites came to offer sacrifices to God and to celebrate religious holidays.

Samuel's infertile mother went there with her husband on just such an occasion. That's when she asked God for a son—vowing to return the boy to full-time service for God. Samuel was born within the year, and after he was weaned from breast milk, he was brought to the Shiloh priest to serve at the worship center.

Shiloh is where Joshua divided the land of Israel among the tribes and where the Israelites met in times of crisis.

The Philistines apparently destroyed the village and worship center after routing the Israelite army, killing the priest's two sons, and capturing Israel's sacred chest that contained the Ten Commandments. The Philistines later returned the chest because it caused a plague wherever it went. With Shiloh gone, the chest was kept in storage until David brought it to his new capital in Jerusalem.

What's left of Shiloh is a seven-acre mound of ruins known as Seilun. Archaeological evidence seems to support the theory that the Philistines destroyed it in about 1050 BC.

SHITTIM
(SHIT um)
Sittim, Hebrew
"acacia," a kind of tree
First mention: Numbers 25:1

MAP 1
D5

Before invading Israel, the Hebrews camped at Shittim, about eight miles east of the Jordan River in what is now Jordan. This is where some Hebrew men took part in fertility rites with local women, causing a plague that killed twenty-four thousand people. In this place also called "Acacia" in some translations, Moses later declared Joshua his successor, then gave his farewell message before dying. From this camp, Joshua sent scouts to explore the border town of Jericho. Many scholars say the one-time village of Shittim lies beneath the mound of ruins called Tell el-Hamman.

SHUNEM

(SHOE num)
Sunem, Hebrew
First mention: Joshua 19:18

It was in Shunem—a village in the rolling hills about seven miles south of where Jesus grew up in Nazareth—that the prophet Elisha raised the dead son of a widow. Elisha lay on the boy's body, placing "his mouth on the child's mouth" (2 Kings 4:34). The boy's cold body warmed up and came back to life.

Shunem, in what is now Sulam, is also where the Philistine army camped the night before overrunning the nearby Israelite army, killing Saul and his three sons.

SHUR DESERT

(SURE)
Sur, Hebrew
"wall"
First mention: Genesis 16:7

After Moses and the Hebrews crossed the Red Sea, "they moved out into the Shur Desert" (Exodus 15:22). It's unclear where the Hebrews crossed the Red Sea, so it's impossible to tell exactly where the Shur Desert was. But the general location was along the northwest part of the Sinai Peninsula. The Bible also occasionally refers only to Shur, without mentioning a desert. Since the word means "wall," some scholars say it's possible that Shur also refers to a line of Egyptian forts defending the eastern border and located near what is now the Suez Canal. If so, the Shur Desert may have been just east of those forts.

SIDON

(SIGH done)
Sidon, Hebrew
First mention: Genesis 10:19

In Lebanon, about thirty-five miles north of the Israeli border and more than halfway to Beirut, lies the coastal city of Sayda. In Bible times, it was Sidon, a city of Phoenicia that was famous for its wine and purple dyes. Lumberjacks from Sidon cut cedars of Lebanon for the Jews to use in building Solomon's temple as well as the replacement temple five hundred years later. At least one of Solomon's thousand wives came from Sidon, perhaps bringing her idols with her. God split

347

Israel in two because Solomon worshiped the gods of his wives.

SILAS
(SI luhs)
Silas, Greek
Silvanus, Latin
First century AD
First mention: Acts 15:22

Silas, also called in the New Testament by his Roman name, Silvanus, is best known as Paul's associate who spent a night in prison with him. As the two sang hymns at midnight in Philippi, in what is now Greece, an earthquake shook the doors open. But the two stayed inside and converted the jailer's entire family.

Before traveling with Paul, Silas was chosen as a church leader in Jerusalem. He was apparently well educated, because Peter—a fisherman who probably wasn't well educated—credits him with helping write the eloquent letter of 1 Peter.

SILOAM POOL
(suh LOW uhm)
Siloam, Greek
Siloah, Hebrew
"sent"
First mention: Nehemiah 3:15

See Jerusalem

MAP 2
C5

Jerusalem got its water from the Gihon Spring outside the city walls.

A woman draws water from Siloam Pool, where Jesus told a blind man to wash his eyes for healing.

King Hezekiah wanted to make sure the people had all the water they needed when invaders surrounded the city. So he assigned miners to chisel a tunnel nearly six hundred yards through solid rock, from the spring to what became the Siloam Pool inside the city. This is the pool where Jesus sent a blind man to wash his eyes. Jesus mixed spit with dirt and gently rubbed it into the man's eyes. "So the man went and washed, and came back seeing!" (John 9:7).

SIMEON

(SIM ee uhn)
Simon, Hebrew
"one who hears"
1800s BC
First mention: Genesis 29:33

Jacob's second of twelve sons, Simeon took the lead in wiping out the village of a Canaanite prince who raped his young sister, Dinah. Simeon, along with his younger brother Levi, decided to avenge their sister—all three were born to Jacob's first wife, Leah. The two brothers killed all the men of Shechem, and the other brothers joined in to plunder the village and take the women and children as slaves.

In his deathbed blessing, Jacob complained about the habitual violence of Simeon and Levi and predicted their descendants would be scattered throughout Israel. In fact, Levi's tribe of priests received only forty-eight cities scattered throughout Israel. And Israel's southland tribes of Simeon and Judah eventually took the name of the larger tribe—Judah.

SIMON

(SI muhn)
Simon, Greek and Hebrew
First century AD
First mention: 1. Matthew 10:4
2. Matthew 26:6
3. Matthew 27:32
4. Acts 8:9
5. Acts 9:43

1. **Zealot and disciple of Jesus.** Jesus had two disciples named Simon, one of whom he renamed. The other was Simon the Zealot. What Simon was zealous about remains debatable.

The Greek word translated as "zealot" or "zealous one" could mean he was an intense person and zealous about a lot of concerns or perhaps about God and the Jewish way of life. But the word also applied to a revolutionary movement to free Israel from the Romans. If Simon was this kind of a zealot, he would have had difficulties with his fellow disciple Matthew, who collaborated with the Romans by collecting taxes.

2. **Leper.** There's confusion over whether or not this Simon was also a Jewish scholar, called a Pharisee. Matthew and Mark identify Simon only as a leper—presumably a healed one—who lived in the village of Bethany. Simon hosted a meal for Jesus. At that meal a woman anointed Jesus with expensive oil, and Jesus' disciple Judas complained about this wasted money. But in Luke's similar account of what may have been the same meal, Simon was a Jewish scholar, the woman who anointed Jesus had a bad reputation, and the person complaining was Simon.

Simon's complaint was that Jesus was a fake prophet who couldn't even tell that the woman was immoral. Jesus read Simon's mind and told him a parable. One man wrote off the debts of two others—one debtor owed ten times as much as the other. Jesus asked Simon who would be most grateful. Simon answered, "I suppose the one

At a meal hosted by Simon the leper, Simon wonders why Jesus allows an immoral woman to anoint his feet with oil. Jesus says she's expressing gratitude for sins forgiven.

for whom he canceled the larger debt" (Luke 7:43). Jesus said that Simon hadn't even welcomed him properly, but the grateful woman was still welcoming him.

3. **Cross-carrying Cyrene.** Roman soldiers beat and tortured Jesus to the point that he may not have been able to carry his cross to the execution site. Perhaps that's why soldiers forced that job onto a spectator in the crowd—Simon of Cyrene, a city in northern Africa. Simon "was coming in from the country just then" (Luke 23:26). He may have been among thousands of Jews who came from abroad to celebrate the religious holiday of Passover. Mark added that Simon was the father of Alexander and Rufus, suggesting

that Simon's sons later became well-known leaders in the church.

4. **Sorcerer.** Many Christians fled Jerusalem after a Jewish mob stoned Stephen to death and launched an assault on the new religious movement. Philip, one of Stephen's associates, traveled north to Samaria. His preaching, backed up by miracles of healing, won many converts—including a sorcerer named Simon. When the apostles heard about Philip's success, they sent Peter and John to investigate. The apostles not only approved; they prayed for these new Christians to receive the Holy Spirit.

The Holy Spirit's arrival must have included some show of power—perhaps like the sudden ability to speak in foreign languages, as happened when the Spirit first came to the apostles. Simon offered to pay Peter for the ability to give people the Holy Spirit.

"May your money perish with you for thinking God's gift can be bought!" Peter answered (Acts 8:20). The last we hear of Simon, he's asking Peter to pray for him. Simon's name, however, lives on in the word "simony," referring to a person buying or selling a church job or title.

5. **Leatherworker.** Peter was staying at the seaside home of Simon, a tanner in Joppa, when he had a vision that helped him see the spiritual potential in Gentiles. Simon's home was a fitting place for Peter to have this vision because Gentiles and tanners were both considered to be ritually unclean—tanners because they worked with dead animals. Jews who came in contact with them had to go through cleansing rituals before entering the temple courtyard.

Peter seemed to have no problem staying with a Jewish tanner, perhaps because he had seen Jesus among other ritually unclean people, such as lepers. But Peter needed convincing before taking his ministry to the Gentiles. A vision of God telling him to eat nonkosher food, followed by a divine call to the home of a Roman soldier who converted, helped Peter understand that the Good News about Jesus was for everyone.

SISERA

(SIS ur uh)
Sisera, Hebrew
1100s BC
First mention: Judges 4:2

A woman with a hammer and a tent peg put an end to this Canaanite commander, whose army and chariot corps had terrorized the Israelites for twenty years.

Sisera lived in Hazor, a city north of the Sea of Galilee. He led his troops and nine hundred iron chariots on a two-day march south to engage Deborah's Israelite militia at Mount Tabor. But as he approached along the river valley, a rainstorm bogged down his chariots. That's when the Israelites attacked.

Sisera ran for his life. He didn't stop until he came to the tent of a traveling metalworker. The nomad's wife, Jael, invited the weary Sisera to lie down. When Sisera asked for water, she gave him warm milk—which acts as a sedative.

"When Sisera fell asleep from exhaustion, Jael quietly crept up to him with a hammer and tent peg. Then she drove the tent peg through his temple and into the ground, and so he died" (Judges 4:21).

SMYRNA

(SMUR nah)
Smyrna, Greek
First mention: Revelation 1:11

MAP 5
B2

Revelation's end-time prophecies are addressed to seven churches in what is now Turkey. Only two got good news from Jesus—Smyrna and Philadelphia.

Jesus had this to say about Christians in Smyrna, a coastal city with three pagan temples: "I know about your suffering and your poverty—but you are rich!" (Revelation 2:9). Jesus added that if they endured suffering even in the face of death, he would give them eternal life.

SODOM

(SOD dum)
Sedom, Hebrew
"field" or "burning"
First mention: Genesis 10:19

MAP 1
D6

Lot thought he made a good choice when he moved to Sodom. He and his uncle Abraham agreed to separate so their huge flocks wouldn't have to compete for pasture and water. Lot chose the fertile plains of the Jordan River valley.

In time, Sodom and the neighboring city of Gomorrah grew wicked. "Sodom's sins were pride, laziness, and gluttony, while the poor and needy suffered" (Ezekiel 16:49). Lot's story also reveals sex sins: rape and homosexuality. In fact, *sodomy*—homosexual sex—takes its name from this city.

God sent two angels to warn Lot to get out of town. The men of Sodom surrounded Lot's house, intending to rape the angels. But the angels blinded

WHERE WAS SODOM?

There are two theories.

1. North Dead Sea. The Bible puts Sodom and Gomorrah in "the fertile plains of the Jordan Valley" (Genesis 13:10). The Jordan River ends where it empties into the Dead Sea, about five miles south of Jericho. The five cities of the plain, including Sodom and Gomorrah, may have been there. But no cities of that era have been found. And the geological details in the story—tar pits, sulfur, and salt—better fit the southern theory.

2. South Dead Sea. The valley continues into the Dead Sea, the lowest spot on earth, about thirteen hundred feet below sea level.

When the cities of the plains gathered their armies to fight off an invader, some soldiers fell into "tar pits" (Genesis 14:10). Those are in and around the southern shallows of the Dead Sea—an area now desolate, but perhaps fertile in ancient times. What's left of Sodom and Gomorrah may be submerged in those shallows.

Some scholars, however, suggest several ruins above water, along the southeast shoreline—such as Bab edh-Dra. Excavations show several were inhabited in ancient times and were destroyed by fire.

them. Before dawn, the angels took the hands of Lot, his wife, and their two daughters and rushed them out of town, telling them to run for their lives and not to look back.

At dawn, "the LORD rained down fire and burning sulfur from the heavens on Sodom and Gomorrah. He utterly destroyed them. . . . Lot's wife looked back as she was following along behind him, and she became a pillar of salt" (Genesis 19:24–26).

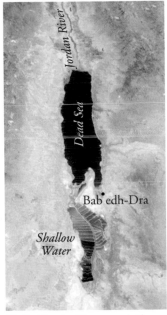

The Dead Sea, viewed from a space shuttle. Various theories place Sodom under the light-colored shallows to the south, along the southeast shoreline near Bab edh-Dra ruins, or in the Jordan River valley north of the sea.

SOLOMON

(SAH luh muhn)
Selomoh, Hebrew, from the similar-sounding word *shalom*
"peace"
Reigned about 970–930 BC
First mention: 2 Samuel 5:14

Solomon, the Bible says, was the wisest man on earth. But he did the dumbest thing in the world.

He proved himself dumber than the donkey herder, King Saul, and dumber than the shepherd, King David. Late in his life, when wisdom generally soars, he did what neither of the kings before him had tolerated—he broke God's first and most important commandment. He worshiped other gods.

Perhaps the pensive essay of Ecclesiastes, often attributed to him, gives a glimpse into why he did this: "I said to myself, 'Come now, let's give pleasure a try.' . . . While still seeking wisdom, I clutched at foolishness" (Ecclesiastes 2:1, 3).

GOD GRANTS ONE WISH
Solomon's wisdom came from a dream conversation with God.

Before Solomon built his famous Jerusalem temple, he went to a shrine at Gibeon a few miles north of Jerusalem and offered a thousand sacrifices to God. That night God came to him in a dream and invited him to ask for anything.

"I am like a little child who doesn't know his way around," Solomon replied. "Give me an understanding mind so that I can govern your people

SOLOMON AT HIS WISEST

Two prostitute roommates had babies within three days of each other. While sleeping one night, one prostitute rolled over on her son and accidentally suffocated him. She quietly swapped sons with the other woman, and insisted it was her baby. The other woman knew better.

Two women and a baby showed up in Solomon's court.

"All right, bring me a sword," Solomon said. "Cut the living child in two and give half to each of these women!" (1 Kings 3:24–25).

In today's culture, that sounds like an obvious trick. But in the ancient Middle East, all-powerful rulers sometimes did crazy things like that. An Egyptian ruler named Haremhab had a law for anyone interfering with boat traffic on the Nile: "His nose shall be cut off." Assyrian rulers sometimes cut off noses, ears, and even lips. One Ammonite king in what is now Jordan gouged out the right eye of every Hebrew he could find east of the Jordan River. Kings with sharp instruments were taken seriously.

The baby snatcher was fine with Solomon's ruling. But the horrified mother replied, "Oh no, my lord! Give her the child—please do not kill him!" (1 Kings 3:26).

That's when everyone knew who the real mother was.

well and know the difference between right and wrong. For who by himself is able to govern this great nation of yours?" (1 Kings 3:7, 9).

"I will give you a wise and understanding mind such as no one else has ever had or ever will have!" God replied (1 Kings 3:12).

Solomon became a widely sought-after sage and a prolific writer. "He composed some 3,000 proverbs and wrote 1,005 songs" (1 Kings 4:32). He's credited with writing or at least influencing many of the wise sayings in Proverbs, in addition to Ecclesiastes, a reflective book that explores the meaning of life, as well as the Song of Solomon, a tribute to love.

Solomon hosted representatives from many neighboring nations who came to learn from him. Most famous was his visit from the queen of Sheba, possibly from a kingdom in what is now southern Saudi Arabia or Yemen. She brought a caravan of camels loaded with spices, gold, and jewels to honor Solomon—and perhaps to jump-start trade between the two nations. Though the queen was used to luxury and probably surrounded herself with wise advisers, Solomon's wisdom and wealth left her breathless.

"Everything I heard in my country about your achievements and wisdom is true!" she said. "Truly I had not heard the half of it!" (1 Kings 10:6–7).

SETTLING SCORES

Solomon came close to missing out on all this fame and fortune. As one of King David's many younger sons—well over a dozen of them—Solomon nearly got brushed aside when it came time to choose the next king.

As Solomon's father lay dying, the oldest son, Adonijah—the person most people expected would become the next king—was already celebrating his upcoming coronation with a banquet. Celebrating with him, showing their support, were the military commander Joab, a chief priest named Abiathar, and many of David's other sons.

It was Solomon's mother, Bathsheba, along with the prophet Nathan, who reported the banquet to David and reminded him of his promise to transfer the throne to Solomon. David honored that promise and gave some advice to the new king. In addition to urging Solomon to obey God's laws, David asked his son to settle some old scores. For Joab, who had murdered two of David's commanders and killed his coup-leading son Absalom, David instructed, "Don't let him die in peace" (1 Kings 2:6). And for Shimei, who cursed David as he fled during Absalom's attempted coup, the king said, "You will know how to arrange a bloody death for him" (1 Kings 2:9).

Solomon settles a case in which two women each claim they are the mother of a living child, while neither claims the dead one.

SOLOMON AT HIS DUMBEST

There's a tie for first place.

• Marriage can be plenty stressful with just one partner. "He had seven hundred wives and three hundred concubines [secondary wives]" (1 Kings 11:3).

• In his old age Solomon worshiped idols.

Actually the two dumbnesses were connected. Solomon married foreign women as part of peace treaties and trade deals. A foreign ruler was less likely to attack Israel or renege on a trade deal if his daughter was living in the harem of Israel's king.

Solomon's brides, however, didn't just bring their baggage to Jerusalem; they brought their gods, as well: "In Solomon's old age, they turned his heart to worship their gods instead of trusting only in the LORD" (1 Kings 11:4).

In time, Solomon found other reasons to justify executing both men. He also executed his brother Adonijah for asking to marry one of David's young wives, apparently in an attempt to position himself for a coup—passing himself and his wife off as the rightful king and queen.

GOLDEN AGE, HIGH PRICE TAG

Israel was never bigger or richer than it was during Solomon's day. Solomon owed a lot of that to his father, a gifted warrior who overpowered Israel's enemies and expanded the nation's borders.

Solomon didn't have to fight any major battles. He controlled the land from Egypt's border in the south to the Euphrates River in what is now northern Syria, more than two hundred miles beyond Damascus. His kingdom stretched eastward from the Mediterranean Sea to deep within what is now Jordan. That means he controlled both of the main caravan routes connecting Arabia, Egypt, and the rest of Africa in the south to all the nations in the north—the Way of the Sea along the coast and the King's Highway through Jordan.

He used those routes to develop international trade relations, to collect taxes from caravans, and to receive representatives delivering tax tribute from neighboring kingdoms. "Each year Solomon received about twenty-five tons of gold. This did not include the additional revenue he received from merchants and traders, all the kings of Arabia, and the governors of the land" (1 Kings 10:14–15).

He needed it all. And more.

He needed it to maintain his army, with a massive infantry, twelve thousand horses, and fourteen hundred charioteers. He needed it to fund his unprecedented building program—fortifying cities throughout the nation, undertaking the seven-year building project of the temple, and the thirteen-year project of his palace. And he needed it to feed his palace staff. "The daily food requirements for Solomon's palace were 150 bushels of choice flour and 300 bushels of meal, ten oxen from the fattening pens, twenty pasture-fed cattle, one hundred sheep or goats, as well as deer, gazelles, roebucks, and choice fowl" (1 Kings 4:22–23).

The price tag was high. At one point, Solomon gave twenty Galilean cities to the king of Tyre, in what is now Lebanon, in return for lumber and gold for his building projects. In the long run, however, Solomon lost

SOLOMON'S PREFAB TEMPLE

Jews worshiped at a tent for several hundred years, from the time of Moses through David. That changed when Solomon built Israel's first permanent worship center—a temple in Jerusalem that would stand for more than four hundred years.

Surprisingly, this white limestone temple that glistened on the capital's hilltop like a jewel was a prefabricated building: "The stones used in the construction of the Temple were prefinished at the quarry, so the entire structure was built without the sound of hammer, ax, or any other iron tool at the building site" (1 Kings 6:7).

This was out of respect for the holy site. Jews had been worshiping there for decades, since King David bought a bedrock threshing floor from a farmer and built an altar on it.

Solomon's temple, following a rectangular floor plan, stood some ninety feet long, thirty feet wide, and forty-five feet high. Priests offered sacrifices in the courtyard outside and burned incense inside the main sanctuary. Only once a year, on Yom Kippur (the Day of Atonement), could the high priest enter the most sacred room, which was entirely paneled with gold. That room, a thirty-square-foot cube, was called the Most Holy Place. It held Israel's most sacred relic—the Ark of the Covenant, a gold-covered chest containing the Ten Commandments. There, the priest sprinkled blood of a sacrificed bull on the ark as one of the many rituals to atone for Israel's sins that year.

Solomon's grand temple was destroyed in 586 BC, when Babylonian invaders from what is now Iraq stripped away the gold, then ripped this magnificent jewel from Jerusalem's mountaintop.

far more of his kingdom because of the high taxes and forced labor he imposed on his own people. To make the temple alone, he drafted nearly two hundred thousand workers.

By the time Solomon died after his forty-year reign, the overworked, overtaxed Israelites were demanding relief. But Solomon's son and successor, Rehoboam—in a show of strength—promised nothing but more of the same. Much more.

So the ten northern tribes broke from the union and formed their own Jewish country—Israel. Solomon's son ruled Judah, named after the largest tribe still loyal to David's dynasty.

Israel's glory days were over.

STEPHEN

(STEVE un)
Stephanos, Greek
"crown"
First century AD
First mention: Acts 6:5

Following Jesus' advice on how to stay alive forever is what killed Stephen, the first Christian martyr. Jesus had said, "People need more than bread for their life; they must feed on every word of God" (Matthew 4:4).

Stephen was in the bread business. He was one of seven Christians chosen by the disciples to pass out food each day to destitute widows. That got him into no trouble, as far as the Bible says. But when he started feeding people the word of God—teaching them in the synagogue—a mob formed.

A WISE, RESPECTED MAN

Stephen got his job because of grumblers. Jewish Christians who moved to Jerusalem from Greek-speaking communities abroad complained that their widows weren't getting as much food as the local widows. So the apostles appointed seven men to handle the food distribution. These leaders had to be wise, respected, and full of the Holy Spirit.

All seven men had Greek names, suggesting the disciples wanted no hint of discrimination against the immigrants.

Back in the synagogues, Jews started debating about this new religious movement that could evolve into another branch of Judaism—one whose distinctive teaching was that the Messiah had come with a new covenant that replaced the old Jewish laws of Moses.

Stephen worshiped at a synagogue popular among Greek-speaking Jews who had moved from Africa, Turkey, and other regions. And he got swept into the debate. He must have been a masterful debater, because the competition couldn't overcome his arguments. So they convinced some men to lie about him, then took him before the same Jewish council that had tried Jesus. There, Stephen was charged with blasphemy against God and Moses.

A BLISTERING SPEECH

Stephen didn't seem particularly gifted

A Jewish mob turns Stephen into Christianity's first martyr, stoning him to death while Saul holds the killers' cloaks.

at subtlety. With his life on the line, he gave his esteemed Jewish audience a lesson about the not-so-esteemed Jewish tradition of rejecting God and killing his messengers.

"You stubborn people!" Stephen said. "You are heathen at heart and deaf to the truth. Must you forever resist the Holy Spirit? But your ancestors did, and so do you! Name one prophet your ancestors didn't persecute! They even killed the ones who predicted the coming of the Righteous One—the Messiah whom you betrayed and murdered" Acts 7:51–52).

As Jewish leaders shook their fists in rage, Stephen saw a vision of Jesus standing beside God. When he started describing it, the Jews dragged him outside and threw their coats at the feet of Paul—a witness who would later convert and become Christianity's best-known missionary.

As the stones flew, Stephen spoke his last words: "Lord, don't charge them with this sin!" (Acts 7:60).

The persecution of Christians that followed drove believers out of Jerusalem in all directions. But they took their faith with them and spread it around.

SUCCOTH

(SUE kohth)

"shelters"

Sukkot, Hebrew

First mention: 1. Exodus 12:37 (Succoth in Egypt)

2. Genesis 33:17 (Succoth in Jordan)

MAP 1
C4

Two cities in the Bible were named Succoth—one in Egypt and another in Jordan. Moses and the Hebrews camped at Succoth, somewhere in the Nile River delta, before they reached the Red Sea. Jacob, with his family and flocks, camped at Succoth in Jordan on his return trip home to what is now Israel. By about a thousand years later, Israelites lived there. When they refused to feed Gideon's soldiers, who were chasing Midianite raiders, he beat the city leaders with thorny switches.

SUSA

(SUE sah)

Susan, Hebrew

First mention: Ezra 4:9

MAP 3
E3

Two famous Jews in Iran called this city home: Queen Esther and the survivor of the lions' den, Daniel.

They lived in Susa because it was the capital of the Persian Empire. Daniel served as adviser for a king before Esther's time. Cyrus the Great, conqueror of Babylon, made this ancient city his capital. One of the oldest cities in the Middle East— about six thousand years old—it was already some twenty-five hundred years old when Cyrus arrived. The location was great, along a riverbank on fertile plains near the Persian Gulf. Today the city is called Shush, and it's about forty miles from the Iraqi border.

SYCHAR

(SY car)

Sychar, Greek

First mention: John 4:5

MAP 4
B4

After Jesus' baptism and temptation, he headed home to Galilee and stopped at about noon in the Samaritan village of Sychar. He waited by Jacob's well for someone with a rope and a bucket. What followed was his talk with a Samaritan woman about living water that forever quenches thirst—a metaphor about spiritual satisfaction and eternal life.

Sychar was probably near Shechem in central Israel, where Jacob once lived and perhaps dug a well. Many scholars associate Sychar with a modern village that has a similar-sounding name— Askar. Nearby is an old well about one hundred feet deep, just as the woman described it to Jesus: "This is a very deep well" (John 4:11).

SYRACUSE

(SEER ah kuse)

Syrakousa, Hebrew

First mention: Acts 28:12

See Map
Page 322

After his shipwreck on the voyage to Rome for trial, Paul spent three days in the port city of Syracuse, Sicily. His earlier ship had gotten caught in a storm off the coast of Crete and pushed five hundred miles before being rammed aground at Malta, a small island about fifty miles south of Sicily. Paul and his military escort booked passage on an Egyptian ship that had spent the winter at Malta. Their first stop was Syracuse. They may have stayed for three days to deliver cargo or perhaps to wait for favorable winds.

SYRIA
(SEER ee uh)
Aram, Hebrew
Syria, Greek
First mention: Numbers 23:/ (Aram)

MAP 1
E1

Syria, Israel's neighbor to the northeast, has been generally hostile toward the Jews since ancient days—and at about three hundred miles long and wide, it's nearly seven times larger. It's like comparing New Jersey (representing Israel) to Pennsylvania and West Virginia combined (representing Syria). In population, though, the desert nation of Syria is only about three times larger—6.5 million Israelis compared to 17.2 million Syrians.

Syria's oasis capital of Damascus, at five thousand years old, is one of the oldest continually occupied cities in the world. The capital lies a mere forty miles from Israel's northern border and about 130 miles from Jerusalem.

Israel's warrior king, David, overpowered several Syrian forces and made Damascus a kingdom subject to him. But late in Solomon's reign, Syria broke free. Throughout most of Bible history, the two nations dueled for control, each over the other. But when Assyria threatened them both, during Ahab's time, they joined forces in a battle that repelled the Assyrians. It was only a temporary victory. Assyria eventually swallowed both nations.

TAANACH

(TAY ah knock)
Tanak, Hebrew
First mention: Joshua 12:21

MAP 1
B3

A Jewish woman with an army made the fortified city of Taanach famous. Taanach controlled one of the key passes through the Mount Carmel range. It was in that area by the Kishon River valley that a Canaanite chariot corps engaged an Israelite militia of foot soldiers led by Deborah. She was one of Israel's heroic leaders before the time of the kings. The battle had all the makings of a Jewish Custer's Last Stand, but a sudden downpour bogged the chariots deep in mud. The Canaanites abandoned their chariots and ran for their lives, chased by the Israelites.

TAMAR

(TAY mar)
Tamar, Hebrew
"palm tree"
1. 1800s BC
2. About 1000 BC
First mention: 1. Genesis 38:6
2. 2 Samuel 13:1

1. **Pregnant by her father-in-law.** Judah was not only the father of the Israelite tribe of Judah; he was the father of twin sons by his daughter-in-law, Tamar. But in fairness to Judah, he thought she was a prostitute.

Tamar's husband died before they had children, so according to Jewish law, she became one of the wives of his younger brother, Onan. Tamar's first son with Onan would inherit the dead father's property. But the only children Onan wanted were his own heirs. So when he had sex with Tamar, he didn't release his semen inside of her. The Bible says God killed him for that.

Judah told Tamar to go home to her parents and wait for the next brother, Shelah, to grow up. But when he did, there was no marriage. Judah was afraid that marriage to Tamar would somehow kill Shelah, too.

Tamar found out that Judah would be going to a neighboring city to supervise the sheep shearing, so she veiled herself as a prostitute and waited by the city gate. Judah propositioned her, offering to pay with a goat he would send from his flock. As collateral, he gave her his walking stick, identification seal, and a cord. Later, when he sent the goat, Tamar was gone.

She turned up pregnant three months later, and Judah ordered her executed—until he saw the collateral. "She is more in the right than I am," Judah said, "because I didn't keep my promise to let her marry my son Shelah" (Genesis 38:26).

Tamar delivered twin sons, Perez and Zerah. Judah never slept with her again.

2. Raped by her half brother. David's oldest son, the crown prince Amnon, fell in lust with his beautiful half sister, Tamar. She was the full sister of Absalom. Amnon lured her into his bedroom by saying he was sick and asking if she would bring him food, He raped her, then chased her off, dooming her to a life without marriage. In that culture, she would have regained her respect if Amnon had married her. But he didn't. Tamar lived as a desolate woman in the home of her brother, Absalom.

King David was furious with Amnon but did nothing. Absalom, however, patiently waited for revenge. Two years later, at a sheep-shearing banquet, he had his servants kill Amnon.

TARSHISH

Location Unknown

(TAR shish)
Tarsis, Hebrew
First mention: Psalm 48:7

One thing is clear about the mysterious Tarshish: It was in the opposite direction God told Jonah to go.

Jonah was a Jewish prophet, and God ordered him east to Nineveh, near what is now Mosul, Iraq. Jonah was to warn his nation's Assyrian enemies that their capital was about to fall. Instead, Jonah boarded a ship bound for Tarshish. Some scholars speculate Jonah was headed to Tartessus, a kingdom in Spain. But Tarshish could have been any number of places west of Israel, including Africa and Europe.

TARSUS

MAP 5
E3

(TAR suhs)
Tarsos, Greek
First mention: Acts 9:11

The apostle Paul was a Turk by today's map. He grew up on the fertile plains in what is now Tarsus, Turkey—a riverside town about ten miles from the Mediterranean coast. Paul was also a Roman citizen. That's because his city, several decades before he was born, warmly welcomed the Romans. Mark Antony, in turn, declared the people free Roman citizens.

Tarsus grew rich because of its location on the coastal side of the Cilician Gates, a narrow mountain pass. Caravans loaded with taxable products passed through Tarsus on their journey between Turkey and the lower Middle Eastern countries, such as Syria and Israel. About a quarter of a million people live in Tarsus today.

TEKOA

MAP 1
C5

(uh KOH uh)
Teqoa, Hebrew
First mention: 2 Samuel 14:2

Tekoa, home of the shepherd-prophet Amos, was once a small village in the grazing fields about six miles south of Bethlehem. God sent Amos beyond the border of his own country of Judah, into the northern Jewish nation of Israel. There, Amos condemned the sins of Israel, Judah, and their neighbors.

A woman from Tekoa once used a parable to convince King David to welcome his son Absalom back from

A model of Herod's temple and courtyard. The tall building is the sanctuary, where only priests could enter. The large courtyard surrounding the walled temple complex—which had interior courtyards for Jews only—was the closest non-Jews could get to the sanctuary.

exile. She said she was a widow and one of her sons had killed the other in a fight. Now, she said, the family wanted to execute her only surviving son. When David vowed to protect him, the woman asked him to do the same for Israel's crown prince. Absalom had fled the country after killing his half brother for raping Absalom's sister. David called Absalom home.

Tekoa is now a ruins where herders pitch their tents. Nearby is an Arab village called Tequa and an Israeli settlement called Tekoa.

TEMPLE MOUNT

Har Habayit, Hebrew
First mention: 2 Chronicles 3:1

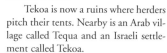

See Jerusalem

**MAP 4
B5**

Nearly three thousand years ago, on a hilltop in Jerusalem, Solomon built the first Jewish temple. The Bible calls that hill Mount Moriah, as many locals still do. Others call it the Temple Mount.

It's easy to spot. Sitting on top of it today is a gold-domed building that dominates the Jerusalem skyline. It's the Dome of the Rock, a thirteen-hundred-year-old Muslim shrine built around a huge boulder. The boulder is said to be where:

- Abraham almost sacrificed his son
- David built an altar
- Muhammad ascended to heaven

The Babylonians leveled Solomon's temple in 586 BC, but the Jews rebuilt it a few decades later. Herod the Great, in about 20 BC, launched an eighty-year temple renovation project. He started by doubling the size of the hilltop to about 525 yards by 330 yards. He used fill dirt held in place by a massive retaining wall. The Western Wall—also called the Wailing Wall—is part of that wall. And it's all that remains of the Jewish temple—which is why it's the most sacred site in Judaism.

The Roman army destroyed the temple in AD 70. When Muslims took over the region about six hundred years later, they built the Dome of the

A B C D E F G H I J K L M N O P Q R S T U V W X Y Z

Rock on that site. Many scholars say the Dome of the Rock sits directly above the temple ruins, but archaeological excavations are prohibited.

TERAH
(TAIR uh)
Terah, Hebrew
Perhaps "ibex," a mountain goat
2200s BC
First mention: Genesis 11:24

Abraham's father, Terah, raised his family in the cosmopolitan city of Ur, along the Euphrates River in what is now southern Iraq. For some unknown reason, he decided to pack up and move to the shepherd's frontier of Canaan, in what is now Israel.

He got only about halfway. Following the main caravan trail up the river, he stopped at the village of Haran, in what is now southern Turkey, and apparently liked what he saw. He stayed there until he died at age 205. His son finished what Terah started and continued to Canaan.

THEBES
(THEEBS)
No, Hebrew
Niwt, Egyptian
Thebes, Greek
"city"
First mention: Jeremiah 46:25

MAP 3
B5

About 450 miles upriver from Cairo is the modern city of Luxor, known in Bible times as Thebes, capital of Egypt

for many centuries. One prophet warned, "Thebes will be torn apart" (Ezekiel 30:16). A later prophet reported it as fact: "Thebes fell, and her people were led away as captives" (Nahum 3:10). Nahum was likely referring to Assyria's sack of Thebes in 663 BC. Ancient temples linger as a testimony to this once-glorious city on the Nile River.

Jackal-headed images of Anubis—Egypt's god of the dead—flank two walls leading into a tomb at Thebes. As Bible prophets predicted, this one-time capital of Egypt is now a ghost town full of ruins.

THESSALONICA
(thess uh low NI kuh)
Thessalonike, Greek
First mention: Acts 17:1

MAP 5
A1

One of many towns that ran off the apostle Paul, Thessalonica is located on the coast of northern Greece. Paul converted many people there, but some Jews stirred up a mob and charged the house where Paul had been staying. He wasn't there, so they took the homeowner before the city council and charged him with treason for giving allegiance to Jesus as king. The council threw out the case, but believers convinced Paul to leave town that night. Paul visited the church again and wrote the people two letters preserved in the New Testament as First and Second Thessalonians. The letters show that believers there were confused about the Second Coming and about what happens to people who die before Jesus returns.

"Doubting Thomas" checks the nail scars on the hands of Jesus.

Most of the ancient city lies in ruins beneath the modern town of Thessaloniki.

THOMAS

(TOM us)
Thomas, Greek
First century AD
First mention: Matthew 10:3

One of Jesus' twelve disciples, Thomas had a nickname—"the Twin." But people today know him better as Doubting Thomas.

That's because when the other disciples told him they had seen Jesus risen from the dead, Thomas replied, "I won't believe it unless I see the nail wounds in his hands" (John 20:25). Eight days later, Jesus returned to the group and invited Thomas to touch the wounds. Thomas simply replied, "My Lord and my God!" (John 20:28).

Thomas wasn't just a skeptic; he was a brave soul. When Jesus said he was going back to Jerusalem, shortly after word leaked out that Jewish leaders were planning to kill him, Thomas told the other disciples, "Let's go, too—and die with Jesus" (John 11:16).

Christian books written during the next two centuries are filled with legends about Thomas. One persistent story is that in AD 52, he arrived on India's southwestern coast, in what is now the state of Kerala. There he started several churches, before moving to the east coast, where he was martyred. India's Syro-Malabar Catholic Church, with three million members, claims Thomas as founding minister.

THREE TAVERNS
Treis Tabernai, Greek
First mention: Acts 28:15

See Map
Page 322

Three Taverns sounds like a rest stop for drinkers, but it was a place where travelers could spend the night. Paul and his military escort probably stopped there on the trip to Rome for Paul's trial. Their ship made port about one hundred miles south of Rome, in Puteoli, near Pompeii and what is now Naples. They continued their journey on foot—which would have taken them about a week. Christians in Rome heard that Paul had arrived, so they rushed to meet him. One group reached him at Three Taverns, about thirty-five miles south of Rome on the Appian Way road.

TIBERIAS
(tie BEER ee us)
Tiberias, Greek
First mention: John 6:23

MAP 4
C3

Herod Antipas, a son of Herod the Great, founded the lakeshore city of Tiberias in AD 20 as a new capital of Galilee—to replace Sepphoris, in the hills near Nazareth. Certainly the

location seemed better, on the Sea of Galilee's western shore. Unfortunately, builders discovered the site had once been a cemetery. That made Tiberias off-limits and ritually unclean to observant Jews. If they went there, they had to perform cleansing rituals before worshiping. Perhaps that's why the Bible has only a single passing reference to this city, reporting people from Tiberias arriving by boats to hear Jesus (John 6:23).

Tiberias, a village on the Sea of Galilee's west shoreline—as seen in 1839. Jews stayed away because it rested on a cemetery.

TIBERIUS CAESAR
(tie BEER ee us SEE zur)
Tiberias, Greek
Reigned AD 14-37
First mention: Luke 3:1

Rome's emperor during the last half of Jesus' life was Tiberius, the adopted son of the previous emperor, Augustus. Though Tiberius was a skilled soldier, Roman historians say he became a cruel and decadent ruler.

Jesus referred to him once, when Jewish scholars asked a trick question intended to get Jesus in trouble no matter how he answered: Should Jews pay taxes to Caesar? Jesus held up a coin and asked whose picture was stamped on it. Caesar's, the scholars answered. "Well, then," Jesus replied, "give to Caesar what belongs to him. But everything that belongs to God must be given to God" (Matthew 22:21).

TIGRIS RIVER

(TIE gris)
Tigris, Greek
Hiddeqel, Hebrew
First mention: Genesis 2:14

Two main rivers flow out of the Turkish mountains and into Iraq, running roughly parallel for more than a thousand miles before emptying into the Persian Gulf. The land between was Mesopotamia, a Greek word meaning "between the rivers." In this fertile swath of land, empires grew: Sumer, Babylon, and Assyria. Many cities were built on the banks of the Tigris, including Nineveh, Assyria's capital.

Tigris was the smaller river, stretching about twelve hundred miles before joining with the Euphrates and flowing together for about one hundred miles before entering the Persian Gulf. The Tigris and Euphrates are two of four branches from the river that nourished the Garden of Eden.

TIMNAH

(TIM nah)
Timna, Hebrew
First mention: Joshua 15:10

Several Israelite towns were named Timnah, including one where the widower Judah was fooled into thinking his widowed daughter-in-law was a prostitute. That case of mistaken identity produced twin sons.

Another Timnah may actually be the same city, nearly a thousand years later. It was the hometown of Samson's Philistine bride, and here is where Samson's clashes with the Philistines began. After his bride gave thirty wedding guests the answer to his riddle, Samson had to pay up on his bet—a set of robes for each guest. He stormed off and killed thirty Philistines, then removed their robes to settle his debt.

Philistine discoveries at a ruin called Tell el-Batashi, about twenty miles west of Jerusalem, lead archaeologists to speculate it was once Timnah.

TIMOTHY

(TIM uh thee)
Timotheos, Greek
Joined Paul's ministry about AD 50
First mention: Acts 16:1

Tender and heartbreaking, the last letter Paul wrote to his young associate, Timothy, is the most moving in all of the New Testament. Facing imminent execution in Rome, Paul took pen in hand to write to "Timothy, my dear son" (2 Timothy 1:2).

Timothy wasn't really his son—

Paul just loved him that much. Timothy was the son of a Jewish Christian mother and a Gentile father. Paul probably met Timothy on the first missionary trip, which included a stop in Timothy's hometown of Lystra in what is now Turkey. That's the town where Jews stoned Paul and left him for dead. On Paul's second missionary trip, he stopped in Lystra and invited Timothy to join his ministry team. When Timothy agreed, Paul arranged to have him circumcised, so Jews would have no reason to criticize the half Jew for refusing to honor God's covenant with Abraham.

Paul soon started using Timothy as a troubleshooter, carrying messages to problem churches and staying to help work out solutions—even in the toughest church of all, at Corinth, Greece. That's where a church member in good standing was having sex with his stepmother. "I am sending Timothy," Paul wrote the fragile church. "He will remind you of what I teach" (1 Corinthians 4:17).

As Paul's execution neared, probably in the mid-60s AD, Timothy was pastoring in Ephesus, Turkey. Paul offered fatherly advice along with assurances intended to soften the blow of his death: "Remain faithful to the things you have been taught. . . . The time of my death is near. I have fought a good fight, I have finished the race, and I have remained faithful" (2 Timothy 3:14; 4:6–7).

Timothy apparently went to Rome at Paul's request. Church leaders later wrote that Timothy returned to Ephesus, where he became the first bishop of that church and where he was martyred in AD 97 during another wave of Roman persecution.

Titus

(TIE tus)
Titos, Greek
Joined Paul's ministry about AD 50
First mention: 2 Corinthians 2:13

Before Titus became Paul's associate minister during the apostle's last two missionary journeys, Titus was a Gentile guinea pig—a prototype of a Christian who didn't observe Jewish traditions, the most painful of which was circumcision.

In the early days of the church, most believers were Jewish Christians. But as Gentiles began professing faith in Jesus, church leaders started debating whether or not Gentiles needed to obey Jewish laws. Paul said they didn't. And he took Titus with him to Jerusalem to help make his case. The leaders agreed with Paul, to the great relief of Titus.

Like Timothy, Titus served as one of Paul's trusted troubleshooters, delivering Paul's letters to confused congregations and helping solve their problems when Paul was busy somewhere else.

Titus was pastoring the church at Crete when Paul wrote him advice preserved in the New Testament. It began with an old saying from a Cretan prophet—a generalization that would be considered politically incorrect today. "The people of Crete are all liars; they are cruel animals and lazy gluttons," Paul said, quoting the prophet. "This is true. So rebuke them as sternly as necessary to make them strong in the faith" (Titus 1:12–13).

Perhaps Titus discovered Crete wasn't as bad as the prophet and Paul made it out to be. A church historian named Eusebius, writing about three hundred years later, said Titus stayed there and became the island's first bishop.

TROAS

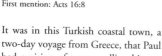

(TROW as)
Troas, Greek
First mention: Acts 16:8

It was in this Turkish coastal town, a two-day voyage from Greece, that Paul had a vision of a man calling him to Europe. It's at this very point in the history of the early church, recorded in Acts, that the writer starts using the word "we," inserting himself into Paul's second missionary journey. For this reason, scholars speculate that the author, a physician named Luke, joined Paul's entourage in Troas.

But the standout event in this town, located a mere ten miles south of legendary Troy, is one that argues for short sermons. Paul preached until midnight. A young man named Eutychus fell asleep, fell three stories from a window ledge, and died. Paul raised him from the dead and continued to preach until dawn.

TYRE

(TIRE)
Sor, Hebrew
Tyrus, Latin
First mention: Joshua 19:29

Tyre was a busy seaport in what is now Sur, Lebanon, about fifteen miles north of the Israeli border. David and Solomon were both on good terms with the city's king, Hiram, and bought from him cedar for the temple. Solomon also went into a joint business venture with Hiram, using sailors from Tyre as crew for his fleet of trading ships in the Red Sea.

Tyre was really two cities—with one on an island about seven hundred yards offshore. The prophet Ezekiel said invaders would "scrape away its soil and make it a bare rock!" (Ezekiel 26:4). Two hundred years later, Alexander the Great did just that. He overran the coastal city, then used the city's debris to build a causeway to the island.

UR
(URR)
Ur, Hebrew
First mention: Genesis 11:28

MAP 3
E3

Abraham—father of the Jews—was an Iraqi. By today's map, at least.

He was born, raised, and married in Ur, just across the Euphrates River from the southern Iraqi town of Nasiriya, a hard-fought holdout during the 2003 war in which American and British troops ousted dictator Saddam Hussein. It's also precariously near an Iraqi air base.

Ur was the New York City of four thousand years ago—the world's hub of culture, power, and wealth. One of the oldest cities discovered—at about sixty-five hundred years old—Ur grew to become the control center for the world's first known empire—Sumer. It was also a religious center for the moon goddess Nanna—with a temple devoted to her. Built around the time of Abraham, the temple was a step pyramid called a ziggurat, perhaps thirty stories high.

In Abraham's day, about 2100 BC, Ur was at its peak. A century later, however, invaders destroyed the city. Abraham's father may have seen it coming, which would explain why he moved six hundred miles upriver and settled in the caravan town of Haran.

"Ur of the Chaldeans" is how the Bible often refers to Abraham's cosmopolitan hometown. But the Chaldeans—who became the Babylonians—didn't show up in the Persian Gulf area until more than a thousand years after Abraham, arriving in the 800s BC. So the reference to Chaldea was to help

In Abraham's hometown of Ur, worshipers follow a priest up a stair-stepped pyramid called a ziggurat, to honor their moon goddess Nanna.

later readers place the city, much like a reference to Iraq does today.

Ur died a slow death. The river shifted course, gradually isolating Ur from river traffic. Today, Ur is about twelve miles from the Euphrates.

DIGGING UP UR

Desert sands blew over the ghost town ruins for centuries, creating an oval mound nearly a mile long, half a mile wide, and about sixty feet high. The mound, discovered in 1625, is called Tell el-Mukayyar. Excavations began in 1849 and continued for nearly a century, ending in 1934.

The best-known archaeologist at Ur was Sir Leonard Woolley, who spent a dozen years digging through the mound, from 1922 through 1934. He uncovered the massive ziggurat, beautiful objects such as a golden goat standing and nibbling on a flowering tree, and sixteen royal tombs rivaling those of Egypt—complete with riches and the bodies of servants sacrificed and buried with their kings.

Woolley's biggest headline came in 1929, when he said he had found evidence of Noah's flood. Tunneling into Ur's burial pits, at the lower levels of the mound, he discovered an eight-foot-thick layer of water-deposited silt that he dated to around 4000 BC.

Certainly *a* flood, but scholars say not *the* Flood. Since neighboring cities show no evidence of a similar flood, the one Woolley found at Ur was probably just local.

URIAH
(your EYE uh)
Uriyah, Hebrew
"The Lord is my light"
About 1000 BC
First mention: 2 Samuel 11:3

An Israelite special forces soldier, Uriah was murdered at King David's command for two reasons:

- His beautiful wife, Bathsheba
- His loyalty to the king who killed him

URIAH THE MERCENARY?

Uriah the Hittite, as the Bible calls him, may not have been a Hittite at all. The Hittites lived in northern Syria and Turkey and sometimes hired themselves out as mercenaries. But Uriah may have had some Hittite blood in him, netting him the nickname.

He was, however, a brave and skilled warrior, part of an elite force called the Thirty.

While Uriah and the rest of the army were three days away, laying siege to the city of Rabbah, near what is now Jordan's capital of Amman, King David was back in Jerusalem committing adultery with Uriah's wife, Bathsheba. The king had seen her bathing as he took an afternoon walk on the palace roof. He sent for her, slept with her, and she got pregnant.

A BUNGLED COVER-UP

David tried twice to cover up his sin.

He sent for Uriah, pretending to ask how the war was going. But his real motive was to get Uriah in bed with Bathsheba so Uriah would think he was the child's father.

David told the warrior to go home and rest, but Uriah chose instead to follow his military code of honor—a high standard of loyalty to king, comrades, and country. He slept at the palace entrance with other servants. The next morning, he explained that he couldn't rest in the comfort of his home while the king's army and the nation's most sacred object—the golden chest containing the Ten Commandments—camped in open fields.

That night, David tried again. This time he got Uriah drunk. But even drunk, Uriah had more honor than David did sober. Uriah slept again at the palace entrance.

So David sent Uriah back to the battle with a sealed note: "Station Uriah on the front lines where the battle is fiercest. Then pull back so that he will be killed" (2 Samuel 11:15).

After Uriah's death, David married Bathsheba, but their baby son died. Solomon was born to them later and became Israel's next king.

Uz

(UHZ)
Us, Hebrew
First mention: Job 1:1

Location Unknown

Job lived in the land of Uz. Unfortunately, the Bible never says where Uz was.

Partly because a man named Uz descended from Aram, the Hebrew word for Syria, some speculate Uz was in Syria. That fits with Job's story about the attack of Chaldean raiders. Chaldeans later called themselves Babylonians. And Babylon was in Iraq, which is Syria's eastside neighbor. Yet other evidence hints at Jordan or even southern Israel.

UZZAH

(YOU zuh)
Uzza, Hebrew
"God is my strength"
About 1000 BC
First mention: 2 Samuel 6:3

Uzzah's death makes God look bad.

God struck Uzzah dead simply for trying to keep Israel's most sacred object from tipping over and falling. Uzzah and his brother were transporting the gold-covered chest that held the Ten Commandments—also called the Ark of the Covenant. When the oxen pulling the cart stumbled, Uzzah reached out to steady the ark. "The LORD's anger blazed out against Uzzah for doing this, and God struck him dead" (2 Samuel 6:7).

Why God did this is unknown. Even King David didn't understand. Among the many guesses scholars make is that the ark was holy and Uzzah was not. He was ritually unclean and should not have touched it for any reason.

Three months later, David moved the ark successfully to Jerusalem, treating it with respect and offering sacrifices along the way.

ZACCHAEUS

(zack KEY us)
Zakchaios, Greek
"innocent"
First century AD
First mention: Luke 19:2

Zacchaeus was a tax man who got rich by overcharging his own Jewish people for taxes demanded by the occupying forces of Rome. The Jews hated him and other tax collectors for collaborating with the enemy, and they treated them as ritually unclean —like lepers. Jesus, however, had another approach. He chose one tax collector, Matthew, as a disciple. And when Jesus passed through Jericho and saw short Zacchaeus up a tree, trying to catch a glimpse of him over the crowds, Jesus called him down and spent the night at his home.

The crowd grumbled. But Jesus' kindness changed Zacchaeus. "I will give half my wealth to the poor," he told Jesus, "and if I have overcharged people on their taxes, I will give them back four times as much!" (Luke 19:8).

The Jericho oasis, looking east from the Judean hills toward the Jordan River. When Jesus passed through Jericho, surrounded by crowds, the tax collector Zacchaeus scrambled up a tree to catch sight of him.

ZADOK

(ZAY doc)
Sadoq, Hebrew
900s BC
First mention: 2 Samuel 8:17

Two priests served together in Jerusalem during King David's reign, but only one—Zadok—kept his job when David's son, Solomon, took over.

The other priest, Abiathar, made the mistake of backing the wrong prince, Adonijah, who threw himself a precoronation party as David lay dying. Zadok—intensely loyal to David—refused to attend. Zadok had proved his loyalty years earlier when Prince Absalom attempted a coup that forced David to leave Jerusalem. Zadok stayed behind as a spy for David.

When Solomon became king, he banished the priest Abiathar from Jerusalem. That gave the family of Zadok a monopoly on the Jerusalem priesthood that lasted until Babylon destroyed the temple four hundred years later.

ZAREPHATH

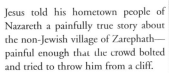

(ZAIR uh fath)
Sarepat, Hebrew
First mention: 1 Kings 17:9

Jesus told his hometown people of Nazareth a painfully true story about the non-Jewish village of Zarephath—painful enough that the crowd bolted and tried to throw him from a cliff.

Here's the story: When Israel rejected God and the prophet Elijah,

God sent a drought. He told Elijah to wait out the drought in Zarephath, a village in what is now Lebanon, about twenty-five miles north of the Israeli border. The point Jesus made was that Jews had a long history of rejecting prophets like himself. When they did, God found people elsewhere. "There were many widows in Israel," Jesus said, "yet Elijah was sent to none of them except to a widow at Zarephath" (Luke 4:25–26 NRSV).

ZEBULUN

(ZEBB u luhn)
Zebulun, Hebrew
First mention: Joshua 19:10

Descendants of Jacob's tenth son, Zebulun, got one of the smaller plots of land in Israel. Using a selection process a bit like drawing straws, they ended up with about a twenty-mile-long stretch of land between the Mount Carmel range and the Galilean hills. Between those highlands, however, lay the fertile valley of Jezreel. Warriors of Zebulun joined Deborah's militia at the battle of Mount Tabor, routing a Canaanite chariot corps that got bogged down in the valley during a rainstorm.

ZECHARIAH

(zech uh RYE uh)
Zekaryah, Hebrew
"The Lord remembers"
1. Prophesied from 520–518 BC
2. First century BC
First mention: 1. Ezra 5:1
2. Luke 1:5

Zechariah is the most popular name in the Bible. There are at least thirty men with this name in the Old Testament, though just one in the New Testament. Two standouts include the prophet who wrote the book of Zechariah and the elderly New Testament priest who became John the Baptist's father.

1. **The prophet.** It took double-barreled prophecies to shake up the Jews enough to convince them to rebuild the temple. The Jews had been back from exile in Babylon for almost twenty years, but they still hadn't rebuilt Jerusalem's temple.

The prophet Haggai was the first barrel. From August to December of 520 BC, he said the crop failures would stop once the temple was rebuilt. Zechariah was the second barrel. Prophesying from October 520 to December 518 BC, he promised a Messiah if the Jews rebuilt the temple.

Matthew's Gospel said Jesus rode into Jerusalem on a donkey before his crucifixion to fulfill Zechariah's prophecy: "Shout in triumph, O people of Jerusalem! Look, your king is coming to you. He is righteous and victorious, yet he is humble, riding on a donkey" (Zechariah 9:9).

2. **The priest.** Several months before the angel Gabriel visited Mary to announce the birth of Jesus, Gabriel made a stop at the Jerusalem temple. Inside, an old and childless priest named Zechariah was burning incense to God. Gabriel said the priest's wife, Elizabeth, would have a son whom they were to name John.

"He must never touch wine or hard liquor, and he will be filled with the Holy Spirit, even before his birth," Gabriel said. "He will precede the coming of the Lord, preparing the people for his arrival" (Luke 1:15, 17).

Zechariah asked how he could be sure this would happen. As a sign, if not a rebuke, Gabriel said Zechariah wouldn't be able to talk until the child was born. His speech came back during John's circumcision ceremony, after Zechariah wrote on a tablet that the boy's name would be John.

ZEDEKIAH

(ZED uh KI uh)
Sidqiyah, Hebrew
"the Lord is my salvation"
Reigned 597–586 BC
First mention: 2 Kings 24:17

The Babylonian king Nebuchadnezzar made a bad decision when he replaced the eighteen-year-old king of Judah with twenty-one-year-old Zedekiah. Nebuchadnezzar wanted a servant king who would pay taxes. But when rebellion broke out later in Babylon, Zedekiah saw his chance to declare Jewish independence.

Nebuchadnezzar, weary of repeated

Invaders overrun Jerusalem's defenders at the temple altar and courtyard, while King Zedekiah flees the city.

Jewish revolts, wiped Judah off the map. When the Babylonians broke through Jerusalem's walls, Zedekiah and his armies ran for their lives. The army of Babylon caught him and forced him to watch his sons die. It was the last thing the king saw. Soldiers blinded him and led him into exile with the other survivors.

ZEPHANIAH

(ZEF ah NI uh)
Sepanyah, Hebrew
Prophesied during Josiah's reign of
640–609 BC
First mention: Zephaniah 1:1

Zephaniah is one of the rare prophets who seemed to make a difference. His warning about the destruction of Judah apparently helped spur King Josiah in the south to launch the religious reform that took place in the 620s BC. The idolatry Zephaniah described was exactly what Josiah tried to stop. The reform movement probably got a burst of energy when Assyria's capital fell in 612 BC, as Zephaniah had predicted.

Zephaniah traced his genealogy back four generations to Hezekiah, perhaps the king. If so, Josiah—great-grandson of Hezekiah—took the advice of a trusted relative.

ZERUBBABEL

(zuh ROO buh buhl)
Zerubbabel, Hebrew
"seed of Babylon"
500s BC
First mention: Ezra 2:2

Born during Israel's fifty-year exile in Babylon, Zerubbabel led the first wave of Jews home—more than forty thousand of them. Persia conquered Babylon in 538 BC, freed the exiles, and appointed Zerubbabel governor of Judah. Governor Zerubbabel gave the people more than a year to settle in before they started rebuilding the temple—a comparatively modest worship center, but one that stood longer than the temples of Solomon and Herod the Great combined.

ZIN WILDERNESS

Sin, Hebrew
First mention: Numbers 13:21

"Wilderness of Zin," is what the Bible calls it. But it's not really a wilderness. Not with forests. Zin looks more like Mars. With lots of rocks and canyons, Zin is Israel's answer to the Dakota Badlands.

It's located in Israel's southland, between the Negev desert and Egypt's triangular Sinai Peninsula. Moses led the Israelites through this nasty stretch of terrain, with the people griping all along the way. They spent most of their forty years in this wilderness at the oasis of Kadesh-barnea, on Zin's northern end.

ZION

See Jerusalem

(ZIE un)
Siyyon, Hebrew
First mention: 2 Samuel 5:7

A word with many meanings, Zion started out in the Bible meaning the tiny, ridgetop city that David captured —later called Jerusalem. But in time the name grew to refer to the entire country, both to the land and the people. In the New Testament, Zion even refers to the heavenly city of God at the end of human history. (See *Jerusalem.*)

ZIPPORAH

(zip POH ruh)
Sippora, Hebrew
1400s BC
First mention: Exodus 2:21

Zipporah—wife of Moses—was the daughter of a Midianite shepherd who grazed his flocks in the Sinai Peninsula. Moses met her when he fled Egypt for killing an Egyptian foreman who was beating a Hebrew slave. Zipporah's father gave Moses a job as shepherd and later allowed Moses to marry his daughter. Zipporah had two sons— Gershom and Eliezer.

When Moses took his family back to Egypt to free the Hebrews, God came to kill one of the males—perhaps an uncircumcised son. Zipporah quickly circumcised the boy and complained, "What a blood-smeared bridegroom you are to me!" (Exodus 4:25).

ZOAR

(ZORE)

Soar, Hebrew

"small"

First mention: Genesis 13:10

When God burned up the cities of Sodom and Gomorrah, along with other cities on the plain, he spared one city—Zoar. This was at Lot's request. When angels ordered him to leave Sodom, he asked them to spare the little village so he could take his family there instead of to the mountains.

Scholars debate where Zoar and the other cities were located. But many place them in or around the shallow water at the bottom half of the Dead Sea—flooded land that in ancient times may have been a dry and fertile plain. Several ancient sources connect Zoar to the Jordanian city of Safi, along the southern rip of the Dead Sea.

ZOPHAR

(ZOH far)

Sopar, Hebrew

Possibly "bird"

Perhaps about 2000 BC

First mention: Job 2:11

The last of Job's three comforters, Zophar followed the approach of Eliphaz and Bildad before him—accusing Job instead of consoling him. All three insisted that Job lost his family, flocks, and health because he had sinned. Zophar was perhaps the most insensitive of all. "Is a person proved innocent just by talking a lot?" Zophar demanded. "Listen! God is doubtless punishing you far less than you deserve!" (Job 11:2, 6). God later humbled the three friends by making them ask Job to pray for them.

ZORAH

(ZOOR uh)

Sora, Hebrew

First mention: Joshua 15:33

Samson grew up in Zorah, a village in the foothills of southern Israel, near the coastal plains. Since the coast was where the Philistines lived, that put Samson dangerously close to several Philistine cities. In fact, he married a Philistine woman from the neighboring village of Timnah, only about five miles west.

After the Philistines executed Samson's wife, he launched a twenty-year, one-man guerrilla campaign against them. In the end, it cost him his life. His brothers retrieved his body and buried him at Zorah.

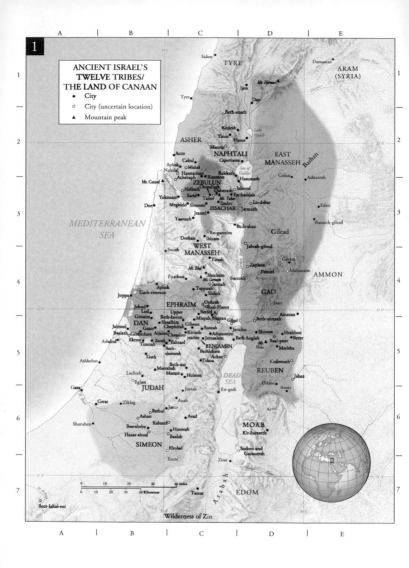

Adapted from the Holman Bible Atlas ©1998. Used by permission.

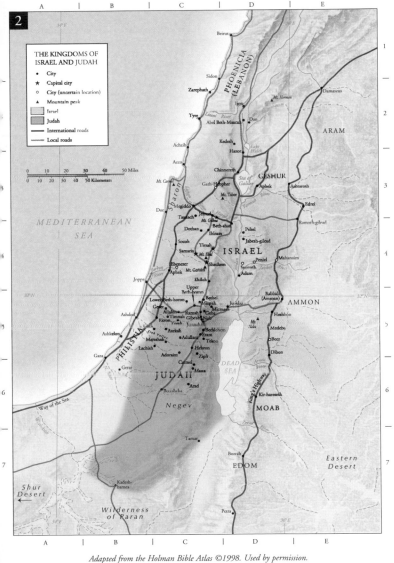

THE KINGDOMS OF
ISRAEL AND JUDAH

- • City
- ★ Capital city
- ○ City (uncertain location)
- ▲ Mountain peak
- Israel
- Judah
- ── International roads
- ── Local roads

0 10 20 30 40 50 Miles
0 10 20 30 40 50 Kilometers

MEDITERRANEAN
SEA

Beirut
Sidon
Zarephath
PHOENICIA
(LEBANON)
Mt. Hermon
Damascus
Tyre
Litani River
Ijon
Abel Beth-Maacah
Dan
ARAM
Achzib
Kedesh
Hazor
Lake
Huleh
Acco
Chinnereth
Mt. Carmel
Gath-Hepher
Sea of
Galilee
GESHUR
Aphek
Ashtaroth
Dor
Megiddo
Mt. Tabor
Taanach
Mt. Gilboa
Beth-shan
Edrei
Dothan
Ibleam
Pehel
Ramoth-gilead
Socoh
Jabesh-gilead
Samaria
Tirzah
Mahanaim
Mt. Ebal
Shechem
Peniel
Succoth
Ebenezer
Mt. Gerizim
Adam
Aphek
Shiloh
Joppa
Upper
Beth-horon
Bethel
Lower Beth-horon
Mizpah
Rabbah
(Amman)
AMMON
Gezer
Aijalon
Ramah
Gibeah
Nob
Geba
Michmash
Ekron
Timnah
Gibeon
Heshbon
Ashdod
Azekah
Bethlehem
Medeba
Elah Valley
Etam
Mt. Nebo
Mareshah
Adullam
Tekoa
Beer
Ashkelon
Lachish
Adoraim
Ziph
Dibon
Gaza
Hebron
DEAD
SEA
Gerar
Carmel
JUDAH
Maon
King's Highway
Kir-hareseth
Beersheba
Arad
Negev
MOAB
Way of the Sea
PHILISTIA
Tamar
Bozrah
Eastern
Desert
Shur
Desert
EDOM
Kadesh-
barnea
Wilderness
of Paran
Petra

Adapted from the Holman Bible Atlas ©1998. Used by permission.

381

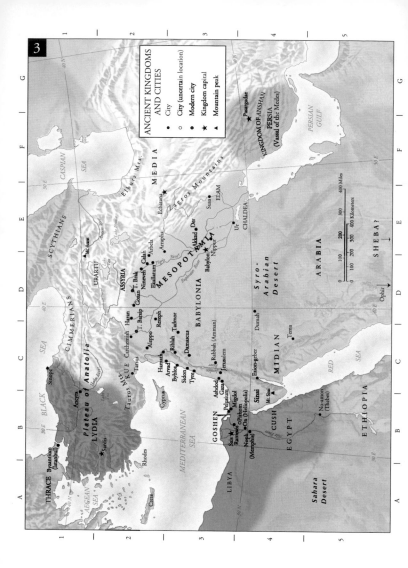

ANCIENT KINGDOMS
AND CITIES

- City
- ○ City (uncertain location)
- ● Modern city
- ★ Kingdom capital
- ▲ Mountain peak

Adapted from the Holman Bible Atlas ©1998. Used by permission.

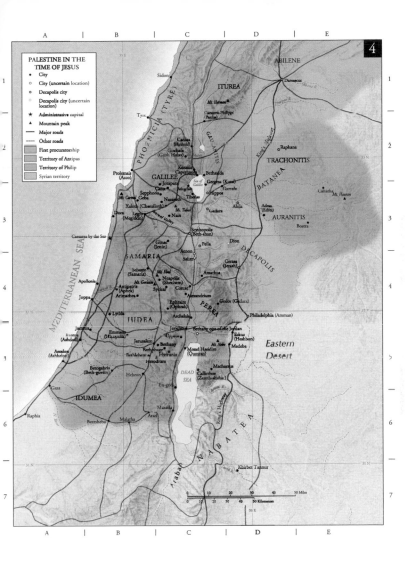

PALESTINE IN THE TIME OF JESUS

- City
- City (uncertain location)
- Decapolis city
- Decapolis city (uncertain location)
- ★ Administrative capital
- ▲ Mountain peak
- — Major roads
- — Other roads
- First procuratorship
- Territory of Antipas
- Territory of Philip
- Syrian territory

ABILENE

Sidon

ITUREA

Damascus

Mt. Hermon

Caesarea Philippi (Paneas)

Tyre

PHOENICIA (TYRE)

GAULANITIS

TRACHONITIS

Raphana

Cadesh (Kadesh)

Gischala (Gush Halav)

BATANEA

Ptolemais (Acco)

Korazin
Capernaum
Bethsaida

GALILEE

Jutapata
Cana

Sea of Galilee

Gergesa (Kursi)

Canatha
Mt. Hauran

Sepphoris
Geba

Magdala
Tiberias

Hippos
Gamala

AURANITIS

Xaloth (Chesulloth)

Mt. Carmel

Nazareth

Mt. Tabor

Gadara

Abila

Adraa (Edrei)

Dora

Legio (Megiddo)

Jezreel Valley

Nain

Scythopolis (Beth-shan)

Bostra

Caesarea by the Sea

Ginae (Jenin)

Dion

Pella

Aenon

Gerasa (Jerash)

DECAPOLIS

SAMARIA

Salim

MEDITERRANEAN SEA

Sebaste (Samaria)

Mt. Ebal

Neapolis (Shechem)

Mt. Gerizim

Amathus

Apollonia

Sychar

Coreae

Antipatris (Aphek)
Arimathea

Joppa

Ephraim (Ophrah)

Alexandrium

Godor (Gadara)

Philadelphia (Amman)

Lydda

JUDEA

Archelais

PEREA

Jamnia (Jabneh)

Jericho

Bethany east of the Jordan

Rabat (Heshbon)

Emmaus (Nicopolis)

Jerusalem

Bethphage
Bethany

Mt. Nebo

Medeba

Azotus (Ashdod)

Bethlehem

Mead Hasidim (Qumran)

Ashkelon

Hyrcania

Herodium

DEAD SEA

Machaerus

Eastern Desert

Beterogabris (Beth-gavrin)

Hebron

Callirrhoe (Zaret-shahar)

Gaza

En-gedi

IDUMEA

Masada

Raphia

Beersheba

Malatha

Arad

NABATEA

Khirbet Tannur

Arabah

King's Highway

0   10   20   30   40   50 Miles

0   10   20   30   40   50 Kilometers

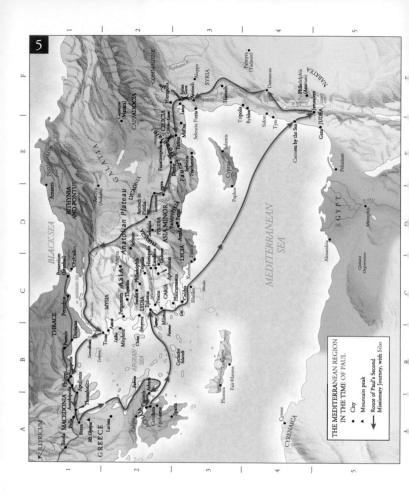

THE MEDITERRANEAN REGION
IN THE TIME OF PAUL

• City
▲ Mountain peak
→ Route of Paul's Second
   Missionary Journey, with Silas

Adapted from the Holman Bible Atlas ©1998. Used by permission.

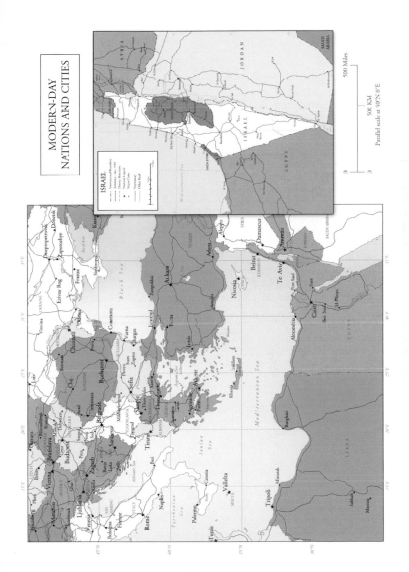

MODERN-DAY
NATIONS AND CITIES

ISRAEL

- - - - International Boundary
- · - · Armistice line, 1949
········ Demarc. boundary
★ National capital
● Major cities
□ Deyr esor
——— Other Road

500 Miles

500 KM
Parallel scale at 30°N 0°E

ART CREDITS

A. M. Rosati / Art Resource, NY: Page 232

Alinari / Art Resource, NY: Pages 54, 62, 312

Alinari/SEAT / Art Resource, NY: Pages 12, 52

Arjan Korthout NL: Page 271

Bible Places/Todd Bolen: Cover, Pages 292, 296, 345

Borromeo / Art Resource, NY: Page 71

Cameraphoto / Art Resource, NY: Pages 50, 377

Cameraphoto Arte, Venice / Art Resource, NY: Pages 99, 181, 301

Corbis Images: Pages 11, 47, 63, 105, 189, 214, 348

Earth Sciences and Images Analysis; NASA-Johnson Space Center: Pages 32, 322 (bottom), 353

Erich Lessing / Art Resource, NY: Pages 9, 17, 27, 42, 97, 113, 120, 132, 137, 138, 215, 236, 237, 238, 279, 310, 316, 342, 355, 359, 374

Giraudon / Art Resource, NY: Page 178

Greg Schneider: Pages 31, 56, 60, 88, 123, 171, 173, 176, 194, 196, 239, 272, 276, 280, 283, 325, 341

Gustave Doré: Page 79

HIP/Scala / Art Resource, NY: Pages 76, 265

Image Select / Art Resource, NY: Page 77

The Jewish Museum, NY / Art Resource, NY: Pages 24, 210, 287

Katrina Thomas / Saudi Aramco World / PADIA: Page 249

Library of Congress: Pages 235, 303, 323, 367

Model Maker R Walsh@www.noahs-ark.net: Page 33

National Geographic: Page 371

ORBIMAGE, Inc. Processing by NASA Goddard Space Flight Center: Pages 8, 319

Oriental Institute of the University of Chicago: Page 44

Réunion des Musées Nationaux / Art Resource, NY: Pages 10, 147, 227, 314, 350

Richard Nowitz Photography: Pages 110, 164, 253, 255

Scala / Art Resource, NY: Pages 8, 9, 21, 43, 83, 90, 130, 135, 143, 144, 160, 165, 167, 202, 211, 240, 242, 243, 297, 322 (top), 328, 329, 334, 365, 366

SEF / Art Resource, NY: Page 273

Smithsonian American Art Museum, Washington, DC / Art Resource, NY: Page 337

Stephen M. Miller: Page 257

Tate Gallery, London / Art Resource, NY: Pages 10, 119, 199, 281

Topham: Pages 48, 186, 284, 286, 335, 343

Vanni / Art Resource, NY: Pages 40, 106

Werner Forman / Art Resource, NY: Pages 8, 41, 94

Zev Radovan: Pages 35, 49, 61, 64, 69, 125, 146, 149, 153, 207, 209, 218, 219, 222, 234, 256, 263, 269, 274, 277, 308, 317, 320, 332, 364